SPAIN &
PORTUGAL'S
BEST TRIPS

32 AMAZING
ROAD TRIPS

This edition written and researched by

Regis St Louis
Stuart Butler, Kerry Christiani, Anthony Ham,
Isabella Noble, John Noble, Josephine Quintero,
Brendan Sainsbury, Andy Symington

SYMBOLS IN THIS BOOK

✓ Top Tips	📖 History & Culture	📷 Essential Photo
S Link Your Trips	👪 Family	🏃 Walking Tour
● Tips from Locals	🍷 Food & Drink	✗ Eating
↪ Trip Detour	🌳 Outdoors	🛏 Sleeping

☎ Telephone Number	@ Internet Access	🗎 English-Language Menu
☉ Opening Hours	🛜 Wi-Fi Access	🚼 Family-Friendly
P Parking	🌱 Vegetarian Selection	🐾 Pet-Friendly
⊖ Nonsmoking	🏊 Swimming Pool	
❄ Air-Conditioning		

MAP LEGEND

Routes
- ▬▬ Trip Route
- ▬▬ Trip Detour
- ▬▬ Linked Trip
- ▬► Walk Route
- ▬ Tollway
- ▬ Freeway
- Primary
- Secondary
- Tertiary
- Lane
- Unsealed Road
- ░ Plaza/Mall
- ▦ Steps
-)=(Tunnel
- ═ Pedestrian Overpass
- --- Walk Track/Path

Boundaries
- --- International
- ---- State/Province
- ⌐⌐⌐ Cliff
- ▬ Wall

Population
- ✪ Capital (National)
- ◉ Capital (State/Province)
- ● City/Large Town
- ○ Town/Village

Transport
- ✈ Airport
- ⊕ Cable Car/Funicular
- P Parking
- ⊕ Train/Railway
- 🚋 Tram
- Ⓤ Underground Train Station

Trips
- 1 Trip Numbers
- 9 Trip Stop
- 🚶 Walking tour
- ↪ Trip Detour

Route Markers
- E44 E-road network
- M100 National network

Hydrography
- ～ River/Creek
- ～ Intermittent River
- ～ Swamp/Mangrove
- ～ Canal
- Water
- Dry/Salt/Intermittent Lake
- Glacier

Areas
- ░ Beach
- Cemetery (Christian)
- Cemetery (Other)
- Park
- Forest
- Urban Area
- Sportsground

PLAN YOU.

ON THE ROAD

MADRID & CENTRAL SPAIN 37

CONTENTS

Northern Spain & Basque Country
p103

Barcelona & Eastern Spain
p181

Portugal
p315

Madrid & Central Spain
p37

Andalucía & Southen Spain
p241

Contents cont.

ROAD TRIP ESSENTIALS

Classic Trips

Look out for the Classic Trips stamp on our favorite routes in this book.

5

Salamanca Plaza Mayor illuminated at night (Trip 1)

WELCOME TO
SPAIN & PORTUGAL

Spectacular beaches, mountaintop castles, medieval villages, stunning architecture and some of the most celebrated restaurants on the planet – Iberia has an allure that few destinations can match.

There's much to see and do amid the enchanting landscapes that inspired Picasso, Velàzquez and the great epic poets of Portugal. You can spend your days feasting on seafood in coastal Galician towns, feel the heartbeat of Andalucía at soul-stirring flamenco shows, hike across the flower-strewn meadows of the Pyrenees, or chart a winding route through the spectacular vineyards of the Douro Valley. The 32 trips in this book offer something for everyone: beach lovers, outdoor adventurers, family travellers, music fiends, foodies and those simply wanting to delve into Iberia's rich art and history.

And if you only have time for a single journey, make it one of our nine Classic Trips, which take you to the very best of Spain and Portugal. Turn the page for more.

➔

SPAIN & PORTUGAL
Classic Trips

28

What is a Classic Trip?

All the trips in this book show you the best of Spain and Portugal, but we've chosen nine as our all-time favourites. These are our Classic Trips – the ones that lead you to the best of the iconic sights, the top activities and the unique, only-in-Iberia experiences. Turn the page to see the map, and look out for the Classic Trip stamp throughout the book.

21 **Costa del Sol Beyond the Beaches** Wander the streets of Málaga, along Spain's most famous coastline.

28 **Alentejo & Algarve Beaches** Marvel at this trip's coastal formations, such as those at Praia de Marinha.

8 **Roving La Rioja Wine Region** Enjoy grape grazing along this peaceful route.

8

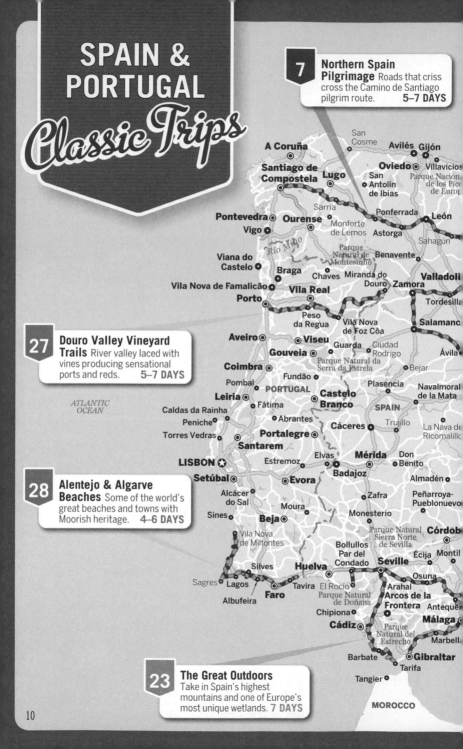

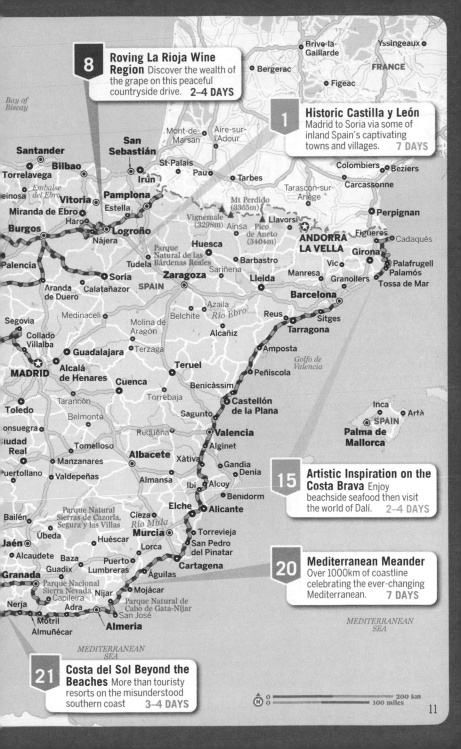

8 **Roving La Rioja Wine Region** Discover the wealth of the grape on this peaceful countryside drive. **2–4 DAYS**

1 **Historic Castilla y León** Madrid to Soria via some of inland Spain's captivating towns and villages. **7 DAYS**

15 **Artistic Inspiration on the Costa Brava** Enjoy beachside seafood then visit the world of Dalí. **2–4 DAYS**

20 **Mediterranean Meander** Over 1000km of coastline celebrating the ever-changing Mediterranean. **7 DAYS**

21 **Costa del Sol Beyond the Beaches** More than touristy resorts on the misunderstood southern coast **3–4 DAYS**

FRANCE

Brive-la-Gaillarde
Yssingeaux
Bergerac
Figeac
Mont-de-Marsan
Aire-sur-l'Adour
Colombiers
Beziers
Carcassonne
St-Palais
Pau
Tarbes
Tarascon-sur-Ariège
Perpignan

Bay of Biscay

Santander
Bilbao
Torrelavega
einosa *Embalse del Ebro*
Vitoria
Miranda de Ebro
Haro
Burgos
Palencia
Nájera
Logroño
Estella
Pamplona
Irún
San Sebastián
Mt Perdido (3355m)
Vignemale (3298m)
Ainsa
Pico de Aneto (3404m)
Llavorsí
ANDORRA LA VELLA
Figueres
Cadaqués
Girona
Palafrugell
Palamós
Tossa de Mar
Vic
Huesca
Parque Natural de las Bárdenas Reales
Tudela
Barbastro
Sariñena
Lleida
Manresa
Granollers
Barcelona
SPAIN
Zaragoza
Soria
Aranda de Duero
Calatañazor
Medinaceli
Azaila
Belchite
Río Ebro
Reus
Sitges
Tarragona
Molina de Aragón
Alcañiz
Amposta
Segovia
Collado Villalba
Guadalajara
Terzaga
Teruel
Peñíscola
Golfo de Valencia
MADRID
Alcalá de Henares
Cuenca
Benicàssim
Torrebaja
Castellón de la Plana
Toledo
Tarancón
Belmonte
Requena
Sagunto
Valencia
Inca
Artà
SPAIN
Palma de Mallorca
onsuegra
Tomelloso
Albacete
Xàtiva
Alginet
iudad Real
Manzanares
Almansa
Gandia
Denia
uertollano
Valdepeñas
Ibi
Alcoy
Benidorm
Bailén
Parque Natural Sierras de Cazorla, Segura y las Villas
Cieza
Río Mula
Elche
Alicante
Jaén
Úbeda
Huéscar
Murcia
Torrevieja
San Pedro del Pinatar
Alcaudete
Baza
Lorca
Granada
Guadix
Puerto Lumbreras
Águilas
Cartagena
Parque Nacional Sierra Nevada
Capileira
Níjar
Mojácar
Nerja
Adra
Parque Natural de Cabo de Gata-Níjar
San José
Motril
Almuñécar
Almería

MEDITERRANEAN SEA

MEDITERRANEAN SEA

N 0 — 200 km
0 — 100 miles

11

Spain & Portugal's best sights and experiences, and the road trips that will take you there.

SPAIN & PORTUGAL
HIGHLIGHTS

Barcelona

Home to cutting-edge architecture, world-class dining and vertiginous nightlife, Barcelona has long been one of Europe's most alluring destinations. Days are spent wandering the cobblestone lanes of the Gothic quarter while nights are spent taking in gilded music halls and first-rate tapas bars. The great city of Gaudí is all the more memorable when visited as part of an epic road trip through Spain, such as **Trip 20: Mediterranean Meander**.

Trips

Barcelona The city comes alive at dusk

Algarve Beaches This Atlanic coastal trip offers stunning rocky coves

La Rioja Wine Country

La Rioja is the sort of place where you could spend weeks meandering along quiet roads in search of the finest drop. Bodegas offering wine-tastings and villages that shelter wine museums are the mainstay in this region. Aside from scenery and fine quaffs, you'll find plenty of surprises (such as a Frank Gehry–designed masterpiece in a tiny village) on **Trip 8: Roving La Rioja Wine Region**.

Trip

Algarve Beaches

Beach-lovers have much to celebrate on a drive along Portugal's southern coast. Sandy islands, cliffs and coastline set the stage for memorable trip exploring the back roads during **Trip 28: Alentejo & Algarve Beaches**. After a day spent surfing or frolicking in the waves, you can roll up to a beautifully sited restaurant for a seafood feast overlooking the crashing waves.

Trip 28

Lisbon

With its mazelike lanes and hilltop panoramas overlooking the Río Tejo, Lisbon is a marvellous place for wanderers. Its neighbourhoods are a delight for the senses, as you pass small grocers, tiled buildings and candlelit taverns, the mournful rhythms of fado drifting on the breeze. The hardest part of visiting will be tearing yourself away (but other delights await) on **Trip 26: Atlantic Coast Surf Trip**.

Trips 26 29

Lisbon Outdoor dining along enchanting cobbled streets

BEST ROADS FOR DRIVING

- -

The Coastal Road to São Vicente Clifftops en route to Europe's southwestern-most tip. **Trip** 28

- -

The Road to Pinhão Terraced vineyards at perilous heights above the meandering Río Douro. **Trip** 27

- -

Valle del Roncal Tower above the clouds on this ascent through the Pyrenees. **Trip** 18

- -

The road to Sant Feliu de Guíxols Spectacular cliffs and crashing waves along the Costa Brava. **Trip** 15

- -

Central Picos Mountain magnificence and gateway to adventure. **Trip** 9

Picos de Europa

Fill up the tank and prepare to be dazzled on a journey through some of the most spectacular mountain scenery in Spain. Jutting out in compact form just back from the rugged coastline of Cantabria and Asturias, the limestone massifs you'll see on **Trip 9: Mountain Roads in Picos de Europa** are unique in Spain but geologically similar to the Alps and jammed with inspiring trails.

Trip 9

Alto Douro Vineyards The terraced landscape of the Douro Valley

Alto Douro Vineyards

The oldest demarcated wine region on earth has steeply terraced hills stitched together with craggy vines that have produced luscious wines for centuries. On **Trip 27: Douro Valley Vineyard Trails**, you'll travel impossibly scenic back roads, with countless vintners offering tours and tastings. Some spots also have heritage accommodation – which comes in mighty handy when you want more than just a sip.

Trip 27

BEST PLACES FOR FOODIES

Valencia Birthplace of paella and home to superb eateries.
Trips 19 20

Galicia Seafood feasting in beautiful coastal settings.
Trips 7 13

Sagres Top spot for traditional Portuguese specialties like *cataplana* (seafood stew).
Trip 28

Basque Country Home to some of the best restaurants in Spain. **Trips** 7 8 18

Segovia Famed for its roast suckling pig and other meaty dishes. **Trip** 1

17

HIGHLIGHTS ★

Madrid City skyline along Gran Vía at night

Sierra Nevada Outdoor adventures through dramatic mountainscapes

Madrid

Madrid has a dizzying array of attractions, not least of which is its astounding collection of fine art. You can spend the day gazing at works by Goya, Velázquez and El Greco, then head out into the night for artfully prepared tapas and roaring nightlife. The wall-to-wall bars, small clubs, live-music venues and cocktail bars make a fine finale to **Trip 4: Spain's Interior Heartland**.

Trips

Sierra Nevada

Spectacular mountain vistas are just one attractive feature on **Trip 23: The Great Outdoors**. Spain's highest peaks aren't just for snapshots. This is the setting for outdoor adventure aplenty: horse riding, rock climbing and mountain biking, with skiing and snowboarding in the winter. There's also wildlife, including ibex. You could spend days exploring Spain's biggest national park and barely scratch the surface.

Trip 23

Asturian Coast

Wild, rugged and unspoilt, the secluded sandy stretches and coves that line the Asturian coast hide some of Spain's most beautiful beaches. On **Trip 7: Northern Spain Pilgrimage**, you'll want to pull over frequently to admire the green hills and rocky headlands. You'll also eat very well at the villages along the way, as the food here is famous throughout Spain.

Trip

Porto

It would be hard to dream up a more romantic city than Portugal's second largest. Laced with pedestrian laneways, it is blessed with baroque churches, epic theatres and sprawling plazas. Its Ribeira district – a Unesco World Heritage site – is a fascinating place to explore. As scenic as it is, this is just a prelude to the gorgeous landscapes you'll encounter on **Trip 30: The Minho's Lyrical Landscapes**.

Trips 27 30

Flamenco

The soundtrack to Europe's most passionate country, flamenco has the power to stir your soul. It's as if by sharing in the pain of innumerable generations of dispossessed misfits you open a door to a secret world of musical ghosts and ancient spirits. There's only one real proviso: you have to hear it live, which you'll have plenty of opportunities to do on **Trip 22: Golden Triangle**.

Trips 22 24

(left) **Porto** View over the rooftops of this historic city;

(below) **San Sebastián** A delectable array of tapas

Pintxos in San Sebastián

Chefs here have turned bar snacks into an art form. *Pintxos* (Basque tapas) are piles of flavour often mounted on a slice of baguette. As you step into any bar in central San Sebastián, the choice lined up along the counter will leave first-time visitors gasping. In short, **Trip 18: The Pyrenees** will take you to Spain's most celebrated eating scene.

Trips

BEST SCENIC VILLAGES

Sos del Rey Católico A gorgeous medieval village in the Pyrenees. **Trip** 18

Ronda A stunner in southern Spain set high above a mountain gorge. **Trip** 24

Tamariu Backed by hills, this is a beautiful settlement on the seaside. **Trip** 15

Trujillo Atmospheric medieval lanes surrounded by 16th-century walls. **Trip** 6

Monsanto A village surrounding an age-old castle, with great walks nearby. **Trip** 32

21

IF YOU LIKE

Madrid Museo Thyssen-Bornemisza (Trip 2)

Beaches

Spain and Portugal have some magnificent stretches of sand, from people-packed beaches to remote shores that invite endless wandering. Despite Iberia's summertime popularity, you can find unspoiled beaches if you know where to look.

15 Artistic Inspiration on the Costa Brava Rugged coast with pine-dappled cliffs, hidden coves and wide beaches.

20 Mediterranean Meander A showcase of coastal charm, with beach-loving favourites such as Cabo de Gata and Sitges.

21 Costa del Sol Beyond the Beaches Spain's most famous coastline, with draws like classy Marbella and beautifully set Nerja.

28 Alentejo & Algarve Beaches Portugal's south coast is a stunner with cliff-backed beaches, seaside villages and great surf.

Wine

In Iberia, wine is king, and the fruits of its picturesque vineyards are famous throughout the world. While Rioja and port are well known, there's much more to discover in this great winery region.

8 Roving La Rioja Wine Region Bodegas, wine museums and vineyards to the horizon – this is Spanish wine's heartland.

27 Douro Valley Vineyard Trails Head to northern Portugal for views over steep, terraced slopes and luscious red wines.

16 Central Catalon's Wineries & Monasteries The Penedès plains are the heart of *cava* (sparkling wine) country, with cellar tours and vast vineyards.

31 Tasting the Dão Surrounded by mountains, this is the spot for some of Portugal's best drops.

Art

Spain's artistic tradition is one of Europe's richest and most original, from local masters to the continent's finest, who flourished under Spanish royal patronage. The result? Art galleries of astonishing depth.

2 Back Roads Beyond Madrid Home to countless galleries and three world-class museums, Madrid looms large in the global art scene.

20 Mediterranean Meander See artwork by Spanish greats, from Picasso in Malaga to Catalan giants in Barcelona.

12 Castles & Cathedrals in Medieval Spain Full of surprises with exhibits in Salamanca and León.

32 Highlands & History in the Central Interior A Portugal ramble that showcases Roman collections, Renaissance art and eclectic global works.

Barcelona The impressive interior of Gaudí's Sagrada Família (Trip 20)

Architecture

The great building designs across Iberia span many centuries, from Roman-era aqueducts and Islamic-era palaces to fantastical 19th-century Modernisme and the cutting-edge works of today.

7 Northern Spain Pilgrimage Marvel at the stunning building in Bilbao that transformed a city. – the Frank Gehry–designed Guggenheim Museum

19 Barcelona to Valencia Take in Barcelona's great Modernista masterpieces followed by stunning 21st-century works in Valencia.

26 Atlantic Coast Surf Trip Great works span the centuries, from 15th-century monasteries to post-modern music halls.

22 Golden Triangle Gaze with awe at exquisite masterpieces built by the Moors.

Outdoor Activities

Adventure comes in many forms in Spain and Portugal, with seaside activities (surfing, swimming, kayaking), cycling, canyoning, white-water rafting and great hikes and walks in nearly every region.

23 The Great Outdoors With surfing, mountain climbs and wildlife watching, the south of Spain seems to have it all.

17 Peaks & Valleys in Northwest Catalonia Get off the beaten path for rafting and hikes through stunning national parks.

9 Mountain Roads in Picos de Europa Dramatic peaks set the scene for kayaking along the Río Sella and magnificent walks.

28 Alentejo & Algarve Beaches Sun-drenched days of surfing, sea kayaking and dolphin watching.

Great Scenery

With soaring peaks and flower-filled valleys, Spain and Portugal have glorious landscapes, which make a fine backdrop to country walks – or for simply taking in the view from the open road.

13 Coast of Galicia Bask in the untamed beauty of Galicia's wild beaches, jagged cliffs and tiny coves.

18 The Pyrenees Stunning scenery lurks around every curve on this soaring drive across northwest Spain.

30 The Minho's Lyrical Landscapes Head to northern Portugal for meandering rivers and granite-strewn peaks.

3 The Forgotten West Enter a world of fertile mountain-backed landscapes and dramatic river valleys.

NEED TO KNOW

CURRENCY
Euro (€)

LANGUAGE
Spain: Spanish, as well as Catalan, Basque and Galician; Portugal: Portuguese.

VISAS
Generally not required for stays of up to 90 days (not at all for members of EU or Schengen countries). Some nationalities need a Schengen visa.

FUEL
Petrol stations (usually open 24 hours) can be found along major highways. Expect to pay €1.35 to €1.80 per litre.

RENTAL CARS
Auto Jardim (www.auto-jardim.com)

Hertz (www.hertz.com)

Holiday Autos (www.holidayautos.com)

Pepecar (www.pepecar.com)

IMPORTANT NUMBERS
Europe-wide emergencies (☎112)

International access code (☎00)

Country code Portugal (☎351)

Country code Spain (☎34)

Climate

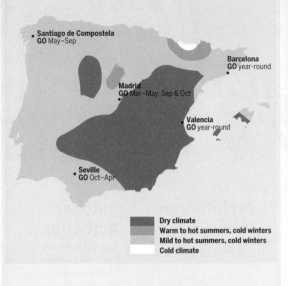

Santiago de Compostela
GO May–Sep

Barcelona
GO year-round

Madrid
GO Mar–May, Sep & Oct

Valencia
GO year-round

Seville
GO Oct–Apr

Dry climate
Warm to hot summers, cold winters
Mild to hot summers, cold winters
Cold climate

When to Go

High Season (Jun–Aug, public holidays)
» Accommodation books out and prices increase by up to 50%. Low season in parts of inland Spain. Expect warm, dry and sunny weather; more humid in coastal areas.

Shoulder (Mar–May, Sep & Oct)
» A good time to travel with mild, clear weather and fewer crowds. In Spain, local festivals can send prices soaring.

Low Season (Nov–Feb)
» Cold in central Spain and Portugal's interior; shorter, rainier days in both countries. Mild temperatures in Andalucía, the Mediterranean coast and the Algarve. This is high season in Spanish ski resorts. Many hotels are closed in beach areas but elsewhere prices plummet.

Your Daily Budget

Spain

Budget: less than €75
» Dorm bed: €18–€25

» Double room in *hostal*: €55–€65 (more in Madrid and Barcelona)

» Self-catering and lunch *menú del día*: €9–€14

Midrange: €75–€175
» Double room in midrange hotel: €65–€140

» Lunch and/or dinner in local restaurant: €20–€40

» Car rental: from €25 per day

Top End: more than €175
» Double room in top-end hotel: €140 and up (€200 in Madrid and Barcelona)

» Fine dining for lunch and dinner: €150–€250

» Regularly stay in Spanish *paradores* and *pousadas* (luxury state-owned hotels): €70–€230

Portugal

Budget: less than €50
» Dorm bed: €15–€22

» Self-catering

» Plan sightseeing around free admission days (often Sunday mornings)

» Youth cards save on sights and transport

Midrange: €50–€120
» Double room in a midrange hotel: €50–€100

» Lunch and dinner in a midrange restaurant: €20–€30

» Book online to save money on accommodation

Top End: more than €120
» Boutique hotel room: from €120

» Three-course meal in a top restaurant: from €40

Eating

Tapas Bar Tapas and drinks; open longer hours than restaurants.

Taberna Rustic place in Spain serving tapas and *raciones* (large tapas).

Panadería/Pasteleria Bakery (Spanish/Portuguese); good for pastries and coffee.

Vinoteca Wine bar where you order by the glass.

Cervecería/Cervejaria (Spanish/Portuguese) Beer hall; the place to go for snacks and draft beer (*cerveza/cerveja*).

Marisqueira Spanish eatery specialising in seafood.

Spain & Portugal
Price categories indicate the cost of a main course:

€	less than €10
€€	€10–20
€€€	more than €20

Sleeping

Casas Rurales/Casa no Campo (Spanish/Portuguese) Comfy village houses or farmhouses for hire in the countryside.

Hostales Simple Spanish guesthouses that have ensuite rooms.

Paradores/pousadas (Spanish/Portuguese) State-funded accommodation often in castles, converted monasteries and old mansions.

Pensión/pensão (Spanish/Portuguese) Inexpensive, extremely basic guesthouses, often with shared bathrooms.

Spain
Price categories indicate the cost of a double room with private bathroom in high season:

	BARCELONA & MADRID	ELSEWHERE
€	less than €75	less than €65
€€	€75–200	€65–140
€€€	more than €200	more than €140

Portugal
Price categories refer to a double room with bathroom in high season. Unless otherwise stated, breakfast is included in the price.

€	less than €60
€€	€60–120
€€€	more than €120

For more, see Road Trip Essentials (p393).

Barcelona Gaudí's otherworldly apartment block, Casa Batlló (p239)

Arriving in Spain

Barajas Airport (Madrid)

Rental cars Major car-rental agencies have desks in the airport at arrival terminals.

Metro & buses Cost around €5 and run every five to 10 minutes from 6.05am to 1.30am; it's 30 to 40 minutes to the centre.

Taxis Cost €30 and reach the centre in 20 minutes.

El Prat Airport (Barcelona)

Rental cars Major car-rental agencies have concessions at arrival terminals.

Buses Cost €5.90 and run every five to 10 minutes from 6.10am to 1.05am; it's 30 to 40 minutes to the centre.

Trains Cost €4.10 and run every 30 minutes from 5.42am to 11.38pm; it takes 25 to 30 minutes to reach the centre.

Taxis Cost €25 to €30 and reach the centre in 30 minutes.

Arriving in Portugal

Aeroporto de Lisboa (Lisbon)

Rental cars There is a wide choice of car-hire companies at the airport.

Metro €1.90 (including €0.50 Viva Viagem card); red line from Aeroporto station; transfer at Alameda for blue line to Rossio and Baixa-Chiado. It's 20 minutes to the centre; frequent departures from 6.30am to 1am.

AeroBus €3.50; every 20 minutes from 7.45am to 8.15pm.

Taxis €12–€16; around 20 minutes to the centre.

Aeroporto de Faro (Faro)

Rental cars Car-rental agencies have desks in the airport.

Buses €1.60; every 30 minutes weekdays, every two hours weekends.

Taxis €10–€14; around 20 minutes to the centre.

Mobile Phones

Local SIM cards are widely available and can be used in European and Australian mobile phones. Not compatible with many North American or Japanese systems.

Internet Access

Wi-fi is available in most lodgings and cafes (and is usually free). Internet cafes are rare.

Money

ATMs are widely available throughout both Spain and Portugal. Credit cards are accepted in most hotels, restaurants and shops.

Tipping

Menu prices indicate a service charge. Most people leave small change if satisfied: 5% is fine; 10% is considered generous.

Useful Websites

Lonely Planet (www. lonelyplanet.com) Destination information, articles, hotel bookings, traveller forums and more.

Tour Spain (www.spain.info) Spanish tourism authority with interactive maps featuring key attractions in every region.

Portugal Tourism (www. visitportugal.com) Portugal's useful and official tourism authority.

RAC (www.rac.co.uk/driving-abroad) Info for British drivers on driving in Spain and Portugal.

CITY GUIDE

BARCELONA

From Gothic to Gaudí, Barcelona bursts with art and architecture. It's also home to celebrated Catalan restaurants, fascinating neighbourhoods and simmering nightlife. Cap it off with pretty beaches, hilltop viewpoints and historical relics dating back to the Romans, and it's no wonder Barcelona continues to be one of Europe's best-loved destinations.

Barcelona Take a stroll through the city along shady La Rambla

Getting Around

Heavy traffic and narrow one-way streets can exasperate even the most diehard city drivers. Luckily Barcelona has a good metro system with stops all across town. A one-way fare costs €2.15, a day pass costs €7.60.

Parking

Street parking can be hard to find. Try a car park (such as those near Plaça de les Glòries or Estació del Nord). Parking costs around €3 per hour or €17 to €20 for 24 hours.

Discover the Taste of Barcelona

For fresh seafood, visit the family-run eateries in La Barceloneta near the seaside. Poble Sec and Sant Antoni have some great local favourites, particularly for tapas.

Live Like a Local

Base yourself in El Born for great restaurants and cocktail bars. Bohemian spirits are drawn to El Raval, with its eclectic eateries and nightlife. L'Eixample has great architecture and the city's top restaurants.

Useful Websites

Lonely Planet (www.lonelyplanet.com/barcelona) Travel tips, accommodation, articles and traveller's forum.

Miniguide (www.miniguide.es) Insight into Barcelona's food, culture, nightlife and fashion.

Barcelona Turisme (www.barcelonaturisme.com) City's official tourism website.

Trips Through Barcelona 18 19 20

TOP EXPERIENCES

➡ Strolling La Rambla

Few pedestrian thoroughfares can rival La Rambla as it cuts through old Barcelona and down to the shores of the Mediterranean. It's a canvas, catwalk and stage all in one.

➡ Historic treasures at La Catedral

Barcelona's cathedral spans the centuries like a silent witness to the city's history. Don't miss the leafy cloister inhabited by geese.

➡ Panoramic views in Park Güell

The playfulness of Gaudí's imagination runs wild in this hilltop park, which is part garden and part Modernista sculptural fantasy.

➡ Tapas tasting at Mercat de la Boqueria

One of Europe's great produce markets, this is also the centre of Barcelona's culinary culture. Browse fruits, seafood and baked goods, then head to the back for a tapas feast.

➡ Gaudí's genius in La Pedrera

One of Gaudí's great gifts to the city, this apartment block is extraordinary outside and in, and only gets better the higher you climb.

➡ Bar-hopping in El Born

Join locals on an evening of bar-hopping and tapas nibbling in one of Barcelona's best-loved neighbourhoods, El Born, whose tangle of streets surround the Basílica de Santa Maria del Mar.

➡ Brilliant artwork at Fundació Joan Miró

There is no finer or more comprehensive collection of Joan Miró's work than this museum on Montjuïc. One of Barcelona's favourite sons, Miró was a towering figure of 20th-century Catalan art.

CITY GUIDE

MADRID

Madrid has transformed itself into one of Spain's premier style centres, and its calling cards are many: astonishing art galleries, relentless nightlife, an exceptional live-music scene, a feast of fine restaurants and tapas bars, and a population that's mastered the art of the good life.

Getting Around

It's easy to get lost in this sprawling metropolis. Luckily you can take advantage of Madrid's extensive metro system (Europe's second-largest network). A single ticket costs €1.50. A 10-ride ticket is €12.20.

Parking

Do yourself a favour and leave your vehicle in a car park (costing around €3 per hour and €20 per day).

Discover the Taste of Madrid

Splendid tapas bars abound everywhere, but La Latina is the undoubted queen. Restaurants in Malasaña, Chueca and

TOP EXPERIENCES

➡ Grand masterpieces at Museo del Prado
One of the great art galleries of the world, this is a showcase of Spanish paintings, including works by Goya and Velàzquez. (www.museodelprado.es)

➡ Idyllic walks in Parque del Buen Retiro
Join locals on a scenic stroll through these beautifully landscaped gardens, laid out in the 17th century by Felipe IV.

➡ Captivating artworks in Centro de Arte Reina Sofia
A spectacular gallery that stages contemporary shows. It's impossible not to be moved while gazing upon Picasso's heart-wrenching *Guernica*.

➡ Royal decadence at the Palacio Real
This palace is a fine place to lose yourself among Italianate baroque decadence. Sumptuous ceiling frescoes and ornate clocks are a few of the eye-catching features found in its 2800 rooms.

Madrid Relax in the serene Parque del Buen Retiro

Huertas range from glorious old tavernas to boutique eateries across all price ranges.

Live Like a Local
Base yourself in Salamanca if you're seeking somewhere quiet and upmarket – plus it's perfect for serial shoppers. Staying in Plaza Mayor and Real Madrid will put you in the heart of the busy downtown area, and if it's nightlife you seek, book a place in Huertas or Lavapiés.

Useful Websites
Es Madrid (www.esmadrid.com) Nicely designed town hall website with info on upcoming events.

Le Cool (http://madrid.lecool.com) Upcoming events with an emphasis on the alternative and avant-garde.

Madrid Diferente (www.madriddiferente. com) Restaurants, shops, upcoming events with a refreshingly offbeat style.

Trips Through Madrid 1 2 4

LISBON

Spread across steep hillsides that overlook the Río Tejo, Lisbon has captivated visitors for centuries. Windswept vistas at breathtaking heights reveal the city in all its beauty: Roman and Moorish ruins, white-domed cathedrals and grand plazas lined with sun-drenched cafes. But the real delight of discovery is delving into the narrow cobblestone lanes.

Getting Around

Driving around Lisbon is challenging, particularly in the narrow winding lanes in the old centre. Lisbon has a good metro system, and tram lines (particularly number 28) are an atmospheric way of getting around town.

Parking

Car park rates can be expensive in the centre, and street parking spaces are often scarce. Good free places to park include Campo de Santa Clara near the Alfama (good daily except Tuesday and Saturday when the market is on) and along Av 24 de Julio west of Cais do Sodré.

Lisbon Ornamental cloisters of Mosteiro dos Jerónimos

TOP EXPERIENCES

➡ Atmospheric lanes of the Alfama

Take a stroll in Lisbon's Moorish time capsule: a medina-like district of tangled alleys, hidden palm-shaded squares and terracotta-roofed houses.

➡ Architectural wizardry in Mosteiro dos Jerónimos

A Unesco World Heritage site, this 16th-century monastery is pure eye candy, with a magnificent facade, tree-trunk-like columns and an elaborate cloister. (www.mosteirojeronimos.pt)

➡ Magnificent views from Castelo de São Jorge

On a windswept hilltop, this centuries-old fortification offers a window into Lisbon's Visigoth, Moorish and Christian past, and the views are jaw-dropping. (http://castelodesaojorge.pt)

➡ Hearing fado in Mesa de Frades

Hear the power of fado at this traditional, dining and concert space in the Alfama. It was once a chapel. (www.mesadefrades.com)

Discover the Taste of Lisbon

Follow the scent of char-grilled sardines and the sound of fado to lively outdoor restaurants in the Alfama. Foodies should head to the Chiado, which has some excellent restaurants. Though better known for its nightlife, nearby Bairro Alto also has some gems.

Live Like a Local

Base yourself in the Chiado for boutique hotels and great restaurants and bars. The lanes of the Alfama have great charm but getting to other parts of the city is challenging. Príncipe Real has some good options and feels less touristy than other areas.

Useful Websites

Visit Lisboa (www.visitlisboa.com) Culture, food, city highlights.

Go Lisbon (www.golisbon.com) Curated info on sights, restaurants, bars and shops.

Trips Through Lisbon 26 29

SPAIN & PORTUGAL
BY REGION

Sparkling beaches, towering peaks, medieval villages and world-class dining: there's much to discover on an Iberian road trip. Here's your guide to what each region has to offer and the best drives to experience.

Madrid & Central Spain (p35)

With celebrated restaurants, vertiginous nightlife and hallowed museums, Madrid is a great place to start the journey. Beyond the capital, you can roll across ancient Roman bridges in Extremadura, explore the many treasures of Toledo and chase the ghosts of La Mancha on the Don Quixote Trail.

Tilt your wheel toward windmills on Trip 5

Portugal (p315)

You can explore lovely Lisbon with its heart-wrenching fado, hilltop views and atmospheric neighbourhoods, then head south for the coastal allure of the Algarve. Up north lies the jaw-dropping scenery (and luscious wines) of the Douro Valley, while the interior is awash with age-old villages and looming castles.

Follow the scent of char-grilled fish on Trip 26

Northern Spain & Basque Country
(p103)

Ruggedly beautiful, northern Spain is a land of towering cliffs and windswept coast – not to mention stellar seafood. Dining is particularly outstanding in Basque Country, home to some of Spain's best restaurants. Add to this the great wines along the Rioja trail and hiking adventures in Picos de Europa.

Discover unspoiled seascapes on Trip 13

Barcelona & Eastern Spain
(p181)

Barcelona has long enchanted visitors with its mad-cap architecture, Gothic quarter and brilliant restaurants. Beyond lies the picturesque beaches and seaside villages of the Costa Brava, the soaring peaks of the Pyrenees and much more to discover in the hinterland (medieval towns, mountain monasteries, vineyards).

Breathe in the crisp mountain air on Trip 18

Andalucía & Southern Spain
(p241)

The cradle of flamenco, Andalucía is a soulful, traditional place of blindingly white castle-topped towns, bustling beaches and elaborate palace-fortresses of unrivaled magnificence. There's much to see and do here, from frolicking off sun-kissed beaches to marvelling at the grandeur of the Alhambra in Granada.

Gaze out to Africa from the 'Rock' on Trip 21

Madrid & Central Spain

WELCOME TO THE SPANISH HEARTLAND, TO THIS MOST SPANISH OF SPANISH REGIONS where history is writ large and magnificently on seemingly every corner. On your journeys across the high plateau that surrounds Madrid you'll encounter some of Spain's most spectacular cities – from Cáceres to Cuenca, Segovia to Salamanca – as well as cathedral towns par excellence (Toledo, León and Burgos). This is also a region to savour castles and Roman relics, tilt at windmills in the finest tradition of Don Quixote, and tread lightly through some of the most beautiful villages (Covarrubias, Atienza, Chinchón) and medieval towns (Trujillo, Sigüenza, Cuenca) in Europe. Above all this is a region to get a taste for Old Spain and the stirring relics it left behind.

Toledo The windmills of Don Quixote (Trip 5)
MATTEO COLOMBO / GETTY IMAGES ©

Madrid & Central Spain

ATLANTIC OCEAN

Bay of Biscay

Ribadesella
Cangas de Onís
Parque Natural de Redes
Torre Cerredo (2648m)
Riaño
Valdecebollas (2136m)
Torrelavega
Santander
Reinosa
Puerto de la Sía
Bilbao
Puerto la Braguia
Amboto (1327m)
San Sebastián
Txindoki (1341m)
Ir

Alto do Poío (1335m)
Catouté (2117m)
León
Astorga
Ponferrada
Aguilar de Campóo
Miranda de Ebro
Vitoria
Estel

Río Sil
Encoro de Prada
Embalse de las Portas
Puebla de Sanabria
Becilla de Valderaduey
Sahagún
Osorno
Burgos
Nájera
Logroño
Calahorra

Chaves
Parque Natural de Montesinho
Benavente
Palencia
Salas de los Infantes
Soria
Calatañazor

Mirandela
Miranda do Douro
Zamora
Valladolid
Aranda de Duero

PORTUGAL
Parque Natural do Douro International
Vila Nova de Foz Côa
Pinhel
Guarda
Lumbrales
Ciudad Rodrigo
Salamanca
Peña de Francia (1732m)
Granadilla
Plasencia

Río Duero
Tordesillas
Peñafiel
Parque Natural del Hoz
Atienza
Medina del Campo
Puerto de Somosierra
Segovia
Puerto de Navacerrada
Collado Villalba
Puerto de Tornavacas
Valverde de la Vera

Pico de Almanzor (2592m)
Bejar
Ávila
Molina de Aragón
Guadalajara

MADRID
Alcalá de Henares
Torrejón de Ardoz
Parla

Alcántara
Navalmoral de la Mata
Talavera de la Reina
Toledo
Aranjuez
Tarancón
Cuen

Río Tejo
Río Tajo
Cáceres
Trujillo
Villacañas
Belmonte

Arroyo de la Luz
Miajadas
Consuegra
Alcázar de San Juan
Socuéllamos

SPAIN
Daimiel
Tomelloso
Albacete

Mérida
Don Benito
Almadén
Ciudad Real
Manzanares
Villanueva de los Infantes

Badajoz
Almendralejo
Almagro
Valdepeñas

Zafra
Puertollano

Fregenal de la Sierra
La Capitana (959m)
Peñarroya-Pueblonuevo
Pozoblanco
Puerto Calatraveño (750m)
La Carolina
Beas de Segura
El Yelmo (1808m)
Río Segura

Castaño (960m)
Monesterio
Hamapega (910m)
Bailén
Empanadas (2107m)
Revolcador (2001m)

Aracena
Parque Natural Sierra Norte de Sevilla
Montoro
Andújar
Linares
Úbeda
María (2045m)
Lorc

Valverde del Camino
Palma del Río
Córdoba
Torredonjimeno
Jaén
Cazorla
Huéscar

Huelva
Seville
Écija
Lucena
Lobatejo (1380m)
El Almadén (2032m)
Baza
Puerto Lumbreras

Puente Genil
Bermejo (1476m)

100 km
50 miles

Classic Trip

1 Historic Castilla y León 7 Days
Madrid to Soria via some of inland Spain's captivating towns and villages. (p41)

2 Back Roads Beyond Madrid 5–7 Days
Route running south and east of the capital through wonderfully historic towns. (p53)

3 The Forgotten West 4–6 Days
Cáceres to deep canyons with villages and quiet back roads en route. (p63)

4 Spain's Interior Heartland 5–7 Days
Journey through northern Spain with Roman and very Spanish attractions along the way. (p75)

5 Route of Don Quixote 4–6 Days
Detective trail across La Mancha in search of Spain's favourite literary hero. (p85)

6 Ancient Extremadura 5–7 Days
Medieval towns, Roman ruins, remote castles and Extremadura's home of *jamón* (cured ham). (p95)

DON'T MISS

Covarrubias
Stunning riverside village. Step behind its walls and into another world on Trip **1**

Café de la Iberia, Chinchón
Eat where Goya ate overlooking a special square on Trip **2**

San Martín del Castañar
Lost in the wilds of Spain's west, this village ranks in Spain's top five for at least one Lonely Planet writer. Find it on Trip **3**

Palacio Episcopal, Astorga
This whimsical Antoni Gaudí structure is surely his most unlikely. Track it down on Trip **4**

El Toboso
If you really want to understand the cult of Don Quixote, visit El Toboso. We take you there on Trip **5**

Museo del Jamón, Monesterio
Extremadura's most celebrated *jamón*-producing town now has a museum dedicated to *jamón*. Get a taste on Trip **6**

Salamanca Plaza Mayor is widely considered to be Spain's most beautiful central plaza

Classic Trip

Historic Castilla y León

1

This journey through Spain's Castilian heartlands takes in some of the country's most beguiling historic cities and larger towns with numerous time-worn pueblos (villages) en route.

671 km
Covarrubias
One of Spain's most beautiful villages

631 km
Burgos
Arguably Spain's foremost Gothic cathedral

9

10

Valladolid

Aranda de Duero

Soria
FINISH

4

2

START
⭐ MADRID

Salamanca
Golden sandstone architecture without peer

254 km

Segovia
Disney castle, Roman aqueduct and lively streets

92 km

7 DAYS
782 KM / 486 MILES

GREAT FOR...

📖

BEST TIME TO GO

Spring (March to May) and Autumn (September and October) to avoid extreme heat and cold.

📷 **ESSENTIAL PHOTO**

Plaza Mayor, Salamanca, floodlit at night.

☑ **BEST FOR CULTURE**

Irresistible Salamanca street life against a glorious architectural backdrop.

Classic Trip

1 Historic Castilla y León

From Segovia to Soria, the towns of Castilla y León rank among Spain's most appealing historic centres. Architecture may be central to their attraction, but these are no museum pieces. Instead, the relentless energy of life lived Spanish-style courses through the streets, all set against a backdrop of grand cathedrals and animating stately squares. Out in the countryside postcard-perfect villages complement the clamour of city life.

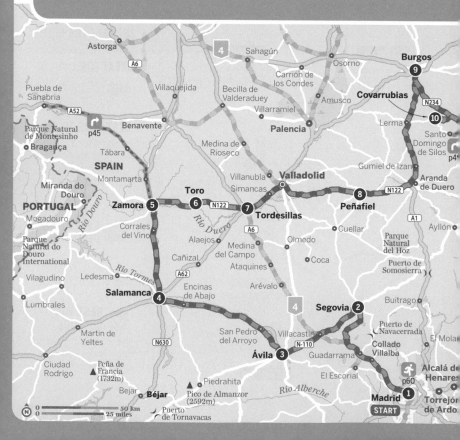

❶ Madrid

Madrid is the most Spanish of all Spanish cities. Its food culture, drawn from the best the country has to offer, makes it one of Europe's more underrated culinary capitals, while its nightlife and its irresistible joie de vivre exist like some Spanish stereotype given form. But there is more to Madrid than just nonstop colour and movement. This is one of the premier art cities on the continent, with three world-class galleries – the Prado, Thyssen and Reina Sofía – all clustered close to one of the city's main boulevards and a short walk from the Parque del Buen Retiro, one of the loveliest and most expansive monumental parks in Europe. In short, this is a city that rewards those who linger and love all things Spanish. To explore Madrid on foot, see p60.

The Drive » Getting out of Madrid can be a challenge, with a complicated system of numbered motorways radiating out from the city. Drive north along the Paseo de la Castellana, turn west along the M50 ring road, then take the A6, direction A Coruña. Of the two main roads to Segovia from the A6, the N603 is the prettier.

TRIP HIGHLIGHT

❷ Segovia

Unesco World Heritage listed Segovia is a stunning confluence of everything that's good about the beautiful towns of Castilla. There are historic landmarks in abundance, among them the Roman **Acueducto**, the fairytale **Alcázar** (📞921 46 07 59; www.alcazardesegovia.com; Plaza de la Reina Victoria Eugenia; adult/concession/child under 6yr €5/3/free, tower €2, EU citizens free 3rd Tue of month; ⏰10am-6pm Oct-Mar, 10am-7pm Apr-Sep; 🚗), which is said to have inspired Walt Disney, and Romanesque gems such as the **Catedral** (📞921 46 22 05; Plaza Mayor; adult/concession €3/2, Sun morning free, tower €5; ⏰9.30am-5.30pm Oct-Mar, 9.30am-6.30pm Apr-Sep) or the **Iglesia de San Martín** (⏰before & after Mass). This is also one of the most dynamic towns in the country, a winning mix of local students and international visitors filling the city's bars and public spaces with an agreeable crescendo of noise. To cap it all, the setting is simply superb – a city strung out along a ridge, its warm terracotta and sandstone hues arrayed against a backdrop of Castilla's rolling hills and the often-snowcapped

Map labels

Río Ebro

Logroño

Nájera

Hontoria del Pinar

Navaleno

FINISH

N234

❶❶ **Soria**

alatañazor

Río Duero

Gormaz

Almazán

Atienza

Imón

Medinaceli

❷

Cifuentes

Torija

Guadalajara

Priego

Pastrana

🔗 LINK YOUR TRIP

2 Back Roads Beyond Madrid

Also starting in Madrid, this loop south and east of the capital takes in the historic towns and villages of Madrid's hinterland.

4 Spain's Interior Heartland

From Santander's ferry port, we take you through Roman ruins, buzzing towns and soaring cathedrals on your way to Madrid.

Sierra de Guadarrama. There are many vantage points to take in the full effect, but our favourite can be found anywhere in the gardens near the entrance to the Alcázar.

 p50

The Drive » It's 66km from Segovia to Ávila along the N110. The road runs southwest, parallel to the Sierra de Guadarrama, with some excellent views en route. At around the halfway mark, you'll cross the A6 motorway.

3 Ávila

Ávila's old city, surrounded by imposing 12th-century *murallas* (walls) comprising eight monumental gates, 88 watchtowers and more than 2500 turrets, is one of the best-preserved medieval-walled cities in Spain. Two sections of the **Murallas** (muralladeav-ila.com; adult/child under 12yr €5/free; ⏲10am-8pm Tue-Sun; 🅿) can be climbed – a 300m stretch that can be accessed from just inside the Puerta del Alcázar, and a longer 1300m stretch that runs the length of the old city's northern perimeter. The best views are those at night from **Los Cuatro Postes**, a short distance northwest of the city. Ávila is also the home city of Santa Teresa, with the **Convento de Santa Teresa** (☎920 21 10 30; Plaza de la Santa; ⏲8.45am-1.30pm & 3.30-9pm Tue-Sun) as its centrepiece. Other important religious high points include the **Catedral del Salvador** (Plaza de la Catedral; admission €4; ⏲10am-7.30pm Mon-Fri, 10am-8pm Sat, noon-6.30pm Sun), the **Monasterio de Santo Tomás** (www.mon-asteriosantotomas.com; Plaza de Granada 1; admission €4; ⏲10am-1pm & 4-8pm) and the sandstone **Basílica de San Vicente** (Plaza de San Vicente; admission €2; ⏲10am-6.30pm Mon-Sat, 4-6pm Sun).

🛏 p50

The Drive » The N501 runs northwest of Ávila to Salamanca, in the process traversing the pancake-flat high *meseta* (plateau) of central Spain and covering 96km en route.

TRIP HIGHLIGHT

4 Salamanca

Salamanca is a special place: its perfect mix of eye-catching architecture and animated streets make it one of our favourite cities in Spain. The city is at its best as day turns the corner into

---

💬 LOCAL KNOWLEDGE: FROG-SPOTTING IN SALAMANCA

Arguably a lot more interesting than trainspotting (and you don't have to wear an anorak and drink tea from a thermos flask), a compulsory task facing all visitors to Salamanca is to search out the frog sculpted into the facade of the **Universidad Civil** (Calle de los Libreros; adult/concession €4/2, Mon morning free; ⏲9.30am-1.30pm & 4-6.30pm Mon-Sat, 10am-1.30pm Sun). Once pointed out, it's easily enough seen, but the uninitiated can spend considerable time searching. Why bother? Well, they say that those who detect it without help can be assured of good luck and even marriage within a year. Some hopeful students see a guaranteed examination's victory in it. If you believe all this, stop reading now. If you need help, look at the busts of Fernando and Isabel. From there, turn your gaze to the largest column on the extreme right of the front. Slightly above the level of the busts is a series of skulls, atop the leftmost of which sits our little amphibious friend (or what's left of his eroded self).

DETOUR:
PUEBLA DE SANABRIA

Start: ❺ Zamora

Northwest of Zamora, close to the Portuguese border, this captivating village is a tangle of medieval alleyways that unfold around a 15th-century castle and trickle down the hill. This is one of Spain's loveliest hamlets and it's well worth the detour, or even stopping overnight: the quiet cobblestone lanes make it feel like you've stepped back centuries. Wandering the village is alone worth the trip here but a few attractions are worth tracking down. Crowning the village's high point and dominating its skyline for kilometres around, the **Castillo** (adult/child under 12yr €3/free; ⏰11am-2pm & 4-8pm Mon-Sat, 4-7pm Sun; P 🚻) has some interesting displays on local history, flora and fauna and superb views from the ramparts. Also at the top of the village, the striking **Plaza Mayor** is surrounded by some fine historical buildings. The 17th-century *ayuntamiento* (town hall) has a lovely arched facade and faces across the square to **Iglesia de Nuestra Señora del Azogue** (admission free; ⏰11am-2pm & 4-8pm Sat & Sun), a pretty village church which was first built in the 12th century. If you're staying the night, the **Posada Real La Cartería** (📞980 62 03 12; www.lacarteria.com; Calle de Rúa 16; r from €81; ❄@📶) captures the essence of Puebla de Sanabria's medieval appeal with both rooms and a restaurant.

night. See p166 for more about Salamanca.

🍴 🛏 p50

The Drive » The N630 runs due north from Salamanca to Zamora (67km), a relatively quiet road by Spanish standards and one that follows the contours of the rolling hill country of Castilla y León's west.

- - - - - - - - - -

❺ Zamora

If you're arriving by road, first appearances can be deceiving and, as in so many Spanish towns, your introduction to provincial Zamora is likely to be nondescript apartment blocks. But persevere as the *casco historico* (old town) is hauntingly beautiful, with sumptuous medieval monuments

that have earned Zamora the popular sobriquet 'Romanesque Museum'. Much of the old town is closed to motorised transport and walking is easily the best way to explore this subdued encore to the monumental splendour of Salamanca. Zamora is also one of the best places to be during Semana Santa, with haunting processions of hooded penitents parading through the streets. Whatever time of year you're here, don't miss the **Museo de Semana Santa** (📞980 53 22 95; semanasantadezamora.com; Plaza de Santa María La Nueva; adult/child €4/1.50; ⏰10am-2pm & 5-8pm Tue-Sat, 10am-2pm Sun).

🍴 🛏 p50

The Drive » The A11 tracks east of Zamora – not far out along the sweeping plains that bake in summer, take the turn-off to Toro.

- - - - - - - - - -

❻ Toro

With a name that couldn't be more Spanish and a stirring history that overshadows its present, Toro is your archetypal Castilian town. It was here that Fernando and Isabel cemented their primacy in Christian Spain at the Battle of Toro in 1476. The town sits on a rise high above the north bank of Río Duero and has a charming historic centre with half-timbered houses and Romanesque churches. The high

Classic Trip

FRANZ MARC FREI / LOOK-FOTO / GETTY IMAGES ©

MARIA GALAN / GETTY IMAGES ©

WHY THIS IS A CLASSIC TRIP
ANTHONY HAM, AUTHOR

The towns north and west of Madrid are windows on the Spanish soul, each with their own distinctive appeal. Segovia, Ávila, Salamanca, Zamora and Burgos are all Spanish classics, dynamic cities with extraordinary architectural backdrops. Throw in some captivating, beautiful villages along the way and you've captured the essence of this remarkable country in just a week.

Top: Tordesillas reflected in the Río Duero
Left: Diners in Covarrubias
Right: Ávila's fortified *murallas* (walls)

point, literally, is the 12th-century **Colegiata Santa María La Mayor** (Plaza de la Colegiata; admission €2; ⏰10.30am-2pm & 5.30-7.30pm Tue-Sun), which rises above the town and boasts the magnificent Romanesque-Gothic Pórtico de la Majestad.

The Drive » Return to the main east–west road that passes to the north of Toro (the A11, then E82), and continue east to Tordesillas.

❼ Tordesillas

Commanding a rise on the northern flank of Río Duero, this pretty little town has a historical significance that belies its size. Originally a Roman settlement, it later played a major role in world history when, in 1494, Isabel and Fernando, the Catholic Monarchs, sat down with Portugal here to hammer out a treaty determining who got what in Latin America. Portugal got Brazil and much of the rest went to Spain. Explaining it all is the excellent **Museo del Tratado del Tordesillas** (📞983 77 10 67; Calle de Casas del Tratado; ⏰10am-1.30pm & 5-7.30pm Tue-Sat, 10am-2pm Sun). Not far away, the heart of town is formed by the delightful porticoed and cobbled **Plaza Mayor**, its mustard-yellow paintwork offset by dark-brown woodwork and black grilles.

Classic Trip

The Drive » From Tordesillas, E80 sweeps northeast, skirts the southern fringe of Valladolid and then continues east as the N122, through the vineyards of the Ribera del Duero wine region all the way into Peñafiel.

⑧ Peñafiel

Peñafiel is the gateway to the Ribera del Duero wine region and it's an appealing small town in its own right. At ground level, **Plaza del Coso** is one of Spain's most stunningly picturesque plazas. This rectangular 15th-century 'square' was one of the first to be laid out for this purpose and is considered one of the most important forerunners to the *plazas mayores* (main squares) across Spain. It's still used for bullfights on ceremonial occasions, and it's watched over by distinctive half-wooden facades. But no matter where you are in Peñafiel, your eyes will be drawn to the **Castillo de Peñafiel** (Museo Provincial del Vino; Peñafiel; castle €3, incl museum €7, audioguides €2; ⏰11am-2.30pm & 4.30-8.30pm Tue-Sun), one of Spain's longest and narrowest castles (the walls and towers stretch over 200m but are little more than 20m across). Within

the castle's crenulated walls is the state-of-the-art **Museo Provincial del Vino**, the local wine museum that tells a comprehensive story of the region's wines.

📑 p51

The Drive » The N122 continues east of Peñafiel. At Aranda del Duero, turn north along the E5 and make for Lerma, an ideal place to stop for lunch – try the roast lamb at Asador Casa Brigant on Plaza Mayor. Sated, return to the E5 and take it all the way into Burgos.

TRIP HIGHLIGHT

⑨ Burgos

Dominated by its Unesco World Heritage–listed cathedral but with plenty more to turn the head, Burgos is one of Castilla y León's most captivating towns. The extraordinary Gothic **Catedral** (📞947 20 47 12; www.catedraldeburgos. es; Plaza del Rey Fernando; adult/child under 14yr incl multilingual audioguide €6/1.50; ⏰10am-6pm) is one of Spain's glittering jewels of religious architecture and looms large over the city and skyline. Inside is the last place of El Cid and there are numerous extravagant chapels, a gilded staircase and a splendid altar. Some of the best cathedral views are from up the hill at the lookout, just below the 9th-century Castillo de Burgos. Elsewhere in town, two monasteries – the **Cartuja de Miraflores**

(📞947 25 25 86; ⏰10.15am-3pm & 4-6pm Mon, Tue & Thu-Sat, 11am-3pm & 4-6pm Sun) and the **Monasterio de las Huelgas** (📞947 20 16 30; www.monasteriodelashuelgas.org; guided tours €7, Wed free; ⏰10am-1pm & 4-5.30pm Tue-Sat, 10.30am-2pm Sun) – are worth seeking out, while the city's eating scene is excellent.

🍴 📑 p51

The Drive » Take the E5 south of Burgos but almost immediately after leaving the city's southern outskirts, take the N234 turnoff and follow the signs over gently undulating hills and through green valleys to the walled village of Covarrubias.

TRIP HIGHLIGHT

⑩ Covarrubias

Inhabiting a broad valley in eastern Castilla y León and spread out along the shady banks of Río Arlanza with a gorgeous riverside aspect, Covarrubias is only a short step removed from the Middle Ages. Once you pass beneath the formidable stone archways that mark the village's entrances, Covarrubias takes visitors within its intimate embrace with tightly huddled and distinctive, arcaded half-timbered houses opening out onto cobblestone squares. Simply wandering around the village is the main pastime, and don't miss the charming riverside pathways or outdoor tables that spill out onto the squares. Otherwise, the main attraction is the **Colegiata de San Cosme y Damián** (admission €2.50; ⏱10.30am-2pm & 4-7pm Mon & Wed-Sat, 4.30-6pm Sun), which has the evocative atmosphere of a mini cathedral and Spain's oldest still-functioning church organ; note also the gloriously ostentatious altar, fronted by several Roman stone tombs, plus that of Fernán González, the 10th-century founder of Castilla. Don't miss the graceful cloisters and the sacristia with its vibrant 15th-century paintings by Van Eyck and tryptic *Adoracion de los Magis*.

The Drive » The N234 winds southwest of Covarrubias through increasingly contoured country all the way to Soria. Along the way there are signs to medieval churches and hermitages marking many minor roads that lead off into the trees. In no time at all you'll see the turn-off to Santo Domingo de Silos.

- - - - - - - - - -

⓫ Soria

Small-town Soria is one of Spain's smaller provincial capitals. Set on Río Duero in the heart of backwoods Castilian countryside, it has an appealing and compact old centre, and a sprinkling of stunning monuments. The narrow streets of the town centre on Plaza Mayor, with its attractive Renaissance-

DETOUR: SANTO DOMINGO DE SILOS

Start: ⓾ **Covarrubias**

Nestled in the rolling hills just off the Burgos–Soria (N234) road, this tranquil, pretty village is built around a monastery with an unusual claim to fame: monks from here made the British pop charts in the mid-1990s with recordings of Gregorian chants. Notable for its pleasingly unadorned Romanesque sanctuary dominated by a multidomed ceiling, the **church** (⏱6am-2pm & 4.30-10pm, chant 6am, 7.30am, 9am, 1.45pm, 4pm, 7pm & 9.30pm) is where you can hear the monks chant. The monastery, one of the most famous in central Spain, is known for its stunning **cloister** (admission €3.50; ⏱10am-1pm & 4.30-6pm Tue-Sat, 4.30-6pm Sun), a two-storey treasure chest of some of Spain's most imaginative Romanesque art. Don't miss the unusually twisted column on the cloister's western side. For sweeping views over the town, pass under the Arco de San Juan and climb the grassy hill to the south to the Ermita del Camino y Via Crucis.

era *ayuntamiento* and the **Iglesia de Santa María la Mayor**, with its unadorned Romanesque facade and gilt-edged interior. A block north is the majestic, sandstone, 16th-century **Palacio de los Condes Gomara** (Calle de Aguirre). Further north is the beautiful Romanesque **Iglesia de Santo Domingo** (Calle de Santo Tomé Hospicio; ⏱7am-9pm), with a small but exquisitely sculpted portal of reddish stone that seems to glow at sunset. Down the hill by the river east of the town centre, the 12th-century **Monasterio de San Juan**

de Duero (Camino Monte de las Ánimas; admission €0.60, Sat & Sun free; ⏱10am-2pm & 5-8pm Tue-Sat, 10am-2pm Sun) has many gracefully interlaced arches in the partially ruined cloister. A lovely riverside walk south for 2.3km will take you past the 13th-century church of the former Knights Templar, the Monasterio de San Polo (not open to the public), and on to the fascinating, baroque **Ermita de San Saturio** (Paseo de San Saturio; ⏱10.30am-2pm & 4.30-7.30pm Tue-Sun).

✕ 🛏 p51

Classic Trip

Eating & Sleeping

Segovia ②

✕ Restaurante
El Fogón Sefardí Sephardic €€

(📞921 46 62 50; www.lacasamudejar.com; Calle de Isabel la Católica 8; mains €15-25, tapas from €2.50; 🕐1.30-4.30pm & 5.30-11.30pm) Located within the Hospedería La Gran Casa Mudéjar, this is one of the most original places in town. Sephardic and Jewish cuisine is served either on the intimate patio or in the splendid dining hall with original, 15th-century Mudéjar flourishes. The theme in the bar is equally diverse. Stop here for a taste of the award-winning tapas. Reservations recommended.

🛏 Hospedería La Gran
Casa Mudéjar Historic Hotel €€

(📞921 46 62 50; www.lacasamudejar.com; Calle de Isabel la Católica 8; r from €80; 🌐@🛜) Spread over two buildings, this place has been magnificently renovated, blending genuine 15th-century Mudéjar carved wooden ceilings in some rooms with modern amenities. In the newer wing, the rooms on the top floors have fine mountain views out over the rooftops of Segovia's old Jewish quarter. Adding to the appeal, there's a small spa and the restaurant comes highly recommended.

Ávila ③

🛏 Hotel El Rastro Historic Hotel €

(📞920 35 22 25; www.elrastroavila.com; Calle Cepedas; s/d €35/55; 🌐🛜) This atmospheric hotel occupies a former 16th-century palace with original stone, exposed brickwork and a natural earth-toned colour scheme exuding a calm understated elegance. Each room has a different form, but most have high ceilings and plenty of space. Note that the owners also run a marginally cheaper, same-name *hostal* (budget hotel) around the corner.

Salamanca ④

✕ Mesón Cervantes Castilian €€

(www.mesoncervantes.com; Plaza Mayor 15; menú del día €13.50, mains €10-22; 🕐10am-midnight) Although there are outdoor tables on the square, the dark wooden beams and atmospheric buzz of the Spanish crowd on the 1st floor should be experienced at least once; if you snaffle a window table in the evening, you've hit the jackpot. The food's a mix of *platos combinados* (meat-and-three-veg dishes), salads and *raciones* (large tapas servings).

🛏 Microtel
Placentinos Boutique Hotel €€

(📞923 28 15 31; www.microtelplacentinos. com; Calle de Placentinos 9; s/d incl breakfast Sun-Thu €57/73, Fri & Sat €88/100; 🌐🛜) One of Salamanca's most charming boutique hotels, Microtel Placentinos is tucked away on a quiet street and has rooms with stone walls and wooden beams. The service is faultless, and the overall atmosphere is one of intimacy and discretion. All rooms have a hydromassage shower or tub and there's a summer-only outside whirlpool spa.

Zamora ⑤

✕ El Rincón
de Antonio Contemporary Castilian €€€

(📞980 53 53 70; www.elrincondeantonio. com; Rúa de los Francos 6; mains €19.50-26, set menus €11-65; 🕐1.30-4pm & 8.30-11.30pm Mon-Sat, 1.30-4.30pm Sun) A fine place offering tapas in the bar, as well as sit-down meals in a classy, softly lit dining area. Amid the range of tasting menus there's one consisting of four tapas for €11, including a glass of wine. In the restaurant, dishes are classic with a contemporary twist, such as Galician scallops served in onion leaves. Reservations recommended.

🛏 Parador Condes de Alba y Aliste
Historic Hotel €€€

(📞980 51 44 97; www.parador.es; Plaza Viriato 5; r €100-168; ❄ @ 🛜 🏊) Set in a sumptuous 15th-century palace, this is modern luxury with myriad period touches (mostly in the public areas). There's a swimming pool and, unlike many *paradores* (luxurious state-owned hotels), it's right in the heart of town. On the downside, there is very limited parking available (just eight places). The **restaurant** (menú del día €33) is predictabe *parador* quality.

Peñafiel ⑧

🛏 Hotel Convento Las Claras
Historic Hotel €€

(📞983 87 81 68; www.hotelconventolasclaras. com; Plaza de los Comuneros 1; s €80-105, d €95-150; ❄ 🛜 🏊) This cool, classy hotel is an unexpected find in little Peñafiel. A former convent, the rooms are luxurious and there's a full spa available with thermal baths and treatments. There's also an excellent restaurant with, as you'd expect, a carefully chosen wine list. Lighter meals are available in the cafeteria.

Burgos ⑨

✕ Cervecería Morito
Tapas €

(Calle Sombrerería 27; tapas €3, raciones €5-7; 🕐12.30-3.30pm & 7-11.30pm) Cervecería Morito is the undisputed king of Burgos tapas bars and it's always crowded, deservedly so. A typical order is *alpargata* (lashings of cured ham with bread, tomato and olive oil) or the *pincho de morcilla* (small tapa of local blood sausage).

The presentation is surprising nouvelle, especially the visual feast of salads.

🛏 Hotel La Puebla
Boutique Hotel €€

(📞947 20 00 11; www.hotellapuebla.com; Calle de la Puebla 20; r from €95; ❄ @ 🛜) This boutique hotel adds a touch of style to the Burgos hotel scene. The rooms aren't huge and most don't have views but they're softly lit, beautifully designed and supremely comfortable. Extra perks include bikes and a pillow menu, while, on the downside, some readers have complained about the level of street noise.

Soria ⑪

✕ Baluarte
Contemporary Castilian €€

(📞975 21 36 58; www.baluarte.info; Caballeros 14; mains €12-25, menú degustación €47; 🕐1.45-3.45pm & 9-11pm Tue-Sat, 1.30-3.30pm Sun) Oscar Garcia is one of Spain's most exciting new chefs and this venture in Soria appropriately showcases his culinary talents. Dishes are based on classic Castilian ingredients but treated with just enough foam and drizzle to ensure that they are both exciting and satisfying, without being too pretentious. Reservations essential.

🛏 Hotel Soria Plaza Mayor
Hotel €€

(📞975 24 08 64; www.hotelsoriaplazamayor. com; Plaza Mayor 10; s/d/ste €65/72/91; ❄ @) This hotel has terrific rooms, each with its own style of decor, overlooking either Plaza Mayor or a quiet side street. There are so many balconies that even some bathrooms have their own. The suites are *very* comfortable.

Cuenca Casas colgadas (hanging houses) jut out precariously over the steep defile of Río Huécar

Back Roads Beyond Madrid

2

This trip through the Spanish capital's hinterland is a cracker, taking in some of Spain's most eye-catching old cities and more beautiful villages.

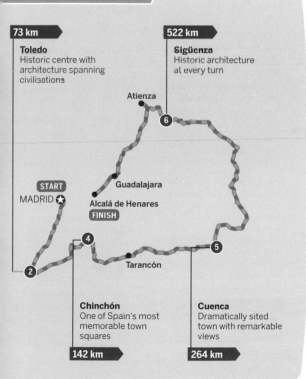

TRIP HIGHLIGHTS

73 km

Toledo
Historic centre with architecture spanning civilisations

522 km

Sigüenza
Historic architecture at every turn

Atienza

6

START
MADRID ✪

Guadalajara

Alcalá de Henares
FINISH

4

2

Tarancón

5

Chinchón
One of Spain's most memorable town squares

142 km

Cuenca
Dramatically sited town with remarkable views

264 km

5–7 DAYS
671KM / 417 MILES

GREAT FOR...

BEST TIME TO GO
April to May or September to October for milder weather.

 ESSENTIAL PHOTO
The 'hanging houses' of Cuenca.

 BEST FOR HISTORY
Toledo is extraordinarily rich in historical landmarks.

Back Roads Beyond Madrid

2

Travel south and east of Madrid and you won't have to go too far to encounter destinations of astonishing variety, taking in former royal playgrounds (Aranjuez), a storied university town (Alcalá De Henares), lovely villages (Chinchón and Atienza) and some of Spain's most spectacular old cities (Toledo, Cuenca and Sigüenza). Throw in castles, quiet back roads and an astonishing architectural portfolio and this trip is definitely a keeper.

① Madrid

Madrid is the kind of city that gets under your skin the longer you stay. Art-lovers will adore the galleries on offer, especially the **Museo del Prado** (www.museodelprado.es; Paseo del Prado; adult/child €14/ free, 6-8pm Mon-Sat & 5-7pm Sun free, audioguides €3.50, admission plus official guidebook €23; ☺10am-8pm Mon-Sat, 10am-7pm Sun; Ⓜ Banco de España), **Museo Thyssen-Bornemisza** (☎902 760 511; www.museothyssen.org; Paseo del Prado 8; adult/child €10/free, Mon free; ☺10am-7pm Tue-Sun, noon-4pm Mon; Ⓜ Banco de España) and **Centro de Arte Reina Sofía** (☎91 774 10 00; www.museoreinasofia.es; Calle de Santa Isabel 52; adult/

concession €8/free, 1.30-7pm Sun, 7-9pm Mon & Wed-Sat free; ☺10am-9pm Mon & Wed-Sat, 10am-7pm Sun; Ⓜ Atocha). Fabulous food and tapas culture is another Madrid speciality, showcasing the best that Spain has to offer in one place. For a walking tour of Madrid, see p60.

The Drive ›› The quickest way to get to Toledo from Madrid by road is along the dual-carriageway N401 that runs southwest of the capital. And in this case there's no advantage to taking quieter B roads – the flatlands between the two cities are not Spain's prettiest.

TRIP HIGHLIGHT

② Toledo

Perched dramatically on a steep ridge high above

the Río Tajo, Toledo looms large in the nation's history and consciousness as a religious centre, bulwark of the Spanish church, and once-flourishing symbol of a multicultural medieval society. The old town today is a treasure chest of churches, museums, synagogues and mosques set in a labyrinth

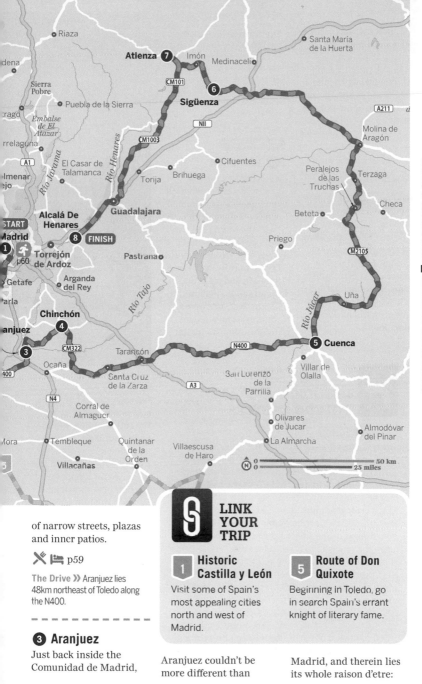

of narrow streets, plazas
and inner patios.

✕ ⊫ p59

The Drive » Aranjuez lies
48km northeast of Toledo along
the N400.

➌ Aranjuez

Just back inside the
Comunidad de Madrid,

LINK YOUR TRIP

1 Historic Castilla y León

Visit some of Spain's
most appealing cities
north and west of
Madrid.

5 Route of Don Quixote

Beginning in Toledo, go
in search Spain's errant
knight of literary fame.

Aranjuez couldn't be
more different than

Madrid, and therein lies
its whole raison d'etre:

Aranjuez was founded as a royal pleasure retreat, an escape for Spanish nobility from the rigours of city life. The town's centrepiece is the 300-room **Palacio Real** (☎91 891 07 40; www.patrimonionacional.es; palace adult/concession €9/4, guide/audioguide €6/4, EU citizens last 3hr Wed & Thu free, gardens free; ☺palace 10am-8pm Apr-Sep, 10am-6pm Oct-Mar, gardens 8am-9.30pm mid-Jun–mid-Aug, reduced hours mid-Aug–mid-Jun), a sprawling, gracefully symmetrical complex filled with a cornucopia of ornamentation. Sweeping out into the palace grounds are stately gardens and royal pavilions.

The Drive >> The expansive royal gardens of Aranjuez segue nicely into pretty riverine woodlands lining the M305, which follows the Río Tajo east of town then breaks away northeast to Chinchón, 21km from Aranjuez.

- - - - - - - - - - -

TRIP HIGHLIGHT

❹ Chinchón

Arriving in Chinchón, you may wonder what all the fuss is about – a modern town has grown out from the town's old core. But persist and you'll discover that Chinchón's old centre may be small, but its main square is one of Spain's more memorable *plazas mayores* (main squares). The village's unique, almost circular **Plaza Mayor** is lined with

MARTIN CHILD / GETTY IMAGES ©

DETOUR: TOLEDO CASTLES

Start: ❷ Toledo

The area around Toledo is rich with castles in varying states of upkeep. Situated some 20km southeast of Toledo along the CM42 is the dramatic ruined Arab castle of **Almonacid de Toledo**. A few kilometres further down the road is a smaller castle in the village of **Mascaraque**. Continue on to Mora, where the 12th-century **Castillo Peñas Negras**, 3km from town, is on the site of a prehistoric necropolis; follow the sandy track to reach the castle for stunning big-sky views of the surrounding plains. Next, head for the small, pretty town of **Orgaz**, which has a handsome, well-preserved 15th-century **castle** (☎925 31 76 85; www.ayto-orgaz.es/castillo; adult/concession €3/2; ☺guided visits 1pm Mon-Fri, 11am, noon, 1pm, 4pm & 5pm Sat, 11pm, noon & 1pm Sun). Around 30km southwest of Toledo, the hulking 12th-century Templar ruin of **Castillo de Montalbán** stands majestically over the Río Torcón valley.

sagging, tiered balconies and is watched over by the 16th-century **Iglesia de la Asunción**. In summer the plaza is converted into a bullring and it's the stage for a popular Passion play shown at Easter. Lunch in one of the *méson* (tavern)-style restaurants around the plaza is a must.

✗ p59

The Drive >> From Chinchón, take the M311 southeast, then head south along the CM322, crossing the Río Tajo en route. At Villarubia de Santiago, turn left (east) along the N400. After 35km you'll pass through Tarrancón. Stay on the N400 for a further 86km to reach Cuenca.

Toledo The old town looks down over the Río Tajo

TRIP HIGHLIGHT

⑤ Cuenca

Coming from the west, Cuenca's modern town sprawls out across the plains with little to inspire, but climbing the hill between the gorges of Ríos Júcar and Huécar to the east is one of Spain's most memorable cities. Its old centre is a Unesco World Heritage stage-set of evocative medieval buildings. Just wandering the narrow streets, tunnels and staircases, stopping every now and again to admire the majestic views, is the chief pleasure of Cuenca. The most striking element of medieval Cuenca, the *casas colgadas* (hanging houses) jut out precariously over the steep defile of Río Huécar. Dating from the 14th century, the houses, with their layers of wooden balconies, seem to emerge from the rock as if an extension of the cliffs; one contains the **Museo de Arte Abstracto Español** (Museum of Abstract Art; www.march.es/arte/cuenca; Calle Canónigos; adult/concession/child €3/1.50/free; ◷11am-2pm & 4-6pm Tue-Fri, 11am-2pm & 4-8pm Sat, 11am-2.30pm Sun), another

an excellent restaurant. For the best views of the *casas colgadas*, cross the Puente de San Pablo footbridge or walk to the mirador at the northernmost tip of the old town. Also don't miss the **Catedral** (Plaza Mayor; adult/child €3.80/2, incl Museo Diocesano & audioguide €5; ◷10am-1pm & 4-6pm) or the **Museo de la Semana Santa** (www.msscuenca.org; Calle Andrés de Cabrera 13; adult/child €3/free; ◷11am-2pm & 4.30-7.30pm Thu-Sat, 11am-2pm Sun; ♿), which celebrates the city's famous Easter processions.

🍴 🛏 p59

The Drive » There are faster ways to get from Cuenca to Sigüenza but we recommend taking the narrow CM2105 to cross the heavily wooded and decidedly craggy Serranía de Cuenca. After tracking northeast across the mountains, continue north to the N211 and then follow the signs to Sigüenza. Plan on at least six hours for this stretch.

TRIP HIGHLIGHT

➏ Sigüenza

Your prize for a long day in the saddle from Cuenca is Sigüenza, sleepy, historic and filled with the ghosts of a turbulent past. The town is built on a low hill cradled by Río Henares and the beautiful 16th-century **Plaza Mayor** is the ideal place to begin exploring. Rising up from the heart of the old town, the city's centrepiece, the **Catedral** (☺9.30am-2pm & 4-8pm Tue-Sat, noon-5.30pm Sun), was badly damaged during the Spanish Civil War but was largely rebuilt. Calle Mayor heads south up the hill from the cathedral to a magnificent-looking castle, which was originally built by the Romans and was, in turn, a Moorish *alcázar* (fortress), a royal palace, an asylum and an army barracks; it's now a luxury hotel.

🛏 p59

The Drive » After the long drive from Cuenca to Sigüenza, the thirty-one pretty kilometres to Atienza will feel like you've hardly had time to get out of third gear. Take the CM110 northwest, then west, then northwest again.

➐ Atienza

Atienza is one of those charming walled medieval villages, crowned by yet another castle ruin, that seems to appear with anything-but-monotonous regularity in the most out-of-the-way places in inland Spain. The main half-timbered square and former 16th-century marketplace, **Plaza del Trigo**, is overlooked by the Renaissance **Iglesia San Juan Bautista**, which has an impressive organ and lavish gilt *retablo* (altarpiece). There are several more mostly Romanesque churches, three of which hold small museums.

The Drive » Meandering generally south from Atienza, the CM101 twists and turns for 33km to Jadraque, from where the equally quiet CM1003 tracks southwest until just short of the regional capital of Guadalajara. Having rejoined the main motorway, the N2, there's nothing for it but to stick with it all the way into Alcalá de Henares. Total distance 111km.

➑ Alcalá de Henares

Alcalá de Henares is first and foremost a university town, replete with historical sandstone buildings seemingly at every turn. Founded in 1486, the **Universidad de Alcalá** (☎91 883 43 84; www.uah.es; guided tours €4; ☺9am-9pm) is one of the country's principal seats of learning. A guided tour gives a peek into the Mudéjar chapel and the magnificent Paraninfo auditorium, where the King and Queen of Spain give out the prestigious Premio Cervantes literary award every year. But Alcalá has another string to its bow – this is the birthplace of Miguel de Cervantes Saavedra, and his birthplace is recreated in the illuminating museum, the **Museo Casa Natal de Miguel de Cervantes** (☎91 889 96 54; www.museocasanatal-decervantes.org; Calle Mayor 48; ☺10am-6pm Tue-Sun), which lies along the beautiful, colonnaded Calle Mayor. Throw in some sunny squares and a young student population and it's an ideal place to catch the buzz you'll find in Madrid without the hassles of being back in the big city.

Eating & Sleeping

Toledo ②

✕ Kumera   Modern Spanish €

(☎925 25 75 53; www.restaurantekumera.
com; Calle Alfonso X El Sabio 2; meals €9-10, set
menus €20-35; ☺8am-2.30am Mon-Fri, 11am-
2.30am Sat & Sun) With arguably the best price-
to-quality ratio in town, this place serves up
innovative takes on local traditional dishes such
as *cochinillo* (suckling pig), *rabo de toro* (bull's
tail) or *croquetas* (croquettes, filled with *jamón* –
cured ham –, squid, cod or wild mushrooms),
alongside gigantic toasts and other creatively
conceived dishes. The dishes with foie gras as
the centrepiece are especially memorable.

⛉ La Posada de
Manolo   Boutique Hotel €€

(☎925 28 22 50; www.laposadademanolo.com;
Calle de Sixto Ramón Parro 8; s/d from €44/55;
✳🖘) This memorable hotel has themed each
floor with furnishings and decor reflecting
one of the three cultures of Toledo: Christian,
Islamic and Jewish. There are stunning views of
the old town and cathedral from the terrace.

Chinchón ④

✕ Café de la Iberia   Spanish €€

(☎91 894 08 47; www.cafedelaiberia.com;
Plaza Mayor 17; mains €13-22; ☺12.30-4.30pm
& 8-10.30pm) This is definitely our favourite
of the *mesones* (home-style restaurants) on
the Plaza Mayor perimeter. It offers wonderful
food, including succulent roast lamb, served by
attentive staff in an atmospheric dining area set
around a light-filled internal courtyard (where
Goya is said to have visited), or, if you can get a
table, out on the balcony.

Cuenca ⑤

✕ Figón del Huécar   Spanish €€€

(☎969 24 00 62; www.figondelhuecar.es;
Ronda de Julián Romero 6; mains €17-25, set
menus €26-36; ☺1.30-4pm & 9-11pm Tue-Sat,
1.30-4pm Sun) With a romantic terrace offering
spectacular views, this is a highlight of old-town
eating. Roast suckling pig, lamb stuffed with
raisins, pine nuts and foie gras and a host of
Castilian specialities are presented and served
with panache. The house used to be the home of
Spanish singer José Luis Perales.

⛉ Posada de San José   Historic Hotel €€

(☎969 21 13 00; www.posadasanjose.com;
Ronda de Julián Romero 4; s with shared/
private bathroom €32/59, d with shared/
private bathroom €45/85 d with view €97)
This 17th-century former choir school retains
an extraordinary monastic charm with its
labyrinth of rooms, eclectic artwork, uneven
floors and original tiles. All rooms are different;
cheaper ones are in former priests' cells, while
more costly doubles combine homey comfort
with old-world charm. Several have balconies
with dramatic views of the gorge. There's a
tapas restaurant and the owners also rent out
tastefully furnished self-contained apartments.

Sigüenza ⑥

⛉ Parador de
Sigüenza   Historic Hotel €€€

(☎949 39 01 00; www.parador.es; Plaza del
Castillo; d €90-175; P ✳🖘) Sigüenza's
luxurious *parador* (state-owned hotels) is set in
the castle, which dates back to the 12th century,
and overlooks the town. The magnificent
courtyard is a wonderful place to pass the time.
The rooms have period furnishings and castle-
style windows so can be on the dark side: ask for
one with a balcony to make the most of natural
light and views.

STRETCH YOUR LEGS MADRID

Start/Finish: Plaza Mayor

Distance: 3.8km

Duration: Two to three hours

Madrid's compact and historic centre is ideal for exploring on foot. So much of Madrid life occurs on the streets and in its glorious plazas, and it all takes place against a spectacular backdrop of architecture, stately and grand.

Take this walk on Trips

Plaza Mayor

So many Madrid stories begin in Madrid's grand central square. Since it was laid out in 1619, the Plaza Mayor has seen everything from bullfights to the trials of the Spanish Inquisition. These days the grandeur of the plaza owes much to the warm colours of the uniformly ochre apartments, with 237 wrought-iron balconies offset by the exquisite frescoes of the 17th-century Real Casa de la Panadería (Royal Bakery).

The Walk » Walk down Calle de Postas off the plaza's northeastern corner, cross the endlessly busy Plaza de la Puerta del Sol, then continue east along Carrera de San Jerónimo. At elegant Plaza de Canalejas, turn right.

Plaza de Santa Ana

There are few more iconic Madrid squares than Plaza de Santa Ana, a local favourite since Joseph Bonaparte carved it out of this crowded inner-city neighbourhood in 1810. Surrounded by classic Madrid architecture of pastel shades and wrought-iron balconies, the plaza presides over the Barrio de las Letras and the outdoor tables are among the most sought-after in the city.

The Walk » Walking west, cross Plaza del Ángel, walk along Calle de la Bolsa, cross Calle de Toledo and make for Calle de la Cava Baja, a glorious, medieval street lined with tapas bars. Keep Iglesia de San Andrés on your right, and stroll down the hill to Plaza de la Paja.

Plaza de la Paja

Delightful Plaza de la Paja (Straw Sq) slopes down into the tangle of lanes that once made up Madrid's Muslim quarter. In the 12th and 13th centuries the city's main market occupied the square and it retains a palpable medieval air, and at times can feel like a Castilian village square. **Delic** (☎91 364 54 50; www.delic.es; Costanilla de San Andrés 14; ◷11am-2am Sun & Tue-Thu, 11am-2.30am Fri & Sat; Ⓜ La Latina), with tables on the square, is brilliant for a mojito, while the **Jardín del Príncipe Anglona** (Plaza de la Paja; ◷10am-10pm Apr-Oct, 10am-6.30pm Nov-Mar; Ⓜ La Latina),

a walled 18th-century garden, is a peaceful oasis in the heart of this most clamorous of cities.

The Walk >> Take any lanes heading west through La Morería, the old Muslim quarter, to Calle de Bailén. Turn right, cross the Viaduct (with fine views on either side), pass the cathedral and continue on to Plaza de Oriente.

Plaza de Oriente

Cinematic in scope, Plaza de Oriente is grand and graceful. It's watched over by the **Palacio Real** (📞91 454 88 00; www.patrimonionacional.es; Calle de Bailén; adult/concession €11/6, guide/audioguide €4/4, EU citizens free last two hours Mon-Thu; ⏱10am-8pm Apr-Sep, 10am-6pm Oct-Mar; **M**Ópera) and the **Teatro Real** (📞91 516 06 96; www.teatro-real.com; Plaza de Oriente; 50min guided tour adult/child under 7yr €8/free; ⏱10.30am-1pm; **M**Ópera) – Madrid's opera house – by sophisticated cafes, and apartments that cost the equivalent of a royal salary. At the centre of the plaza is an equestrian statue of Felipe IV designed by Velázquez, and nearby are some 20 marble statues, mostly of an-

cient monarchs. Local legend holds that these royals get down off their pedestals at night to stretch their legs.

The Walk >> Return south along Calle de Bailén. then turn left (east) up Calle Mayor. After passing the intimate Plaza de la Villa on your right, Mercado de San Miguel appears, also on your right as you climb the hill.

Mercado de San Miguel

One of Madrid's oldest and most beautiful markets, the **Mercado de San Miguel** (www.mercadodesanmiguel.es; Plaza de San Miguel; tapas from €1; ⏱10am-midnight Sun-Wed, 10am-2am Thu-Sat; **M**Sol) is now one of the city's most exciting gastronomic spaces. Within the early-20th-century glass walls, all manner of stalls serve up tapas, from fishy *pintxos* (Basque tapas) atop mini toasts to *jamón* (cured ham) or other cured meats from Salamanca, cheeses, pickled goodies and fine wines.

The Walk >> To get back to where you started, leave the market, walk down Calle de la Cava de San Miguel, turn left and climb the stairs through the Arco de los Cuchilleros to the Plaza Mayor.

La Alberca A historic and harmonious huddle of narrow alleys flanked by gloriously ramshackle houses

The Forgotten West

3

From the medieval Cáceres to the Parque Natural Arribes del Duero, this journey through Spain's west takes you along some of the country's quietest roads and least-visited villages.

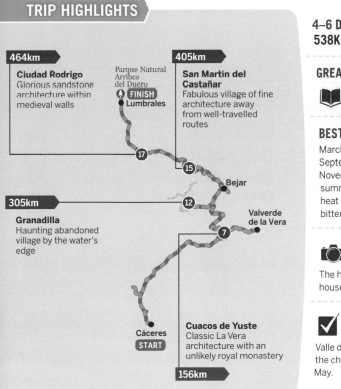

4–6 DAYS
538KM / 335 MILES

GREAT FOR...

464km

Ciudad Rodrigo
Glorious sandstone architecture within medieval walls

Parque Natural Arribes del Duero
FINISH
Lumbrales

405km

San Martín del Castañar
Fabulous village of fine architecture away from well-travelled routes

Bejar

305km

Granadilla
Haunting abandoned village by the water's edge

17

15

12

Valverde de la Vera

7

Cáceres
START

Cuacos de Yuste
Classic La Vera architecture with an unlikely royal monastery

156km

BEST TIME TO GO
March to May and September to November, to avoid summer's searing heat and winter's bitter cold.

ESSENTIAL PHOTO
The half-timbered houses of La Alberca.

BEST FOR FOODIES
Valle del Jerte during the cherry harvest in May.

3 The Forgotten West

This journey begins in Cáceres and ends high above the canyons north of Ciudad Rodrigo. In between, we take you through the forgotten villages and food culture of La Vera and the Sierra de Francia. In Cáceres, Plasencia and Ciudad Rodrigo, you'll experience three of Spain's most underrated cities, but the heart and soul of this journey is the opportunity to soak up village life far from tourist Spain.

❶ Cáceres

The old core of Cáceres can seem like little more than a rumour as you make your way through the modern suburbs that surround it. But no sooner have you set foot in the Plaza Mayor than the city begins to work its magic. The Plaza itself is a glorious variation on the fine Spanish tradition of town squares as the focal point and architectural highpoint of local life. But in Cáceres it's just the beginning. Climb the steps, pass beneath the Arco de la Estrella and you enter another world of cobblestone streets free of traffic, imposing palaces and churches, and the unmistakeable sense of an ancient world, silent and somehow intact five centuries after its heyday.

The Drive >> Casar de Cáceres lies around 12km north of Cáceres and is well signposted off the N630 to Plasencia.

❷ Casar de Cáceres

Extremadura may be well known for its *jamón* (cured ham) but one of its cheeses is equally celebrated in Spanish culinary circles. The Torta del Casar is a pungent, creamy cheese that's aged for 40 days and eaten most often as a spread on *tostas* (toasts) or even with a steak. The otherwise nondescript town of

Casar de Cáceres (population four-thousand-and-something), where the whole place can seem deserted on a summer's afternoon, is where the Torta de Casar was born and its main street is lined with shops selling the local product. There's even the small **Museo de Queso** (Calle Barrionuevo Bajo 7, Casar de Cáceres; ⏰10am-2pm Tue-Sat) dedicated to the cheese.

The Drive » It's just 4km from Casar de Cáceres back to the N630, then 11km north to where the EX302 branches off the west. A further 11km across low, scrubby and strangely appealing hills brings you to Garrovillas.

❸ Garrovillas

At first glance (and the sensation can stay with you longer if you lose yourself in the confusing

LINK YOUR TRIP

1 Historic Castilla y León

To reach Salamanca and join this trip, drive 77km northeast of La Alberca, or 89km northeast of Ciudad Rodrigo.

6 Ancient Extremadura

The trajectories of these two trips intersect at Cáceres before going their separate ways.

tangle of streets), Garrovillas looks like any rural Extremaduran village, with whitewashed houses, shuttered windows and locals who stop to stare as you drive past. But you'll be rewarded if you persist into the village centre and the truly remarkable Plaza Mayor, which is surrounded by arched porticoes. It's one of the prettiest in Extremadura, and that's no small claim.

The Drive 》 Return to the N630, turn left (north) and be ready to stop around 7km further on for a fine lookout over the Embalse de Alcantará (Alcantará dam). The road thereafter sweeps northeast and 45km later you arrive in Plasencia.

❹ Plasencia

JACKF / GETTY IMAGES ©

Rising above a bend of the Río Jerte, Plasencia, which retains long sections of its defensive walls, is quite a sight. Inside the town, life flows through the lively, arcaded Plaza Mayor, meeting place of 10 streets and scene of a Tuesday farmers market since the 12th century. The best-preserved defensive tower of the old city wall, located at the top of the old town, has been converted into the **Centro de Interpretación de la Ciudad Medieval** (Plaza de Torre Lucía; ◷10am-2pm & 5-8pm Tue-Sat Jun-Sep, 10am-2pm & 4-7pm Oct-May), which tells

DETOUR: PARQUE NACIONAL DE MONFRAGÜE

Start: ❹ Plasencia

Spain's 14th and newest national park is a hilly paradise for birdwatchers and a wonderful place to enjoy Extremadura's diverse topography. Straddling the Tajo valley, the park is home to spectacular colonies of raptors and more than 75% of Spain's protected species. Among some 175 feathered varieties are around 300 pairs of black vultures (the largest concentration of Europe's biggest bird of prey) and small populations of two other rare large birds: the Spanish imperial eagle and the black stork. The best time to visit is between March and October, since many bird species winter in Africa.

Signed walking trails crisscross the park and gateways include the pretty hamlet of **Villareal de San Carlos**, from where most trails leave. The EX208 road also traverses the park and the hilltop **Castillo de Monfragüe**, a ruined 9th-century Islamic fort, has sweeping views; the castle can also be reached via an attractive 1½-hour walk from Villareal. Arguably the best spot is the **Mirador del Salto del Gitano**, a lookout point along the main road. From here, there are stunning views across the river gorge to the **Peña Falcón** crag.

To get to the park, drive south from Plasencia along the EX208. The park begins around 24km south of Plasencia.

the history of medieval Plasencia and provides access to a walkable chunk of the wall. Romanesque churches are something of a Plasencia speciality and part of the **Catedral** (Plaza de la Catedral; Catedral Nueva free, Catedral Vieja €2; ☺9am-1pm & 5-7pm Mon-Sat, 9am 1pm Sun) is the Romanesque Catedral Vieja with the classic 13th-century cloister surrounding a trickling fountain and lemon trees, alongside the 16th-century Catedral Nueva, a Gothic-Renaissance blend with a handsome plateresque facade, soaring *retablo* (altarpiece) and intricately carved choir stalls. Also in this double-barreled cathedral is the soaring octagonal Capilla de San Pablo, with a dramatic 1569 Caravaggio painting of John the Baptist.

✖ 🛏 p73

The Drive ›› It's time to leave behind busy roads and disappear into the remote valleys of La Vera. Take the EX203 east of Palencia, and take the turn-off to Pasarón de la Vera after around twenty-five rocking and rolling kilometres.

❺ Pasarón de la Vera

Pasarón de la Vera is a pretty, tranquil village nestled in a valley. It's a suitably gentle introduction to the charms of La Vera with abundant stonework, a stone fountain in the main square and occasional half-timbered houses. Aside from a peaceful time-worn air, the standout attraction is the emotive 16th-century palace **Condes de Osorno**, featuring an open-arcaded gallery decorated with medallions.

RUTA DE LA PLATA

As you travel between Extremadura and Castilla y León, you may see signs designating the route as 'Autovia Ruta de la Plata'. The name of this ancient thoroughfare (aka Ruta de la Plata) probably derives not from the word for 'silver' (*plata* in modern Spanish), but the Arabic *bilath*, meaning tiled or paved. But it was the Romans in the 1st century who laid this artery that originally linked Mérida with Astorga and was later extended to the Asturian coast. Along its length moved goods, troops, travellers and traders – you're following in a fine, ancient tradition. Later, it served as a pilgrim route for the faithful walking from Andalucía to Santiago de Compostela and it's now increasingly a rival to the much more crowded Camino de Santiago. From Seville, it's a 1000km walk or cycle to Santiago or a similar distance to Gijón. Entering Extremadura south of Zafra, the well-marked route passes through Mérida, Cáceres and Plasencia, then heads for Salamanca in Castilla y León. Take a look at www.rutadelaplata.com or pick up the guide (€3) from tourist offices on the route.

The Drive » Twist down along the contours of La Vera's hills for around 8km to Jaraiz de la Vera.

❻ Jaraiz de la Vera

Every Spanish cook knows that *pimentón de la Vera* (La Vera paprika, either sweet and spicy) has no peers, and Jaraiz de la Vera is where much of this fabled condiment comes from. With such success has come a certain prosperity, and for this reason the buildings are a little grander, the atmosphere a touch less charming than other villages in the area. But do stop long enough to buy a tin of *pimentón* at the source. Your Spanish friends will be impressed indeed.

✕ p73

The Drive » Cuacos de Yuste lies just 8km northeast of Jaraiz along a particularly serpentine section of the EX203.

TRIP HIGHLIGHT

❼ Cuacos de Yuste

Cuacos de Yuste ranks among the loveliest of La Vera's villages and it's here that you'll find one of the richest concentrations of La Vera's architectural specialty: half-timbered houses leaning at odd angles, their overhanging upper storeys supported by timber or stone pillars. In particular, seek out lovely Plaza Fuente Los Chorros, which surrounds a 16th-century fountain, and Plaza Juan de Austria, built on a rock, with its bust of Carlos I. And in a surprising twist, in a lovely setting 2km above the village, the **Monasterio de Yuste** (www.patrimonio-nacional.es; adult/child €9/4, audioguide €6; ☉10am-8pm Apr-Sep, to 6pm Oct-Mar) is where Carlos I came

in 1557 to prepare for death after abdicating his emperorship over much of Western and Central Europe. It's a soulful, evocative place amid the forested hills and a tranquil counterpoint to the grandeur of so many formerly royal buildings elsewhere in Spain.

The Drive » Jarandilla de la Vera lies just ten winding kilometres northeast of Cuacos de Yuste along the EX203.

❽ Jarandilla de la Vera

Jarandilla is one of the most appealing stops in La Vera. Its castle-like church, on Plaza de la Constitución, was built by the Templars and features an ancient font brought from the Holy Land. And it's almost worth coming here just to stay in the magnificent, fortress-like parador, set against a backdrop of pretty wooded hillsides.

🛏 p73

The Drive » The EX203 shows no signs of straightening out as it tracks east for 18km from Jarandilla to Valverde de la Vera.

⑨ Valverde de la Vera

Valverde de la Vera is another classic La Vera hamlet – its lovely Plaza de España is lined with timber balconies, and water gushes down ruts etched into the cobbled lanes. It's also the scene for Extremadura's most haunting Easter celebrations, Los Empalaos.

The Drive » Return back down the road to Cuacos de la Yuste (this is one road that's worth driving twice), then climb back up to the Monasterio de Yuste, from where a narrow road with fine views continues 7km further on to Garganta la Olla.

⑩ Garganta la Olla

Garganta la Olla is a picturesque, steeply pitched village with ancient door lintels inscribed with the 16th-century date of construction and name of the original owner. Seek out the Casa de las Muñecas at No 3 on the main Calle Chorillo. The 'House of the Dolls' gets its name from the much-weathered female carving on the stone archway. Painted in blue, the come-on colour of the time, it was a brothel under Carlos I and now houses a far drearier souvenir shop. Another distinctive house is the Casa de Postas Posada de Viajeros (look for the plaque at the top of the street), a travelling inn reputedly used by Carlos I.

The Drive » From Garganta la Olla, take the spectacular drive over the Sierra de Tormantos and the 1269m Puerto de Piornal pass to the Valle del Jerte (around one hour). The road passes through lovely thick forests with breaks in the trees opening out onto some lovely views on both sides of the pass.

⑪ Valle del Jerte

This valley reinforces northern Extremadura's claims as a foodie hub. For a start, Piornal (1200m), on the southeast flank of the valley and the first village you come to as you descend from the Puerto de Piornal, is famous for its Serrano ham. Further down the slopes, the Valle del Jerte grows half of Spain's cherries and is a sea of white blossom in early spring. Visit in May and every second house is busy boxing the ripe fruit. Continue northeast along the valley floor and you'll come to Cabezuela del Valle where the Plaza de Extremadura area has some fine houses with overhanging wooden balconies.

The Drive » A spectacular, winding 35km road leads from just north of Cabezuela over the 1430m Puerto de Honduras to

EASTER SUFFERING

At midnight on the eve of Good Friday in Valverde de la Vera, Los Empalaos (literally 'the Impaled'), in the form of several penitent locals, strap their arms to a beam (from a plough) while their near-naked bodies are wrapped tight with cords from waist to fingertips. Barefoot, veiled, with two swords strapped to their backs and wearing a crown of thorns, these 'walking crucifixes' follow a painful Way of the Cross. Iron chains hanging from the timber clank sinisterly as the penitents make painful progress through the crowds. Guided by *cirineos* (who pick them up should they fall), the *empalaos* occasionally cross paths. When this happens, they kneel and rise again to continue their laborious journey. Doctors stay on hand, as being so tightly strapped does nothing for blood circulation.

Hervás in the Valle del Ambroz. From Hervás, it's around 25km west to Granadilla.

TRIP HIGHLIGHT

⑫ Granadilla

The ghost village of **Granadilla** (⊙10am-1pm & 4-8pm Tue-Sun Apr-Oct, to 6pm Nov-Mar) is a beguiling reminder of how Extremadura's villages must have looked before the rush to modernisation. Founded by the Moors in the 10th century but abandoned in the 1960s when the nearby dam was built, the village's traditional architecture has been painstakingly restored as part of a government educational project. You enter the village through the narrow Puerta de Villa, overlooked by the sturdy castle. From here, the cobblestone Calle Mayor climbs up to the delightfully rustic Plaza Mayor. Some buildings function as craft workshops or exhibition centres in summer; make sure also to walk your way along the top of the Almohad walls, with evocative views of village, lake and pinewoods.

The Drive » Return to the N630, the main and busiest road link between Extremadura and Castilla y León, and soon after crossing into the latter, follow the signs to Béjar and the climb up the steep, narrow and winding mountain road to Candelario (around an hour from Granadilla).

⑬ Candelario

Candelario is your introduction to the Sierra de Béjar, which is home to more delightful villages and rolling mountain scenery; the peaks around here are normally snowcapped until well after Easter. Nudging against a steep rock face, tiny and charming Candelario is easily the pick of the villages, dominated as it is by mountain architecture of stone-and-wood houses clustered closely together to protect against the harsh winter climate. It is a popular summer resort and a great base for hiking.

DETOUR:
SIERRA DE GATA & LAS HURDES

Start: ⑫ **Granadilla**

Remote and forgotten mountain ranges are a specialty in this corner of Extremaura and western Castilla y León, and they don't come much further off the beaten track than the Sierra de Gata and Las Hurdes in Extremadura's far north. The prettiest villages in the Sierra de Gata include Hoyos and San Martín de Trevejo, where people speak their own isolated dialect, a unique mix of Spanish and Portuguese. In Valverde del Fresno, **A Velha Fábrica** (☎927 51 19 33; www.avelhafabrica.com; Calle Carrasco 24, Valverde del Fresno; s/d/f incl breakfast €60/90/140; P✿🔊♿) is a great small hotel set in a former textile mill.

The Las Hurdes region has taken nearly a century to shake off its image of poverty, disease, and chilling tales of witchcraft and even cannibalism. In 1922 the miserable existence of the *hurdanos* prompted Alfonso XIII to declare during a horseback tour, 'I can bear to see no more'. Head for villages such as Casares and Ladrillar, with traditional stone, slate-roofed houses huddled in clusters, while the PR40 is a near-circular 28km route from Casares that follows ancient shepherd trails.

From the N630, the EX205 runs west along the southern shore of the Embalse de Gabriel y Galán and into the Sierra de Gata. Close to the halfway point, the EX204 runs north into the heart of Las Hurdes.

The Drive ›› Return to Béjar, cross the N630 and continue northwest along the marvellously serpentine SA515, passing en route small villages such as Cristóbal and Miranda del Castañar. You'll see Mogarraz, high on a ridge, long before you arrive, around 45 minutes after leaving Candelario.

⑭ Mogarraz

Mogarraz has some of the most evocative old houses in the region and is famous for its *embutidos* (cured meats), as well as the more recent novelty of over 400 portraits of past and present residents, painted by local artist Florencio Maillo and on display outside the family homes. The history of this extraordinary project dates from the 1960s when poverty was rife and many locals were seeking work, mainly in South America. They needed identity cards and it is these that inspired the portraits. Buy some *jamón*, admire the portraits and generally slow down to the pace of village life in this remote corner of the country.

The Drive ›› Roads wind along the walls of the Sierra de Francia's steep hills and by bearing generally north, losing yourself with the greatest of pleasure on occasion, you'll come to San Martín del Castañar. The whole trip shouldn't take longer than 30 minutes.

TRIP HIGHLIGHT

⑮ San Martín del Castañar

If you dream of a village utterly unchanged by the passing years and retaining that sense of unspoiled community and blissful isolation, San Martín del Castañar could just be your place. It's the sort of village where old folk pass the day chatting on doorsteps and there's scarcely a modern building to be seen – it's all half-timbered stone houses, stone fountains, flowers cascading from balconies and a bubbling stream. At the top of the village there's a small rural bullring, next to the renovated castle and historic cemetery.

The Drive ›› Roads west of San Martín straighten out a little and there are fine views of the Peña de Francia, the Sierra's highest, craggiest point, up ahead. At the SA202, turn left and roll on into La Alberca. It should take 20 minutes all up.

⑯ La Alberca

La Alberca is one of the largest and most beautifully preserved of Sierra de Francia's villages; a historic and harmonious huddle of narrow alleys flanked by gloriously ramshackle houses built of stone, wood beams and plaster. Look for the date they were built (typically late 18th century) carved into the door lintels. Numerous stores sell local products such as *jamón*, as well as baskets and the inevitable tackier souvenirs. The centre is pretty-as-a-postcard Plaza Mayor; there's a market here on Saturday mornings. Our only word of warning is this: this is the busiest of the Sierra de Francia's towns, so try to avoid visiting on weekends when the tour buses roll in.

🗙 🛏 p73

The Drive ›› Return back up the SA202, then turn left (northwest) onto the C515 which takes you across less precipitous country into Ciudad Rodrigo (50km from La Alberca).

TRIP HIGHLIGHT

⑰ Ciudad Rodrigo

Close to the Portuguese border and away from well-travelled tourist routes, somnambulant

LA VERA FOOD BOUNTY

Surrounded by mountains often still capped with snow as late as May, the fertile La Vera region produces raspberries, asparagus and, above all, *pimentón* (paprika), sold in charming old-fashioned tins and with a distinctive smoky flavour.

Ciudad Rodrigo is one of the prettier towns in western Castilla y León and its walled old town is home to some of the best-preserved plateresque architecture outside Salamanca. The elegant, weathered sandstone **Catedral de Santa María** (Plaza de San Salvador 1; adult/concession €3/2.50, Sun afternoon free, tower €2; ☺11am-2pm Mon, 11am-2pm & 4-6pm Tue-Sat, noon-2pm & 4-6pm Sun), begun in 1165, towers over the historic centre, while the long, sloping Plaza Mayor is another fine centrepiece – the double-storey arches of the Casa Consistorial are stunning, but the plaza's prettiest building is the **Casa del Marqués de Cerralbo**, an early-16th-century townhouse with a wonderful facade. Elsewhere watch for the 16th-century **Palacio de los Ávila y Tiedra** (Plaza del Conde 3; ☺9am-7pm Mon-Sat), and there are numerous stairs leading up onto the crumbling ramparts of the city walls that encircle the old town. You can follow their length for about 2.2km around the town and enjoy fabulous views over the surrounding plains. And just for something different, there's the **Museo del Orinal** (Chamber Pot Museum; ☏952 38 20 87; www.museodelorinal.es; Plaza Herrasti; adult/child under 12yr €2/free; ☺11am-2pm Tue, Wed, Fri & Sun, 11am-2pm & 4-7pm Sat & Mon; 🚻), Spain's (possibly the world's) only museum dedicated to the not-so-humble chamber pot.

🍴 🛏 p73

The Drive » The quiet SA324 north from Ciudad Rodrigo passes through Castillejo de Martín Viejo (17km) and San Felices de los Gallegos (40km), with a pretty Plaza Mayor and a well-preserved castle. After Lumbrales, a further 10km north, the road (now the SA330) narrows and passes among stone walls – the big views lie just up ahead.

----

⑱ Parque Natural Arribes del Duero

One of the most dramatic landforms in Castilla y León, the Parque Natural Arribes del Duero is a little-known gem. Not far beyond Lumbrales, the **Mirador del Cachón de Caneces** (lookout) offers the first precipitous views. But it's at **Aldeadávila**, around 35km to the north, that you find the views that make this trip worthwhile. Before entering the village, turn left at the large purple sign. After 5.1km, a 2.5km walking track leads down to the **Mirador El Picón de Felipe**, with fabulous views down into the canyon. Returning to the road, it's a further 1km down to the **Mirador del Fraile** – the views of the impossibly deep canyon with plunging cliffs on both sides are utterly extraordinary. This is prime birdwatching territory, with numerous raptors nesting on the cliffs and griffon vultures wheeling high overhead on the thermals. It's a wonderful way to end this wonderful journey.

Eating & Sleeping

Plasencia ④

✖ Casa Juan   Spanish €€
(☎927 42 40 42; www.restaurantecasajuan.
com; Calle de las Arenillas 5; mains €13-18;
⏱1.30-4pm & 8.30-11pm Fri-Wed, closed Jan)
Tucked down a quiet lane, French-owned Casa
Juan does well-prepared *extremeño* meat
dishes, such as shoulder of lamb and suckling
pig. Try the homemade melt-in-the-mouth foie
gras or the expertly hung local *retinto* beef.
Fairly priced wines from all around Spain seal
the deal.

🛏 Palacio Carvajal Girón   Hotel €€
(☎927 42 63 26; www.palaciocarvajalgiron.
com; Plaza Ansano 1; r €85-155; P ✴ 🛜 🏊)
A mightily impressive conversion job on a
formerly ruined palace in the heart of the old
town has resulted in this chic Plasencia address.
Rooms have modern fittings with crisp white
linen juxtaposed with original features of the
building – a most successful combination.

Jaraiz de la Vera ⑥

✖ La Finca   Spanish €€
(☎927 66 51 50; www.villaxarahiz.com; Ctra
203, Km 32.8, Jaraíz de la Vera; mains €14-20;
⏱1-4pm & 8.30-11pm Tue-Sun; 🛜) Offering
spectacular sierra views from the terrace and
the upmarket dining room, this hotel restaurant
just below Jaraíz is one of La Vera's best bets
for smart regional food, featuring local peppers,
caldereta de cabrito (goat stew) and other
quality Extremadura produce. There's also a bar
with an amazing array of gin-and-tonic choices.

Jarandilla de la Vera ⑧

🛏 Parador de
Jarandilla   Historic Hotel €€
(☎927 56 01 17; www.parador.es; Avenida de
García Prieto 1; r €80-120; P ✴ 🛜 🏊) Be king
of the castle for the night at this 15th-century
castle-turned-hotel. Carlos I stayed here for

a few months while waiting for his monastery
digs to be completed. Within the stout walls
and turrets are period-furnished rooms, plus
a classic courtyard where you can dine royally
from the restaurant menu.

La Alberca ⑯

✖ La Taberna   Castilian €€
(☎923 41 54 60; www.latabernadelaalberca.
com; Plaza Mayor 5; mains €12-18; ⏱1-4pm daily,
plus 8pm-12.30am Sat; 🚸) Right on Plaza Mayor
with daily three-course menus including such
surf to turf choices as *rabo de toro* (oxtail) and
grilled trout, plus gut-busting *parrilladas* (grills)
of various meats.

🛏 Hostal La Alberca   Hostal €
(☎923 41 51 16; www.hostallaalberca.com; Plaza
Padre Arsenio; s/d/tr €29/35/49) Housed in one
of La Alberca's most evocative half-timbered
buildings, above a restaurant, this charming
place has comfortable, renovated rooms.
Balconies overlook a small square at the
entrance to the village.

Ciudad Rodrigo ⑰

✖ Mayton   Castilian €€
(Calle Colada 9; menú del día €12, meals €25)
Set in an old stone mansion – but without
the prohibitive price tag you would expect to
find – Mayton promises quality traditional
cooking. The region's outstanding *embutidos*
feature alongside *cordero* (lamb) and there is an
overflowing, atmospheric wine cellar.

🛏 Hospedería
Audiencia Real   Historic Hotel €€
(☎923 49 84 98; www.audienciareal.com;
Plaza Mayor 17; d €50-80; ✴ 🛜) Right on Plaza
Mayor, this fine 16th-century inn has been
beautifully reformed and retains a tangible
historic feel with lovely exposed stone walls.
Rooms have wrought-iron furniture and several
sport narrow balconies overlooking the square;
the very best has a private glassed-in alcove
containing a romantic table for two.

Valladolid Colourful facades fill the streets of this attractive town

Spain's Interior Heartland

4

Take a journey through Spain's northern heartland, from the Bay of Biscay to Madrid, with some of inland Spain's most appealing towns to savour along the way.

TRIP HIGHLIGHTS

375 km

León
Fabulous cathedral and irresistible street life

START
● Santander

● Aguilar de Campóo

5
6

● Palencia

8

Astorga
Winning combination of Romans, Gaudí and chocolate

425 km

592 km

Valladolid
Engaging city with fascinating historical heritage

743 km

9

☆ MADRID
FINISH

San Lorenzo de El Escorial
Unesco-listed, masterpiece-rich royal monastery without peer

5–7 DAYS
802KM / 499 MILES

GREAT FOR...

BEST TIME TO GO
April to May or September to October to avoid extremes of heat and cold.

ESSENTIAL PHOTO
Stained-glass windows from inside León's cathedral.

BEST FOR HISTORY
Villa Romana La Olmeda, Spain's most intact Roman-era villa.

Spain's Interior Heartland

You *could* speed down the motorway and reach Madrid in a little over four hours from Santander. But unless you're in a hurry, why not detour via the stirring cathedral towns of León and Palencia, formerly Roman Astorga, and the dynamic city of Valladolid. For much of the journey, the views of sweeping horizons and distant mountains make this one a real pleasure to drive.

① Santander

Santander often plays second fiddle to the more-famous Basque cities further east, but this is one cool city, home as it is to the belle-époque elegance of El Sardinero neighbourhood and the best of seaside living Spanish-style. Just back from the water, there are good city beaches, bustling shopping streets and a heaving bar and restaurant scene. See p144 for more.

🏨 p82

The Drive » The E5 is a multi-carriageway road that climbs up and over the Cordillera Cantábrica with some stunning mountain views in the early

part of the journey. South of the mountains, track south until the turn-off to Aguilar de Campóo (110km).

② Aguilar de Campóo

Aguilar de Campóo is a worthwhile stop, and the town and surrounding countryside offer some rather lovely views of the Montaña Palentina and the mountains you've just crossed to get here. The town is a pleasing place to wander, take in the fresh mountain air and soak up the bustle of a provincial northern Castilian town. On no account miss the **Monasterio de Santa María la Real** (☎979 12 30 53;

www.santamarialareal.org;
Carretera de Cervera; admission with/without guided visit €5/3; ⏰4-8pm Tue-Fri, 10.30am-2pm & 4.30-7.30pm Sat & Sun Oct-Jun, 10.30am-2pm & 4.30-7.30pm Jul-Sep), a Romanesque monastery with a glorious 13th-century Gothic cloister with delicate capitals.

The Drive » Return to the E5 and follow it south as far as Abia de las Torres, then turn northwest along the P240, bound for Saldaña (65km, around one hour). The turn-off to Villa Romana La Olmeda is 3km south of Saldaña along the CL615.

❸ Villa Romana La Olmeda

On the fertile plains south of the Montaña Palentina, **Villa Romana La Olmeda** (www.villaromanalaolmeda.com; off CL615; adult/concession/child under 12yr €5/3/free,

🔗 **LINK YOUR TRIP**

1 Historic Castilla y León

This loop west and north of Madrid takes in historic towns and gorgeous villages all the way to Soria.

2 Back Roads Beyond Madrid

South and east of Madrid you'll encounter many historic towns and villages, from Toledo to Alcalá de Henares.

3-6.30pm Tue free; ☺10.30am-6.30pm Tue-Sun; [P] [⚐]) is a stunning relic from the days when Spain stood at the crossroads of ancient civilisations. But it's worth the detour for far more than its historical significance – these are some of the most beautiful remnants of a Roman villa anywhere on the Iberian Peninsula. The villa was built around the 1st or 2nd century AD, but was completely overhauled in the middle of the 4th century. It was then that the simply extraordinary mosaics were added: the hunting scenes in El Oecus (the reception room) are especially impressive. The whole museum is wonderfully presented – elevated boardwalks guide you around the floor plan of the 4400-sq-metre villa, with multimedia presentations in Spanish, English and French showing how the villa might once have appeared.

The Drive ≫ Return back down along the P240 to the E5, then follow it south as far as Palencia (70km).

④ Palencia

Palencia is a quintessential Castilian town – subdued at first glance, it's a surprisingly lively town with some magnificent architectural creations. Begin with a walk along the colonnaded main pedestrian street, Calle Mayor, which is flanked by shops and several other churches, then make your way to Palencia's immense Gothic **Catedral** (Calle Mayor Antigua 29; cathedral & crypt €2, incl museum €3; ☺10am-1.30pm & 4.30-7.30pm Mon-Fri, 10am-2pm & 4-5.30pm Sat, 4.30-8pm Sun), where the sober exterior belies the extraordinary riches that await within; it's widely known as 'La Bella Desconocida' (the Unknown Beauty). Inside, the Capilla El Sagrario is the pick with its ceiling-high altar-piece that tells the story of Christ in dozens of exquisitely carved and painted panels. Beyond the cathedral, Palencia is embellished with some

ROMANESQUE DETOURS

Spain's northern interior is littered with outstanding examples of Romanesque architecture, most of which lie close by the main route. Aguilar de Campóo and its surrounds are strewn with Romanesque jewels, with the Monasterio de Santa María la Real, just outside town on the highway to Cervera de Pisuerga, the undoubted highlight. On the road between Villa Romana La Olmeda and Palencia, Frómista is known for its exceptional Iglesia de San Martín, which dates from 1066; it's adorned with a veritable menagerie of human and zoomorphic figures just below the eaves. Further along the road, between Palencia and León, picturesque Sahagún is an important waystation for pilgrims en route to Santiago, particularly for the 12th-century Iglesia de San Tirso with its pure Romanesque design and Mudéjar bell tower laced with rounded arches.

Villa Romana La Olmeda Geometric Roman mosaics

real architectural gems, including the 19th-century **Modernista Mercado de Abastos** (Fresh Food Market) on Calle Colón, the eye-catching **Collegio Vallandrando** on Calle Mayor and the extraordinarily ornate neoplateresque **Palacio Provincial** on Calle Burgos.

✕ ⊨ p82

The Drive » Forsake the motorways and take the quieter N610 east of town, traversing Castilla y León's rural backcountry, before turning onto the N601, which takes you northwest to León. The 125km trip should take around 1½ hours.

TRIP HIGHLIGHT

⑤ León

León is one of our favourite regional cities in Spain. Although its Gothic cathedral and other architecture grab the headlines (see p115), don't miss the showpiece **Museo de Arte Contemporáneo** (Musac; www.musac.org.es; Avenida de los Reyes Leóneses 24; admission €5, 5-9pm Sun free; ⊙10am-3pm & 5–8pm Tue-Fri, 11am-3pm & 5-9pm Sat & Sun), with cutting-edge installation art behind its attractive facade of 37 shades of coloured glass;

the shades were gleaned from the pixelisation of a fragment of one of the stained-glass windows in León's Catedral. And by night León's large student population floods the narrow streets and plazas of the picturesque old quarter, the Barrio Húmedo.

✕ ⊨ p82

The Drive » The AP71 (a toll road) whips you from León to Astorga in less than an hour. If you're not in a hurry, take the quieter (and roughly parallel) N120.

❻ Astorga

Perched on a hilltop on the frontier between the bleak plains of northern Castilla and the mountains that rise up to the west towards Galicia, Astorga is a fascinating small town with a wealth of attractions way out of proportion to its size. The most eye-catching sight is the **Palacio Episcopal** (Museo de los Caminos; Calle de Los Sitios; admission €3, incl Museo Catedralicio €5; ☉10am-2pm & 4-8pm Tue-Sat, 10am-2pm Sun), a rare flight of fancy in this part of the country designed by Antoni Gaudí. There's also the **Museo Romano** (Plaza de San Bartolomé 2; adult/child under 12yr €2.50/free, incl Museo del Chocolate €3; ☉10am-2pm & 4-6pm Tue-Sun; 🚹) – Astorga was once an important Roman settlement called Astúrica Augusta – as well as the plateresque and Gothic **Catedral** (Plaza de la Catedral; cathedral free, museum €3, incl Palacio Episcopal €5; ☉church 9-10.30am Mon-Sat, 11am-1pm Sun, museum 10am-2pm & 4-8pm Tue-Sun) and even a **Museo del Chocolate** (☎987 61 82 22; www.museochocolateastorga.com; Avenida de la Estación 12-16; adult/child under 12yr €2.50/free, incl Museo Romano €3; ☉10.30am-2pm & 4-6pm Tue-Sat, 11am-2pm Sun; 🚹), which is dedicated to the chocolate-making traditions of the town. Less sinfully, the town sees a steady stream of pilgrims passing through along the Camino de Santiago.

✕ 🛏 p82

The Drive » Take the A6 southwest from Astorga. Just after the Benavente turn-off, bear east on the N610, then southeast of the N601 all the way into Medina de Rioseco (126km).

❼ Medina de Rioseco

Medina de Rioseco is another touchstone of Castilla's more illustrious past. A once-wealthy trading centre, it still has a tangible medieval feel and the strong sense of a place that time forgot. Head for Calle Mayor, with its colonnaded arcades held up by ancient wooden columns – market stalls set up here on Wednesday mornings – while two churches hint at the town's former grandeur: the **Iglesia de Santiago** (Calle Santa María; admission €2; ☉11am-noon & 4-7pm Tue-Sun), which blends Gothic, neoclassical and plateresque architectural styles, and the grandiose Isabelline Gothic **Iglesia de Santa María de Mediavilla** (Calle Santa María; guided visits in Spanish €2; ☉11am-noon & 5-7pm Tue-Sun),

---

↱ DETOUR: LAS MÉDULAS

Start: ❻ Astorga

In the remote hill country of northwestern Castilla y León, the ancient Roman gold mines at Las Médulas once served as the main source of gold for the entire Roman Empire – the final tally came to a remarkable three million kilograms. An army of slaves honeycombed the area with canals and tunnels (some over 40km long!) through which they pumped water to break up the rock and free it from the precious metal. The result is a singularly unnatural natural phenomenon and one of the more bizarre landscapes you'll see in Spain. It's breathtaking at sunset.

To get here, drive from Astorga to Ponferrada, then around 20km southwest. To get to the heart of the former quarries, drive beyond Las Médulas village (4km south of Carucedo and the N536 Hwy). Several trails weave among chestnut trees and bizarre formations left behind by the miners. There are also fine views to be had in the vicinity of neighbouring Orellan.

whose Capilla de los Benavente is sometimes referred to as the 'Sistine Chapel of Castilla'. And stop by the **Museo de Semana Santa** (Calle de Lázaro Alonso; admission €3.50; ⊙11am-2pm & 4-7pm Tue-Sun Apr-Sep, weekends only Oct-Mar) – Medina de Rioseco is renowned for the solemnity of its Easter processions.

✗ 🛏 p83

The Drive ≫ The N601 runs southeast to Valladolid and you'll be there in little more than half an hour.

- - - - - - - - - -

TRIP HIGHLIGHT

⑧ Valladolid

Valladolid rivalled Madrid as the seat of royal power until the 16th century, and this noble heritage bequeathed to the city important monuments and some excellent museums (see p165). After dark, the streets around the pretty Plaza Mayor throng with people.

✗ 🛏 p83

The Drive ≫ From Valladolid it's motorways all the way. Take the E80 southwest to Tordesillas, then the A6 before following the signs into San Lorenzo de El Escorial. The 152km journey should take just under two hours.

- - - - - - - - - -

TRIP HIGHLIGHT

⑨ San Lorenzo de El Escorial

The imposing palace and monastery complex of San Lorenzo de El Escorial is an impressive place, rising up from the foothills of the mountains that shelter Madrid from the north and west. The one-time royal getaway is now a prim little town overflowing with quaint shops, restaurants and hotels catering primarily to throngs of weekending *madrileños* (people from Madrid). The main drawcard here is the Unesco World Heritage–listed **Real Monasterio de San Lorenzo** (☎91 890 78 18; www.patrimonionacional.es;

adult/concession €10/5, guide/audioguide €4/4, EU citizens free last 3hrs Wed & Thu; ⊙10am-8pm Apr-Sep, 10am-6pm Oct-Mar, closed Mon), truly one of Spain's most imposing royal complexes. The fresh, cool air here has been drawing city dwellers since the complex was first ordered to be built by Felipe II in the 16th century.

✗ p83

The Drive ≫ San Lorenzo de El Escorial is 59km northwest of Madrid and it takes 40 minutes to drive there. Take the M600 to the A6 highway, then follow the signs to Madrid.

- - - - - - - - - -

⑩ Madrid

Madrid is the start and end point for so many journeys but it's also a destination in its own right, with world class art galleries, a fabulous culinary offering and irresistible street life. Explore it on our walking tour (p60).

Eating & Sleeping

Santander ❶

🛏 Hotel Las Brisas   Boutique Hotel €€

(📞942 27 01 11; www.hotellasbrisas-santander. com; Calle La Braña 14; s/d €69/74; 🕙closed Jan; @🛜) Almost as much gallery as hotel, century-old Las Brisas is a three-storey belle-époque Sardinero villa decked out with art and crafts. The 13 comfy characterful rooms feature coffee- and tea-makers and recently updated bathrooms with huge shower heads. Some enjoy beach views, as does the front terrace. For longer stays consider its nearby apartments.

Palencia ❹

🍴 Gloria
Bendita   Contemporary Castilian €€

(📞979 10 65 04; Calle la Puebla 8; mains €15-25; 🕙1-11.30pm Mon-Sat, 1-5pm Sun; 🛜) Ignore the drab surroundings of modern apartment blocks and seek out this, one of Palencia's new breed of elegant restaurants serving sophisticated Castilian cuisine with a modern twist. Meat and fish dishes are the emphasis here with classics such as braised beef served with oyster mushrooms. There are just a handful of tables in an intimate space so reservations are essential.

🛏 Hotel Colón 27   Hotel €

(📞979 74 07 00; www.hotelcolon27.com; Calle de Colón 27; s/d/tr €40/50/60; ❇🛜) This place is excellent value, with comfortable carpeted rooms sporting light pine furniture, good firm mattresses, shiny green-tiled bathrooms and small flat-screen TVs. Located opposite a school, it can be noisy at recess time.

León ❺

🍴 El Picoteo de la Jouja   Tapas €

(Plaza de Torres de Omaña) This intimate little bar has earned a loyal following for its concentration on traditional local tapas (try the six tapas for €13.50) and local wines, including some from the nearby Bierzo region. The tapas

include cured meats, snails and all manner of León specialities.

🍴 Delirios   Contemporary Castilian €€

(📞987 23 76 99; www.restaurantedelirios.com; Calle Ave Maria 2; mains €12-20; 🕙1.30-3.30pm & 9-11.30pm Tue-Sat, 1.30-3.30pm Sun) One of the city's more adventurous dining options where innovative combinations such as tuna tataki with orange and ginger, and brie and foie gras with coconut hit the mark virtually every time. Staider tastebuds can opt for dishes such as steak with parsnip chips, while the chocolate mousse with passionfruit is designed to put a satisfied waddle in every diner's step. Reservations recommended.

🛏 La Posada Regia   Historic Hotel €€

(📞987 21 31 73; www.regialeon.com; Calle de Regidores 9-11; s/d incl breakfast from €54/59; ❇🛜) This place has the feel of a *casa rural* (village accommodation) despite being in the city centre. The secret is a 14th-century building, magnificently restored (wooden beams, exposed brick and understated antique furniture), with individually styled rooms and supremely comfortable beds and bathrooms. As with anywhere in the Barri Gótic, weekend nights can be noisy.

🛏 Hostal de
San Marcos   Historic Hotel €€€

(📞987 23 73 00; www.parador.es; Plaza de San Marcos 7; d incl breakfast from €134; ❇@🛜) Despite the confusing '*hostal*' in the name, León's sumptuous *parador* (state-owned hotel) is one of the finest hotels in Spain. With palatial rooms fit for royalty and filled with old-world luxury and decor, this is one of the Parador chain's flagship properties, and as you'd expect, the service and attention to detail are faultless. It also houses the Convento de San Marcos.

Astorga ❻

🍴 Aizkorri   Contemporary Castilian €€

(www.aizkorri.es; Plaza España 5; pinchos €3, mains €10-18; 🕙10am-4pm & 7pm-midnight) The modern steely grey-and-black bar here is generally packed with locals here for the palate pleasing *pinchos* (snacks), such as tuna with tartar sauce. More substantial dishes range from tasty salads with artichoke hearts and roasted peppers to innovative takes on traditional cuisine such as baked rabbit on puff pastry with roasted vegetables.

🛏 Hotel Astur Plaza   Hotel €€

(✆987 61 89 00; www.hotelasturplaza.com; Plaza de España 2; s/d/ste from €55/75/110; ❄@🛜) Opt for one of the supremely comfortable rooms that face pretty Plaza de España. On weekends, you'll want to forsake the view for a quieter room out the back. The suites have hydromassage tubs and there are three VIP rooms with 'super kingsize' beds (€85).

Medina de Rioseco ❼

🍴 Casa Manolo   Castilian €€

(Calle Las Armas 4; mains €9-12; ⊙8am-midnight Fri-Wed) The best of a clutch of restaurants on this side street in the historic centre. The courtyard provides a pleasant setting for enjoying reliably good Castilian dishes.

🛏 Vittoria Colonna   Hotel €

(✆983 72 50 87; www.hotelvittoriacolonna.es; Calle de San Juan 2B; s/d €33/55; ❄🛜) This modern three-star hotel with its raspberry-pink frontage offers well-sized and well-appointed rooms. Some are nicer than others, but all have smart grey-and-white bathrooms.

Valladolid ❽

🍴 Martín Quiroga   Contemporary Castilian €€

(✆605 787117; Calle San Ignacio 17; mains €16-18; ⊙1.30-3.30pm & 8.30-11.30pm) With just four tables and a typical waiting list of a month, you would imagine that this extraordinarily high-quality gastrobar would have prices to match. It doesn't. There is no menu, dishes depend on what's fresh in season and available from the market that day, but there's plenty of choice. Special diets are catered to with advance notice. Reservations essential.

🛏 Hotel Mozart   Hotel €

(✆983 29 77 77; www.hotelmozart.net; Calle Menéndez Pelayo 7; s/d €50/60; ❄🛜) Extremely well priced hotel given the recently refurbished quality of the rooms. King-size beds, plush earth-colour furnishings and fabrics, polished parquet floors, dazzling marble bathrooms and space enough for a comfortable armchair. The entrance has a whiff of grandeur about it as well, which contributes to the surprise of this budget bracket price.

San Lorenzo de El Escorial ❾

🍴 La Cueva   Spanish €€€

(✆91 890 15 16; www.mesonlacueva.com; Calle de Floridablanca 24; mains €20-32; ⊙1-4pm & 9-11pm) Just a block back from the monastery complex, La Cueva has been around since 1768 and it shows in the heavy wooden beams and hearty, traditional Castilian cooking – roasted meats and steaks are the mainstays, with a few fish dishes.

Consuegra *Classic La Mancha* molinos
de viento *(windmills) in the sunset*

Route of Don Quixote

Follow the trail of Spain's favourite literary legend, El Quijote (Don Quixote in English), across the endless horizons and amid the castles and ancient windmills of Spain's evocative interior.

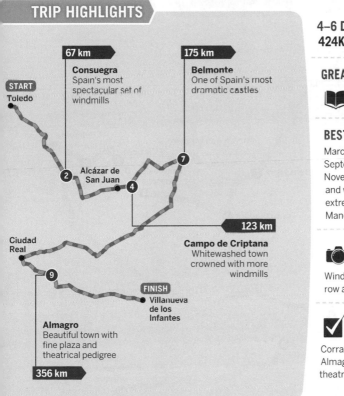

START
Toledo

67 km

Consuegra
Spain's most spectacular set of windmills

175 km

Belmonte
One of Spain's most dramatic castles

Alcázar de San Juan

2

4

7

Ciudad Real

9

123 km

Campo de Criptana
Whitewashed town crowned with more windmills

FINISH
Villanueva de los Infantes

Almagro
Beautiful town with fine plaza and theatrical pedigree

356 km

4–6 DAYS
424KM / 264 MILES

GREAT FOR...

BEST TIME TO GO

March to May and September to November; summer and winter can be extreme across La Mancha.

ESSENTIAL PHOTO

Windmills lined up in a row above Consuegra.

BEST FOR HISTORY

Corral de Comedias in Almagro, Spain's oldest theatre.

5 Route of Don Quixote

Few literary landscapes have come to define an actual terrain quite like the Castilla-La Mancha portrayed in Miguel de Cervantes's *El ingenioso hidalgo don Quijote de la Mancha*. Here is where our noble knight tilted at windmills, fell for Dulcinea, and drove Sancho Panza and his trusty steed Rocinante across a land ripe for adventures. With this itinerary, you get to follow in their footsteps.

1 Toledo

There's nothing to suggest that Don Quixote ever made his way through Toledo's streets, other than, perhaps, the numerous images of the knight in Toledo's souvenir shops, but it is in Toledo that most journeys through Castilla-La Mancha begin. This stunning city is awash in Chirstian, Islamic and Jewish architecture – its **Catedral** (www.catedral primada.es; Plaza del Ayuntamiento; adult/child €11/free; ⊙10.30am-6.30pm Mon-Sat,

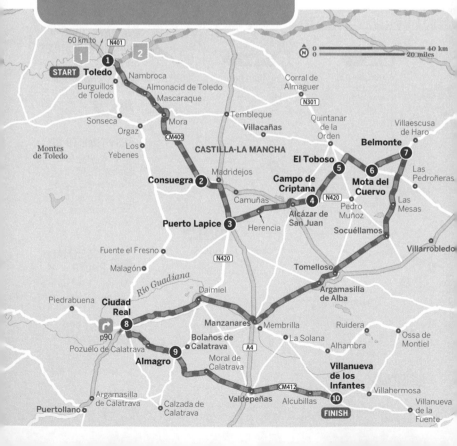

2-6.30pm Sun) is one of Spain's most impressive, the **Mezquita del Cristo de la Luz** (Calle Cristo de la Luz; admission €2.50; ⊙10am-2pm & 3.30-5.45pm Mon-Fri, 10am-5.45pm Sat & Sun) hints at Al-Andalus, and the **Sinagoga del Tránsito** (☎925 22 36 65; museosefardi.mcu.es; Calle Samuel Leví; adult/child €3/1.50, Sat after 2pm & all day Sun free; ⊙9.30am-7.30pm Tue-Sat Mar-Oct, 9.30am-6pm Tue-Sat Nov-Feb, 10am-3pm Sun year-round) is superb. But this is a city to wander, a place of serpentine cobblestone laneways and a brooding atmosphere apt to fire the imagination.

🗙 🛏 p92

The Drive » Drive southeast of Toledo along the CM400. On the final approach into Consuegra (67km), watch for

LINK YOUR TRIP

1 Historic Castilla y León

This classic route begins in Madrid and sweeps through some of inland Spain's most beguiling cities and *pueblos* (villages).

2 Back Roads Beyond Madrid

This route through fabulous towns and villages passes through Toledo.

the line of windmills along a ridge of the kind that struck fear into the heart of El Quijote.

TRIP HIGHLIGHT

② Consuegra

Exactly where Don Quixote tilted at windmills and prepared to do honourable battle against these 'monstrous giants' is not clear from the book, but Consuegra is very much a leading candidate. Here, visible for miles around and strung out along a ridge, are nine *molinos de viento* (windmills) of the classic La Mancha variety. They're the most accessible of La Mancha's windmills (a well-signposted road leads up from the town) and the views from here seem to go on forever. Adjacent to the windmills is a 12th-century **castle** (adult/child €4/free; ⊙10am-1.30pm & 4.30-6.30pm Mon-Fri, 10.30am-1.30pm & 4.30-6.30pm Sat & Sun Jun-Sep, 10am-1.30pm & 3.30-5.30pm Mon-Fri, 10.30am-1.30pm & 3.30-5.30pm Sat & Sun Oct-May; ⊞) – Consuegra once belonged to the Knights of Malta; a few rooms in the castle have been re-created to give a good indication of how the knights would have lived – and down in the town, it's worth tracking down the Plaza Mayor, with its pretty 1st-floor balconies.

🛏 p92

The Drive » It's just under 7km east across pancake-flat plains to the N4 motorway, but you'll find yourself pulling over often to look back at Consuegra's windmills. Once on the N4, Puerto Lapice is 17km south and signposted just off the main highway.

---

③ Puerto Lapice

Many towns and villages in Castilla-La Mancha have tried to lay claim to an El Quijote pedigree, often basing their claims more upon wishful thinking than any close reading of the original text. In fact, few towns are actually mentioned by name in the book. One exception is the now-unremarkable town of Puerto Lapice. It was here that Don Quixote stayed in an inn that he mistook for a castle and, after keeping watch all night, convinced the innkeeper to knight him. It's the sort of town that shimmers in the summer heat, with the only magic of the hallucinatory kind, so drive through town, nod to the noble knight, and keep right on going.

The Drive » From Puerto Lapice, drive east along the N420, bypass Alcázar de San Juan (which some scholars have speculated may have been where El Quijote's journey began), and follow the signs to Campo de Criptana – the whitewashed town crowned by more windmills is unmissable north of the main road. Total journey time is around half an hour.

TRIP HIGHLIGHT

④ Campo de Criptana

Campo de Criptana, one of the most popular stops on the El Quijote route, is Consuegra's main rival when it comes to windmills. And if you think its dramatic windmill crown is impressive, imagine how it must once have seemed – only 10 of Campo de Criptana's original 32 windmills remain. Local legend also maintains that Cervantes himself was baptised in the town's Iglesia de Santa Maria. And unusually for such a small town lost on the La Mancha plains, Campo de Criptana has another claim to fame, although it's one that many locals perhaps would rather forget: revered contemporary film-maker Pedro Almodóvar was born here, but left for Madrid in his teens, later remarking that in this conservative provincial town, 'I felt as if I'd fallen from another planet'.

🍴 🛏 p92

The Drive » Around 3km east of Campo de Criptana along the N420, turn left at the signpost for El Toboso, which is 19km further on along a quiet, flat road.

⑤ El Toboso

To see the cult of El Quijote in full swing, come to El Toboso, a small town far from the main roads northeast of Campo de Criptana. The most entertaining of El Toboso's numerous Cervantes-influenced locations is the 16th-century **Casa-Museo de Dulcinea** (Calle Don Quijote 1; admission €0.60; ⏱10am-2pm & 4.30-7.30pm Tue-Fri, until 6.30pm Sat, 10am-2pm Sun), which was apparently the home of Doña Ana, the *señorita* who inspired Cervantes' Dulcinea, the platonic love of Quijote. Also scattered around the town are the obligatory Don Quixote statue and a library with more than 300 editions of the book in various languages. To make the most of your visit, stop by the small **tourist office** (☎925 56 82 26; www.turismocastillalamancha.com; Plaza Juan Carlos I 1; ⏱10am-2pm & 4-6pm Tue-Sat, 10am-2pm Sun).

DON QUIXOTE

Few literary landscapes have come to define an actual terrain quite like the La Mancha portrayed in Miguel de Cervantes' *El ingenioso hidalgo don Quijote de la Mancha*, better known as El Quijote (in Spanish) or Don Quixote (in English). Published in two volumes in 1605 and 1615, El Quijote went on to become the most famous Spanish novel ever published; in 2002 the Norwegian Nobel Institute asked 100 leading authors from 54 countries to vote for the greatest novel of all time and El Quijote polled 50% more votes than any other book. It is also the most widely translated book on earth after the Bible.

Belmonte Castillo de Belmonte rises dramatically above the village

The Drive » Drive northeast a short distance and then turn right (southeast) along the N301 – the next town you come to is Mota del Cuervo (20km).

6 Mota del Cuervo

If there weren't any windmills here, you'd struggle to find a reason to stop. And if you've already had enough windmills, what are you doing on this trip? But we can't get enough of them and windmills there are – seven of them – standing in the fields around town. Position yourself in the right place on a good day and there are outstanding sunset photos to be had with the windmills in the foreground.

The Drive » Finding Belmonte couldn't be easier – drive northeast of Mota del Cuervo for 16km along the N420 and there you are. As elsewhere on Spain's high inland plateau, the horizons here are vast and you'll see Belmonte's castle well before you arrive.

TRIP HIGHLIGHT

7 Belmonte

Quiet little Belmonte is notable for its fine castle, the 15th-century **Castillo de Belmonte** (www.castillodebelmonte.com; adult/child €8/4; ⏱10am-2pm &

4.30-8.30pm Tue-Sun Jun-Sep, 10am-2pm & 3.30-6.30pm Oct–mid-Feb, 10am-2pm & 4-7pm mid-Feb–May). This is how castles *should* look, with turrets, largely intact walls and a commanding position over the village. It's been recently done up inside, and has a slick display with multilingual audio commentary. And the connection to Don Quixote? Some scholars believe that the castle did serve as inspiration for Cervantes when creating the knight's imaginary world and at least one film-maker agreed – the castle appeared in the

89

DETOUR: VILLADIEGO

Start: ⑧ Ciudad Real

Queso manchego (Manchego cheese) is an icon of the Spanish table and you're travelling through its heartland. For many visitors, their Manchego initiation will be the neat little tapas triangles often served free with a drink. These are usually *semicurado* (semicured) rather than the crumbly stronger (and more expensive) *curado* (cured); the former is aged for approximately three to four months, the latter six to eight months. To receive official Manchego accreditation, the milk must come from a local Manchegan breed of sheep that has evolved over hundreds of years.

To learn more, visit **Villadiego** (www.quesosvilladiego.com; Carretera Poblete-Alarcos Km 2.2, Poblete), 7km southwest of Ciudad Real along the CM420, the cheese equivalent of visiting a winery. During the course of a one-hour tour of the farm (where they've been making the cheese since 1840), you learn what it takes to make *queso manchego*, with tasting an essential part of the visit. Needless to say, they've a shop where you can buy what you've tried.

2002 Spanish production of *El Caballero Don Quijote*. And while you're in town, stop by the **Iglesia Colegial de San Bartolomé** (Colegiata; ◷11am-2pm & 4.30-7.30pm Tue-Sat, 11am-2pm Sun), a magnificent golden-sandstone church with an impressive altarpiece.

🛏 p92

The Drive » The distances on this trip have so far been quite short, but today is a longer day in the saddle. From Belmonte, drive south along the quieter-than-quiet CM3102 for 56km to Tomelloso. Then join the N310 as far as Manzanares (42km), before changing to the N430 to Ciudad Real (55km).

---

⑧ Ciudad Real

Despite being the one-time royal counterpart of Toledo, these days Ciu-dad Real is an unspectacular Spanish working town. The town centre has a certain charm with its pedestrianised shopping streets and distinctive Plaza Mayor, complete with carillon clock (topped by Cupid), flamboyant neo-Gothic town-hall facade and modern tiered fountain. But the main reason to visit is to track down the museum-library, the **Museo del Quijote y Biblioteca Cervantina** (☎926 20 04 57; Ronda de Alarcos 1; ◷10am-2pm & 6-9pm Tue-Sat). The museum has audiovisual displays, while the Cervantes library is stocked with 3500 Don Quixote books, including some in Esperanto and Braille, with most of them now digitised, and others dat-ing back to 1724. It helps if you speak Spanish. Entry is by guided tour every half-hour.

🍽 🛏 p93

The Drive » Head south of Ciudad Real along the N412 and Almagro is just 28km southeast down a road that crosses the flat La Mancha plains.

TRIP HIGHLIGHT

⑨ Almagro

Not even the marketing departments of local tourist authorities can come up with a Quijote connection for Almagro, but it's one of Castilla-La Mancha's prettiest towns and we recommend that you visit for that reason alone. The jewel in Al-magro's crown is the ex-traordinary 16th-century Plaza Mayor, with its wavy tiled roofs, stumpy columns and faded bottle-green porticoes. Right on the square, the **Corral de Comedias** (www.corraldecomedias.com; Plaza Mayor 18; adult/child incl English audioguide €3/free; ⊙10am-2pm & 5-8pm Mon-Fri, to 6pm Sat, 11am-2pm Sun Apr-Oct, 10am-2pm & 4-7pm Mon-Fri, to 5pm Sat, to 1pm Sun Nov-Mar) showcases a literary heritage of a different kind: this is the oldest theatre in Spain, an evocative 17th-century stage with rows of wooden balconies facing the original stage, complete with dressing rooms. Performances are still held here in July during the **Festival Internacional de Teatro Clásico** (www.festivaldealmagro.com). Just around the corner is the **Museo Nacional de Teatro** (museoteatro.mcu.es; Calle de Gran Maestre 2; adult/child €3/free, Sat afternoon & Sun

free; ⊙10am-2pm & 4-7pm Tue-Fri, 11am-2pm & 4-6pm Sat, 11am-2pm Sun), which has exhibits on Spanish theatre from the golden age of the 17th century displayed in rooms surrounding a magnificent 13th-century courtyard. Otherwise, the town is a delight to wander around, although it can be deathly quiet in the depths of winter.

✗ ⌷ p93

The Drive ≫ Return to the N412, turn southeast and, 34km later, you'll cross the N4 motorway, pass the wine centre of Valdepeñas and continue east. Some 34km east of Valdepeñas is Villanueva de los Infantes.

- - - - - - - - - - -

❿ Villanueva de los Infantes

'In a village in La Mancha whose name I cannot recall, there lived long ago a country gentle-

man...' Thus begins the novel and thus it was that the village where our picaresque hero began his journey had always remained a mystery. That was, at least, until 10 eminent Spanish academics marked the 400th anniversary of the book's publishing in 1605 by carefully following the clues left by Cervantes. Their conclusion? That Villanueva de los Infantes, now with an ochre-hued Plaza Mayor surrounded by wood-and-stone balconies and watched over by the 15th-century Iglesia de San Andrés, was Don Quixote's starting point. It's also the end point of our journey, unless, of course, you wish to retrace your steps and set out to follow once again the path trod by Spain's most quixotic knight.

⌷ p93

Eating & Sleeping

Toledo ❶

✗ La Abadía — Castilian, Tapas €€

(www.abadiatoledo.com; Plaza de San Nicolás 3; raciones €4-15; ⊗ bar 8am-midnight, restaurant 1-4pm & 8.30pm-midnight) In a former 16th-century palace, this atmospheric bar and restaurant has arches, niches and subtle lighting spread over a warren of brick-and-stone-clad rooms. The menu includes lightweight dishes and tapas, but the 'Menú de Montes de Toledo' (€19) is a fabulous collection of tastes from the nearby mountains.

✗ Casa Aurelio — Spanish €€€

(☎925 22 41 05; www.casa-aurelio.com; Calle de la Sinagoga 6; mains €18-22; ⊗1-4.30pm & 8-11.30pm Tue-Sat, 1-4.30pm Mon) This place ranks among the best of Toledo's traditional eateries. Game, fresh produce and time-honoured dishes are prepared with panache. There's another **branch** (Plaza del Ayuntamiento) near the cathedral.

🛏 Casa de Cisneros — Boutique Hotel €€

(☎925 22 88 28; www.hostal-casa-de-cisneros. com; Calle del Cardenal Cisneros; s/d €40/66; ❄ 🛜) Right by the cathedral, this lovely 16th-century house was once the home of the cardinal and Grand Inquisitor Cisneros (often known as Ximénes). It's a top choice, with cosy, seductive rooms with original wooden beams and walls, and voguish bathrooms. Archaeological works have revealed the remains of Roman baths and part of an 11th-century Moorish palace in the basement.

🛏 Parador Conde de Orgaz — Hotel €€€

(☎925 22 18 50; www.parador.es; Cerro del Emperador; r €105-207; P ❄ 🛜 🏊) High above the southern bank of Río Tajo, Toledo's low-rise *parador* (luxurious state-owned hotel) boasts a classy interior and breathtaking city views. The *parador* is well signposted: turn right just after crossing the bridge northeast of the old centre. You'll need a car or be prepared to pay taxis.

Consuegra ❷

🛏 La Vida de Antes — Hotel €€

(☎925 48 06 09; www.lavidadeantes.com; Calle Colón 2; s/d incl breakfast €55/75; P ❄ @ 🛜 🏊) Charming La Vida de Antes has old tiled floors, antique furnishings and a pretty patio that really evoke a bygone era. The duplex rooms are particularly cosy and there's interesting art exhibited throughout the building.

Campo de Criptana ❹

✗ Cueva La Martina — Spanish €€

(☎926 56 14 76; www.cuevalamartina.com; Rocinante 13; mains €16-20; ⊗1.30-4pm Mon, 1.30-4pm & 8.30-midnight Tue-Sun) The best place to eat is atmospheric Cueva La Martina, opposite the windmills. The cavelike dining area is dug into the rock, and there's a breezy upstairs terrace with views over town.

🛏 Hospedería Casa de la Torrecilla — Hotel €€

(☎926 58 91 30; www.lacasadelatorrecilla. es; Calle Cardenal Monescillo 17; s/d €45/80; ❄ @ 🛜) The lovely Hospedería Casa de la Torrecilla has a vividly patterned and tiled interior patio. Housed in an early-20th-century nobleman's house, the rooms have parquet floors and are spacious and atmospheric.

Belmonte ❼

🛏 Palacio Buenavista Hospedería — Boutique Hotel €€

(☎967 18 75 80; www.palaciobuenavista. es; Calle José Antonio González 2; s/d/ste incl breakfast €48/78/98; P ❄ 🛜) Palacio Buenavista Hospedería is a classy boutique hotel set in a 17th-century palace next to the Colegiata. Rooms are stylish and set around a sumptuous central patio with skylight; several have views of the castle. There's an excellent restaurant.

Ciudad Real ❽

✖ El Ventero
Tapas €

(Plaza Mayor 8; tapas from €3.50) Time your chair on the square here to enjoy the carillon clock display (generally noon, 1pm, 2pm, 6pm and 8pm), when Don Quixote, Sancho and Cervantes emerge for a congenial spin around a small stage. The vast menu of *raciones* (large tapas servings) includes *salmorejo* (thick garlicky gazpacho), *almoronía* (similar to ratatouille topped with cheese) and *perdiz roja* (partridge in a sherry sauce).

🛏 Palacio de la Serna
Hotel €€

(📞926 84 22 08; www.hotelpalaciodelaserna. com; Calle Cervantes 18; r €89-140, ste €180-220; 🅿 ❄ 🛜 🏊) Just 20 minutes' drive south of Ciudad Real (and an equivalent distance from Almagro) in the sleepy village of Ballesteros de Calatrava, this superb hotel feels a world away. Set around a courtyard, it combines rural comfort with most appealing design; the owner's evocative modern sculptures feature heavily. Rooms are a little avant-garde, with open showers and numerous thoughtful touches. There's a good on-site restaurant.

Almagro ❾

✖ Bar El Gordo
Tapas €

(Plaza Mayor 12; raciones €6-12; 🕐 noon-4pm & 8-11pm) The best and liveliest tapas option on the square, this has a good mix of visitors and locals and buzzes with good cheer on weekend evenings. El Gordo means 'the Fat Man', and the cheerful boss Domingo lives up to his name.

✖ Restaurante Abrasador
Castilian €€

(📞926 88 26 56; www.abrasador.es; Calle San Agustín 18; tostas €1.50, mains €11.50-25, set menus from €25; 🕐 noon-4pm & 8-11pm Mon, Tue & Thu-Sat, noon-4pm Sun) Thoughtfully prepared cooking dominates the restaurant out the back (snaffle the table next to the open fire in winter if you can), with perfectly grilled meats. Out the front, you'll find some of the most creative tapas in Almagro – the famed local eggplant features prominently and it's our pick of the orders whatever guise it's in.

🛏 La Casa del Rector
Hotel €€

(📞926 26 12 59; www.lacasadelrector.com; Calle Pedro Oviedo 8; s/d €85/99; ❄ @ 🛜 🏊) This extraordinary hotel has a wide variety of rooms ranging from sumptuous antique-filled classics to those reflecting cutting-edge modern design, complete with vast private hot tubs and dramatic artwork. Service is faultless and facilities include a classy spa.

🛏 Parador de Almagro
Historic Hotel €€€

(📞926 86 01 00; www.parador.es; Ronda de San Francisco 31; r €80-164; 🅿 ❄ @ 🛜 🏊) A luxurious, old-world charm, despite the mildly incongruous, brightly coloured beams in the rooms.

Villanueva de los Infantes ❿

🛏 La Morada de Juan de Vargas
Hotel €€

(📞926 36 17 69; www.lamoradadevargas. com; Calle Cervantes 3; d €50-75; ❄ 🛜) Exceptionally welcoming and intelligent hosts combined with a prime location just off the main square make La Morada de Juan de Vargas the best of the town's several appealing rural hotel options.

Mérida Home to the most impressive set of Roman ruins in all of Spain

Ancient Extremadura

6

This journey traverses Spain's ancient past, from stirring Roman ruins to tight tangles of medieval old quarters and castles that evoke a picaresque past.

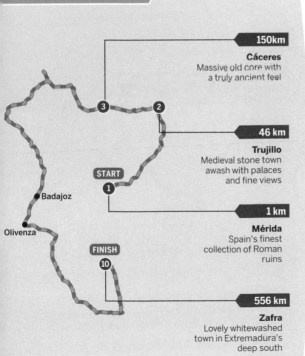

150km
Cáceres
Massive old core with a truly ancient feel

46 km
Trujillo
Medieval stone town awash with palaces and fine views

START

1 km
Mérida
Spain's finest collection of Roman ruins

FINISH

556 km
Zafra
Lovely whitewashed town in Extremadura's deep south

Badajoz

Olivenza

5–7 DAYS
556KM / 346 MILES

GREAT FOR...

BEST TIME TO GO
March to May or September to October, when you should enjoy milder weather.

ESSENTIAL PHOTO
On stage at Mérida's Teatro Romano.

BEST FOR FAMILIES
Wandering through the Ciudad Monumental in Cáceres.

6

Ancient Extremadura

Extremadura is one of Spain's least-visited corners, but that would surely change if only people knew what was here. This is a land where the stories of ancient civilisations, the golden age of Spanish exploration and untold medieval riches are written in stone, with so many magnificent old cities and villages strung out across a splendid terrain of rolling hills and big horizons.

TRIP HIGHLIGHT

❶ Mérida

Mérida, capital of Extremadura, is a marvellous place to begin your journey, home as it is to the most impressive set of Roman ruins in all Spain. Once capital of the Roman province of Lusitania, Emerita Augusta (the Roman forerunner to Mérida) has so much to turn the head. The glittering jewels are the 1st-century-BC **Teatro Romano** (Paseo Álvarez Sáez de Buruaga; entry by combined

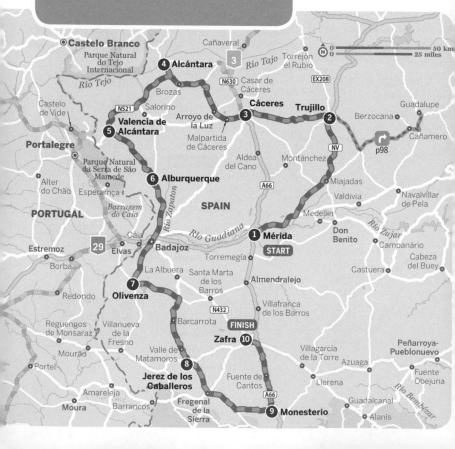

ticket adult/concession/child €12/6/free; ◷9am-9pm Apr-Sep, 9.30am-2pm & 4 6.30pm Mon-Fri, 9am-6.30pm Sat & Sun Oct-Mar), a classical theatre still used for performances during the summer **Festival del Teatro Clásico** (www.festivaldemerida.es; admission €15-45), and the adjacent **Museo Nacional de Arte Romano** (☏924 31 16 90; museoarteromano.mcu.es; Calle de José Ramón Mélida; adult/child €3/free, EU seniors & students free, after 2pm Sat & all day Sun free; ◷9.30am-8pm Tue-Sat, 10am-3pm Sun Apr-Sep, 9.30am-6.30pm Tue-Sat, 10am-3pm Sun Oct-Mar). But in Mérida such splendours are just the beginning. There's the 60-arch **Puente Romano** that spans the Río Guadi-

LINK YOUR TRIP

3 The Forgotten West

Begin in Cáceres then disappear off the map through some of the loveliest, least-known villages in the country.

29 Medieval Jewels in the Southern Interior

It's a 110km drive northwest from Zafra to Elvas, where you'll find striking landscapes and medieval lore in Portugal's southern interior.

ana, the **Templo de Diana** (Calle de Sagasta) that rises improbably from the modern city centre, and the **Alcazaba** (Calle Graciano; entry by combined ticket adult/concession/child €12/6/free; ◷9am-9pm Apr-Sep, 9.30am-2pm & 4-6.30pm Mon-Fri, 9am-6.30pm Sat & Sun Oct-Mar), a fortress that has been occupied by just about everyone down through the ages, from Visigoths and Romans to the enlightened Muslims of Al-Andalus.

✗ ⊨ p101

The Drive ≫ Getting from Mérida to Trujillo couldn't be easier – take the A5 motorway heading northeast of the city and Trujillo lies just 94km up the road.

- - - - - - - - - - - - -

TRIP HIGHLIGHT

❷ Trujillo

The core of Trujillo is one of the best-preserved medieval towns in Spain. It begins in the Plaza Mayor, which is surrounded by towers and palaces, and the splendour continues up the hillside with a labyrinth of mansions, leafy courtyards, fruit gardens, churches and convents all enclosed within 900m of walls circling the upper town and dating back to the 16th century when Trujillo's favourite sons returned home as wealthy conquistadors. At the top of the hill, Trujillo's impressive **Alcazaba** (adult/child €1.40/free; ◷10am-2pm & 4.30-7pm)

has 10th-century Islamic origins. Patrol the battlements for magnificent 360-degree sweeping views. From here, from just about any vantage point, whether bathed in the warm light of a summer sunset or shrouded in the mists of winter, Trujillo can feel like a magical place.

✗ ⊨ p101

The Drive ≫ The A58 connects Trujillo with Cáceres, just 46km to the west.

- - - - - - - - - - - - -

TRIP HIGHLIGHT

❸ Cáceres

The old core of Cáceres, its Ciudad Monumental (Old Town), is truly extraordinary. Narrow cobbled streets twist and climb among ancient stone walls lined with palaces and mansions, while the skyline is decorated with turrets, spires, gargoyles and enormous storks' nests. Protected by defensive walls, it has survived almost intact from its 16th-century heyday and so much of the monumental beauty is clustered around three connected squares, the Plaza de Santa María, Plaza de San Jorge, and the Plaza de San Mateo. At dusk or after dark, when the crowds have gone, you'll feel like you've stepped back into the Middle Ages. Stretching at the feet of the old city, the lively and arcaded Plaza Mayor is one of Spain's finest public squares.

✕ 🍴 🛏 p101

The Drive » Drive 13km west of Cáceres along the N521, then turn right (northwest) onto the EX207 (the sign will say Arroyo de la Luz). Some 17km further on, turn left onto the EX207 – Alcántara is 26km away to the northwest.

➍ Alcántara

Out in Extremadura's wild, remote and rarely travelled west, Alcántara is best known for its magnificent Roman bridge. The bridge – 204m long, 61m high and much reinforced over the centuries – spans the Río Tajo below a huge dam.

The town itself retains old walls, a ruined castle, several imposing mansions and the enormous Renaissance **Convento de San Benito** (www. fundacionsanbenito.com; Calle Trajano; ⏱10.30am-1.30pm & 5-7pm Wed-Sat, 10.30am-1.30pm Sun). The highlights of the down-at-heel monastery, built in the 16th century to house the Orden de Alcántara, an order of Reconquista knights, include the Gothic cloister and the perfectly proportioned three-tier loggia. Admission is by free hourly guided visits.

The Drive » Leaving Alcántara, return along the EX207 for around 6km, then take the EX117. Where that road

LIANEM / GETTY IMAGES ©

ends, just after Membrío, turn right onto the N521. Just when you think you're headed for Portugal, Valencia de Alcántara appears up ahead.

➎ Valencia de Alcántara

Not many travellers stop out here, 7km from the Portuguese border, and its well-preserved old centre is a curious labyrinth of whitewashed houses and mansions. One side of the old town is watched over by the ruins of a medieval castle and the 17th-century **Iglesia de Rocamador**. The surrounding countryside

DETOUR: GUADALUPE

Start: ➋ Trujillo

Guadalupe's revered **Real Monasterio de Santa María de Guadalupe** (📞927 36 70 00; www. monasterioguadalupe.com; Plaza de Santa María de Guadalupe; church free, monastery by guided tour adult/child €5/2; ⏱church 8.30am-9pm, monastery 9.30am-1pm & 3.30-6.30pm) is located, according to legend, on the spot where a shepherd found an effigy of the Virgin, hidden years earlier by Christians fleeing the Muslims. A sumptuous church-monastery (complete with works attributed to El Greco, Goya, Zurbarán and even Michelangelo) was built on the site and this is still one of Spain's most important pilgrimage sites. One-hour guided tours leave every half-hour. While the monastery is the obvious highlight, take some time to wander the picturesque streets off the Plaza Mayor. Guadalupe is a nearly-two-hour drive along narrow mountain roads. Take the EX208 for 27km southeast of Trujillo, then the EX102 for 50km into Guadalupe.

Valencia de Alcántara Ancient dolmens (stone circles of prehistoric monoliths)

is known for its cork industry and some 50 ancient dolmens (stone circles of prehistoric monoliths).

The Drive » Unless you plan on crossing the border, return a few clicks back up the N521 heading northeast, then turn right (southeast) onto the EX110 along which, 32km later, you'll encounter Alburquerque.

❻ Alburquerque

Looming large above this small town, 38km north of Badajoz, is the intact **Castillo de la Luna** (⊘11am-2pm & 4-6pm Tue-Sun). The centrepiece of a complex frontier defence system of forts, the castle was built on the site of its Islamic antecedent in the 13th century and subsequently expanded. From the top, views take in the Portuguese frontier (the Portuguese actually took the town for a few years in the early 18th century).

The Drive » Head roughly south along the EX110, shadowing the Portuguese border, crossing low hills and quiet farmlands all the way into Badajoz. This provincial capital has little to recommend it – carry right on through, looking for the EX107 and the signs to Olivenza.

❼ Olivenza

Pretty Olivenza, 24km south of Badajoz, clings to its Portuguese heritage – it has only been Spanish since 1801. The cobbled centre is distinctive for its whitewashed houses, typical turreted defensive walls and penchant for blue-and-white ceramic tile work. Smack-bang in its centre is the 14th-century castle, dominated by the **Torre del Homenaje**, 36m high, from which there are fine views. The most impressive section of the original defensive walls is around the 18th-century

Puerta del Calvario, on the western side of town.

The Drive » It's 29km east-southeast along the EX105 to the N435 at Barcarrota – after all this time in the backblocks, the sudden rush of traffic may come as a surprise. From there it's 25km south into Jerez de los Caballeros.

⑧ Jerez de los Caballeros

Walled and hilly Jerez de los Caballeros was a cradle of conquistadors. It has a 13th-century castle that was built by the Knights Templar. You can wander around at will, but it's basically just the impressive walls that are preserved. There are several handsome churches scattered across the town, three with towers emulating the Giralda in Seville.

The Drive » Take the N435 southeast to Fregenal de la Sierra, then the EX201, then the EX103 over the hills, watching for signs to Monesterio (and black pigs fattening up in stone-walled fields).

⑨ Monesterio

Since the completion of the A66 motorway, many bypassed towns have disappeared into quiet obscurity, but not Monesterio, because this is one of Spain's (and certainly Extremadura's) most celebrated sources of *jamón* (cured ham). Occupying pride of place at the southern end of the town is the outstanding **Museo del Jamón** (☏924 51 67 37; www.museodeljamon-demonesterio.com; Paseo de Extremadura 314; ⏱9.30am-2pm & 6-8pm Mon- Sat, 10am-2pm Sun), arguably the best of its kind in Spain. Its exhibits take visitors through the process of *jamón* production, from ideal pig habitats, to the *matanza* (killing of the pigs) right through to the finished product.

The Drive » It's 40km north from Monesterio to Zafra, either along the motorway or the quieter N630 that shadows it.

TRIP HIGHLIGHT

⑩ Zafra

Looking for all the world like an Andalucian *pueblo blanco* (white town), gleaming-white Zafra is a serene, attractive place to rest at journey's end. Originally a Muslim settlement, Zafra's narrow streets are lined with baroque churches, old-fashioned shops and traditional houses decorated by brilliant red splashes of geraniums. Zafra's 15th-century castle, a blend of Gothic, Mudéjar and Renaissance architecture, is now a *parador* (luxury hotel) and dominates the town's roofscape. Plaza Grande and the adjoining Plaza Chica, arcaded and bordered by bars, are the places to see Zafra life. The southern end of the Plaza Grande, with its palm trees, is one of Extremadura's prettiest corners.

Eating & Sleeping

Mérida ❶

✗ Tábula Calda Spanish €€

(☎924 30 49 50; www.tabulacalda.com; Calle Romero Leal 11; mains €10-18, set menu €13.50-27; ⏱1-4pm & 8pm-midnight Mon-Sat, 1-4pm Sun) This inviting space, with tilework and abundant greenery, serves up well-priced meals that cover most Spanish staples and everything either comes from its garden or is sourced from within 100km of the kitchen. Before your food arrives, you'll be plied with a complimentary tapa, house salad (orange, sugar and olive oil, reflecting the family's Jewish roots) and olives. Manuel is a warm and welcoming host.

⌂ Hotel Adealba Hotel €€

(☎924 38 83 08; www.hoteladealba.com; Calle Romero Leal 18; s €50-80, d €60-90; ⓟ ❄ 🛜) This chic but cordial hotel occupies a 19th-century townhouse close to the Templo de Diana and does so with a classy, contemporary look. Although some of the installations are starting to show their age, the beds are super comfy and the bigger the room, the better the deal. There's a compact on-site spa complex Valet parking (€18) is available.

Trujillo ❷

✗ Restaurante La Troya Traditional Spanish €

(☎927 32 13 64; www.mesonlatroya.com; Plaza Mayor 10; menus €15; ⏱1-4pm & 8.30-11pm) Famed across Spain for its copious servings of no-frills *comida casera* (home-style cooking), Troya enjoys a prime location on the main town square. On entering, you'll be directed to one of several dining areas, to be presented with plates of tortilla and chorizo and a lettuce-and-tomato salad. And that's even before you've ordered

your three-course *menú* (set menu). It's all about quantity, and queues stretch out the door on weekends.

⌂ Posada dos Orillas Historic Hotel €€

(☎927 65 90 79; www.dosorillas.com; Calle de Cambrones 6; d €50-70; ❄ 🛜) This tastefully renovated 16th-century mansion is in a great location in the walled town. Rooms replicate Spanish colonial taste and are named for the countries in which towns called Trujillo are found. Personal service from the owners is excellent here, and the nights are quiet as as can be.

Cáceres ❸

✗ Restaurante Torre de Sande Fusion €€

(☎927 21 11 47; castillodelaarguijuela.com; Calle Condes 3; menus €25-45; ⏱1-4pm & 7pm-midnight Tue-Sat, 1-4pm Sun) Dine in the pretty courtyard on dishes such as *salmorejo de cerezas del Jerte con queso de cabra* (cherry-based cold soup with goat's cheese) at this elegant gourmet restaurant in the heart of the Ciudad Monumental. More modestly, stop for a drink and a tapa at the interconnecting *tapería* (tapas bar).

⌂ Hotel Casa Don Fernando Boutique Hotel €€

(☎927 62 71 76; www.casadonfernando.com; Plaza Mayor 30; d €50-150; ⓟ ❄ 🛜) The classiest midrange choice in Cáceres, this boutique hotel sits on Plaza Mayor directly opposite the Arco de la Estrella. Spread over four floors, the designer rooms and bathrooms are tastefully chic; superior rooms (€30 more than the standards) have the best plaza views (although nights can be noisy especially on weekends). Attic-style top-floor rooms are good for families.

Northern Spain & Basque Country

THIS IS THE SPAIN THAT MOST INTERNATIONAL VISITORS ARE YET TO DISCOVER. Spain's north coast and its hinterland are home to some of the most dramatic scenery in the country, from snow-speckled mountains to a storm-lashed coastline peppered with picture-perfect villages.

As far as driving country goes there can be few parts of the Iberian Peninsula more rewarding than northern Spain. Many of the roads are quiet and wend through small fishing ports, across mountain pastures and along ancient pilgrim trails. The scenic and cultural variety awaiting the road tripper here is astounding. You can pause in food-obsessed cities, climb castle turrets, stand among rolling vineyards and even play Lawrence of Arabia in a barren semidesert.

La Rioja Fertile soils producing outstanding Spanish wines (Trip 8)
I. LIZARRAGA / GETTY IMAGES ©

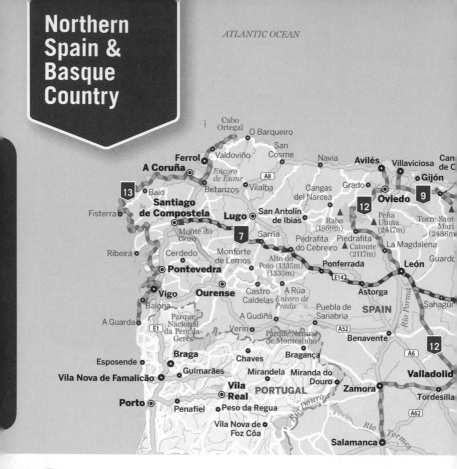

Northern Spain & Basque Country

ATLANTIC OCEAN

Food

Northern Spain's united love of food means the freshest shellfish, tapas, or rabbit stew can be found on Trips **10** **11** **13**

Wine Tasting

La Rioja is home to the best red wines in Spain – bodegas, tours, tastings and museums will inform as you consume on Trip **8**

Seaside Villages

Spain's northwestern coast lingers long in the memory. Quaint fishing villages such as Muxía and Combarro add a gentle touch on Trip **13**

Meeting God

From rock-cut churches to the Camino de Santiago, Islamic monuments to the pagan hills of Fisterra, there's always somewhere to commune with your god along Trips **7** **8** **11** **12** **13**

Wildlife

There are bears in the hills of Asturias, eagles in the mountains of Cantabria and dinosaurs in the desert valleys of La Rioja. Enjoy a Spanish safari on Trips **9** **11** **12**

Bodegas Ysios Vineyards and an architectural masterpiece

Camino de Santiago *A pilgrimage that attracts walkers of all backgrounds and ages from around the world*

Classic Trip

Northern Spain Pilgrimage

7

Travel in the footprints of thousands of pilgrims past and present as you journey along the highroads and backroads of the legendary Camino de Santiago pilgrimage trail.

TRIP HIGHLIGHTS

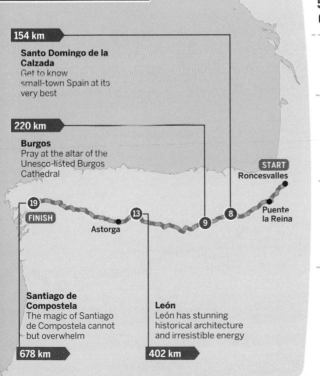

154 km

Santo Domingo de la Calzada
Get to know small-town Spain at its very best

220 km

Burgos
Pray at the altar of the Unesco-listed Burgos Cathedral

START
Roncesvalles

19
FINISH

13

Astorga

9

8

Puente la Reina

Santiago de Compostela
The magic of Santiago de Compostela cannot but overwhelm

678 km

León
León has stunning historical architecture and irresistible energy

402 km

5–7 DAYS
678 KM / 423 MILES

GREAT FOR...

BEST TIME TO GO

April to June for fields of poppies, September and October for golden leaves.

ESSENTIAL PHOTO

Standing outside the Cathedral de Santiago de Compostela.

BEST FOR CULTURE

Santiago de Compostela

Classic Trip

7 Northern Spain Pilgrimage

For over a thousand years pilgrims have marched across the top of Spain on the Camino de Santiago (Way of St James) to the tomb of St James the Apostle in Santiago de Compostela. Real pilgrims walk, but by driving you'll enjoy religious treasures, grand cathedrals, big skies and wide open landscapes – and no blisters.

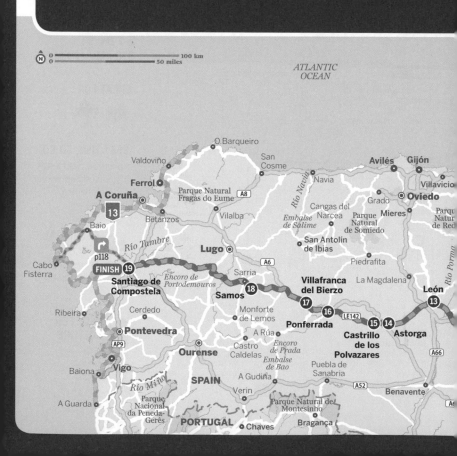

❶ Roncesvalles

Long a key stopping point on the Camino de Santiago, history hangs heavily in the air of the monastery complex of Roncesvalles, where pilgrims give thanks for a successful crossing of the Pyrenees. The main event here is the **monastery complex** (www.roncesvalles.es; adult/child €4.30/2.50; ☺10am-2pm & 3.30-7pm Apr-Oct, shorter hours Nov-Mar), which contains a number of different buildings of interest. The 13th-century Gothic **Real Colegiata de**

Santa María (admission free; ☺9am-8.30pm) houses a much-revered, silver-covered statue of the Virgin beneath a modernist-looking canopy. There's also a statue of **Santiago** (St James) dressed as a pilgrim (with scallop shell and staff). Also of interest is the cloister, which contains the tomb of King Sancho VII (El Fuerte) of Navarra, the apparently 2.25m-tall victor in the Battle of Las Navas de Tolosa, fought against the Muslims in 1212. Nearby

LINK YOUR TRIP

13 Coast of Galicia
With the Camino de Santiago ticked off carry on to Fisterra and the end of the world on the Coast of Galicia drive.

18 The Pyrenees
Before you commune with God, commune with Mother Nature as you travel the breadth of the gorgeous Pyrenees.

Classic Trip

is the 12th-century **Capilla de Sancti Spiritus**.

If you need some exercise there's lots of good walking around here.

The Drive » It's basically 47km (one hour) downhill all the way from Roncesvalles to Pamplona. It's a pretty drive through mountainscapes, forests and gentle farmland. The N135 road passes through innumerable hamlets and villages painted in the red and white Basque colours and centred on old stone churches, many of which are crammed with religious treasures.

-- -- -- -- -- -- --
❷ Pamplona

Renowned across the world for the Sanfermines festival, when bulls tear through the streets at dawn causing chaos as they go (and alcohol-fueled revellers cause chaos for the remainder of the day – and night), Pamplona is a quiet and low-key city at any other time of the year. Animal rights groups oppose bullrunning as a cruel tradition and increasing left-wing influence in local government has called the future of Pamplona's bullrun into question.

Pamplona's history stretches back to Roman times, and is best traced in the city's fantastic **Museo de Navarra** (www.cfnavarra.es/cultura/museo; Calle Cuesta de Santo Domingo 47; adult/student/child €2/1/ free, free Sat afternoon & Sun; ☺9.30am-2pm & 5-7pm Tue-Sat, 11am-2pm Sun), whose highlights include huge Roman mosaics. The **Catedral** (www.catedraldepamplona.com; Calle Dormitalería; adult/child €5/3; ☺10.30am-7pm Mon-Sat) is late-medieval Gothic with a neoclassical facade. The cathedral tour is a highlight and takes you up to the top of the bell tower, into the pretty

WHAT IS THE CAMINO DE SANTIAGO?

The Camino de Santiago (Way of St James) originated as a medieval pilgrimage and ever since people have taken up the challenge of the Camino and walked to Santiago de Compostela. It all began back in the 9th century when a remarkable event occurred in the poor Iberian hinterlands: following a shining star, Pelayo, a religious hermit, unearthed the tomb of the apostle James the Greater (or, in Spanish, Santiago). The news was confirmed by the local bishop, the Asturian king and later the pope.

Compostela became the most important destination for Christians after Rome and Jerusalem. Its popularity increased with an 11th-century papal decree granting it Holy Year status: pilgrims could receive a plenary indulgence – a full remission of your life's sins – during a Holy Year. These occur when Santiago's feast day (25 July) falls on a Sunday: if you've been naughty then you'll need to wait until 2021 for the next one – but driving there doesn't count...

The 11th and 12th centuries marked the heyday of the pilgrimage. The Reformation was devastating for Catholic pilgrimages and by the 19th century the Camino had nearly died out. In its startling late-20th-century reanimation, which continues today, it's most popular as a personal and spiritual journey of discovery, rather than one primarily motivated by religion.

Today the most popular of the several *caminos* (paths) to Santiago de Compostela is the Camino Francés, which spans 783km of Spain's north and attracts walkers of all backgrounds and ages from across the world. It's the Council of Europe's first Cultural Itinerary and a Unesco World Heritage site but, for pilgrims, it's a pilgrimage equal to visiting Jerusalem, and by finishing it you're guaranteed a healthy chunk of time off purgatory.

cloisters and a museum with religious treasures, a Roman-era house and finishes all surreal with a room full of Virgins!

 p120

The Drive » Leave Pamplona on the A12 westbound and after about 10 minutes turn off at exit 9, onto the more driver-friendly NA1110. Drive through Astraín and continue along this peaceful country road for 10 minutes to Legarda, then to Muruzábal and, finally, 2km southeast to Santa María de Eunate.

❸ Santa María de Eunate

Surrounded by cornfields and brushed by wildflowers, the near perfect octaganal Romanesque chapel of **Santa María de Eunate** (⊙10am-2pm & 4-7.30pm Tue-Sun) is one of the most picturesque chapels along the whole Camino. Dating from around the 12th century its origins – and the reason why it's located in the middle of nowhere – are something of a mystery.

The Drive » From the chapel it's just a 5km drive along the NA6064 to gorgeous Puente la Reina.

❹ Puente la Reina

The chief calling card of Puente la Reina (Basque: Gares), 22km southwest of Pamplona on the A12, is the spectacular six-arched **medieval bridge** that dominates the

western end of town, but Puente la Reina rewards on many other levels. A key stop on the Camino de Santiago, the town's pretty streets throng with the ghosts of a multitude of pilgrims. Their first stop here is at the late-Romanesque **Iglesia del Crucifijo**, erected by the Knights Templar and still containing one of the finest Gothic crucifixes in existence.

The Drive » The fastest way between Puente la Reina and Estella is on the A12 (20 minutes, 22km), but the more enjoyable drive is along the slower, more rural, NA1110, for which you should allow about half an hour. You'll probably spy a few Camino pilgrims trudging along.

❺ Estella

Estella (Basque: Lizarra) was known as 'La Bella' in medieval times because of the splendour of its monuments and buildings, and though the old dear has lost some of its beauty to modern suburbs, it's not without

charms. During the 11th century Estella became a main reception point for the growing flood of pilgrims along the Camino de Santiago. Today most visitors are continuing that same plodding tradition. There's an attractive old quarter and a couple of notable churches, including the 12th-century **Iglesia de San Pedro de la Rúa**. It's cloisters are a fine example of Romanesque sculptural work. Across the river and overlooking the town is the **Iglesia de San Miguel**, with a fine Romanesque north door. Close to Estella are a couple of interesting monasteries: the **Monasterio de Irache** (⊙10am-1.15pm & 4-7pm Wed-Sun, closed 1-17 Jan) and **Monasterio de Iranzu** (www.monasterio-iranzu.com; admission €2.50; ⊙10am-2pm & 4-8pm).

The Drive » It's a 40km (50 minute) drive from Estella to Viana. When you leave Estella take the A12 westward and turn onto the NA1110 at junction 58. Follow the NA1110 through the sleepy towns of Los Arcos, Sansol

---

TOP TIP: FUENTE DE VINO

Even the most adamant nonwalker might wish they'd donned hiking boots when they get to the Monasterio de Irache near Estella and find the **Fuente de Vino** (Spring of Wine), just behind the Bodega de Irache. Yes, it really is a spring of wine and yes, you really can drink some for free – though only if you're a pilgrim walking, not driving! – to Santiago.

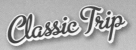

Classic Trip

JUERGEN RICHTER / LOOK-FOTO / GETTY IMAGES ©

JOSÉ ANTONIO MORENO / GETTY IMAGES ©

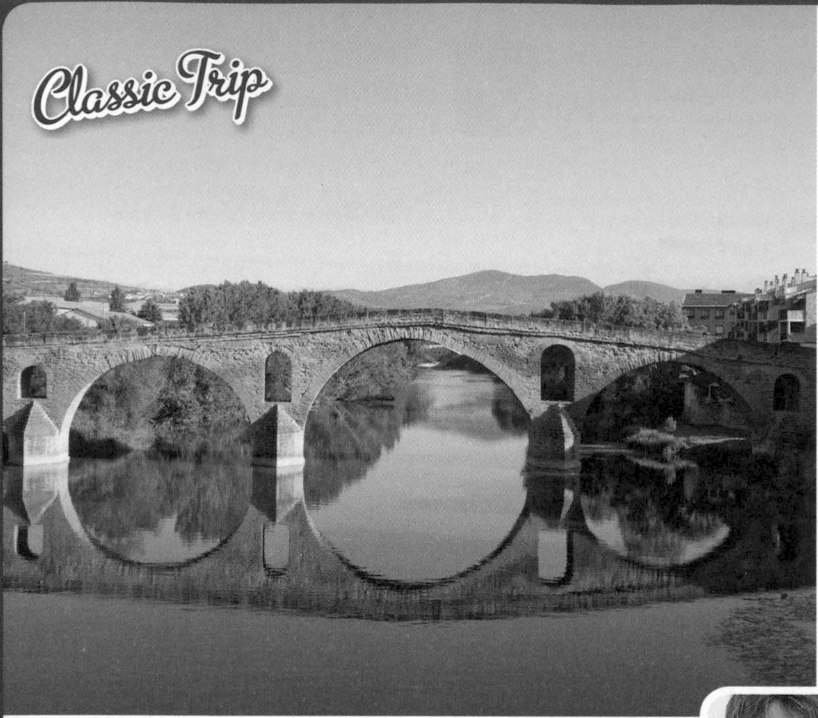

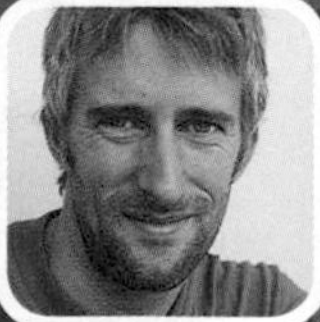

WHY THIS IS A CLASSIC TRIP
STUART BUTLER, AUTHOR

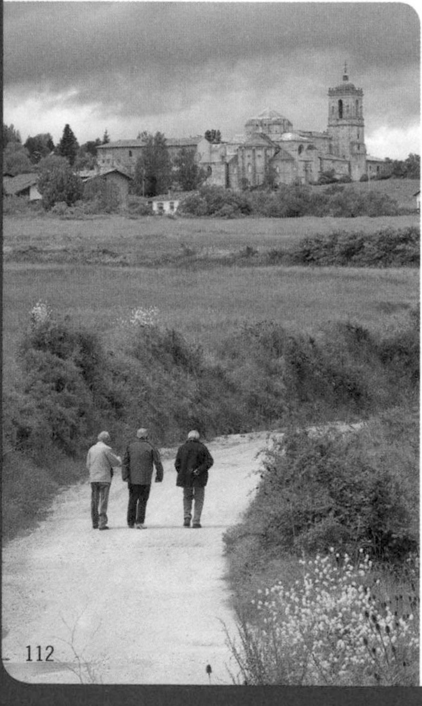

This is a drive on an epic scale. The Camino de Santiago has been drawing people to northern Spain for a millennia, and although religion plays no part in it for me I still consider the Camino the ultimate way of seeing northern Spain. Drive it. Cycle it. Walk it. Just do it!

Top: Puente la Reina bridge
Left: Camino de Santiago
Right: Pilgrims near Burgos

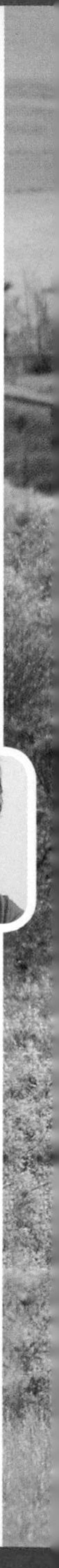

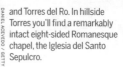

and Torres del Rıo. In hillside Torres you'll find a remarkably intact eight-sided Romanesque chapel, the Iglesia del Santo Sepulcro.

- - - - - - - - -

⑥ Viana

Overlooked by many nonpilgrim tourists, Viana, the last town in Navarra, started life as a garrison town defending the kingdom of Navarra from Castilla. Today, the old part of the town, which sits atop a hill, is still largely walled and is an interesting place to wander about for a couple of hours. The **Iglesia de Santa María** and **Iglesia de San Pedro** are the chief attractions. Work started on Santa María in the 13th century and it is one of the more impressive religious structures on this eastern end of the Camino. The Iglesia de San Pedro is today a ruin that hosts concerts and weddings. The former **bull ring** is today a plaza in the middle of town, where children booting footballs are considerably more common than bulls.

The Drive » It's 10km and 20 minutes from Viana to Logroño. The first half of the drive is through open, big-sky countryside; the last part through the city suburbs. There's a large car park underneath the main plaza by the old town.

Classic Trip

❼ Logroño

Logroño, capital of La Rioja and Spain's wine-growing region par excellence, doesn't feel the need to be loud and brash. Instead it's a stately town with a heart of tree-studded squares, narrow streets, hidden corners and a monumentally good selection of *pintxos* (Basque tapas) bars. All up, this is the sort of place that you cannot help but feel contented in – and it's not just the wine. The superb **Museo de la Rioja** (Plaza San Agustin 23; ⏰10am-2pm & 4-9pm Tue-Sat, 10am-2pm Sun) in the centre of Logroño takes you on a wild romp through Riojan history and culture – from the days when dinner was killed with arrows to re-creations of the kitchens that many a Spanish granny grew up using. The other major attraction is the **Catedral**

de Santa María de la Redonda (Calle de Portales; ⏰8am-1pm & 6-8.45pm Mon-Sat, 9am-2pm & 6.30-8.45pm Sun), which started life as a Gothic church before maturing into a full-blown cathedral in the 16th century.

✕ 🛏 p120

The Drive » For the short 45km (35 minute) hop to Santo Domingo de la Calzada, the Camino walking trail virtually traces the route of the fast, and dull, A12 motorway. There's really not much reason for you to veer off the motorway (none of the quieter, smaller roads really follow the Camino).

TRIP HIGHLIGHT

❽ Santo Domingo de la Calzada

Santo Domingo is small-town Spain at its very best. A large number of the inhabitants continue to live in the partially walled old quarter, a labyrinth of medieval streets where the past is alive and the sense of community is strong. The **Catedral de Santo Domingo de la Calzada** (www.catedralsantodomingo. es; Plaza del Santo 4; adult/

student/child €4/3/free; ⏰10am-8.30pm Mon-Fri, 9am-7.10pm Sat, 9am-12.20pm & 1.45-7.10pm Sun Apr-Oct, shorter hours Nov-Mar) and its attached museum glitter with the gold that attests to the great wealth the Camino has bestowed on otherwise backwater towns. The cathedral's most eccentric feature is the white rooster and hen that forage in a glass-fronted cage opposite the entrance to the crypt. Their presence celebrates a long-standing legend, the Miracle of the Rooster, which tells of a young man who was unfairly executed only to recover miraculously, while the broiled cock and hen on the plate of his judge suddenly leapt up.

The Drive » From Santo Domingo to Burgos it's just 57km and 50 minutes. Again you're sort of stuck with using the A12.

TRIP HIGHLIGHT

❾ Burgos

On the surface, conservative Burgos seems to embody all the stereotypes of a north-central Spanish town, with sombre grey-stone architecture, the fortifying cuisine of the high *meseta* (plateau) and a climate of extremes. But Burgos is a city that rewards. The historic centre is austerely elegant, guarded by monumental gates and with the cathedral as its centrepiece. This Unesco

✓

TOP TIP: PILGRIM HOSTELS

In towns and villages all along the Camino you will see very cheap pilgrim hostels. These are *only* for pilgrims travelling to Santiago by foot or bicycle (and able to prove it). As a driver you will be reliant on normal hotel-style accommodation.

WHO WAS ST JAMES THE APOSTLE?

St James, or James the Greater, was one of the 12 disciples of Jesus. He may even have been the first disciple. He was also the first to be martyred by King Herod in AD 44. So, if St James was living in the Holy Lands 2000 years ago, an obvious question persists: what were the remains of St James doing in northwest Spain a thousand years later? The accepted story (and we're not standing by its authenticity) suggests that two of St James's own disciples secreted his remains onto a stone boat which then set sail across the Mediterranean and passed into the Atlantic to moor at present-day Padrón (Galicia). Continuing inland for 17km, the disciples buried his body in a forest named Liibredon (present-day Santiago de Compostela). All was then forgotten until a thousand years later, when a religious hermit found the remains.

World Heritage–listed Catedral is a masterpiece that originally started life as a modest Romanesque church, but over time became one of the most impressive cathedrals in a land of impressive cathedrals. For more on the Catedral and the other stellar attractions of Burgos, see p46.

✕ 🍴 p120

The Drive » It's 58km (45 minutes) from Burgos to little castle-topped Castrojeriz. Take the A12 out of town to junction 32 and turn off northwest along the minor BU400.

⑩ Castrojeriz

With it's mix of old and new buildings huddled around the base of a hill that's topped with what's left of a crumbling **castle**, Castrojeriz is your typical small *meseta* town. It's worth a climb up to the castle if only for the views. The town's church, **Iglesia de San Juan**, is worth a look as well.

The Drive » From Castrojeriz it's only 30km (35 minutes) along the BU403 and P432 to Frómista. The scenery is classic *meseta* and if you're lucky you'll catch a glimpse of such evocative sights as a flock of sheep being led over the alternately burning or freezing plateau by a shepherd.

⑪ Frómista

The main (and some would say only) reason for stopping here is the village's exceptional Romanesque church, the **Iglesia de San Martín** (admission €1; ⊘9.30am 2pm & 4.30-8pm). Dating from 1066 and restored in the early 20th century, this harmoniously proportioned church is one of the premier Romanesque churches in rural Spain, adorned with a veritable menagerie of human and zoomorphic figures just below the eaves. The capitals within are also richly decorated.

The Drive » From Frómista to Sahagún is 59km (45 minutes)

via the P980 to Carrión de los Condes, where the Camino basically starts following the major A231 road.

⑫ Sahagún

Despite appearances, Sahagún was an immensely powerful and wealthy Benedictine centre by the 12th century. The Mudéjar-influenced brick Romanesque churches merit a visit.

The Drive » The 59km (50 minute) stretch from Sahagún to León along the A231 and N601 isn't one of the more memorable driving moments of this route. Still, you have to feel for those walking the Camino as they're virtually walking along beside you (some pilgrims bus between Burgos and León because so much of the route is next to the motorway).

TRIP HIGHLIGHT

⑬ León

León is a wonderful city, combining stunning historical architecture with an irresistible energy. Its standout attraction is the

NORTHERN SPAIN & BASQUE COUNTRY 7 NORTHERN SPAIN PILGRIMAGE

13th-century **Catedral**
(📞987 87 57 70; www.
catedraldeleon.org; adult/
concession/child under 12yr
€5/4/free; ⏰9.30am-1.30pm
& 4-8pm Mon-Sat, 9.30am-
2.30pm & 5-8pm Sun), one
of the most beautiful
cathedrals in Spain.
Whether spotlit by night
or bathed in glorious
sunshine, the cathedral,
arguably Spain's premier
Gothic masterpiece,
exudes a glorious, almost
luminous quality. The
show-stopping facade has
a radiant rose window,
three richly sculpted
doorways and two mus-
cular towers. After going
through the main en-
trance, lorded over by the
scene of the Last Supper,
an extraordinary gallery
of *vidrieras* (stained-
glass windows) awaits.
Even older than León's
cathedral, the **Real
Basílica de San Isidoro**
(⏰7.30am-11pm) provides
a stunning Romanesque
counterpoint to the
former's Gothic strains,
with extraordinary
frescoes in the attached
Panteón, the main high-
light. Fernando I and
Doña Sancha founded the
church in 1063 to house
the remains of the saint,
as well as the remains of
themselves and 21 other
early Leónese and Castil-
ian monarchs. The main

basilica is a hotchpotch
of styles, but the two
main portals on the
southern facade are pure
Romanesque. Attached
to the Real Basílica de
San Isidoro, **Panteón
Real** (admission €5;
⏰10am-1.30pm & 4-6.30pm
Mon-Sat, 10am-1.30pm Sun)
houses the remain-
ing sarcophagi, which
rest with quiet dignity
beneath a canopy of some
of the finest Romanesque
frescoes in Spain. Motif
after colourful motif of
biblical scenes drench the
vaults and arches of this
extraordinary hall.

✕ 🛏 p120

The Drive » Taking the N120
from León to Astorga will keep
you on the route of the Camino.
It's a 50km (one hour) drive.
There's also the much faster
AP71 motorway, but what's the
point in coming all this way to
drive on a road like that?!

- - - - - - - - - - - -

⑭ **Astorga**

On a map of Spain,
Astorga comes across as
rather insignificant, but
this medium-sized town
has history and attrac-
tions totally out of pro-
portion to its provincial
status today. For more on
Astorga, see p80.

The Drive » It's just a 7km
(15 minute) drive from Astorga
to Castrillo de los Polvazares
along the rural LE142. Note that
nonresidents are not allowed
to drive into Castrillo de los
Polvazares, so park up in one of
the parking areas on the edge of
the village.

BRAIS SEARA / GETTY IMAGES ©

- - - - - - - - - - - -

⑮ **Castrillo de los
Polvazares**

One of the prettiest vil-
lages along the Camino – if
a little twee – is Castrillo
de los Polvazares. It consists of little but one main
cobbled street, a small
church and an array of
well-preserved 18th-
century stone houses. If
you can be here before or

Ponferrada Castillo Templario's imposing entrance

after all the tour buses have left then it's an absolute delight of a place and one in which the spirit of the Camino can be strongly felt.

The Drive » Continue along the LE142 towards Ponferrada (one hour 20 minutes, 53km). The road runs pretty much beside the Camino and you'll pass through a string of attractive stone villages, most of which have churches topped with storks nests. It's worth stopping in Rabanal del Camino with its 18th-century Ermita del Bendito Cristo de la Vera Cruz (a hermitage).

- - - - - - - - - -

16 Ponferrada

Ponferrada is not the region's most enticing town, but its castle and remnants of the old town centre (around the stone clock tower) make it worth a brief stop. Built by the Knights Templar in the 13th century, the walls of the fortress-monastery **Castillo Templario** (adult/concession €4/2, Wed free; ⊘10am-2pm & 4.30-8.30pm Tue-Sat, 10am-2pm Sun) rise high over Río Sil, and the square, crenelated towers ooze romance and history. The castle has a lonely and impregnable air, and is

Classic Trip

a striking landmark in Ponferrada's otherwise bleak urban landscape.

Among Ponferrada's churches, the Gothic-Renaissance **Basílica de Nuestra Señora de la Encina** (📞987 41 19 78; 🕑9am-2pm & 4.30-8.30pm), up the hill past the tourist office, is the most impressive, especially its 17th-century painted wood altarpiece from the school of Gregorio Fernández.

The Drive ≫ Take the NVI from Ponferrada to Villafranca del Bierzo (23km, 25 minutes), which runs almost right next to both the A6 motorway and the Camino.

DETOUR: CABO FISTERRA

Start: ⑲ Santiago de Compostela

In popular imagination Cabo Fisterra (86km, 1½ hours; take the AC441) is not just the western edge of Spain (it's not, that honour goes to Cabo da Nave, 5km north), but in the days way before sat-nav it was considered the very end of the world. This has long made it a popular extension to the Camino de Santiago. People today may not come here to ponder what might lie beyond the western horizon, but they do come with equal awe to watch the setting sun and admire the views from beside the powerful lighthouse that sits at the edge of these high cliffs. Fisterra itself is a fishing port with a picturesque harbour, and a tourist destination growing ever more popular among Camino pilgrims. See p174 for more.

⑰ Villafranca del Bierzo

Villafranca del Bierzo has a very well preserved old core and a number of interesting churches and other religious buildings. Chief among the sights are the **San Nicolás El Real**, a 17th-century convent with a baroque altarpiece, and the 12th-century **Iglesia de Santiago**. The northern doorway of this church is called the 'door of forgiveness'. Pilgrims who were sick, or otherwise unable, to carry onto Santiago de Compostela were granted the same Godly favours as if they'd made it all the way.

The Drive ≫ The Camino, and the driving road, leaves Villafranca del Bierzo and starts to wind uphill before entering

Galicia at tiny O Cebreiro, which at 1300m is the highest point on the whole Camino. From here continue to Samos. Total drive length is 90km (two hours) using the NVI, or reduce the journey time a little by taking the neighbouring A6.

---

⑱ Samos

Samos is built around the very fine Benedictine **Mosteiro de Samos** (www.abadiadesamos.com; tours €3; 🕑tours every 30min 10am-12.30pm Mon-Sat, 12.45-1.30pm Sun, 4.30-6.30pm daily). This monastery has two beautiful big cloisters (one Gothic, with distinctly unmonastic Greek nymphs adorning its fountain; the other neoclassical and filled with roses).

The Drive ≫ Between Samos and Santiago de Compostela (136km 2½ hours on the LU633 and N547) there's a whole load of attractive little villages (Sarria, Portomarín and Melide) – there's not a lot to see at each, but it's worth an amble around any of them. Once in Santiago de Compostela dump the car and head to the cathedral.

TRIP HIGHLIGHT

⑲ Santiago de Compostela

This, then, is it. The end of The Way. And what a spectacular finish. Santiago de Compostela, with its granite buildings and frequent drizzle, is one of the most attractive cities in Spain. It goes without saying that your first port of call should be the

Catedral de Santiago de Compostela (www.catedraldesantiago.es; Praza do Obradoiro; ⊙7am-8.30pm), which soars above the city centre in a splendid jumble of moss-covered spires and statues. Built piecemeal over several centuries, its beauty is a mix of the original Romanesque structure (built between 1075 and 1211) and later Gothic and baroque flourishes. The tomb of Santiago beneath the main altar is a magnet for all who come to the cathedral. The artistic high point is the Pórtico de la Gloria inside the west entrance, featuring 200 masterly Romanesque sculptures. After you've given thanks for a safe journey head to the **Museo da Catedral**, which spreads over four floors and includes the cathedral's large, 16th-century Gothic/plateresque cloister. The **Grand Praza do Obradoiro**, in front of the cathedral's west facade, is traffic- and cafe-free and has a unique atmosphere. At its northern end, the Renaissance Hostal dos Reis Católicos (p121) was built in the early 16th century by order of the Catholic Monarchs, Isabel and Fernando, as a refuge for pilgrims and a symbol of the crown's power in this ecclesiastical city. Today it's a hotel, but its four courtyards and some other areas are open to visitors.

✕ 🛏 p121

Santiago de Compostela The city's magnificent Catedral

Eating & Sleeping

Pamplona ❷

✗ Bar-Restaurante Gaucho   Pintxos €

(Travesía Espóz y Mina 7; pintxos €2-3; ⏱7am-3pm & 6.30-11pm) This bustling bar serves multi-award-winning *pintxos* that, despite some serious competition, many a local will tell you are the finest in the city – and we agree! Try the ones made of sea urchins or the crispy spinach and prawn caramel creations.

🛏 Palacio Guendulain   Historic Hotel €€€

(📞948 22 55 22; www.palacioguendulain. com; Calle Zapatería 53; s/d incl breakfast from €132/143; P ❄ 🛜) To call this stunning hotel, inside the converted former home of the viceroy of New Granada, sumptuous is an understatement. On arrival, you're greeted by a museum-piece 17th-century carriage and a collection of classic cars being guarded beside the viceroy's private chapel. The rooms contain *Princess and the Pea*–soft beds, enormous showers and regal armchairs.

Logroño ❼

✗ La Cocina de Ramon   Spanish €€€

(📞941 28 98 08; www.lacocinaderamon.es; Calle de Portales 30; menús €28-37; ⏱1-4pm & 8-11pm Tue-Sat, 1-4pm Sun) It looks unassuming from the outside, but Ramon's mixture of high-quality, locally grown market-fresh produce and tried-and-tested family recipes gives this place a lot of fans. But it's not just the food that makes it so popular: the service is outstanding, and Ramon likes to come and explain the dishes to each and every guest.

🛏 Hotel Calle Mayor   Boutique Hotel €€€

(📞941 23 23 68; www.hotelcallemayor.com; Calle Marqués de San Nicolás 71; r incl breakfast €120-160; P ❄ 🛜) This delicious hotel is *the* place to stay in Logroño. It has huge rooms with cheeky touches such as modern lamps atop ancient columns, it's bathed in light and simply oozes class. The staff are highly efficient.

Burgos ❾

✗ El Huerto de Roque   Contemporary Castilian €€

(www.elhuertoderoque.com; Calle de Santa Águeda 10; mains €10-12, menú del día €15; ⏱restaurant 1-4pm Tue-Sat, gastrobar 8pm-2am Thu-Sat; ✍) Come here for an inexpensive lunch with plenty of choice of dishes. The emphasis is on fresh market and ecological produce with typical plates including vegetable spring rolls with a sweet and sour sauce, and crab in a Thai green curry sauce. The atmosphere throughout is boho-rustic with original tiles, wooden furniture and edgy artwork.

🛏 Hotel Norte y Londres   Historic Hotel €€

(📞947 26 41 25; www.hotelnorteylondres.com; Plaza de Alonso Martínez 10; s/d €66/100; P @ 🛜) Set in a former 16th-century palace and with understated period charm, this fine hotel promises spacious rooms with antique furnishings, polished wooden floors and pretty balconies; those on the 4th floor are more modern. The bathrooms are exceptionally large, the service exceptionally efficient.

León ⑬

✗ Delirios · Contemporary Castilian €€

(☏987 23 76 99; www.restaurantedelirios.
com; Calle Ave Maria 2; mains €12-20; ⏱1.30-
3.30pm & 9-11.30pm Tue-Sat, 1.30-3.30pm
Sun) One of the city's more adventurous
dining options where innovative combinations
such as tuna tataki with orange and ginger,
and brie and foie gras with coconut hit the
mark virtually every time. Those with more
conservative taste buds can opt for dishes
such as steak with parsnip chips, while
the chocolate mousse with passionfruit is
designed to put a satisfied waddle in every
diner's step. Reservations recommended.

🛏 La Posada Regia · Historic Hotel €€

(☏987 21 31 73; www.regialeon.com; Calle de
Regidores 9-11; s/d incl breakfast from €54/59;
❄🏠) This place has the feel of a *casa rural*
(village accommodation) despite being in
the city centre. The secret is a 14th-century
building, magnificently restored (wooden
beams, exposed brick and understated antique
furniture), with individually styled rooms and
supremely comfortable beds and bathrooms.
As with anywhere in the Barri Gòtic, weekend
nights can be noisy.

🛏 Hostal de San Marcos · Historic Hotel €€€

(☏987 23 73 00; www.parador.es; Plaza de San
Marcos 7; d incl breakfast from €134; ❄@🏠)
Despite the confusing *'hostal'* in the name,
León's sumptuous *parador* (state-owned
hotel) is one of the finest hotels in Spain. With
palatial rooms fit for royalty and filled with
old-world luxury and decor, this is one of the
Parador chain's flagship properties and as you'd
expect, the service and attention to detail are
faultless. It also houses the **Convento de
San Marcos**.

Santiago de Compostela ⑲

✗ O Curro da Parra · Contemporary Galician €€

(www.ocurrodaparra.com; Rúa do Curro da Parra
7; mains €17-23, tapas €4-8; ⏱1.30-3.30pm &
8.30-11.30pm Tue-Sat, 1.30-3.30pm Sun) With
a neat little stone-walled dining room upstairs
and a narrow tapas and wine bar below, O Curro
da Parra serves up a broad range of thoughtfully
created, market-fresh fare. You might go for
pork cheeks with apple purée and spinach – or
just ask what the fish and seafood of the day
are. On weekday lunchtimes there's a good-
value €12 *menú mercado* (market menu).

🛏 Hotel Costa Vella · Boutique Hotel €€

(☏981 56 95 30; www.costavella.com; Rúa
da Porta da Pena 17; s €59, d €81-97; ❄🏠)
Tranquil, thoughtfully designed rooms – some
with typically Galician *galerías* (glassed-in
balconies) – a friendly welcome and a lovely
garden cafe make this old stone house a
wonderful option, and the €6 breakfast is
substantial. Even if you don't stay, it's an ideal
spot for breakfast or coffee. Book ahead from
May to September.

🛏 Parador Hostal dos Reis Católicos · Historic Hotel €€€

(☏981 58 22 00; www.parador.es; Praza
do Obradoiro 1; r incl breakfast from €205;
P ❄@🏠) Opened in 1509 as a pilgrims'
hostel, and with a claim to be the world's oldest
hotel, this palatial *parador* just steps from the
cathedral is Santiago's top hotel, with regal (if
rather staid) rooms. If you're not staying, stop
in for a **look round** (⏱noon-2pm & 4-6pm
Sun-Fri; admission €3) and coffee and cakes at
the elegant cafe.

Elciego The spectacular Frank Gehry–designed Hotel Marqués de Riscal

Classic Trip

Roving La Rioja Wine Region

8

Learn all about the gift of the grape on this quiet road trip through vine-studded countryside. Along the way you can visit wine museums and bodegas and admire stunning architecture.

TRIP HIGHLIGHTS

98 km

Dinastía Vivanco
Obtain wine-fuelled knowledge in this space-age museum

1 km

Logroño
Delve into the fabulous culinary scene of this understated city

Haro

⑥

⑧

① START/ FINISH

Nájera

San Millán de Cogolla

Laguardia
Spin back the wheels of time in this wine-soaked fortress town

105km

2–4 DAYS
140 KM / 97 MILES

GREAT FOR...

BEST TIME TO GO
September and October when the grapes are being harvested.

ESSENTIAL PHOTO
Waving at the camera from in front of the Hotel Marqués de Riscal.

BEST FOR FOODIES
Logroño has some of the best tapas in Spain.

8

Roving La Rioja Wine Region

La Rioja is home to the best wines in Spain and on this short and sweet road trip along unhurried back roads you'll enjoy gorgeous vine-striped countryside and asleep-at-noon villages of honey-coloured stone. But the real interest is reserved for food and drink: cutting-edge museums, bodega tours and some of the best tapas in Spain will make this drive an essential for any foodie.

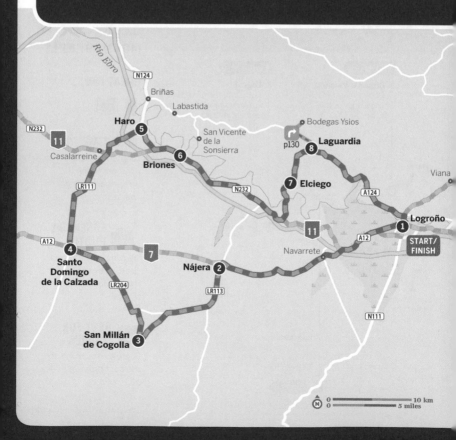

❶ Logroño

Small and low-key Logroño is the capital of La Rioja. The city doesn't receive all that many tourists and there aren't all that many things to see and do, but there is a monumentally good selection of tapas bars. In fact, Logroño is quickly gaining a culinary reputation to rival anywhere in Spain.

Based in the small village of Fuenmayor (10 minutes west of Logroño), **Rioja Trek** (☏941 58 73 54; www.riojatrek.com; wine experience €28 per person) offers three-hour wine 'experiences' where you visit a vineyard and bodega and participate in the process of actually making wine

LINK YOUR TRIP

7 **Northern Spain Pilgrimage**

Drive alongside pilgrims on the road to Santiago de Compostela. You can join 'the Way' in Logroño.

11 **Along the Río Ebro**

From Logroño you can join this tour and explore deserts and Islamic palaces, churches carved into rock and castles with hanging gardens.

yourself. It also offers family-friendly wine-related activities. For more on things to see and do in Logroño, see p114.

 p131

The Drive » It's only a short drive of 28km (25 minutes) from Logroño to Nájera along the N232, which transforms into the A12 motorway around the halfway point.

---

❷ Nájera

The main attraction of this otherwise unexciting town, which lies on the Camino de Santiago, is the Gothic **Monasterio de Santa María la Real** (admission €3; ⊙10am-1pm & 4-7pm Tue-Sat, 10am-12.30pm & 4-6pm Sun), in particular its fragile-looking, early-16th-century cloisters. The monastery was built in 1032, but was significantly rebuilt in the 15th-century.

The Drive » The dry landscapes around Nájera become greener and more rolling as you head southwest along the LR113 and LR205 for 18km (20 minutes) to San Millán de Cogolla. In the far distance mountains, which are snow-capped in winter, rise up.

---

❸ San Millán de Cogolla

The hamlet of San Millán de Cogolla is home to two remarkable monasteries, which between them helped give birth to the Castilian (Spanish) language. On account of

their linguistic heritage and artistic beauty, they have been recognised by Unesco as World Heritage sites.

The **Monasterio de Yuso** (☏941 37 30 49; www. monasteriodeyuso.org; adult/child €6/2; ⊙10am-1.30pm & 4-6.30pm Tue-Sun) contains numerous treasures in its museum. You can only visit as part of a guided tour. Tours last 50 minutes and run every half-hour or so. In August it's also open on Mondays.

A short distance away is the **Monasterio de Suso** (☏941 37 30 82; admission €4; ⊙9.30am-1.30pm & 3.30-6.30pm Tue-Sun). It's believed that in the 13th century a monk named Gonzalo de Berceo wrote the first Castilian words here. Again, it can only be visited on a guided tour. Tickets, which must be bought in advance, can be reserved by phone and can be picked up at the Monasterio de Yuso.

The Drive » It's a 23km (20 minute) drive along the delightfully quiet LR204 to Santo Domingo de la Calzada. The scenery is a mix of vast sunburnt fields, red tinged soils, vineyards and patches of forest.

---

❹ Santo Domingo de la Calzada

The small, walled old town of Santo Domingo is the kind of place where you can be certain that the baker knows all his customers by name and

Classic Trip

that everyone will turn up for María's christening. Santiago-bound pilgrims have long been a part of the fabric of this town, and that tradition continues to this day, with most visitors being foot-weary pilgrims. All this helps to make Santo Domingo one of the most enjoyable places in La Rioja. The biggest attraction in town, aside from the very worthwhile pursuit of just strolling the

streets and lounging in the main old-town plaza, is a visit to the cathedral. See p114 for more.

📖 p131

The Drive » The LR111 goes in an almost ruler-straight line across fields of crops and under a big sky to the workaday town of Haro (20km, 20 minutes).

- - - - - - - - - - -

⑤ Haro

Despite its fame in the wine world, there's not much of a heady bouquet to Haro, the capital of La Rioja's wine-producing region. But the town has a cheerful pace and the compact old quarter,

leading off Plaza de la Paz, has some intriguing alleyways with bars and wine shops aplenty.

There are plenty of wine bodegas in the vicinity of the town, some of which are open to visitors (almost always with advance reservation). One of the more receptive to visitors is the **Bodegas Muga** (📞941 30 60 60; www. bodegasmuga.com; Barrio de la Estación; winery tour €10), which is just after the railway bridge on the way out of town. It gives daily guided tours (except Sunday) in Spanish, and tastings. Although

LOCAL KNOWLEDGE: TAPAS IN LOGROÑO

Make no mistake about it: Logroño is a foodie's delight. There are a number of very good restaurants, and then there are the tapas (which here are sometimes called by their Basque name of *pintxos*). Few cities have such a dense concentration of excellent tapas bars. Most of the action takes place on Calle Laurel and Calle de San Juan. Tapas cost around €2 to €4, and most of the bars are open from about 8pm through to midnight, except on Mondays. The following are some of our favourites.

Torrecilla (Calle Laurel 15; pintxos from €2) OK, we're going to stick our necks out here and say that this place serves the best *pintxos* in town. Go for the pyramid of *jamón* (cured ham) or the miniburgers (which come with mini bottles of ketchup!). In fact, what the heck, go for anything. It's all good!

Bar Soriano (Travesía de Laurel 2; pintxos from €2) The smell of frying food will suck you into this bar, which has been serving up the same delicious mushroom tapa, topped with a shrimp, for more than 30 years.

La Taberna de Baco (Calle de San Agustín 10; pintxos from €2) This place has a cracking list of around 40 different *pintxos*, including *bombitas* (potatoes stuffed with mushrooms) and a delightful mess of toast with pate, apple, goat cheese and caramel.

La Fontana (Calle Laurel 16; pintxos from €2) Another stellar *pintxo* bar with a welcoming atmosphere. This one's speciality is *sepia fontana*. And when you order this what emerges from the kitchen? A pile of egg, mushroom, aubergine and foie gras. The octopus isn't bad either.

THE WEALTH OF THE GRAPE

La Rioja, and the surrounding areas of Navarra and the Basque province of Álava, is Spain's best-regarded wine-producing region. La Rioja itself is further divided into three separate wine-producing areas: Rioja Alta, Rioja Baja and Rioja Alavesa. The principal grape of Rioja is the tempranillo. The first taste of a tempranillo is of leather and cherries and the wine lingers on the tongue.

The Riojans have had a long love affair with wine. There's evidence that both the Phoenicians and the Celtiberians produced and drank wine here and the earliest written evidence of grape cultivation in La Rioja dates to 873. Today, some 250 million litres of wine bursts forth from the grapes of La Rioja annually. Almost all of this (around 85%) is red wine, though some quality whites and rosés are also produced. The Riojan love of wine is so great that in the town of Haro they even have a fiesta devoted to wine. It culminates with a messy 'wine battle' in which thousands of litres of wine gets chucked around, turning everyone's clothes red in the process. This takes place on 29 June.

How to find a good bottle? Spanish wine is subject to a complicated system of classification, similar to the ones used in France and Italy. La Rioja is the only wine region in Spain classed as Denominación de Origen Calificada (DOC), the highest grade and a guarantee that any wine labelled as such was produced according to strict regional standards. The best wines are often marked with the designation 'Crianza' (aged for a year in an oak barrel), 'Reserva' (aged for two years, at least one of which is in an oak barrel) and 'Gran Reserva' (aged for two years in an oak barrel and three years in the bottle).

technically you should book in advance in high season, you can often just turn up and latch on to the back of a tour.

The Drive ❯❯ Briones is almost within walking distance of Haro. It's just 9km away (10 minutes) along the N124.

6 Briones

One man's dream has put the small, obscenely quaint village of Briones firmly on the Spanish wine and tourism map. The sunset-gold village crawls gently up a hillside and offers commanding views over the surrounding vine-carpeted plains. It's on these plains where you will find the fantastic **Dinastía Vivanco** (Museo de la Cultura del Vino; www.dinastiavivanco.com; adult/child €8/free; ◷11am-6pm Tue-Fri & Sun, 10am-8pm Sat Jul-Aug, shorter hours rest of year). Over several floors you will learn all about the history and culture of wine and the various processes that go into its production. All of this is done through interesting displays brought to life with computer technology. The treasures on display include Picasso-designed wine jugs; Roman and Byzantine mosaics; gold-draped, wine-inspired religious artifacts; and the world's largest collection of corkscrews. At the end of the tour you can enjoy some wine tasting, and by booking in advance, you can join a tour of the winery (€20 including museum entry; in Spanish only).

The Drive ❯❯ It's 19km (25 minutes) along the N232 to Elciego. The scenery, which is made up of endless vineyards, will delight anyone who enjoys wide open spaces. In the distance are strange sheer-faced table-topped mountains.

7 Elciego

When the owner of the Bodegas Marqués de Riscal, in the village of Elciego, decided he wanted to

WHY THIS IS A CLASSIC TRIP
STUART BUTLER, AUTHOR

How can anyone not love an area sloshing in wine?! Well, for me, wine is only a part of my love for this region. The light and huge skies is what draws me here. It's so very different to the often grey and damp north coast where I live. It feels so, well, Spanish!

Top: La Rioja vineyards
Left: Bodegas Palacio cellar, Laguardia
Right: Hotel Marqués de Riscal, Elciego

create something special, he didn't hold back. The result is the spectacular Frank Gehry–designed Hotel Marqués de Riscal. Costing around €85 million, the building is a flamboyant wave of multicoloured titanium sheets that stands in utter contrast to the village behind. It's like a rainbow-flavoured Guggenheim museum (not surprisingly, perhaps, as that was also designed by Gehry). Casual visitors are not really welcome to look around the hotel, but there is an excellent wine shop and interesting **wine tours** (☎945 18 08 88; www. marquesderiscal.com; tour €11) take place – there's at least one English-language tour a day.

🛏 p131

The Drive » It's only 15 minutes (9km) along the A3210 from Elciego to wonderful Laguardia, which rises up off the otherwise flat, vine-striped countryside.

- - - - - - - - - -

TRIP HIGHLIGHT

8 Laguardia

It's easy to spin back the wheels of time in the medieval fortress town of Laguardia, or the 'Guard of Navarra' as it was once appropriately known, sitting proudly on its rocky hilltop. As well as memories of long-lost yesterdays, the town further entices visitors with its wine-producing present. **Bodegas Palacio** (☎945 60 01 51; www.bodegaspalacio.com;

Carretera de Elciego; tour €5; ⏰ tours 11am & 1pm Mon & Sat, 4.30pm Tue-Fri, 1.30pm Sun, closed afternoons Jul & Aug) is only 1km from Laguardia on the Elciego road; reservations are not essential but are a good idea (especially out of season). Also just outside Laguardia is the **Centro Temático del Vino Villa Lucia** (📞945 60 00 32; www.villa-lucia.com; Carretera de Logroño; museum €11; ⏰11am-6.30pm Tue-Fri, 10.15am-6.30pm Sat, 11am-12.30pm Sun), a wine museum and shop. Museum visits are

DETOUR: BODEGAS YSIOS

Start: 8 Laguardia

Just a couple of kilometres to the north of Laguardia is the **Bodegas Ysios** (📞941 27 99 00; www.ysios.com; Camino de la Hoya, Laguardia; per person €10; ⏰tours 10.30am, 1pm & 3pm Mon-Fri, 10.30am & 1pm Sat & Sun, advance booking required). Architecturally it's one of the most gob-smacking bodegas in Spain. Designed by Santiago Calatrava as a 'temple dedicated to wine', it's wavelike roof made of aluminium and cedar wood matches the flow of the rocky mountains behind it. Daily tours of the bodega are an excellent introduction to wine production.

by guided tour only and finish with a 4D film and wine tasting.

🍴 🛏 p131

The Drive » From Laguardia it's a short 18km (20 minutes) down the A124 back to Logroño and the start of this tour.

CARLOS SANCHEZ PEREYRA / GETTY IMAGES ©

Bodegas Ysios

Eating & Sleeping

Logroño ❶

🛏 Hotel Marqués
de Vallejo   Design Hotel €€

(☏941 24 83 33; www.hotelmarquesdevallejo.
com; Calle del Marqués de Vallejo 8; s/d from
€50/75; **P ❄ 🛜**) From the driftwood art to
cow skins, beach pebbles and photographic
flashlights it's clear that a lot of thought and
effort has gone into the design of this stylish,
modern and very well-priced hotel.

Santo Domingo de la Calzada ❹

🛏 Hostal R Pedro   Hotel €

(☏941 34 11 60; www.hostalpedroprimero.
es; Calle San Roque 9; s/d €48/59; 🛜) This
carefully renovated townhouse, which has
terracotta-coloured rooms with wooden roof
beams and entirely modern bathrooms, is a
terrific deal.

🛏 Parador
Santo Domingo   Historic Hotel €€

(☏941 34 03 00; www.parador.es; Plaza del
Santo 3; r from €105; **P 🛜**) The Parador Santo
Domingo is the antithesis of the town's general
air of piety. Occupying a 12th-century former
hospital, opposite the cathedral, this palatial
hotel offers anything but a frugal medieval-like
existence. The in-house restaurant is reliably
good.

🛏 Parador Santo Domingo
Bernado de Fresneda   Hotel €€

(☏941 34 11 50; www.parador.es; Plaza de San
Francisco 1; r from €90; **P 🛜**) Just on the edge
of the old town is the Parador Santo Domingo
Bernado de Fresneda, which occupies a former
convent and pilgrim hostel, although quite
honestly, with its divine beds and rooms that
gush luxury, you probably wouldn't describe it
as a 'hostel' anymore.

Elciego ❼

🛏 Hotel Marqués
de Riscal   Design Hotel €€€

(☏945 18 08 80; www.hotel-marquesderiscal.
com; Calle Torrea 1; r from €310; **P ❄ 🛜**) When
the owner of Elciego's Bodegas Marqués de Riscal
decided he wanted to create something special,
he didn't hold back. The result is the spectacular
Frank Gehry–designed Hotel Marqués de Riscal.
Costing around €85 million, the building is a wave
of multicoloured titanium sheets that stand in
utter contrast to the village behind.

Laguardia ❽

✕ Restaurante Amelibia   Spanish €€

(☏945 62 12 07; www.restauranteamelibia.com;
Barbacana 14; menú del día €17; ⏱1-3.30pm
Sun-Mon & Wed-Thu, 1-3.30pm & 9-10.30pm Fri &
Sat) This classy restaurant is one of Laguardia's
highlights: stare out the windows at a view over
the scorched plains and mountain ridges while
dining on sublime traditional Spanish cuisine.

🛏 Posada Mayor
de Migueloa   Historic Hotel €€

(☏945 600 187; www.mayordemigueloa.com;
Calle Mayor 20; s/d incl breakfast €99/105; ❄🛜)
For the ultimate in gracious La Rioja living, this
old mansion-hotel with its rickety rooms full
of polished wood is irresistible. The in-house
restaurant (menus from €24), which is open to
nonguests, is recommended and offers original
twists on local cuisine. Under the hotel is a small
wine bodega (guided visits for non-guests €5).

🛏 Castillo el Collado   Historic Hotel €€€

(☏945 62 12 00; www.hotelcollado.com; Paseo
el Collado 1; d €125-185; 🛜) Like a whimsical
Disney dream castle, this place, which from the
outside is all sturdy turrets and pretty flower
gardens, is a truly unique place to stay. The
half-dozen rooms are all different but combine
quirky style with luxury living. The open-to-all
restaurant (menus from €25) is also excellent.

Lagos de Covadonga *A verdant walking trail leads you to the beautiful Lago de Enol and Lago de la Ercina*

Mountain Roads in Picos de Europa

9

These jagged, deeply fissured mountains peppered with small stone villages and laced with beautiful lakes amount to some of the most spectacular country in Spain.

TRIP HIGHLIGHTS

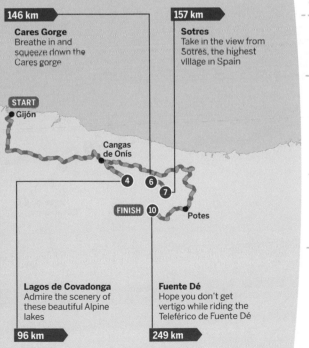

146 km

Cares Gorge
Breathe in and squeeze down the Cares gorge

157 km

Sotres
Take in the view from Sotres, the highest village in Spain

START
Gijón

Cangas de Onís

FINISH

Potes

Lagos de Covadonga
Admire the scenery of these beautiful Alpine lakes

96 km

Fuente Dé
Hope you don't get vertigo while riding the Teleférico de Fuente Dé

249 km

2–4 DAYS
249 KM / 220 MILES

GREAT FOR...

BEST TIME TO GO
June and September have the best combination of reliable(ish!) weather and lower crowds.

ESSENTIAL PHOTO
The gorgeous blue Lagos de Covadonga.

BEST FOR AN ADRENALINE RUSH
Swaying in the breeze on the Teleférico de Fuente Dé.

9 Mountain Roads in Picos de Europa

Rising snow-capped and majestic off the coastal plain, the Picos de Europa mark the greatest, most dramatic heights of the Cordillera Cantábrica, with enough awe-inspiring mountainscapes to make them, arguably, not just the finest hill-walking country in Spain but also some of the most exciting car-touring country. You can drive up towards high-level alpine lakes, peer over free-falling precipices or squeeze through the magnificent Garganta del Cares gorge.

① Gijón

Gritty Gijón (khi-*hon*) is a serious industrial city, but it has been given a thorough facelift and is now, thanks to pedestrianised streets, parks, seafront walks, cultural attractions and a lively food and drinks scene, one of the most enjoyable urban centres in northern Spain.

The ancient core of Gijón is concentrated on the headland known as **Cimadevilla**. The harmonious, porticoed **Plaza Mayor** marks the

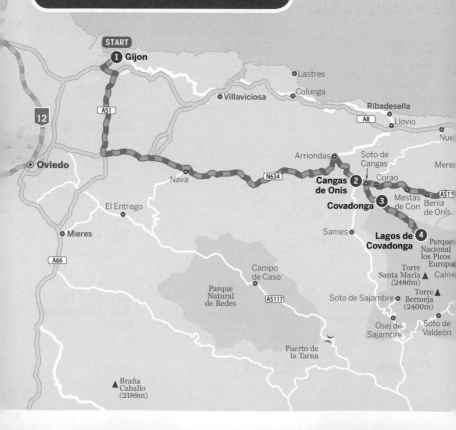

southern end of the promontory. To the west stretch the **Puerto Deportivo** (marina) and the broad **Playa de Poniente**, while to the south is the more modern, 19th- to 20th-century city centre bounded on its east side by the **Playa de San Lorenzo**.

On Playa de Poniente, 1.5km west from Cimadevilla, **Acuario** (☑958 18 52 20; acuario.gijon. es; adult/senior & student/child €15/10/7.50; ☺10am-10pm mid-Jul–Aug, shorter hours rest of year) is an impressive aquarium housing 4000 specimens, from otters to sharks and penguins, in 12 separate underwater environments, including tropical oceans and an Asturian river.

✕ ⊨ p141

The Drive ❯❯ This first part of the drive is more about getting you to the mountains than anything else, so take the fast AS1 and N634 roads from Gijón to Cangas de Onís at the western edge of the Picos.

- - - - - - - - - - - - -

❷ Cangas de Onís

This largely modern and rather unremarkable town bustles with Picos-related tourism activity throughout the summer months. There are a couple of minor historical sights including the **Puente Romano**, the so-called Roman Bridge that spans the Río Sella. However, there's nothing Roman about it – it was actually built in the 13th century, but is no less beautiful for the mistaken identity. From it hangs a copy of the Cruz de la Victoria, the symbol of Asturias that resides in Oviedo's cathedral. The **Capilla de Santa Cruz** (Avenida Contranquil; admission €2; ☺11am-2pm & 5-7pm Thu-Tue, reduced hour mid-Sep–mid-Jun) is a tiny chapel built in 1943 to replace its 8th-century predecessor, which was destroyed during the Spanish Civil War. The

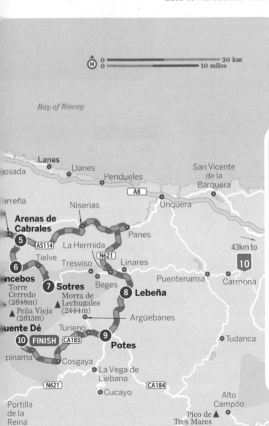

LINK
YOUR
TRIP

10 Cantabria's Eastern Valleys

Rural backwaters your thing? After finishing this trip head to Santander and start meandering through Cantabria's eastern valleys.

12 Castles & Cathedrals in Medieval Spain

From Gijón head 30km west to Avilés to drive through days past and over massive open vistas.

1940s rebuilders discovered that the mound the chapel sits on was an artificial one containing a megalithic tomb 6000 years old, now visible beneath the chapel's floor. Visits are guided in Spanish, English or French.

The Drive » After the big drive from Gijón to Cangas de Onís it's a mere 9km (15 minutes) along the AS262 to Covadonga, during which the scenery gets ever more impressive.

❸ Covadonga

The importance of the tiny village of Covadonga lies in what it represents rather than what it is. Somewhere hereabouts, in approximately AD 722, the Muslims received their first defeat in Spain, at the hands of the Visigothic nobleman Pelayo – an event considered to mark the beginning of the 800-year Reconquista.

The place is an object of pilgrimage, for in a cave here, the **Santa Cueva**, the Virgin supposedly appeared to

Pelayo's warriors before the battle. On weekends and in summer long queues of the faithful and curious line up to enter the cave, now with a chapel installed. The two tombs in the cave claim to be those of Pelayo himself, his daughter Hermesinda and her husband Alfonso I. The **Fuente de Siete Caños** spring, by the pool below the cave, supposedly ensures marriage within one year to women who drink from it.

Landslides destroyed much of Covadonga in the 19th century and the main church, the **Basílica de Covadonga**, is a neo-Romanesque affair built between 1877 and 1901.

The Drive » It's 12km (30 minutes) along a very narrow mountain road to Lago de Enol, the first of the mountain lakes around these parts. At peak visitor periods, private vehicles may only drive up to the lakes before 8.30am or after 8pm, but can drive back down at any time. A shuttle bus runs from Cangas de Onís and Covadonga.

TOP TIP: WARNING

The weather in and around the Picos can change very fast and sudden bouts of mist, rain, cold and snow are common. If you're motoring around higher roads anytime between late October and early May be prepared for sudden snowfall, which can block routes and even leave you stranded.

PAUL HARRIS / GETTY IMAGES ©

TRIP HIGHLIGHT

❹ Lagos de Covadonga

Summer crowds don't distract from the beauty of these two little lakes. Most of the trippers don't get past patting a few cows' noses near the lakes, so walking here is as nice as anywhere else in the Picos.

Lago de Enol is the first lake you reach, with the main car park just past it. It's linked to **Lago de la Ercina**, 1km away, not only by the paved road but also by a footpath via the **Centro**

Garganta del Cares gorge Wild goats feasting on wild grasses

de Visitantes Pedro Pidal (☺10am-6pm mid-Jul–mid-Sep), which has displays on Picos flora and fauna. There are rustic restaurants near both lakes (closed in winter).

A marked circuit walk, the **Ruta de los Lagos** (PRPNPE2; 5.7km, about 2½ hours), takes in the two lakes, the visitors centre and an old mine, the Minas de Buferrera.

When mist descends, the lakes, surrounded by the green pastures and bald rock that characterise this part of the Picos, take on an eerie appearance.

The Drive ≫ After you've finished delighting in the lakes, backtrack all the way to the AS114 and head east along the northern fringe of the Picos to Arenas de Cabrales (44km, one hour). The drive is through rollicking farmland with a daunting mountain backdrop.

SPOTTING PICOS WILDLIFE

Although a few wolves survive in the Picos and the odd brown bear might wander through, you stand a much better chance of spotting the *rebeco* (chamois), some 6000 of which skip around the rocks and steep slopes. Deer, badgers, wild boar, squirrels and martens, in various quantities, inhabit wooded areas.

Eagles, hawks and other raptors soar in the Picos' skies. Keep your eyes peeled for the majestic *águila real* (golden eagle) and the huge scavenging *buitre leonado* (griffon vulture). Choughs, with their unmistakable caws, accompany walkers at high altitudes.

137

⑤ Arenas de Cabrales

Arenas lies at the confluence of the bubbling Ríos Cares and Casaño. The busy main road is lined with hotels, restaurants and bars, and just off it lies a little tangle of quiet squares and back lanes. You can learn all about and sample the fine smelly Cabrales cheese at Arenas' **Cueva-Exposición Cabrales** (☏ 985 84 67 02; www.fundacioncabrales.com; adult/child €4.50/3; ⏱ 10.15am-1.15pm & 4.15-7.15pm, reduced hour Oct-Mar), a cheese-cave museum 500m from the centre on the Poncebos road, with 45-minute guided visits in Spanish.

✖ 🛏 p141

The Drive ›› Hop onto the CA-1 and head south for 6km (10 minutes) to Poncebos.

TRIP HIGHLIGHT

⑥ Poncebos

Poncebos, a tiny straggle of buildings at the northern end of the incredible Cares gorge, is set amid already spectacular scenery. A side road uphill from here leads 1.5km to the hamlet of **Camarmeña**, where there's a lookout with views to El Naranjo de Bulnes in the Macizo Central. And one of the most impressive easy day walks in Spain starts from here – even if you don't normally like to get out the car this one's well worth the huff and puff.

The Drive ›› From Poncebos the minor CA1 leads 11km (20

minutes) to small and often chilly Sotres.

TRIP HIGHLIGHT

⑦ Sotres

If you want a room with a view, then Sotres, the highest village in the Picos and the starting point for a number of good walks, is where you should be looking to retire too. The setting, under a shaft of bare limestone mountain peaks, is breathtaking.

A popular walking route goes east to the village of Tresviso and on down to Urdón, on the Potes–Panes road. As far as Tresviso (10km) it's a paved road, but the final 7km is a dramatic walking trail, the Ruta de Tresviso (PRPNPE30), snaking 850m down to

GARGANTA DEL CARES WALK

Ten kilometres of well-maintained path (the PRPNPE3) high above the Río Cares between Poncebos and Caín constitutes the Garganta del Cares walk, the most popular mountain walk in Spain; in August the experience can feel like Saturday morning on London's Oxford St. But the walk is still a spectacular and at times vertiginous excursion along the gorge separating the Picos' western and central massifs. It's possible to walk the whole 10km and return in one (somewhat tiring) day's outing; it takes six to seven hours plus stops. A number of agencies in Picos towns will transport you to either end of the walk and pick you up at the other end, usually for around €115 for up to four people.

Follow the 'Ruta de Cares' sign pointing uphill about 700m along the road from the top end of Poncebos. The beginning involves a steady climb in the wide and mostly bare early stages of the gorge. After about 3km you'll reach some abandoned houses. A little further and you're over the highest point of the walk.

As you approach the regional boundary with Castilla y León, the gorge becomes narrower and its walls thick with vegetation, creating greater contrast with the alpine heights above. The last stages of the walk are possibly the prettiest, and as you descend nearer the valley floor, you pass through a series of low, wet tunnels to emerge at the end of the gorge among the meadows of Caín.

the Desfiladero de la Hermida gorge. Doing this in the upward direction, starting from Urdón, is at least as popular.

The Drive » Head back to Arenas de Cabrales and follow the AS114 east to where it meets the north–south N621, at the humdrum town of Panes. South of Panes, the N621 to Potes follows the Río Deva upstream through the impressive Desfiladero de la Hermida gorge before reaching Lebeña. Total journey distance 60km (one hour 20 minutes).

POTES FIREWATER

The potent liquor *orujo*, made from grape pressings, is drunk throughout northern Spain and is something of a Potes speciality. People here like to drink it as an after-dinner aperitif as part of a herbal tea called *té de roca* or *té de puerto*. Plenty of shops around town sell *orujo*, including varieties flavoured with honey, fruits and herbs, and many will offer you tastings if you're thinking of buying. Potes' jolly **Fiesta del Orujo** (www.fiestadelorujo.es) kicks off on the second weekend in November, and involves practically every bar in town setting up a stall selling *orujo* shots for a few cents, the proceeds of which go to charity. Of course, you'll have to fight over whose turn it is to drive...

8 Lebeña

About 600m east off the N621 and just outside the village of Lebeña stands the fascinating little **Iglesia de Santa María de Lebeña** (admission €1.50; ⏱10am-1.30pm & 4-7.30pm Tue-Sun; **P**), built in the 9th or 10th century. The horseshoe arches that are in the church are a telltale sign of its Mozarabic style – rarely seen this far north in Spain. The floral motifs on the columns are Visigothic, while below the main *retablo* (altarpiece) stands a Celtic stone engraving. They say the yew tree outside (finally reduced to a sad stump by a storm in 2007) was planted 1000 years ago.

The Drive » Keep following the N621 south to Potes for 9km (10 minutes).

9 Potes

Potes is a popular staging post on the southeastern edge of the Picos, with the Macizo Ándara mountain rising close at hand. The heart of town is a cluster of bridges, towers and quaint back streets restored in traditional slate, wood and red tile after considerable damage during the civil war.

Christian refugees, fleeing from Muslim-occupied Spain to this remote, Christian enclave of Spain in the 8th century, brought with them the **Lígnum Crucis**, purportedly the single biggest chunk of Christ's cross and featuring the hole made by the nail that passed through Christ's left hand. The **Monasterio de Santo Toribio de Liébana** (santotoribiodeliebana.org; ⏱10am-1pm & 4-7pm; **P**), 3km west

of Potes, has housed this holy relic ever since. The monastery is also famous for being the home of medieval monk and theologian Beato de Liébana, celebrated around Europe for his commentary on the Apocalypse.

You can drive 500m past the monastery to the tiny **Ermita de San Miguel**, a chapel with great valley and Picos views.

🍴 🛏 p141

The Drive » It's 23km (30 minutes) along the CA185 to Fuente Dé. This route takes you properly into the mountains and is spectacular at any time, but best outside high summer, when you can really get a better feel for the majesty of the Picos.

TRIP HIGHLIGHT

10 Fuente Dé

At 1078m Fuente Dé lies at the foot of the stark southern wall of the Macizo Central. In four minutes the dramatic (and frankly rather terrifying!) **Teleférico de Fuente Dé** (☎942 73 66 10; www.cantur.com; adult/child return €16/6; ☺9am-8pm Easter & Jul–mid-Sep, 10am-6pm rest of year, closed 2nd half Jan) cable car whisks people 753m up to the top of that wall, from where walkers and climbers can make their way deeper into the central massif.

It's an easy 3.5km, one-hour walk from the top of the *teleférico* (cable car) to the Hotel Áliva, where you can get refreshments. From here several other walks of varying length will reveal the beauty of the mountains to you.

Be warned that during the high season (especially August) you can wait an hour or more for a place in the cable car, going up or down. Good job the scenery is worth lingering for!

ARTURO CANO MIÑO / GETTY IMAGES ©

Poncebos Walking trail over the Río Cares

Eating & Sleeping

Gijón ❶

✕ La Galana   Sidrería, Asturian €€

(www.restauranteasturianolagalana.es; Plaza Mayor 10; mains & raciones €15-24; ⏰1.30-4pm & 8pm-midnight; 🅿️) The front bar is a boisterous *sidrería* (cider bar) where you can snack on tapas (€9 to €15) accompanied by torrents of cider. Up a few steps at the back is a spacious, colourful dining room. Fish, such as *pixín* (anglerfish) with clams or wild sea bass, is the strong suit. It also does excellent vegetarian adaptations of dishes on request, including beautifully prepared salads.

✕ Restaurante Ciudadela   Asturian €€

(ciudadela@grupogravia.com; Calle de Capua 7; mains & raciones €15-25; ⏰1.30-4pm & 9pm-midnight, closed Sun dinner & Mon) Like many Gijón eateries, the Ciudadela has a front bar for nibbling tapas backed by a dining room, in this case combined with a unique cavelike basement that attempts to re-create a Castilian bodega of yesteryear. The carefully concocted dishes range over the best of Asturian offerings, from daily *pucheros* (casseroles/stews) to excellent seafood and meat, and even a low-calorie selection.

🛏️ Hotel Pasaje   Hotel €€

(📞985 34 49 15; www.hotelpasaje.es; Calle del Marqués de San Esteban 3; s/d €50/85; 🛜) A pleasant, friendly, family-owned hotel with good, clean, bright rooms, many enjoying sea views. It's conveniently and centrally located facing the Puerto Deportivo and staff are a wonderful source of local information.

Arenas de Cabrales ❺

✕ Restaurante Cares   Asturian €€

(📞985 84 66 28; mains €14-22, menús €15; ⏰8am-midnight, closed Mon Oct-Jun, closed Jan-Mar) Beside the Poncebos junction on the main road, this is one of the best-value restaurants for miles around. It does great-value *menús* (set menus) for both lunch and dinner, as well as *platos combinados* (meat-and-three-veg dishes) and à la carte fish and meat dishes. Dig into a hearty *cachopo* (veal steak stuffed with ham and cheese) and finish with *delicias de limón* (between lemon mousse and yoghurt).

🛏️ Hotel Rural El Ardinal   Hotel €

(📞985 84 64 34; www.ardinal.com; Barriu del Riu, r incl breakfast €60, ⏰closed Dec & Jan; 🅿️🛜) In a lovely tranquil spot with good views, the cosy little Ardinal offers eight smallish rooms with a cottagey feel (plenty of wood, wrought iron and flowery prints) and a warm sitting-room-cum-bar with a fireplace. It's on the north edge of Arenas, 400m up a lane opposite the central Restaurante Cares.

Potes ❾

✕ Asador Llorente   Cantabrian €€

(Calle de San Roque; mains €8-18; ⏰1-4pm & 8.30-11.30pm, closed Tue Sep-Jul) For super-generous helpings of high-quality, fresh local food, head upstairs to this warm, wood-beamed loftlike space. Carnivores are in for a treat: try the Liébana speciality *cocido lebaniego* (a filling stew of chickpeas, potato, greens, chorizo, black pudding, bacon and beef) or tuck into a half-kilogram *chuletón* (giant beef chop). The lovely, crisp salads are good too.

🛏️ Casa Cayo   Hostal €

(📞942 73 01 50; www.casacayo.com; Calle Cántabra 6; s/d €35/50; ⏰ closed late Dec–mid-Mar; 🛜) Easily the best value in Potes, with friendly service and attractive, comfy, timber-beamed rooms. Ask for room 206, 207 or 305 to look down on the burbling river below. You can eat well in the **restaurant** (mains €8 to €18), which has particularly good meat such as *solomillo* (sirloin) with blue Tresviso cheese or the local speciality *lechazo asado* (roast young lamb or kid).

Castro Urdiales Historic bridge and
lighthouse in the ruins of the town's
old defensive bastion

Cantabria's Eastern Valleys

10

Rich in unspoiled rural splendour, the valleys of eastern Cantabria are ripe for exploration and will please anyone who enjoys poking about tiny mountain hamlets and chilling on the beach.

TRIP HIGHLIGHTS

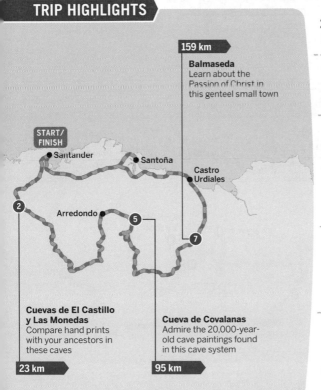

159 km

Balmaseda
Learn about the Passion of Christ in this genteel small town

START/FINISH

● Santander

● Santoña

Castro Urdiales

● Arredondo

2

5

7

Cuevas de El Castillo y Las Monedas
Compare hand prints with your ancestors in these caves

23 km

Cueva de Covalanas
Admire the 20,000-year-old cave paintings found in this cave system

95 km

2–4 DAYS
296KM / 184 MILES

GREAT FOR...

BEST TIME TO GO
May, June and September: temperatures are up, rainfall and prices are down, crowds are away.

ESSENTIAL PHOTO
Snap the breathtaking views from the Puerto de la Braguía pass.

BEST FOR ART
The prehistoric paintings of Cueva de Covalanas.

10 | Cantabria's Eastern Valleys

This short route is one for art-lovers. Nature herself has painted a grand canvas of pretty beaches and stormy oceans, while the inland valleys, sprinkled with sleepy towns and villages, are a feast for the eyes. And this is also where humankind first experimented with art in the form of long-extinct animals painted onto cave walls tens of thousands of years ago.

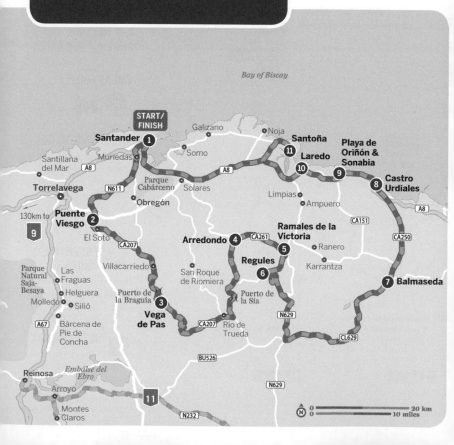

❶ Santander

Santander is not the most beautiful of cities. A huge fire raged through the centre back in 1941, leaving little that's old or quaint. But Cantabria's capital makes the most of its setting along the northern side of the handsome Bahía de Santander, and has good city beaches, a heaving bar and restaurant scene, and a few cultural attractions.

The parklands of the Península de la Magdalena, 2km east of the centre, are perfect for a stroll. Kids will enjoy the seals and penguins and the little train that choo-choos around the headland. The **Palacio de la Magdalena** (☎942 20 30 84; http://palaciomagdalena. com; tours €3; ☺tours hourly 10am-1pm & 4 -6pm Mon-Fri, hourly 10am-noon & 4-5pm Sat, 10am-noon Sun, late Sep–mid-Jun) was built between 1908 and 1912. It's an eclectically styled building which you can visit by 50-minute guided tours, except in summer when the palace hosts the **Universidad Internacional Menéndez Pelayo**, a global get-together for specialists in all sorts of disciplines.

✗ ⊨ p149

The Drive » It's a 30km drive (45 minutes, depending on the

LINK YOUR TRIP

11 Along the Río Ebro

It's simple enough to join this trip up with the leisurely drive along the mighty Río Ebro.

9 Mountain Roads in Picos de Europa

Mountainscapes – and driving routes – don't get much more heartstopping than those found on the Picos de Europa drive.

traffic escaping Santander) along the major S20 and the far more relaxed N611 to Puente Viesgo via Oruña.

- - - - - - - - - - - - -

TRIP HIGHLIGHT

❷ Puente Viesgo

The valley town of Puente Viesgo lies at the foot of the conical Monte Castillo. About 2km up this hill are the Cuevas de Monte Castillo, a series of caves frequented by humans since 150,000 years ago. Two of the four World Heritage–listed caves, **Cuevas de El Castillo y Las Monedas** (☎942 59 84 25; cuevas.culturadecantabria. com; per cave adult/child €3/1.50; ☺9.30am-2.30pm & 3.30-7.30pm Tue-Sun, reduced hours & closed Tue mid-Sep–mid-Jun) – are open for 45-minute guided visits. Booking ahead is highly advisable, especially for the more spectacular El Castillo, which contains the oldest cave art in the world. The 275 paintings and engravings of deer, bison, horses, goats, aurochs, mammoths, handprints and mysterious symbols found within El Castillo date from 39,000 to 11,000 BC. Las Monedas has less art (black animal outlines, from around 10,000 BC) but contains an astounding labyrinth of stalactites and stalagmites.

The Drive » From El Soto, just off the N623 shortly south of Puente Viesgo, take the CA270 and CA262 southeast to Vega de Pas (36km, one hour). The views

from the Puerto de la Braguía pass, 6km before Vega de Pas, are stunning. You can pull over to admire the view by the bus stop. This is a popular cycling route.

- - - - - - - - - -

❸ Vega de Pas

Vega de Pas is the 'capital' of the Valles Pasiegos (the Pas, Pisueña and Miera valleys; www.valles-pasiegos.org), which is one of Cantabria's (and therefore one of Spain's) most traditional rural areas. There's not a whole lot to see in the classic tourist sense but the countryside is outrageously picturesque: it's all jealous greens and steep-sided hills with miniscule villages of stone houses. There are plenty of opportunities to ditch the car and get out for a walk all around here.

The Drive » From Vega de Pas continue southeast on the CA631 into Castilla y León, before turning north again near Las Nieves to follow the BU571 up over the Puerto de la Sía pass towards Arredondo. The road is full of switchbacks and has a couple of mountain passes and waterfalls.

- - - - - - - - - -

❹ Arredondo

Arredondo, a tiny place in Cantabria's southeastern Alto Asón district (www.citason.com), is rather outclassed by its majestic setting at the foot of cloud-scraping pillars of rock and hulking great mountains. There is, though, a small, neo-classical church, **Iglesia de San Pelayo**, which was built in 1860.

The Drive » From Arredondo head east along the N629 to Ramales de la Victoria (13km, 15 minutes). The drive takes you through lush green valleys and below buckled hills and mountains.

- - - - - - - - - - - -

TRIP HIGHLIGHT

⑤ Ramales de la Victoria

The Alto Asón region claims more than half of the 9000 known caves in Cantabria, and Ramales de la Victoria, a small valley town, has two outstanding visitable caves. The **Cueva de Cullalvera** (☎942 59 84 25; cuevas.culturadecantabria. com; adult/child €3/1.50; ☺9.30am-2.30pm & 3.30-7.30pm Tue-Sun, reduced hours & closed Tue-Thu mid-Oct–mid-Apr) is an impressively vast cavity with some signs of prehistoric art. The **Cueva de Covalanas** (☎942 59 84 25; cuevas. culturadecantabria.com; adult/child €3/1.50; ☺9.30am-2.30pm & 3.30-7.30pm Tue-

Sun, reduced hours & closed Tue-Thu mid-Oct–mid-Apr), 3km up the N629 south from Ramales, then 650m up a footpath, is World Heritage listed for its numerous excellent animal paintings from around 18,000 BC, done in an unusual dot-painting technique. Guided visits to either cave last 45 minutes and it's best to book ahead.

The Drive » It's 10km (15 minutes) from Ramales de la Victoria to Regules along the N629 and the CA256. You'll be unlucky if you share the road with more than one or two other cars.

- - - - - - - - - - - -

⑥ Regules

In a lovely, tranquil spot beside the Río Gándara, Regules, is a mere pinprick on many a map. The surrounding Valle de Soba has lots of opportunities for walking and generally moseying about in a deliciously rural tonic from hectic city life. There's also a wonderful place to stay here.

🛏 p149

AGE FOTOSTOCK / ALAMY ©

The Drive » Head back on yourself for a couple of kilometres before veering onto the very minor, and winding, CA662.This joins the N629 and heads south. Turn east onto the CL629 in Bercedo and wiggle your way over the border into Basque country and pretty Balmaseda (54km, one hour).

- - - - - - - - - - - -

TRIP HIGHLIGHT

⑦ Balmaseda

Balmaseda is a genteel and stately small town full of sturdy old houses. The town was originally founded in the late 12th century and its position on the borders of Biscay and Castilla meant that it grew wealthy on trade

---

PASSION OF CHRIST

Balmaseda is renowned throughout northern Spain for its Semana Santa (Easter) festivities, which centre on an elaborate Passion of Christ theatre performance that re-creates the last hours of the life of Christ. The performance, which first came into being at the end of the 19th century, is held in the town streets, using a cast of hundreds of locals. It takes place on the Thursday evening and Good Friday morning.

Ramales de la Victoria Gateway to prehistoric cave art

between the two, but also suffered at the hands of a number of violent takeovers. With the industrial revolution the town was linked to Bilbao, 30km away, by train and its importance was further bolstered.

Walking the streets of the riverside old quarter is pleasure enough for most. The **ayuntamiento** (town hall) is an impressive 18th-century construction and the **Palacio Horastios**, a now derelict mansion dating from the 17th century, has a classic facade.

The small **Museo de Historia de Balmaseda**

(☏946 802 974; www.balmaseda.net; Iglesia de San Juan de Moral; adult/child €1/free; ☺11am-1.30pm & 5-7pm Tue-Thu, 11am-1.30pm Fri-Sun) showcases the town's past.

The Drive » Head down the crowd-free CA250 to Castro Urdiales by the seaside. It's a 27km (40 minute) drive.

- - - - - - - - - - - - - -

⑧ Castro Urdiales

The haughty Gothic jumble that is the **Iglesia de Santa María de la Asunción** (☺10am-1pm & 4-6pm Mon-Sat) stands out above the harbour and the tangle of narrow lanes that make up the

medieval centre of Castro Urdiales. The church shares its little headland with the ruins of the town's old defensive bastion, now supporting a lighthouse.

Of Castro's two beaches, the northern **Playa de Ostende** is the more attractive.

🛏 p149

The Drive » It's just 16km along the coast to Playa de Oriñón. You can go on the marginally faster A8 motorway all the way or take the N634 in half an hour.

❾ Playa de Oriñón & Sonabia

The broad sandy strip of Playa de Oriñón is set deep behind protective headlands, making the water calm and comparatively warm. The settlement here consists of drab holiday flats and caravan parks. Continue 1.7km past Oriñón to the smaller but wilder **Playa de Sonabia**, set in a rock-lined inlet beneath high crags. An up-and-down 10km walking trail links Oriñón with Laredo via Playa de Sonabia and the even more isolated **Playa de San Julián**.

The Drive ⟫ It's 15km (15 minutes) along the A8 to Laredo.

❿ Laredo

Laredo's long, sandy and normally very calm beach is backed by ugly 20th-century blocks. But at the east end of town the cobbled streets of the old **Puebla Vieja** slope down from the impressive 13th-century **Iglesia de Santa María**, with the remains of the 16th-century **Fuerte del Rastrillar** fortress on La Atalaya hill above. The Puebla Vieja has a lively food and drinks scene.

The Drive ⟫ It's a 20-minute (13km) hop around the bay on the N634 and CA241 to Santoña. Traffic can be bad in the summer.

⓫ Santoña

The fishing port of Santoña is famed for its anchovies, which are bottled or tinned here with olive oil to preserve them. Santoña is dominated by two fortresses, the **Fuerte de San Martín** and, further east, the abandoned **Fuerte de San Carlos**. You can take a pleasant walk around both, or take the shuttle ferry (€1.70; March to November) across the estuary to the western end of Laredo beach. Or head off for a hike in the **Parque Cultural Monte Buciero**, which occupies the hill-cum-headland rising northeast of the town. You could also head north along the C141 to **Playa Berria**, a magnificent sweep of sand and surf on the open sea.

🛏 p149

The Drive ⟫ To get back to Santander, and the trip start point, merely head along the A8 and S10 for 46km (35 minutes).

Eating & Sleeping

Santander ❶

🍴 Asubio
Gastrobar   Contemporary Cantabrian €€

(www.asubiogastrobar.com; Calle de Daoíz
y Velarde 23; pinchos €2-4, mains €14-20;
🕐noon-4pm & 8pm-midnight) Creatively
prepared, prize-winning *pinchos* (snacks)
infused with Cantabrian flavours and colourfully
chalked up on a blackboard are the order of
the day here. Try baked octopus with potato
mousse or a local *pasiego* cheese bake, along
with one of the 50 wines on display, and finish
off with a tangy *pizarra de quesucos regionales*
(platter of local cheeses).

🍴 La Conveniente   Tapas, Tablas €€
(Calle de Gómez Oreña 9; raciones & tablas €6-
20; 🕐7pm-midnight Mon-Sat) This cavernous
bodega has high stone walls, wooden pillars
and more wine bottles than you may ever have
seen in one place. Squeeze into the tramline
enclosure at the front, line up for the cavelike
dining room or just snack at the bar. The food
offerings are straightforward – *tablas* (platters)
of cheese, *embutidos* (sausages), ham, pâtés –
and servings are generous.

🛏 Jardín Secreto   Boutique Hotel €€
(🕿942 07 07 14; www.jardinsecretosantander.
com; Calle de Cisneros 37; s/d €65/80; 🛜)
Named for its tiny, tranquil back garden, this
is a charming little six-room world of its own
in a two-centuries-old house near the city
centre. It's run by an engaging brother-and-
sister team, and designed by their mother in a
stylish, contemporary blend of silvers and greys
with exposed stone, brick and wood. The free
morning coffee hits the spot.

🛏 Hotel Bahía   Hotel €€€
(🕿902 570627; www.hotelbahiasantander.com;
Avenida de Alfonso XIII 6; s €167, d €177-197;

🅿️❄@🛜) Central Santander's top hotel,
opposite the UK ferry port, offers large, very
comfortable rooms with thick carpets and solid
wood furnishings. Many have sea views. The
hotel sports an elegant restaurant and cafe.

Regules ❻

🛏 La Casa del Puente   Hotel €€
(🕿942 63 90 20; www.lacasadelpuente.com;
r €85-150; 🅿️🛜) This beautifully restored
casa de indianos (mansion built by a returned
emigrant from Latin America or the Caribbean).
It's in a fantastic, tranquil riverside position: a
step further and you'd be *in* the Río Gándara.
Rooms follow a comfy, funky-coloured, modern-
rustic style, with exposed stonework, floral
finishes, the odd oriental trinket, and up-to-date
installations such as hydromassage showers.

Castro Urdiales ❽

🛏 Ardigales 11   Hotel €€
(🕿942 78 16 16; www.pensionardigales11.com;
Calle de Ardigales 11; s/d from €56/78; 🛜)
Behind a solid stone exterior in the old town
centre hides this somewhat futuristic hotel,
with 11 slick modern rooms decked out in blacks
and whites.

Santoña ⓫

🛏 Hotel Juan de la Cosa   Hotel €€
(🕿942 66 12 38; www.hoteljuandelacosa.
com; Playa de Berria 14; s €65-95, d €65-125;
🕐closed Nov-Mar; 🅿️❄@🛜🏊) Hotel Juan
de la Cosa may be in an unsympathetic-looking
building, but about two-thirds of its spacious,
blue-hued rooms have beach views. It has a
good restaurant with a seafood emphasis, too.

Parque Natural de las Bárdenas Reales

Where now there is desert there was once forest

Along the Río Ebro

11

Follow the mighty Río Ebro on a journey that reveals something of almost everything that Spain has to offer.

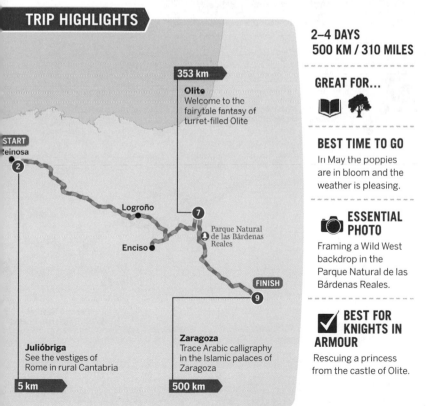

353 km

Olite
Welcome to the fairytale fantasy of turret-filled Olite

START
Reinosa
2

Logroño

7

Parque Natural de las Bárdenas Reales

Enciso

FINISH
9

Julióbriga
See the vestiges of Rome in rural Cantabria

5 km

Zaragoza
Trace Arabic calligraphy in the Islamic palaces of Zaragoza

500 km

**2–4 DAYS
500 KM / 310 MILES**

GREAT FOR...

BEST TIME TO GO

In May the poppies are in bloom and the weather is pleasing.

ESSENTIAL PHOTO

Framing a Wild West backdrop in the Parque Natural de las Bárdenas Reales.

BEST FOR KNIGHTS IN ARMOUR

Rescuing a princess from the castle of Olite.

11 | Along the Río Ebro

Stand at the top of a castle turret in Olite and think back over everything you have, and will, see on this stunning drive and you'll probably end up agreeing with us that this is perhaps the single most diverse and fascinating drive you can cover in northern Spain. Just look at what there is: dinosaurs and deserts, wine and Romanesque churches, Islamic palaces and superb tapas. This is a drive you won't forget.

❶ Reinosa

Southern Cantabria's main town is an unexceptional place, but it is the closest centre to the start of the Río Ebro, which begins life approximately 6km east at Fontibre. While there's not much to the town itself you can head 5km south to the **Colegiata de San Pedro** in Cervatos, which is one of Cantabria's finest Romanesque churches, with rare erotic carvings on its corbels.

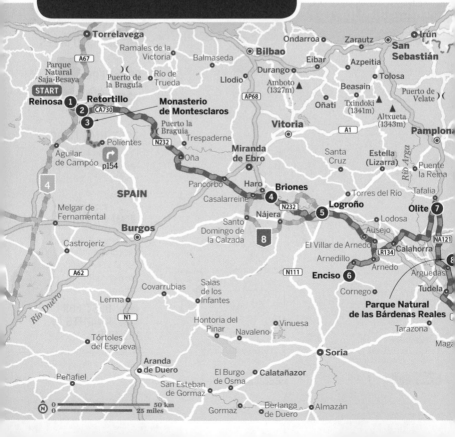

The Drive >> To Retortillo is just a 5km meander (10 minutes) along the CA730 and CA732.

TRIP HIGHLIGHT

❷ Retortillo

In tiny Retortillo you'll discover the remains of Cantabria's most significant Roman town, **Julióbriga** (☎942 59 84 25; centros.culturadecantabria. com; adult/child €3/1.50; ⏰9.30am-2.30pm & 3.30-7.30pm Tue-Sun mid-Jun–mid-Sep, shorter hours rest of year; **P**). The guided visit at Julióbriga includes

dropping into the **Museo Domus**, a full-scale re-creation of a Roman house.

The Drive >> It's a 10km drive along the banks of the impressive Embalse del Ebro reservoir, where the Río Ebro first makes its presence felt, to Arroyo, where you turn south down the SV6427 following signs 6km to the Monasterio de Montesclaros in Montes Claros.

❸ Monasterio de Montesclaros

The Monasterio de Montesclaros has a fine site overlooking the Ebro valley. The monastery, which sits atop a cave, dates from at least the 12th century, but the site itself is thought to have provided a refuge for Christian monks and spiritual hermits from as far back as the 4th century.

LINK YOUR TRIP

8 **Roving La Rioja Wine Region**

Once you hit Logroño, take a few days to enjoy the gift of the grape on our La Rioja Wine Region drive.

4 **Spain's Interior Heartland**

Cross half the breadth of Spain – and probably more than half the diversity.

The Drive >> Return to Arroyo and continue east on the CA730 along the southern edge of the Embalse del Ebro reservoir. If it's hot you might want to unpack your swimming things somewhere along the pretty lake shore. Hook up with the N232 and follow it for 118km to Briones in the La Rioja region. The scenery all the way is gentle, green and intensely rural. Allow 2¼ hours.

❹ Briones

Even without the marvel that is the **Dinastía Vivanco** (Museo de la Cultura del Vino; www.dinastiavivanco.com; adult/child €8/free; ⏰11am-6pm Tue-Fri & Sun, 10am-8pm Sat Jul-Aug, shorter hours rest of year) wine museum, pretty Briones, in the heart of La Rioja's world-renowned wine-growing country, would be worth a stop. The tiny village sits commandingly atop a hill with views to the vine-striped plains. There's a cute little church and a small park built around the remains of a castle. For more on the museum see p127.

The Drive >> Seeing as the navigator is likely to have tried to satisfy their wine cravings in Briones, you'll be pleased to know that it's just a 30-minute straight-line dash down the N232 to the wine capital of Spain: Logroño. Lucky navigator!

❺ Logroño

Logroño, the capital of La Rioja, is one of those towns that on the surface

153

doesn't have much to attract tourists, yet everyone who comes here seems to end up having a good time. The food and, of course, the wine is exceptional, and there's a superb museum and attractive old town. For more on the city's sights, see p114.

 p157

The Drive » With the navigator now likely singing songs about wine in the seat next to you, it's time to see what life was like here in the days before wine. Take the N232 southeast for 33km to El Villar and turn south onto the LR123 to drive another 32km to pretty Enciso. The road leads through some stunning semidesert countryside riven by red-tinged gorges.

- - - - - - - - - - - -

❻ Enciso

Today eagles and vultures are commonly seen

prowling the skies above Enciso, but if you had been travelling around these parts some 120 million years ago, it wouldn't have been prowling vultures you'd need to keep an eye out for but prowling tyrannosauruses. Perhaps a little disappointingly, the dinosaurs are long gone. But if you know where to look, you can still find clues to their passing. Enciso is the centre of Jurrasic activity in these parts. The **El Barranco Perdido** (☏941 39 60 80; www.barrancoperdido.com; over 12yr/4-12yr €24/18; ☉11am-8pm) is a dino theme park containing a museum with complete dinosaur skeletons and an outdoor swimming pool complex. The real highlight of a visit to Enciso, though, is the chance to see

---

🡒 DETOUR:
IGLESIA RUPESTRE DE
SANTA MARÍA DE VALVERDE

Start: ❸ Monasterio de Montesclaros

Follow the CA741 down to Arroyal de los Carabeos, then head south on the CA272 to a roundabout where it meets the CA273. Nine kilometres west on the CA273 is the remarkable **Iglesia Rupestre de Santa María de Valverde**. This beautiful, multiarched church, hewn from the living rock, is the most impressive of several *iglesias rupestres* (rock-cut churches) in this area, dating from probably the 7th to 10th centuries, the early days of Christianity in the region. Santa María church itself is often locked outside July and August, but you can arrange visits in advance through the **tourist office** (☏942 77 61 46; www.valderredible.es; Avenida Cantabria; ☉10am-2pm & 5-8pm Tue-Sat, 11am-2pm Sun) in Polientes, the area's biggest village. Next to the church, the **Centro de Interpretación del Rupestre** (☏942 776 146; adult/child €1/free; ☉10am-2pm & 4-7pm Tue-Sun mid-Jun–mid-Sep, shorter hours rest of year) tells the story of the area's curious rock-church phenomenon through photos, maps, video and multimedia – well worth a visit even if you don't understand Spanish – and can provide plenty of useful information.

Iglesia Rupestre de Santa María de Valverde A church hewn from the living rock

some real-life dinosaur footprints scattered across former mudflats (now rock slopes) in the surrounding countryside. The nearest prints can be found just a kilometre or so east of the village – look for the terrifying T-Rex and dippy diplodocus on the hillside and you're in the right place.

The Drive » With the navigator now scared into a sober state they can direct you back up the LR123 and, just past Arnedo, onto the LR134, which takes you through Calahorra and onto the NA653, the NA624 and, finally, a brief zoom up the AP15 and into the medieval fantasy of Olite. Total distance 78km (1¼ hours).

7 Olite

The turrets and spires of Olite are filled with stories of kings and queens, brave knights and beautiful princesses – it's as if it has burst off the pages of a fairy tale. Though it might seem a little hard to believe today, this insignificant, honey-coloured village was once the home of the royal families of Navarra, and the walled old quarter is crowded with their memories. It's Carlos III that we must thank for the exceptional **Palacio Real** (Castillo de Olite; www.guiartenavarra.com; adult/child €3.50/2; ⊘10am-8pm Jul & Aug, 10am-7pm Mon-Fri, 10am-8pm Sat & Sun May-Jun & Sep, shorter hours Oct-Apr), which towers over the village. Back in Carlos' day, the inhabitants of the castle included not just princes and jesters but also lions, giraffes and other exotic pets, as well as Babylon-inspired hanging gardens. Your navigator won't want to miss the **Museo de la Viña y el Vino de Navarra** (www.guiartenavarra.com; Plaza de los Teobaldos 10; adult/child €3.50/2; ⊘10am-2pm & 4-7pm Mon-Sat, 10am-2pm Sun Mar-Oct, shorter hours Nov-Feb), which is a fascinating journey through wine and wine culture.

📖 p157

The Drive » Start dressing like Lawrence of Arabia as you head south along the N121 to Arguedas on the edge of the semidesert Parque Natural de las Bárdenas Reales. It's a pleasant 40-minute drive (47km).

❽ Parque Natural de las Bárdenas Reales

In a region largely dominated by wet mountain slopes, the last thing you'd expect to find is a sunburnt desert, but in the Parque Natural de las Bárdenas Reales a desert is exactly what you'll find. As well as spectacular scenery, the park plays host to numerous birds and animals, including the great bustard, golden eagles, vultures, mountain cats and wild boar. This may look like an almost pristine wilderness, but it is, in fact, totally artificial. Where now there is desert there was once forest, but humans, being quite dumb, chopped it all down, let his livestock eat all the lower growth, and suddenly found himself living in a desert. There are a couple of dirt motor tracks and numerous hiking and cycling trails, all of which are only vaguely signposted. There's a **park information office** (☎948 83 03 08; www.bardenasreales.es; Km 6 military zone rd; ⏰9am-2pm & 4-7pm Apr-Aug, shorter hours rest of year) on the main route into the park from Arguedas, which can supply information on routes.

The Drive » Head south to Tudela (its old quarter is worth a quick stop if time allows) and join the A68 for the dash to Zaragoza. Total distance 100km (1¼ hours).

TRIP HIGHLIGHT

❾ Zaragoza

Most tourists to Spain tend to overlook Zaragoza, which is a real pity for them but a bonus for those sensible enough to visit, because this is truly one of the most interesting and beautiful cities in northern Spain. For more on the city and it's melange of sights that include Christian and Islamic wonders, see p232.

✗ 📖 p157

JOANOT / GETTY IMAGES ©

Zaragoza A beautiful city sparkling in the night sky

Eating & Sleeping

Logroño ⑤

✕ Marinée Restaurante Seafood €€

(☎941 24 39 10; Plaza de Mercardo 2-3; mains €15-20; ◷1.45-3.45pm Tue & Wed, 1.45-3.45pm & 9-11.30pm Thu-Sun) It's the seafood that really garners all the attention at this resturant on the main square, and that's no surprise: the prawns, cod, seabass and shellfish are all perfectly executed. But don't limit yourself to the fruits of the sea: the landlubber dishes are decent too. The €22 lunch menu is the deal of the day.

🛏 Hotel
Calle Mayor Boutique Hotel €€€

(☎941 23 23 68; www.hotelcallemayor.com; Calle Marqués de San Nicolás 71; r incl breakfast €120-160; 🅿 ❋ 🛜) This delicious hotel is *the* place to stay in Logroño. It has huge rooms with cheeky touches such as modern lamps atop ancient columns, it's bathed in light and simply oozes class. The staff are highly efficient.

Olite ⑦

🛏 Principe de Viana Historic Hotel €€

(☎948 74 00 00; www.parador.es; Plaza de los Teobaldos 2; r from €120; ❋ 📷) Situated in a wing of the castle (though the cheaper rooms are in a newer extension), this offering from the Parador chain is in a sumptuous, atmospheric class of its own. Though there might be good rooms available elsewhere in town for considerably fewer euros, they don't come with a castle attached.

🛏 Hotel
Merindad de Olite Historic Hotel €€

(☎948 74 07 35; www.merindaddeolitehoteles. com; Rúa de la Judería 11; s €58-68, d €68-78; ❋ 🛜) Built almost into the old town walls, this charming place has small but comfortable rooms and masses of medieval style. Get in fast because it fills quickly.

Zaragoza ⑨

✕ El Ciclón Contemporary Spanish €€

(Plaza del Pilar 10; raciones €7-8.50, set menus €15-20; ◷11am-11.30pm) Opened in November 2013 by three acclaimed Spanish chefs (all with Michelin-star restaurant experience), the dishes here are superbly prepared. Choose between set menus and tapas and *raciones* (large-size tapas) such as the Canary Island favourite, *papas arrugadas* (new potatoes with a spicy coriander sauce), noodles with mussels, and artichokes with *migas* (breadcrumbs) and cauliflower cream.

🛏 Hotel Sauce Boutique Hotel €€

(☎976 20 50 50; www.hotelsauce.com; Calle de Espoz y Mina 33; s from €45, d €51-66; ❋ 🛜) This chic, small hotel has a great central location and a light and airy look, with white wicker, painted furniture, stripy fabrics and tasteful watercolours on the walls. The superior rooms are well worth the few euros extra. Breakfast (€8) includes homemade cakes and a much-lauded *tortilla de patatas* (potato omelette).

Valladolid *Decorative balconied buildings overlooking pristine paved streets*

Castles & Cathedrals in Medieval Spain

12

This diverse and all-encompassing drive takes you to breathtaking cities and way off the beaten track to stand in awe of vast plains, spectacular mountain peaks and evocative medieval towns.

TRIP HIGHLIGHTS

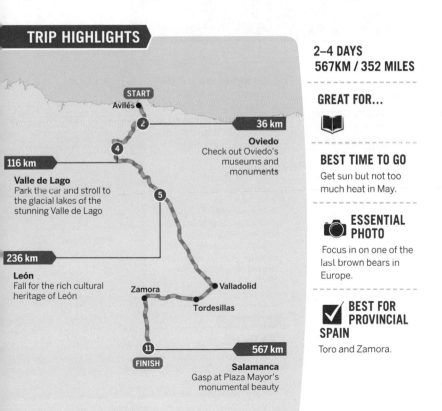

2–4 DAYS
567KM / 352 MILES

GREAT FOR...

BEST TIME TO GO
Get sun but not too much heat in May.

ESSENTIAL PHOTO
Focus in on one of the last brown bears in Europe.

BEST FOR PROVINCIAL SPAIN
Toro and Zamora.

START
Avilés

36 km
Oviedo
Check out Oviedo's museums and monuments

116 km
Valle de Lago
Park the car and stroll to the glacial lakes of the stunning Valle de Lago

236 km
León
Fall for the rich cultural heritage of León

Zamora
Valladolid
Tordesillas

567 km
FINISH
Salamanca
Gasp at Plaza Mayor's monumental beauty

12

Castles & Cathedrals in Medieval Spain

If you're looking for a window on the Spanish soul, head from Christian Spain's rebirth in Asturias over high mountains to the weather-beaten plains of Castilla y León. Experience fabled cities like Salamanca, with its lively student population, and León, with its imposing cathedral. But this is also a drive along quiet back roads, past half-timbered hamlets and isolated castles to a hidden Spain most travellers never imagined still existed.

1 Avilés

You might visit this old estuary port and steel-making town to attend one of the innovative, independent Spanish and global music, theatre, cinema or art events at the **Centro Cultural Internacional Oscar Niemeyer** (Centro Niemeyer; ☎984 83 50 31; www.niemey-ercenter.org; ⊙10am-10pm Sun-Thu, 10am-midnight Fri & Sat). The Niemeyer arts centre, founded in 2011, was designed by Brazilian architect Oscar Niemeyer (the creator of Brasilia) as a gift to Asturias and as a cultural nexus between the Iberian Peninsula and Latin America. While you're

here, the old town's attractive colonnaded streets and central **Plaza de España**, fronted by two elegant 17th-century buildings, make for a lovely stroll.

The Drive » It's all fairly built up between Avilés and Oviedo, but by turning off the main A6 at Tabaza and taking the much more rural AS17 south as far Fonciello you can make the drive a little more pleasing. At Fonciello it's just easier to rejoin the motorway for the last few kilometres to Oviedo. Total drive time 50 minutes (36km).

TRIP HIGHLIGHT

2 Oviedo

The compact but characterful *casco antiguo* (old town) of Oviedo is agreeably offset by

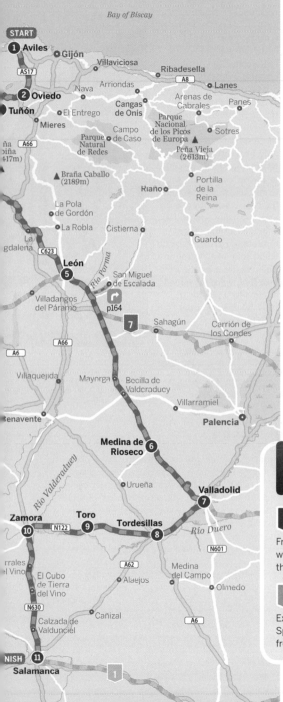

elegant parks and busy shopping streets. The big deal here, alongside just enjoying the old town, is the **Catedral de San Salvador**. The cathedral's origins and main interest lie in the **Cámara Santa** (admission €3, incl museum & cloister €5, free Thu afternoon; ⏰10am-8pm Jul & Aug, shorter hours rest of year), a pre-Romanesque chapel built by Alfonso II to house holy relics. The chapel now contains several key symbols of medieval Spanish Christianity and is a small part of a much bigger complex that was built piecemeal over many years. The **Museo Arqueológico de Asturias** (www.museoarqueologicodeasturias.com; Calle de San Vicente 3; ⏰9.30am-8pm Wed-Fri, 9.30am-2pm & 5-8pm Sat, 9.30am-3pm Sun) has informative displays from prehistoric cave art to *castro* (pre-Roman fortified village) culture, Roman times and the

LINK YOUR TRIP

7 Northern Spain Pilgrimage

From León you could head west to the setting sun on the Camino de Santiago.

1 Historic Castilla y León

Explore the grand heart of Spain by joining this tour from Salamanca.

medieval Kingdom of Asturias. The **Museo de Bellas Artes de Asturias** (Fine Arts Museum; www.museobbaa.com; Calle de Santa Ana 1; ⊘10.30am-2pm & 4.30-8.30pm Tue-Sat, 10.30am-2.30pm Sun), housed in two of Oviedo's finest urban palaces, has a large and rewarding collection, including paintings by Spanish and European greats such as Goya, Zurbarán, Picasso, Titian and Brueghel the Elder, and plenty by Asturians, such as Evaristo Valle.

✖ 🛏 p167

The Drive » It's just 22km (35 minutes) along delicious quiet country roads to the equally delightful village of Tuñón. Take the N634 and the AS228.

- - - - - - - - - - - -

❸ Tuñón

Tuñón itself is just a small village popular with walkers, cyclists and nature lovers. And why do they come here? Bears is the answer! The wild mountains that stretch around and beyond here are the last real refuge of Spain's biggest animal, the brown bear. While you'd have to be lucky to see genuine free-ranging wild bears, the **Cercado Osero**, about 5.5km south of Tuñón (or a 1.1km walk from the Área Recreativa Buyera), a 40,000-sq-metre hillside compound is home to three female Cantabrian brown bears, Paca, Tola and Molinera. The two older bears, Paca and Tola, were orphaned as cubs by a hunter in 1989. The bears hibernate in winter.

The Drive » From Tuñón take the spectacular AS265 and AS227 westward and then south through San Martín and La Riera, via the Puerto de San Lorenzo pass (1347m, often snowed under in winter).

IAKOV FILIMONOV / SHUTTERSTOCK ©

THERE'S A BEAR IN THERE

The wild mountain area of southwest Asturias and northwestern Castilla y León, including Parque Natural de Somiedo, is the main stronghold of the *oso pardo* (brown bear). Bear numbers in the Cordillera Cantábrica have climbed to over 200 from as low as 70 in the mid-1990s, including a smaller population of about 30 in a separate easterly area straddling southeast Asturias, southwest Cantabria and northern Castilla y León. Killing bears has been illegal in Spain since 1973 but only since the 1990s have concerted plans for bear recovery been carried out. The year 2012 saw a record 62 new cubs in the Cordillera Cantábrica, 56 of them in the western area. Experts are further heartened by the fact that there has been at least one recent case of interbreeding between the western and eastern groups.

This lumbering beast can reach 250kg and live 25 to 30 years, and has traditionally been disliked by farmers even though it is almost entirely vegetarian. Public support has played a big part in its recent recovery in the Cordillera Cantábrica, which owes a lot to the celebrated bears of Asturias' **Senda del Oso**. Experts warn that the bear is not yet completely out of the woods – illegal snares set for wild boar and poisoned bait put out for wolves continue to pose serious threats, as do forest fires, new roads and ski stations, which reduce the bears' habitat and mobility, while poaching has claimed the lives of at least two bears in the last few years.

Oviedo A city with a compact but characterful *casco antiguo* (old town)

At tiny Pola de Somiedo veer onto a smaller road heading southeast for 8km to Valle de Lago. Total distance 58km (1½ hours).

TRIP HIGHLIGHT

❹ Valle de Lago

Few foreigners reach the 292-sq-km Parque Natural de Somiedo, a Unesco-listed biosphere reserve on the northern flank of the Cordillera Cantábrica. Composed chiefly of five valleys descending from the Cordillera's 2000m-plus heights, the park combines thick woodlands, rocky mountains and high pastures.

One of the best (and most popular) walking areas is the **Valle de Lago**, whose upper reaches contain glacial lakes and high summer pastures. You must leave vehicles in Valle de Lago village.

The Drive » After you've marveled over the lakes backtrack to Pola de Somiedo and continue southeast all the way to León (120km; 2¼ hours). You could reduce this journey time by speeding the last part along the A66, but we think you'll prefer the lazy, and awfully scenic, C623.

TRIP HIGHLIGHT

❺ León

You'll remember León long after you leave. By day you'll encounter a city with its roots firmly planted in the soil of northern Castilla, with its grand monuments, loyal Catholic heritage and role as an important staging post along the Camino de Santiago. By night León is taken over by its large student population. It's a fabulous mix. The big three attractions here are the **Catedral, Real Basílica de San Isidoro**

163

DETOUR:
MONASTERIO DE SAN MIGUEL DE ESCALADA

Start: ❺ León

Rising from Castilla's northern plains, **Monasterio de San Miguel de Escalada** (admission by donation; ⏱10.15am-2pm & 4.30-8pm Tue-Sun) is one of the region's little-known treasures, a typically remote Castilian church rich in history. It was built in the 9th century by refugee monks from Córdoba on the remains of a Visigoth church dedicated to the Archangel Michael, and various orders of monks and nuns lived here from the 9th century until the 19th century. It's best known for its beautifully simple horseshoe arches of the kind that are rarely seen this far north in Spain. The graceful exterior porch with its portico is balanced by the impressive marble columns within; all of the interior columns (and three of those outside) are of Roman origin. Inside, two stone slabs and an arch are all that remains of the original Visigoth church, while other features are clearly Mozarabic (post Islamic). Note also the windows with alabaster instead of glass.

To get here, take the N601 southeast of León. After about 14km, take the small LE213 to the east; the church is 16km after the turn-off.

and **Panteón Real**. After you're done with religion, explore the **Barrio Gótico** (old quarter). Highlights include stately Plaza de San Marcelo, home to the **ayuntamiento** (town hall), which occupies a charmingly compact Renaissance-era palace. The Renaissance theme continues in the form of the splendid **Palacio de los Guzmanes** (1560), where the facade and patio stand out; the latter is accessible only on a free guided tour that leaves regularly from 11.30am to 4.30pm. Next door is Antoni Gaudí's contribution to León's skyline, the castlelike, neo-Gothic **Casa de Botines** (1893), now a bank. For details on these see p115.

The Drive » It's a straight-line dash down the N601 to forgotten Medina de Rioseco. Allow an hour and a quarter to cover the 100km. Along the way you'll motor past endless flat fields of wheat. In summer it's relentlessly sun baked and in winter it can often be bitterly cold. In a strange way this vast landscape is bewitching.

- - - - - - - - - - - -

❻ Medina de Rioseco

Medina de Rioseco, a once-wealthy trading centre, still has a tangible medieval feel although, given the number of boarded-up frontages around Plaza Mayor, is sadly a lot poorer these days. Head for Calle Mayor with its colonnaded arcades held up by ancient wooden columns; market stalls set up here on Wednesday mornings. The **Iglesia de Santa María de Mediavilla** (Calle Santa María; guided visits in Spanish €2; ⏱11am-noon & 5-7pm Tue-Sun) has three star-vaulted naves and the rightfully famous **Capilla de los Benavente** chapel. Anchored by an extravagant altarpiece by Juan de Juní and carved over eight years from 1543, it's sometimes referred to as the 'Sistine Chapel of Castilla'. Medina de Rioseco is famous for its Easter processions, but if you can't be here during Holy Week, the **Museo de Semana Santa** (Calle de Lázaro Alonso; admission €3.50; ⏱11am-2pm & 4-7pm Tue-Sun Apr-Sep, weekends only Oct-Mar) provides an insight into the ceremonial passion of Easter here.

The Drive » Continue down the N601 for 45km (35 minutes) to Valladolid. After what feels like endless kilometres of wide open space, the suburbs of Valladolid come as something of a shock.

TRIP HIGHLIGHT

➐ Valladolid

Valladolid is an attractive place with a very Spanish character. The city's appeal is in its sprinkling of monuments, the fine Plaza Mayor and some excellent museums. By night, Valladolid comes alive as its large student population overflows from the city's boisterous bars. The nicest part of town centres on the Plaza de San Pablo, an open square dominated by the exquisite **Iglesia de San Pablo**. The church's main facade is an extravagant masterpiece of Isabelline Gothic, with every square centimetre finely worked, carved and twisted to produce a unique fabric in stone. Also fronting the square is the **Palacio de Pimentel** (🕙10am-2pm & 5-7pm Tue-Sat), where, on 12 July 1527, Felipe II was born. The palace hosts occasional exhibitions. The **Museo Nacional de Escultura** (🖉983 25 03 75; http://museoescultura. mcu.es; Calle de San Gregorio 2; adult/concession €3/1.50, Sat afternoon & Sun free; 🕙10am-2pm & 4-7.30pm Tue-Sat, 10am-2pm Sun) houses Spain's premier showcase of polychrome wood sculpture. The museum's home is inside the former Colegio de San Gregorio (1496), a flamboyant Isabelline Gothic–style building where exhibition rooms line a splendid two-storey galleried courtyard.

✕ 🛏 p167

The Drive » There's a whole load of wide open space and big light to marvel at on the 30km drive (30 minutes) down the E80 to Tordesillas.

➑ Tordesillas

The historically important and pretty town of Tordesillas doesn't make it onto all that many tourist itineraries, which is great news for those who do stop off here. The highlight of a visit is the Real Convento de Santa Clara. For more on Tordesillas, see p45.

The Drive » The A11 might be faster but we would suggest taking the N122 from Tordesillas to Toro. The scenery is no different (and in both cases is a world away from the damp hills and mountains you started in way up north), but it's just a more pleasant drive (50km, 50 minutes).

➒ Toro

The typically Castilian town of Toro has a grand past but a very provincial present. It's a good place to stop off for some well-off-the-beaten-tourist-track exploration. After you've enjoyed the attractive old quarter and its historical attractions, head to the **Monasterio Sancti Spiritus** (Calle del Canto 27; admission €4; 🕙guided tours in Spanish 10.30am-12.30pm & 4.30-5.30pm Tue-Sun), just southwest of town, which

SLOW DEATH

Many tranquil villages of Castilla y León have a dark secret: they could soon be extinct. Spain's economic boom in the late 1990s and beyond drove a massive shift from rural villages into urban centres. In the last 50 years, Spain's largest autonomous region has lost a million inhabitants. Its population of just over 2.5 million people is now the same as it was in 1901.

Award-winning documentary film-maker Mercedes Alvarez has warned of 'the dying without sound of a culture with over a thousand years of history'. At the same time, the renowned Spanish writer Julio Llamazares, a Castilla y León native, blamed 'the uncontrolled development of the 1960s and 1970s, which generated a total disdain for everything rural'.

features a fine Renaissance cloister and the striking alabaster tomb of Beatriz de Portugal, wife of Juan I. For more on Toro, see p45.

The Drive >> Keep to the N122 for the 40-minute (35km) drive into Zamora. Fields of wheat. Loads of them. Still.

----

⑩ Zamora

Quiet Zamora is your typical town of the high Spanish plateau, except that beyond the apparently endless suburbs you'll discover a marvelous *casco vieja* (old town) and some fascinating sights. For more

on this underrated town, see p45.

The Drive >> You might just as well take the A66 motorway for this last leg of the journey from Zamora to fantastical Salamanca. It's 67km and will take roughly an hour.

TRIP HIGHLIGHT

⑪ Salamanca

Whether floodlit by night or bathed in the sunset, there's something magical about Salamanca. This is a city of rare beauty, awash with golden sandstone overlaid with ochre-tinted Latin inscriptions; an extraordinary virtuosity of plateresque and

Renaissance styles. The monumental highlights are many, with the exceptional Plaza Mayor (illuminated to stunning effect at night) an unforgettable highlight. But this is also Castilla's liveliest city; home to a massive Spanish and international student population that throngs the streets at night and provides the city with so much youth and vitality. Built between 1729 and 1755, Salamanca's exceptional Plaza Mayor is widely considered to be Spain's most beautiful central plaza.

🛏 p167

MATTEO COLOMBO / GETTY IMAGES ©

Salamanca Plaza Mayor's golden lights at night

Eating & Sleeping

② Oviedo

✗ Naguar
Tapas, Fusion €€

(naguar.es; Avenida de Galicia 14; raciones €10-19; ⊘11am-midnight) Under the watch of acclaimed Asturian chef Pedro Martino, Naguar oozes cool. It's an incredibly popular spot for top-notch creative, contemporary tapas, often with an Asian touch, such as teriyaki sesame chicken with seaweed. Head past the open-plan kitchen to the dining area or just pull up a stool in the orange-lit bar with everyone else.

⊨ Hotel Fruela
Hotel €€

(☑985 20 81 20; www.hotelfruela.com; Calle de Fruela 3; r €75-85; P ❄ �@) With a pleasing contemporary style and a touch of original art, plus professional yet friendly service, the 28-room Fruela achieves a cosy, almost intimate feel and is easily the top midrange option in central Oviedo. Rooms are bright and welcoming. Breakfast, tapas and other meals are available in its cafe-restaurant.

⑦ Valladolid

✗ Martín Quiroga
Contemporary Castilian €€

(☑605 787117; Calle San Ignacio 17; mains €16-18; ⊘1.30-3.30pm & 8.30-11.30pm) With just four tables and a typical waiting list of a month, you would imagine that this extraordinarily

high-quality gastrobar would have prices to match. It doesn't. There is no menu, dishes depend on what's fresh in season and available from the market that day, but there's plenty of choice. Special diets are catered to with advance notice. Reservations essential.

⊨ Hotel Mozart
Hotel €

(☑983 29 77 77; www.hotelmozart.net; Calle Menéndez Pelayo 7; s/d €50/60; ❄ @) Extremely well priced hotel given the quality of its refurbished rooms. Here you'll find king-size beds, plush earth-colour furnishings and fabrics, polished parquet floors, dazzling marble bathrooms and space enough for a comfortable armchair. The entrance has a whiff of grandeur about it as well, which contributes to the surprise of the budget-bracket price.

Salamanca ⑪

⊨ Don Gregorio
Boutique Hotel €€€

(☑923 21 70 15; www.hoteldongregorio.com; Calle de San Pablo 80; r/ste incl breakfast from €216/360; P ❄ @) A palatial hotel with part of the city's Roman wall flanking the garden. Rooms are decorated in soothing shades of cappuccino with crisp white linens and extravagant extras, including private saunas, espresso machines, complimentary minibar, king-size beds and vast hydromassage tubs. Sumptuous antiques and medieval tapestries adorn the public areas.

Baiona *Excellent replica of the Pinta — one of Columbus' ships that docked here in 1493*

Coast of Galicia

Driving along the wild coastline of Galicia rewards with majestic rías (inlets), dramatic cliffs, beaches and islands, and quaint fishing ports. And some of the best seafood around!

TRIP HIGHLIGHTS

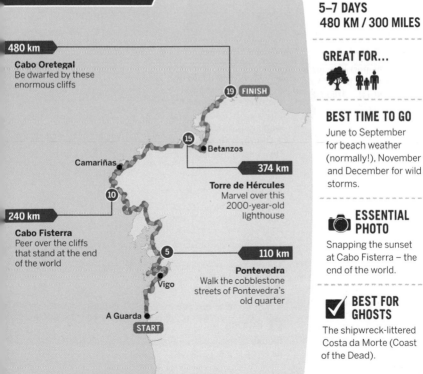

480 km

Cabo Oretegal
Be dwarfed by these enormous cliffs

⑲ FINISH

⑮

● Betanzos

Camariñas

374 km

Torre de Hércules
Marvel over this 2000-year-old lighthouse

⑩

240 km

Cabo Fisterra
Peer over the cliffs that stand at the end of the world

⑤

110 km

Pontevedra
Walk the cobblestone streets of Pontevedra's old quarter

Vigo

A Guarda ●
START

5–7 DAYS
480 KM / 300 MILES

GREAT FOR...

BEST TIME TO GO
June to September for beach weather (normally!), November and December for wild storms.

ESSENTIAL PHOTO
Snapping the sunset at Cabo Fisterra – the end of the world.

BEST FOR GHOSTS
The shipwreck-littered Costa da Morte (Coast of the Dead).

169

13 Coast of Galicia

Rocky headlands, winding inlets, small fishing towns, narrow coves, wide sweeping bays and many a remote, sandy beach – this is the eerily beautiful coastline of Galicia and it's a world away from the popular images of Spain. Bleak and storm wracked, this is a coast of legends and ghosts, and when the cold mists roll in it's easy to see why.

ATLANTIC OCEAN

Camelle

Camariñas 12
p176 Muxia 11 Vim

Fisterra 10
O Pindo
Carnota

Mur
Porto do

Xu

Corrubed

1 A Guarda

A fishing port just north of where the Río Miño spills into the Atlantic, A Guarda (Castilian: La Guardia) has a pretty harbour and good seafood restaurants, but its unique draw is beautiful **Monte de Santa Trega** (adult/child in vehicle Tue-Sun Feb-Dec €1/0.50, other times free), whose summit is a 4km drive or 2km uphill walk (the PRG122) from town. On the way up, poke around the partly re-stored Iron Age **Castro de Santa Trega**. At the top, you'll find a 16th-century chapel, an interesting small **archaeological museum** (⏰10am-8pm Tue-Sun) on *castro* (fortified villages) culture, a couple of cafes and souvenir stalls – and majestic panoramas up the Miño, across to Portugal and out over the Atlantic. It's also nice to take the 3km **walking path** south from A Guarda's harbour along the coast to the heads of the Miño.

🗙 p179

The Drive >> Follow the PO552 north along a straight, cliff-lined coastal road to Baiona (30km, 35 minutes). Enjoy not fighting the steering wheel much – this is about the one and only straight stretch of road you're going to encounter!

2 Baiona

Baiona (Castilian: Bayona) is a popular

resort with its own little place in history: the shining moment came on 1 March 1493, when one of Columbus' small fleet, the *Pinta,* stopped in for supplies, bearing the remarkable news that the explorer had made it to the (West) Indies. Today you can visit a replica of the **Pinta** (admission €2; ⊙10am-8pm; 🅿) in Baiona's harbour.

You can't miss the pine-covered promontory **Monte Boi**, dominated by the **Fortaleza de Monterreal** (pedestrian/car €1/5; ⊙10am-10pm). The fortress, erected between the 11th and 17th centuries, is protected by a 3km circle of walls, and an enjoyable 40-minute walking trail loops round the promontory's rocky shoreline, which is

LINK YOUR TRIP

7 Northern Spain Pilgrimage

Go against the flow and work your way in reverse along the history soaked Camino de Santiago. Start in Santiago de Compostela.

30 The Minho's Lyrical Landscapes

Cross the border to Guimarães in Portugal and enjoy some of the most magical scenery in Western Europe.

broken up by a few small beaches.

A tangle of inviting lanes, with a handful of 16th- and 17th-century houses and chapels, makes up Baiona's **casco histórico** (historic centre), behind the harbourfront road, Rúa Elduayen.

The Drive ›› It's twenty-nine twisting kilometres (50 minutes) along the PO552 and PO325 via the small towns of Patos and Oya – and numerous stunning sandy beaches – to Vigo.

❸ Vigo

Vigo is both a historic and cultured city and a gritty industrial port that's home to Europe's largest fishing fleet. At the heart of the old town's jumbled lanes is elegant **Praza da Constitución**, a perfect spot for a drink. Head down **Rúa dos Cesteiros**, with its quaint wicker shops, and you'll come upon the **Igrexa de Santa María**, built in 1816 – long after its Romanesque predecessor had been burnt down by Sir Francis Drake. Vigo

is something of a modern art centre, with several museums and galleries to prove it. The **Museo de Arte Contemporánea de Vigo** (Marco; www.marcovigo.com; Rúa do Príncipe 54; ☺11am-2.30pm & 5-9pm Tue-Sat, 11am-2.30pm Sun) is the number-one venue for exhibitions ranging from painting and sculpture to fashion and design.

The Drive ›› It's 39km (45 minutes) along the CO41 from built-up Vigo to the tranquil Cabo de Home. On the way pass through Hío for a look at Galicia's most famous *cruceiro*, a small but elaborate 19th-century cross standing outside the San Andrés de Hío church.

❹ Cabo de Home

Windswept Cabo de Home is a rocky cape with walking trails, three lighthouses and great views of the offshore Illas Cíes. The partly excavated Iron Age **Castro de Berobriga** sits atop panoramic Monte Facho nearby. There are some beautiful beaches in the area as well (some nudist).

TOP TIP: BRING YOUR UMBRELLA

Swept by one rainy front after another, Galicia has, overall, twice as much rain as the Spanish national average. Galicians have more than 100 words to describe different kinds of rain, from *babuxa* (a variety of drizzle) to *xistra* (a type of shower) and *treboada* (a thunderstorm).

The Drive ›› Technically you should be able to cover the 38km between Cabo de Home and Pontevedra in around an hour, but the amount of sand and sea temptation along the way is likely to string it out to a half-day journey.

TRIP HIGHLIGHT

❺ Pontevedra

Back in the 16th century Pontevedra was Galicia's biggest city and an important port, where Columbus' flagship, the *Santa María,* was built. Today it's an inviting, small, riverside city that combines history, culture and style into a

Vigo Museo de Arte Contemporánea de Vigo

lively overnight stop. The interlocking lanes and plazas of the compact old town are abuzz with shops, markets, cafes and tapas bars.

Pontevedra's eclectic museum, **Museo de Pontevedra** (☎986 80 41 00; www.museo.depo.es; ⊙10am-9pm Tue-Sat, 11am-2pm Sun), is scattered over five city-centre buildings. If time is limited, head for the bright new **Sexto Edificio** and the adjoining **Edificio Sarmiento**. The Sexto Edificio contains Galician and Spanish art from the 14th to 20th centuries. The Edificio Sarmiento houses an absorbing col-

lection ranging over Galician Sargadelos ceramics, modern art and more.

Art of a different kind can be found at the **Basílica de Santa María a Maior** (Praza de Alonso de Fonseca; ⊙10am-1.30pm & 5-9pm, except during Mass), Pontevedra's most impressive church. It's a mainly Gothic affair with a whiff of plateresque and Portuguese Manueline influences.

✕ 🛏 p179

The Drive » You'll likely be a bit sad to leave lovely old Pontevedra, but don't be too downhearted because you're off to equally enticing Combarro, which is just a 7km (15 minute) skip away up the PO308.

━ ━ ━ ━ ━ ━ ━ ━ ━

⑥ Combarro

Combarro's postcard-perfect old quarter unfurls around a tidy bay and looks like it was plucked straight out of the Middle Ages. With a jumble of seaside *hórreos* (traditional stone grain stores) and crooked lanes (some of them hewn directly out of the rock bed) dotted with *cruceiros,* and a smattering of waterside restaurants, this is some people's favourite stop in the Rías Baixas. It can get extremely busy in high summer.

The Drive » When you're done exploring Combarro take the PO303 northwest to Seixinos and then the PO550 on to Cambados (30km, 30 minutes). The route works its way through farmland and over wide estuaries of greeny-blue waters.

- - - - - - - - - -

7 Cambados

The capital of the **albariño wine country**, famed for its fruity whites, the pretty little *ría*-side town of Cambados has a compact core of old streets lined by stone architecture and dotted with inviting taverns and eateries. The most easily visited wineries are two small establishments in the **Pazo de Fefiñáns**, a handsome 16th-century mansion on broad Praza de Fefiñáns: **Bodegas del Palacio de Fefiñanes** (www.fefinanes.com; visits incl tasting per person €4-9, minimum per group €24-50; 🕙10am-1pm & 4-7pm Mon-Fri Mar-Dec) and **Gil Armada** (bodegagilarmada.com; house tour & tasting €7; 🕙1hr tour noon & 6pm Mon-Sat). Visits to the latter include a house tour. Pay a visit to the ruined 15th-century church, **Igrexa de Santa Mariña Dozo** (Rúa do Castro), which is now roofless but still has its four semicircular roof arches intact. It's surrounded by a well-kept cemetery with elaborate graves – quite spooky at dusk! Just beyond, Monte de A Pastora park provides

expansive views over the Ría de Arousa.

The Drive » You'll need to use a combination of the N640, CP1104 and AC550 to get to Muros. It's a very impressive drive with plenty of reason to stop and swim or, at less benign times of year, to walk windblown sands. Allow two hours to cover the 100km.

- - - - - - - - - -

8 Muros

Muros is an agreeable halt en route to the Costa da Morte. Behind the bustling seafront extends a web of stone-paved lanes dotted with taverns and lined with dignified stone houses. The 14th-century **Igrexa de San Pedro** is a fine example of Galician sailors' Gothic architecture. Stop by **Licores Luisa** (Praza de Galicia 2; 🕙9.30am-2pm & 4.30-7pm Mon-Sat) to sample home-made *orujo* (a firewater made from grape pressings) or liqueurs with an amazing variety of flavours from coffee to banana.

The Drive » As you leave Muros the real excitement of this drive begins (can you believe that all you just drove through was a mere taster...?) for this is where the famed Costa da Morte begins. It's so named because of the number of shipwrecks it's claimed. To get to Carnota take the roundabout AC550 (16km, 20 minutes).

- - - - - - - - - -

9 Carnota

Carnota village is renowned as home

to Galicia's largest *hórreo* – 34.5m long and constructed in an 18th-century *hórreo*-building contest with nearby Lira. However, many people come here not for the grain store but for the spectacular, if exposed, 7km curve of nearby **Praia de Carnota**.

The Drive » Driving to the end of the world has never been so easy. Just follow the AC550 north past O Pindo (which has some great short walks including a four-hour round trip hike up 627m high Monte Pindo) to Fisterra (38km; 40min).

- - - - - - - - - -

TRIP HIGHLIGHT

10 Fisterra

Cabo Fisterra (Castilian: Cabo Finisterre) is the western edge of Spain, at least in popular imagination. The real westernmost point is Cabo da Nave, 5km north, but that doesn't stop throngs of people from heading out to this beautiful, wind-swept cape, which is also the end-point of an 86km extension of the Camino de Santiago. Pilgrims ending their journeys here ritually burn smelly socks, T-shirts etc on the rocks just past the lighthouse.

The cape is a 3.5km drive past the town of Fisterra. On the edge of town you pass the 12th-century **Igrexa de Santa María das Areas.** The hills around here were once used as a site of pagan fertility rites, and they say childless couples used to come up here to improve their chances of conception.

Fisterra itself is a fishing port with a picturesque harbour. The spectacular beach **Praia da Mar de Fora**, over on the ocean side of the promontory, is reachable via an 800m walk.

✗ ⊨ p179

The Drive » The route north from Fisterra to Muxía (take the very minor coastal roads via Castrexe and Nemiña; 37km, one hour) passes along enchanting lanes through thick woodlands; along the way is a nice detour to Cabo Touriñán, a very picturesque spot for a breezy walk. Just south of Muxía, Praia de Lourido is an unspoilt stretch of sand.

- - - - - - - - - -

⑪ Muxia

Muxía is a photogenic little fishing port with a handful of cosy bars. Follow signs to the **Santuario da Virxe da Barca** to reach one of Galicia's most beloved pilgrimage points. This church marks the spot where (legend attests) the Virgin Mary arrived in a stone boat and appeared to Santiago (St James) while he was preaching here. Two of the rocks strewn before the chapel are, supposedly, the boat's sail and tiller. A lightning-sparked fire on Christmas Day 2013 gutted the church's interior (now restored).

The Drive » Heading on from Muxía towards Camariñas, take the pretty road via the inviting beach Praia do Lago, the *hórreo*-studded hamlet Leis and the riverside village of Cereixo (28km, 45 minutes).

- - - - - - - - - -

⑫ Camariñas

The fishing village of Camariñas is known for its fine traditional lacework, with several specialist shops and the interesting **Museo do Encaixe** (Lace Museum; Praza Insuela; admission €2; ◷11am-2pm & 5-8pm Tue-Sun

LOCAL KNOWLEDGE: GALICIA SEAFOOD TIPS

Galicia's ocean-fresh seafood, from *pulpo á feira* (tender, spicy octopus slices) to melt-in-mouth *lubiña* (sea bass), is a reason in itself to come here. In any coastal town or village (and many inland) you can get a meal to remember. Tuck into any of these and you'll never want to eat red meat again.

Pulpo á feira Galicia's signature dish (known as *pulpo a la gallega* elsewhere in Spain): tender slices of octopus tentacle sprinkled with olive oil and paprika. It's available almost everywhere that serves food, but most Galicians agree that the best *pulpo á feira* is cooked in the inland town of O Carballiño, 30km northwest of Ourense. Cooks here invented the recipe in the Middle Ages, when the local monastery received copious supplies of octopus from tenants on its coastal properties. Around 70,000 people pile into O Carballiño on the second Sunday of August for the Festa do Pulpo de O Carballiño.

Percebes (goose barnacles) Galicia's favourite shellfish delicacy, pulled off coastal rocks at low tide and looking like miniature dragon claws. Cedeira is famed for its rich *percebes*.

Shellfish fans will also delight in *ameixas* (clams), *mexillons* (mussels), *vieiras* and *zamburiñas* (both types of scallop), *berberechos* (cockles) and *navajas* (razor clams). These can be bought in any coastal town.

Crabs are also a local favourite and come in a dizzying variety of types, from little *nécoras* to huge *centollos* (spider crabs).

mid-Jun–Aug, noon-2pm & 6-8pm Wed-Sat Oct–mid-Jun).

The Drive » The rugged coast between Camariñas and Camelle, to the northeast, is one of the most beautiful stretches of the Costa da Morte. Take your time (not that you have a choice: the roads are s-l-o-w...) and follow your nose down random country lanes to hidden beaches or dramatic headlands.

- - - - - - - - - - - -

⑬ Camelle

Camelle has no outstanding charm, but it does have the so-called **Museo do Alemán**, beside the pier, a quirky and touching open-air sculpture garden made from rocks and ocean bric-a-brac by 'Man' (Manfred Gnädinger), an eccentric long-time German resident

who died in 2002 just weeks after the Prestige oil tanker went down just offshore. The resulting oil slick devastated this fragile coastline (and beaches as far away as southwest France) and, so people say, caused Man to die of a broken heart. **Praia de Traba**, a little-frequented 2.5km stretch of sand with dunes and a lagoon, is a lovely 4km walk east along the coast, and from there footpath PRG114 continues 8km to Laxe.

The Drive » It's 24km (40 minutes) from Camelle to Laxe via the AC433. If walking just isn't you then the coastal road takes you past the aforementioned Praia de Traba as well as lots of farmland that merges near seemlessly with moorland and sand dune.

Fisterra might by the end of the world but we think this area feels more like it.

- - - - - - - - - - - -

⑭ Laxe

A sweeping bay beach runs right along the lively waterfront of Laxe, and the 15th-century Gothic church of **Santa María da Atalaia** stands guard over the harbour. Much of this area's appeal lies beyond the town. Laxe's **tourist office** (☎981 72 83 13; www. concellodelaxe.com/turismo; Avenida Cesáreo Pondal 26; ◷10am-2pm & 5-8pm Tue-Sun) and its website have information on **walks** in the area, including the 8km coastal walk west to Praia de Traba via the surf beach Praia de Soesto.

For a fascinating archaeological outing, drive inland past Canduas, then 2.4km south on the AC430 to find the turnoff for the **Castro A Cidá de Borneiro**, a pre-Roman *castro* amid thick woodlands. One kilometre further along the AC430, turn right and go 1km to the **Dolmen de Dombate** (◷9am-8pm or dusk, whichever earlier), a large 3700 BC megalithic tomb recently encased in a protective pavilion. A full-size replica, which (unlike the real thing) you can go inside, stands in the adjacent visitors centre.

The Drive » It's only 90km along the coastal road from Laxe to the big city of A Coruña but

---

DETOUR: RUTA DEL LITORAL

Start: ⑫ Camariñas

It takes longer than the direct route but don't miss the scenic coastal road (part paved, part potholed dirt/gravel) from Camariñas 5km northwest to the **Cabo Vilán lighthouse** (with a cafe and an exhibition on shipwrecks and lighthouses) then east to Camelle, a further 21km. The route winds past secluded beaches such as **Area de Trece** – a picturesque set of short sandy strands divided by groups of boulders – across windswept hillsides and past weathered rock formations, and there are many places to stop along the way, such as the **Ceminterio dos Ingleses** (English Cemetery), the sad burial ground from an 1890 shipwreck that took the lives of 172 British naval cadets. Signposting after the cemetery is almost nonexistent: go left at forks after 2km and 3km, straight on at the junction after 5.7km, and left at the fork after 8.5km.

the nature of the roads along the Costa da Morte means it takes at least two hours. For the most scenic route we would suggest skirting the coastline all the way via the villages of Malpica de Bergantiños, Razo da Costa and Leira.

TRIP HIGHLIGHT

⓯ A Coruña

A Coruña (Castilian: La Coruña) is a port city, beachy hot spot and cruise-ship stop; a busy commercial centre and a cultural enclave; a historic city and a modern metropolis. The Ciudad Vieja (old city) has shady plazas, charming old churches, hilly cobbled lanes and a good smattering of cafes and bars. The Unesco-listed **Torre de Hércules** (Tower of Hercules; www. torredeherculescoruna.com; Avenida de Navarra; adult/ senior & child €3/1.50, Mon free; ☺10am-9pm Jun-Sep, 10am-6pm Oct-May; Ⓟ) sits near the windy northern tip of the city. Legend attributes its construction to one of the labours of Hercules, but it was actually the Romans who originally built this lighthouse in the 1st century AD – a beacon on what was then the furthest edge of the civilised world. Kids love the seal colony and the underwater Nautilus room (surrounded by sharks and 50 other fish species) at the excellent **Aquarium Finisterrae** (☎981 18 98 42; mc2coruna.

org/aquarium; Paseo Marítimo 34; adult/senior & child €10/4; ☺10am-9pm, shorter hours Sep-Jun; ♿) on the city's northern headland.

✕ ⌂ p179

The Drive » The straight, yes straight, E70 will see you get into Betanzos in just 20 minutes (24km) – traffic depending...

⓰ Betanzos

Once a thriving estuary port rivalling A Coruña, Betanzos has a well-preserved medieval old town and is renowned for its welcoming taverns with local wines and good food. To explore the old town take Rúa Castro up into the oldest part of town. Handsome **Praza da Constitución** is flanked by a couple of appealing cafes along with the Romanesque/Gothic **Igrexa de Santiago**, whose main portico inspired Santiago de Compostela's Pórtico de la Gloria. A short stroll northeast, two beautiful Gothic churches, **Santa María do Azougue** and **San Francisco**, stand almost side by side. The latter is full of particularly fine stone carving, including many sepulchres of 14th- and 15th-century Galician nobility.

The Drive » There's more fast, but rather dull, driving for the 26km sprint (20 minutes) from Betanzos to Pontedeume. Take the E1/AP9.

⓱ Pontedeume

This hillside town overlooks the Eume estuary, where fishing boats bob. The old town is an appealing combination of handsome galleried houses, narrow cobbled streets and occasional open plazas, liberally sprinkled with taverns and tapas bars. Several parallel narrow streets climb up from the main road, the central one being the porticoed Rúa Real.

The Drive » Heading north from Pontedeume, the coast is studded with small maritime towns and pretty beaches. The naval port of Ferrol, 17km from Pontedeume, is large but has little to detain you. Continuing north, you reach Valdoviño, with the beautiful Praia Frouxeira, and just beyond Valdoviño there's surfy Pantín. Allow about an hour for the 46km journey to Cedeira.

⓲ Cedeira

The fishing port and very low-key resort of Cedeira has a cute little old town sitting on the west bank of the Río Condomiñas, while **Praia da Magdalena** fronts the modern, eastern side of town. Around the headland to the south (a 7km drive) is the much more appealing **Praia de Vilarrube**, a long, sandy beach with shallow waters between two river mouths, in a protected dunes and wetlands area.

For a nice stroll of an hour or two, walk along the waterfront to the fishing port, climb up beside the old fort above it and walk out to **Punta Sarridal**, overlooking the mouth of the Ría de Cedeira. The rocky coast around here produces rich harvests of *percebes* (goose barnacles), a much-coveted seafood delicacy.

The Drive » The narrow CP2205 will have the honour of taking you on the last part of your journey to Cabo Oretegal. The road crosses the Serra da Capelada and has incredible views. Six kilometres beyond San Andrés is Garita de Herbeira lookout; the best place to be wowed over southern Europe's highest sea cliffs. Total journey 26km (45 minutes).

- - - - - - - - - - - -

TRIP HIGHLIGHT

⑲ Cabo Oretegal

This drive finishes with the mother of all Spanish capes, Cabo Ortegal, where the Atlantic Ocean meets the Bay of Biscay. Great stone shafts drop sheer into the ocean from such a height that the waves crashing on the rocks below seem pitifully benign. **Os Tres Aguillóns**, three islets, provide a home to hundreds of marine birds, and with binoculars you might spot dolphins or whales.

Cedeira Fishing boats harbouring in the quaint fishing port

MERCEDES RANCAÑO OTERO / GETTY IMAGES ©

Eating & Sleeping

A Guarda ❶

✖ Restaurante Bitadorna Seafood €€€

(☏986 61 19 70; www.bitadorna.com; Rúa do Porto 30; mains €18-26, menús for 2 €55-78; ⏱11am-4.30pm & 7.30-11.30pm, closed Sun-Tue evenings Sep-Jun) A Guarda is famed for its *arroz con bogavante* (rice with European lobster). A dozen seafood eateries line up facing the harbour. The relatively upscale Bitadorna offers both traditional and creative treatments of whatever comes in fresh from the local fishing boats. A good plan is to go for one of its daily *menús* (set menus) of up to five courses including wine.

Pontevedra ❺

✖ Eirado da Leña Galician, Fusion €€€

(☏986 86 02 25; www.eiradoeventos.com; Praza da Leña 3; mains €18-25; ⏱1.30-4pm & 9-11.30pm Wed-Sat, 1.30-4pm Mon & Tue) A creative culinary experience in a little stone-walled restaurant, set with white linen and fresh flowers. The €24 set menu, available lunchtime and evening, comprises four beautifully presented courses, served with a smile and some curious little surprises!

⌦ Parador
Casa del Barón Historic Hotel €€€

(☏986 85 58 00; www.parador.es; Rúa do Barón 19; r €130-178; 🅿❄🛜) This elegant refurbished 17th-century palace is equipped throughout with antique-style furniture and historical art, and has a lovely little garden.

Fisterra ❿

✖ O Fragón Contemporary Galician €€

(☏659 077320; Praza da Cerca 8; mains €9-20, menú €30; ⏱1.15-3.30pm & 8-10.45pm May-Sep, 1.15-3.30pm Oct & Dec-Apr, closed Tue Sep-Jun,

last week Jun, Carnaval week) Neat O Fragón prepares original, tasty dishes from locally available ingredients. The *menú gastronómico*, available for all meals, is a diverse feast that includes fish, shellfish and meat dishes and a starter and dessert (drinks are extra). It's just round the corner, past the main restaurant strip.

⌦ Hotel Mar da Ardora Design Hotel €€

(☏981 74 05 90; hotelmardaardora.com; Rúa Atalaia 15; s/d incl breakfast €99/110; 🅿🛜♿) This delightful little family-run hotel sits at the top of town with fantastic westward ocean views from the big windows and terraces of its six rooms. Everything is in impeccably contemporary but comfortable style, from the cubist architecture to the soothing white/grey/silver colour schemes.

A Coruña ⓯

✖ Adega O Bebedeiro Galician €€

(☏981 21 06 09; www.adegaobebedeiro.com; Calle de Ángel Rebollo 34; mains €13-25; ⏱1.30-4pm & 8pm-midnight Tue-Sat, 1.30-4pm Sun) It's in a humble street on the northern headland and it looks a dump from outside, but the inside is rustically neat with a conversation-inspiring assortment of Galician bric-a-brac. The food is classic home-style cooking with some inventive touches, such as scallop-stuffed sea bass in puff pastry, or spiced venison with chestnuts, all in generous quantities. Packed on weekends.

⌦ Hotel Zenit Coruña Hotel €€

(☏981 21 84 84; www.zenithoteles.com; Calle Comandante Fontanes 19; s €76-110, d €80-115; 🅿❄@🛜) The sunny, stylishly minimalist rooms – all with outside views – have glass wardrobe doors and washbasins, big bathroom mirrors, tasteful modern art and a menu of pillows, and there's a creative but not overpriced restaurant. And it's just a block from Playa del Orzán.

Barcelona & Eastern Spain

WILD AND GORGEOUS COASTLINE, CHISELLED MOUNTAIN PEAKS AND ENCHANTING CITYSCAPES set the stage for awe-inspiring drives around Catalonia and eastern Spain. Barcelona makes a fine gateway to the region, with its madcap architecture and brilliant restaurants. Just northeast of there, the coastline known as the Costa Brava is studded with villages and beaches against headlands topped with pine forests and the odd lighthouse. West of Barcelona, the coastal plains give way to lowland mountains, and you'll drive through medieval towns and monasteries, serenely set over the vineyards of the Penedès region. The views only get more spectacular as you go north and enter the alpine world of the Pyrenees: you'll roll past old stone villages and flower-strewn meadows, with the mountains all around you.

Barcelona A bird's-eye view over this vibrant city
LEONID ANDRONOV / GETTY IMAGES ©

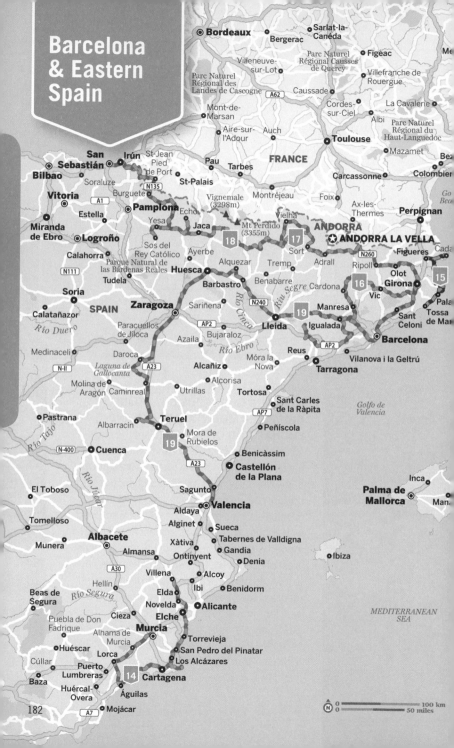

Unsung Wonders of Murcia & Alicante
14 **2–4 Days**

Relax in seaside villages, wander through Roman ruins, and hike highland trails. (p185)

Classic Trip

Artistic Inspiration on the Costa Brava
15 **2–4 Days**

Feast on seafood off beautiful beaches, then visit the wondrous world of Dalí. (p193)

Central Catalan's Wineries & Monasteries
16 **2–4 Days**

Stroll medieval lanes, ride the funicular up Montserrat and visit Penedès vineyards. (p203)

Peaks & Valleys in Northwest Catalonia
17 **2–4 Days**

Go white-water rafting in Llavorsí, hike past waterfalls and visit charming hilltop villages. (p211)

The Pyrenees 5–7 Days
18 Breathe in the mountain air on this epic drive over the Pyrenees. (p219)

Barcelona to Valencia 5–7 Days
19 Explore historic villages and revel in buzzing city life. (p229)

DON'T MISS

The palm groves of Elche

Take a refreshing walk along the wandering paths of this surprising oasis in Murcia. See it on Trip **14**

Cadaqués

Wander the rocky shores and hilly streets that inspired the great artist Salvador Dalí. Stroll in the surrealist's footsteps on Trip **15**

Estany de Sant Maurici

Enjoy spectacular views on a hike past this mountain lake in Catalonia's only national park. Experience it on Trip **17**

Teruel

Visit the tombs of two star-crossed lovers from the 13th century in a stirring but kitschy display. Catch it on Trip **19**

Zugarramurdi

Walk through the caves where witches once held covens and pagan rituals in the 11th century. See it on Trip **18**

Barcelona A wanderer's delight

Elche Marvellous palm groves –
Europe's largest, originally
planted by the Phoenicians

Unsung Wonders of Murcia & Alicante

14

This rollicking ramble takes you from old-fashioned villages to picturesque shorelines, with a vibrant mix of culture, history and outdoor adventure crammed into one easy-going journey.

TRIP HIGHLIGHTS

40 km

Parque Natural de Sierra Espuña
Walking trails amid dramatic highlands

FINISH
● Villena

338 km

Elche
Strolling through enchanting groves of date palms

9

● Murcia
START

2

● Lo Pagán

3

● Cabo de Palos

Cartagena

4

Lorca
Seeing the world in blue and white

72 km

Águilas
Exploring picturesque coves

108 km

2–4 DAYS
402 KM / 241 MILES

GREAT FOR...

BEST TIME TO GO
March to June
or September to
November to escape
the heat and crowds.

ESSENTIAL PHOTO
Limestone cliffs in
Parque Natural de
Sierra Espuña.

BEST FOR OUTDOORS
Strolling the palm
groves in Elche.

185

14 Unsung Wonders of Murcia & Alicante

This winding route through Murcia and Alicante Provinces takes you to some of the unsung wonders of southeast Spain. You'll find great hiking amid rocky forests, striking coastal scenery and a trove of historical treasures (Roman ruins, Gothic cathedrals and Modernista architecture). This 402km journey offers plenty of surprises, from strolling among ancient groves of date palms to swimming in untouched coves in the Mediterranean.

---

① Murcia

Bypassed by most tourists and treated as a country cousin by many Spaniards, this laid-back provincial capital nevertheless more than merits a visit.

Murcia's most striking site is the **Real Casino de Murcia** (www.casinodemurcia.com; Calle de la Trapería 18; adult/child €5/3; ⊗10.30am-7pm), which first opened as a gentlemen's club in 1847. Painstakingly restored to its original glory, the building is a fabulous combination of historical design and opulence. A few blocks south, the **Catedral de Santa María** (Plaza del Cardinal Belluga; ⊗7am-1pm & 6-8pm, to 9pm Sat & Sun Jul & Aug, 7am-1pm & 5-8pm Tue-Sat, 10am-1pm Sun Sep-Jun) was built in 1394 on the site of a mosque. It has a stunning facade facing on to Plaza Belluga.

For a break from the heat, stroll through the lovely **Jardín Floridablanca** with its banyan trees, jacarandas, cypress and palms. A larger park and botanical garden, **Murcia Parque** (Jardín Botánico) lies just west of the Puente del Malecón footbridge.

✗ p191

The Drive » It's a short and easy 37km drive west along the toll-free A7 from Murcia to Alhama de Murcia, gateway to the national park.

TRIP HIGHLIGHT

❷ Parque Natural de Sierra Espuña

The Sierra Espuña is an island of pine forest and limestone formations rising high above an ocean of heat and dust down below. The natural park that protects this fragile and beautiful environment has more than 250 sq km of unspoilt highlands covered with trails and is popular with walkers and climbers.

Access to the park is best via Alhama de Murcia. The informative Ricardo Codorniu Visitors Centre is located in the heart of the park. A few walking trails leave from here, and it can provide good maps for picturesque hikes.

📄 p191

 LINK YOUR TRIP

20 Mediterranean Meander

For a longer drive, join up with this trip at Cartagena, and take in the splendour of coastal Spain.

19 Barcelona to Valencia

From Villena, take the A7 90km north to Valencia, to hook up with this memorable route between two great cities.

The Drive » It's a straight shot (30 minutes or so) along the A7 from Alhama de Murcia to Lorca, 36km to the southwest.

TRIP HIGHLIGHT

③ Lorca

The market town of Lorca has long been known for its historic centre crowned by a 13th-century castle and for hosting one of Spain's most flamboyant Holy Week celebrations.

Among the highlights of Lorca is **La Fortaleza del Sol** (www.lorcatallerdel-tiempo.com; adult/child €5/4; ⏰10.30am-dusk; 🚗), the castle that looms high over Lorca. In the old town, take a stroll through the **Plaza de España**. It's surrounded by a group of baroque buildings, including the **Pósito**, a 16th-century former granary, and the golden limestone **Colegiata de San Patricio**.

Peculiar to Lorca are various small museums exhibiting the magnificent Semana Santa costumes. The big two are the **Museo de Bordados del Paso Azul** (www.pasoa-zul.com; Calle Nogalte 7; adult/child €2.50/2; ⏰10am-1.30pm & 5-7.30pm Mon-Fri, 10am-1.30pm Sat), which competes in splendour with the **Museo de Bordados del Paso Blanco** (Mubbla; www.mubbla.org; Calle Santo Domingo 8; adult/child €2.50/2; ⏰10.30am-2pm & 5-7.30pm Tue-Sat, 10.30am-2pm Sun).

The Drive » The journey takes you from the southern slopes of the Siera del Cano down to to the coast. It's a speedy 37km ride along the RM11 from Lorca to Águilas.

④ Águilas

This easy-going waterfront town is beautiful, and still shelters a small fishing fleet. Town beaches are divided from each other by a low headland topped by an 18th-century fortress. The real interest, though,

SER-Y-STAR / GETTY IMAGES ©

🗨 LOCAL KNOWLEDGE: ADDING COLOUR TO SEMANA SANTA

In Lorca locals tend to see things in blue and white – the colours of the two major brotherhoods that have competed every year since 1855 to see who can stage the most lavish Semana Santa display.

Lorca's Easter parades move to a different rhythm, distinct from the slow, sombre processions elsewhere in Murcia. While still deeply reverential, they're full of colour and vitality, mixing Old Testament tales with the Passion story.

If you hail from Lorca, you're passionately *Blanco* (White) or *Azul* (Blue). Each brotherhood has a statue of the Virgin (one draped in a blue mantle, the other in white, naturally), a banner and a spectacular museum. The result of this intense and mostly genial year-round rivalry is just about the most dramatic Semana Santa you'll see anywhere in Spain.

Cartagena Magnificent Spanish fortifications

are the Cuatro Calas a few kilometres south of town. These four coves are largely unmolested by tourist development (though they get very busy in summer) and have shimmering waters which merge into desert rock. Take RM33 to get there.

🛏 p191

The Drive ≫ Take the Carretera de Lorca (the RM11) 2.5km northward, then head east some 70km along the toll-road AP7. Take exit 815 toward Cartagena Oeste and continue onto RM332.

⑤ Cartagena

Inhabited for over 2000 years, Cartagena wears its history with pride. From ancient Roman ruins to Modernista architecture, the city has a dazzling array of eye candy, made all the more photogenic against its magnificent mountain-fringed harbor.

For a sweeping panoramic view of it all, stride up to **Castillo de la Concepción** (adult/child €3.75/2.75; ⊙10am-5.30pm or 7pm Tue-Sun, plus Mon Jul–mid-Sep), or hop on the lift. Within the castle's gardens, decorated by strut-

ting peacocks, a small museum offers a history of Cartagena through the centuries via audio screens and a 10-minute film. For more about Cartagena, see p252.

🛏 p191

The Drive ≫ From Paseo Alfonxo XIII, take the A30 toward Murcia. After 3km, take exit 190 onto CT32. Continue for 5km then take Autovía de La Manga/RM12 20km east. It's a 30-minute drive total.

⑥ Cabo de Palos

The Mar Menor is a 170-sq-km saltwater lagoon. Its waters are a

189

good 5°C warmer than the open sea and excellent for water sports. Cabo de Palos, at the southern base of a narrow 22km peninsula, is delightful with a picturesque small harbour filled with pleasure boats. The waters around the tiny offshore Islas Hormigas (Ant Islands) are great for scuba diving and the harbour is lined with dive shops.

The Drive » Start off this 50km journey by retracing your route (heading west) along RM12. After 20km, take exit 1 onto AP7. After 25km take exit 774 toward San Pedro del Pinatar. Go straight through the roundabout as it leads you down to Lo Pagán.

- - - - - - - - - - - - - -

❼ Lo Pagán

At the northern end of the lagoon, Lo Pagán is a mellow, low-rise resort with great water views, a long promenade, a pleasant beach, and plenty of bars and restaurants. Get locals to show you where to walk out on jetties for natural mud treatments.

The Drive » It's a speedy trip (five minutes) to travel the 2.5km up to the salt pans. Take Carretera Quintín north and turn right on Av de las Salinas.

- - - - - - - - - - - - - -

❽ Salinas de San Pedro

Just east of Lo Pagán lie the Salinas de San Pedro (salt pans), where you can follow a well-signposted *senda verde* (footpath).

This relatively easy walk of just over 4km passes by several lagoons favoured by flocks of pink flamingos trawling for small fry.

The Drive » Skip the high-speed AP7 and take the more scenic coastal route (60km total). Head back to San Pedro del Pinatar and take the N332 north. You'll pass sea-fronting but over-developed beach towns such as Torrevieja on the way. A few kilometres after the Dunas de Guadamar (a fine beach for swimming), exit onto CV853 and follow signs north to Elche.

- - - - - - - - - - - - - -

TRIP HIGHLIGHT

❾ Elche

Thanks to Moorish irrigation, Elche is an important fruit producer and also a Unesco World Heritage site twice over: for the Misteri d'Elx, its annual mystery play, and for its marvellous, extensive palm groves, Europe's largest, originally planted by the Phoenicians.

Around 200,000 palm trees, each with a lifespan of some 250 years, make the heart of this busy industrial town a veritable oasis. A signed 2.5km walking trail leads from the **Museu del Palmerar** (Porta de la Morera 12; adult/child €1/free; ☺10am-2pm & 3-6pm Tue-Sat, 10am-2pm Sun) through the groves.

The city's most beautiful private garden is the **Huerto del Cura** (www.huertodelcura.com; Calle Porta de la Morera 49; adult/child €5/2.50, audioguide €2; ☺10am-sunset). Don't miss

the water features and the cactus gardens. The **Museo Arqueológico y de Historia de Elche** (MAHE; Calle Diagonal del Palau 7; adult/child €3/free, Sun free; ☺10am-6pm Mon-Sat, to 3pm Sun) gives a superb introduction to the town's long and eventful history.

✖ p191

The Drive » Take Calle Fulgencio west and turn right onto CV8510. Merge onto AP7 toward Alicante. After 3.5km take A31 north toward Alicante. Take exit 185 toward Villena. The 55km drive takes about 40 minutes.

- - - - - - - - - - - - - -

❿ Villena

Villena, between Alicante and Albacete, is the most attractive of the towns along the corridor of the Val de Vinalopó.

Plaza de Santiago is at the heart of its old quarter. Within the imposing 16th-century town hall is Villena's **Museo Arqueológico** (www.museovillena.com; Plaza de Santiago 1; adult/child €2/1; ☺10am-2pm Tue-Fri, 11am-2pm Sat & Sun). There are some magnificent late Bronze Age pieces, with bowls, bracelets and brooches made from solid gold.

Perched high above the town, the 12th-century **Castillo de Atalaya** (adult/child €3/1.50; ☺ guided tours 10am-noon, 3.30pm-4.30pm Tue-Fri, 11am-1pm, 3.30-4.30pm Sat, 11am-1pm Sun) is splendidly lit at night.

🛏 p191

Eating & Sleeping

Murcia ❶

✖ Los Zagales
Spanish €

(www.barloszagalesmurcia.com; Calle Polo Medina 4; dishes €3-12; ☺9.30am-4pm & 7pm-midnight) Lying within confessional distance of the cathedral, Los Zagales dishes up superb, inexpensive tapas, *raciones* (large tapas), *platos combinados* (mixed platters), homemade desserts (and homemade chips). It's locally popular so you may have to wait for a table. It's worth it.

Parque Natural de Sierra Espuña ❷

🛏 Bajo el Cejo
Boutique Hotel €€

(☎968 66 80 32; www.bajoelcejo.com; s/d €80/90; 🅿 ❄ 🛜 🏊) This delicious countryside hideaway is located inside a converted watermill and is absolutely dripping in style and glamour. The 13 rooms are superb but it's the swimming pool and the setting, overlooking the lemon groves and a deep valley, that are the real stars of the show. There's an excellent in-house restaurant.

Águilas ❹

🛏 Hotel Mayarì
Hotel €€

(☎964 41 97 48; www.hotel-mayari.com; Calle Río de Janeiro 14, Calabardina; s/d incl breakfast €65/98; 🅿 ❄ 🛜) In the seaside settlement of Calabardina, 7km from Águilas, this villa offers exceptional hospitality among dry hillscapes. Rooms are all themed differently, with cool, fresh decor. Some have sea views, and there are brilliant home-cooked dinners available, as well as helpful hill-walking advice.

Cartagena ❺

🛏 Pensión Oriente
Pensión €

(☎968 50 24 69; Calle Jara 27; s/d with shared bathroom €25/35; 🛜) Behind a Modernista facade in a central street, this offers simple, comfortable rooms in a noble building that preserves original features such as colourful floor tiles and ceiling mouldings. It's by far Cartagena's most characterful option; helpful management make it a solid all-round choice. All but the spacious room with private bathroom (€40) have well-modernised shared bathrooms. Don't confuse it with a nearby bar, also numbered 27.

Elche ❾

✖ El Granaino
Spanish €€

(☎966 66 40 80; www.mesongranaino.com; Carrer Josep María Buck 40; mains €14-22; ☺9.30am-4pm & 8pm-midnight Mon-Sat; 🛜) Across the river from the centre, it's worth the 10-minute walk to get to this place, where the bar is lined with people scarfing down a quick, quality lunch. Top seafood, delicious stews and a fine range of tapas showcase a classic, quintessentially Spanish cuisine. Fuller meals can be enjoyed outside or in the adjacent dining room. Excellent service and quality.

Villena ❿

🛏 Hotel Salvadora
Hotel €€

(☎965 80 09 50; www.hotelsalvadora.com; cnr Calles Luis García & Jacinto Benavente; s/d/tw €43/60/66; 🅿 ❄ 🛜) This is the town's sole hotel, featuring simple, clean, well-priced rooms, a popular bar with a great range of tapas, and a gourmet restaurant that does a mean *triguico picao* (€6.50), the local speciality – a thick gruel of wheat, beans, pork and turnip.

Tossa de Mar Take a boat out to glide over the bay's crystal-clear waters

Classic Trip

Artistic Inspiration on the Costa Brava

15

This seaside stunner takes you to some of Spain's prettiest beaches, with unspoilt coves, flower-trimmed villages and sweeping panoramas lurking around nearly every bend in the road.

TRIP HIGHLIGHTS

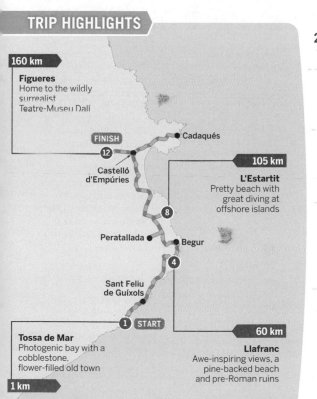

160 km
Figueres
Home to the wildly surrealist
Teatre-Museu Dalí

FINISH
12
Cadaqués
Castelló
d'Empúries

105 km
L'Estartit
Pretty beach with great diving at offshore islands

8
Peratallada
Begur

4
Sant Feliu
de Guíxols

1 **START**

Tossa de Mar
Photogenic bay with a cobblestone, flower-filled old town

60 km
Llafranc
Awe-inspiring views, a pine-backed beach and pre-Roman ruins

1 km

2–4 DAYS
160 KM / 99 MILES

GREAT FOR...

BEST TIME TO GO
May or September for beach weather with fewer crowds.

📷 ESSENTIAL PHOTO
The weird and wonderful Teatre-Museu Dalí in Figueres.

✔ BEST FOR FAMILIES
Playing in the sand on pretty Llafranc beach.

Classic Trip

15 Artistic Inspiration on the Costa Brava

Just north of Barcelona, the Costa Brava has long captivated visitors with its beautiful bays, dramatic headlands and quaint, cobblestone villages just inland from the surf. Great views aside, there's much to do in this picturesque corner of Catalonia: you can visit ancient Roman ruins, clamber around medieval castles, go eye-to-eye with marbled rays off the Iles Mendes, and wander wide-eyed through fantastical Salvador Dalí creations.

TRIP HIGHLIGHT

❶ Tossa de Mar

Curving around a boat-speckled bay and guarded by a headland crowned with impressive defensive medieval walls and towers, Tossa de Mar is a picturesque village of crooked, narrow streets onto which tourism has tacked a larger, modern extension.

The deep-ochre, fairy-tale walls and towers on the pine-dotted headland, **Mont Guardí**, at the end of the main beach, were built between the 12th and 14th centuries. The area they girdle is known as the Vila Vella – or Old Town – full of steep little cobbled streets and picturesque whitewashed houses, garlanded with flowers.

🍴 p201

The Drive » A snaking road hugs the spectacular ups and downs of the Costa Brava for the 23km from Tossa de Mar to Sant Feliu de Guíxols with – allegedly – a curve for each day of the year. From Tossa de Mar take Carretera Blanes a Sant Feliu and stick to the shoreline.

❷ Sant Feliu de Guíxols

Sant Feliu has an attractive waterside promenade and a handful of curious leftovers from its long past, the most important being the so-called **Porta Ferrada** (Iron Gate): a wall and entrance, which is all that remains of a 10th-century monastery. The gate lends its name to an annual music festival held here every July since 1962.

Just north along the coast is **S'agaró**, with each of its Modernista houses designed by Gaudí disciple Rafael Masó. Leave your wheels behind and take the Camí de Ronda to **Platja Sa Conca** – one of the most attractive beaches in the area.

The Drive » Take the Carretera de Palamós (located just a few blocks north of the marina) east. After 1.5km take the Carretera Castelo d'Aro and follow this north onto C31. After 17km on C31, take exit 331. Continue through the historic village of Mont-Ras, skirting the southern edge of bigger Palafrugell. Then take Av del

Mar into Calella de Palafrugell. It takes about a half-hour to make the 28km drive.

- - - - - - - -

❸ Calella de Palafrugell

Halfway up the coast from Barcelona to the French border begins one of the most beautiful stretches of the Costa Brava. Start off in Calella, the southernmost of Palafrugell's crown jewels. The settlement is strung Aegean-style around a bay of rocky points and small, pretty beaches, with a few fishing boats still hauled up on the sand. The seafront is lined with year-round restaurants serving the fruits of the sea. Atop **Cap Roig**, 2.5km from the centre, the **Jardí Botànic**

LINK YOUR TRIP

16 Central Catalan's Wineries & Monasteries

After ending in Figueres, travel 44km south to Girona to the start of this scenic drive around Catalonia's interior.

18 The Pyrenees

From Figueres it's just 25km east to Besalú, where you can drive the Pyrenees trip in reverse, traveling across the mountains to San Sebastián.

Classic Trip

(adult/child €6/3; ⏰10am-8pm Apr-Sep, to 6pm Oct-Mar, closed Mon-Fri Jan & Feb) is a beautiful garden of 500 Mediterranean species, set around an early-20th-century castle-palace.

✖ p201

The Drive » The next stop is barely 2km northeast of Calella. If you need to stretch your legs, you can also walk to Llafranc along coastal footpaths. Driving, take Av Joan Pericot i García east. Go straight through the roundabout at Plaça Doctor Trueta, then veer to the right on Carrer de Lluís Marquès Carbó.

TRIP HIGHLIGHT

④ Llafranc

Llafranc has a smaller bay but a longer, handsome stretch of sand, cupped on either side by pine-dotted craggy coastline. Above the east side of town, the **Cap de Sant Sebastià** is a magical spot that offers fabulous views in both directions and out to sea. There's a lighthouse here, as well as a defensive tower and chapel now incorporated into a hotel. There's also the ruins of a pre-Roman Iberian settlement with multilingual explanatory panels. It's a 40-minute walk up: follow the steps from the harbour and the road up to the right.

The Drive » From Llafranc, head north along GIV6541 towards Palafrugell. Take GIP6531 and follow the signs down to Tamariu; you'll pass through piney forest on the way. Again, if you'd prefer to walk, it's a magnificent 4km walk along the coast.

⑤ Tamariu

Tamariu is a fabulous, small, crescent-shaped cove redolent with the scent of pine. Its beach has some of the most translucent waters on Spain's Mediterranean coast. The gently sloping sands and shallow waters

---

➔ DETOUR:
CASTELL DE PÚBOL

Start: ❸ Calella de Palafrugell

Northwest of Palafrugell, the **Castell de Púbol** (www.salvador-dali.org; Plaça de Gala Dalí; adult/concession €8/6; ⏰10am-6pm Tue-Sun mid-Mar–early Jan) forms the southernmost point of the 'Salvador Dalí triangle', other elements of which include the Teatre-Museu Dalí in Figueres and his home in Portlligat.

Having promised to make his wife Gala, his muse and the love of his life, 'queen of the castle', in 1969 Dalí finally found the ideal residence to turn into Gala's refuge, since at the age of 76 she no longer desired Dalí's hectic lifestyle – a semi-dilapidated Gothic and Renaissance stronghold which included a 14th-century church in the quiet village of Púbol.

The sombre castle, its stone walls covered with creepers, is almost the antithesis to the flamboyance of the Teatre-Museu Dalí or Dalí's seaside home: Gala had it decorated exactly as she wished and received only whom she wished. Legend has it that Dalí himself had to apply for written permission to visit her here.

The interior reflects her tastes, though Dalí touches creep in here and there. In the dining room is a replica of *Cua d'oreneta i violoncels* (Swallow's Tail and Cellos) – his last painting, completed here in 1983 during the two years of mourning following Gala's death.

The Castell is 2km from the village of La Pera, just south of the C66 and 22km northwest of Palafrugell.

are a great place for small children to play.

The Drive >> It's 6km or so to Begur. Take Carrer Aigublava north on a scenic uphill journey, then turn right on GIP6531 and follow this to Begur.

⑥ Begur

Attractive little Begur is dotted with tempting restaurants and cafes and topped by a 10th-century *castell* (castle), towering above the hill village. The sublime coastline around Begur, with its pocket-sized coves hemmed in by pine trees and subtropical flowers and lapped by azure water, is magical.

📖 p201

The Drive >> Head west out of Begur along GI653. In Regencós, take C31, then a few kilometres north of Pals, turn left onto GI651. Drive time to Peratallada is about 20 minutes.

⑦ Peratallada

One of Catalonia's most gorgeous villages, Peratallada is blessed with beautifully preserved narrow lanes, heavy stone arches, a 12th-century Romanesque church and an 11th-century castle-mansion (now a luxury hotel and restaurant). It's a characterful spot, particularly at night.

The Drive >> Get back on GI651 and retrace the drive to C31. But this time turn north onto C31 and continue for 6km. You'll cross the attractive

THE COSTA BRAVA WAY

The 255km-long stretch of cliffs, coves, rocky promontories and pine groves that make up the signposted Costa Brava Way, stretching from Blanes to Colliure in France, unsurprisingly offers some of the best walks in Catalonia, ranging from gentle rambles to high-octane scrambles (or one long, demanding hike if you want to do the whole thing).

For the most part, the trail follows the established GR92, but also includes a number of coastal deviations. A choice route is Cadaqués to the Cap de Creus Lighthouse (2½ hours), a relatively easy walk from the centre of Cadaqués that passes Portlligat before continuing along windswept, scrub-covered, rocky ground past several isolated beaches and reaching the lighthouse.

medieval town of Torroella de Montgrí, then continue on Carretera de L'Estartit. At the roundabout continue straight, along GI641. The 18km drive takes about 25 minutes.

TRIP HIGHLIGHT

⑧ L'Estartit

L'Estartit has a long, wide beach of fine sand but it's the diving that stands out. The protected **Illes Medes**, a spectacular group of rocky islets barely 1km offshore, are home to some of the most abundant marine life on Spain's Mediterranean coast. Eateries serving mostly fresh seafood as well as standard Spanish fare are plentiful along the seafront.

The Drive >> Retrace the drive back through Torroella de Montgrí, then continue onto C31 northwest (don't cross back over the bridge). After about 3km turn right onto GI632, which leads straight into town

(depositing you at the town hall if you so wish). The 19km drive takes about 22 minutes.

⑨ L'Escala

Travel back millennia to the ancient Greco-Roman site of **Empúries** (www.mac.cat; adult/child €5/free; ⏰10am-8pm Jun-Sep, to 5pm Oct-May, closed Mon Nov-Feb), set behind a near-virgin beach facing the Mediterranean. Its modern descendant, L'Escala, 11km north of Torroella de Montgrí, is a sunny and pleasant medium-sized resort on the often-windswept southern shore of the Golf de Roses.

The Empúries is a picturesque two-part site that was an important Greek, and later Roman, trading port, though the site was originally used by Phoenicians. There are fine pieces – including

WHY THIS IS A CLASSIC TRIP
REGIS ST LOUIS, AUTHOR

As a lifelong admirer of the strange and captivating works of Salvador Dalí, I've always felt a deep affinity for the wild coastal scenery around Cadaqués where Dalí spent his formative (and later) years. Yet the whole Costa Brava easily passes for artistic inspiration, with its serene bays, rugged headlands and golden beaches. This coastal drive is pure magic.

Top: A flying leap over Tossa de Mar waters
Left: A misty sunrise over the Cost Brava
Right: Figueres streetscape

198

mosaics – in the museum here, which gives good background information. Empúries is 2km north-west of the L'Escala town centre along the coast.

✕ p201

The Drive ›› Start this 25-minute drive by taking Carretera Sant Martí d'Empúries to Sant Pere Pescador. After crossing a small river, look for GIV6216 leading north. From here, it's a straight shot 8km or so to Castelló d'Empúries.

- - - - - - - - - - -

⑩ Castelló d'Empúries

This well-preserved ancient town was once the capital of Empúries, a medieval Catalan county that maintained a large degree of independence up to the 14th century. Today it makes a superb base for birdwatching at the nearby **Parc Natural dels Aiguamolls de l'Empordà** (www.parcsde-catalunya.net; parking €2; ⊙El Cortalet information centre 9.30am-2pm & 3.30-7pm), as well as at a number of wind-blown but peaceful beaches. The park lies 4km to the northeast along Carretera Castelló d'Empúries. Away from the feathered treats of the natural park, architec-tural beauty can be found in the town centre's **Església de Santa Maria** on Plaça de Jacint Ver-daguer. It's a voluminous 13th- and 14th-century Gothic church with a

Classic Trip

sturdy Romanesque bell tower.

📖 p201

The Drive » It's 23km to Cadaqués – a 30-minute trip, though you could take much longer, with stops to admire the view on this stunning drive. From Castelló d'Empúries, take Carrer Santa Clara to C260. Pass through La Garriga and get on GI614, which will take you the rest of the way. As you ascend, the scenery gets stunning.

⓫ Cadaqués

A whitewashed village around a rocky bay, Cadaqués' narrow, hilly streets are perfect for wandering. The iconic town and its surrounding area have a special magic – a fusion of wind, sea, light and rock – that isn't dissipated even by the throngs of summer visitors.

A portion of that magic owes itself to Salvador Dalí, who spent family holidays here during his youth, and lived much of his later life at nearby Portlligat. At the **Museu de Cadaqués** (Carrer de Narcís Monturiol 15; adult/child €4/3; ⊘10.30am-1.30pm & 4-7pm Mon-Sat Apr-Jun & Oct, 10am-8pm daily Jul-Sep), Dalí often features strongly in the temporary exhibitions on display, as do his contemporaries, also connected to Cadaqués, such as Picasso.

✖ p201

The Drive » Backtrack to Castelló d'Empúries. Stay on C260 as it skirts the southern edge of town, and follow it all the way to Figueres. Total drive time is about 45 minutes for the 35km drive.

TRIP HIGHLIGHT

⓬ Figueres

Twelve kilometres inland, Figueres is a busy town with a French feel and an unmissable attraction: Salvador Dalí. The artist was born in Figueres in 1904 and although his career took him to Madrid, Barcelona, Paris and the USA, he remained true to his roots. In the 1960s and '70s he created here the extraordinary **Teatre-Museu Dalí** (www. salvador-dali.org; Plaça de Gala i Salvador Dalí 5; admission incl Dalí Joies & Museu de l'Empordà adult/child under 9yr €12/free; ⊘9am-8pm Jul-Sep, 9.30am-6pm Tue-Sun Mar-Jun & Oct, 10.30am-6pm Tue-Sun Nov-Feb) – a monument to surrealism and a legacy that outshines any other Spanish artist, both in terms of popularity and sheer flamboyance.

This red castlelike building, topped with giant eggs and studded with plaster-covered croissants, is an entirely appropriate final resting place for the master of surrealism. 'Theatre-museum' is an apt label for this trip through the incredibly fertile imagination of one of the great performers of the 20th century. The inside is full of surprises, tricks and illusions, and contains a substantial portion of Dalí's life's work.

Eating & Sleeping

Tossa de Mar ❶

🍴 La Cuina de Can Simon   Catalan €€€

(📞972 34 12 69; www.lacuinadecansimon.com; Carrer del Portal 24; mains €22-35, taster menus €68-98; ⏰1-3.30pm & 8-10.30pm Wed-Sat, 1-3.30pm Sun) Tossa's culinary star nestles by the old walls in a former fisherman's stone house and distinguishes itself by serving the most imaginative creations in town. Taking the *mar i muntanya* (sea and mountains) theme to its logical extreme, it presents stunning combinations of fresh seafood and succulent meat. Even if you're not splurging on the gob-stoppingly good taster menu, stop by for the delicious desserts. Opens daily in summer.

Calella de Palafrugell ❸

🍴 La Croissanteria de Calella   Ice Cream €

(www.lacroissanteriadecalella.com; Carrer Chopitea 3-5; ice cream €2.50; ⏰10am-5pm; 🛜♿) The main reason for stopping by here is the truly exceptional **Sandro Desii ice cream** (www.sandrodesii.com). The pistachio, *canela con café* (cinnamon with coffee), or even the humble vanilla will leave you in raptures.

Begur ❻

🛏 Hotel Classic   Hotel €€

(📞656 906995; www.hotelclassicbegur.com; Carrer de Pi i Ralló 3; d €120-145; ❄🛜) In the heart of the old town, this warmly welcoming year-round spot has beautiful rooms themed on various notable dates in Begur's history. All are spacious and comfortable, with top modern bathrooms. There are endearing details throughout – we liked the fairly priced in-room wine selection. There's a good restaurant – breakfast is praiseworthy – and a downstairs spa zone. A bargain in the low season.

L'Escala ❾

🍴 La Gruta   Fusion €€

(📞972 77 62 11; www.restaurantlagruta.com; Carrer del Pintor Enric Serra 15; 3-course menu €27; ⏰12.30-3.30pm Mon, 12.30-3.30pm & 8-10.30pm Tue-Sat) This innovative place with slick service is definitely one of the most interesting places to eat in town: as well as catch-of-the-day, it sources top-grade beef fillets and does some inventive fusion and pasta dishes; the desserts are delightful.

Castelló d'Empúries ❿

🛏 Hotel Casa Clara   Hotel €€

(📞972 25 02 15; www.hotelcasaclara.com; Carrer de la Fruita 27; s/d €65/90; 🅿❄🛜) The spacious, tiled rooms at this adorable little hotel all feature plenty of natural light, an individual colour scheme and very comfortable beds – some with wrought-iron bedsteads. The attached restaurant features a changing weekly menu of imaginative, beautifully executed dishes, such as courgette-and-hazelnut bake and sea bream with shitake mushrooms (three courses €15).

Cadaqués ⓫

🍴 Es Baluard   Seafood €€

(📞972 25 81 83; www.esbaluard-cadaques.net; Riba Nemesi Llorens; mains €16-22; ⏰1-3.30pm & 8.30-11pm) The family that runs this old-school restaurant that's set into the old sea wall clearly worships at the throne of Poseidon, because the tastiest of his subjects wind up on your plate. Fish dishes drawing on local market produce, such as the *anchoas de Cadaqués* (anchovies from Cadaqués) and *gambitas de Roses* (prawns from Roses), dominate the menu and you shouldn't shy away from the *crema catalana* (crème-brûlée-like custard desserts), either.

Montserrat *The Monestir de Montserrat – one of Catalonia's most important shrines*

Central Catalan's Wineries & Monasteries

16

On this dramatic drive into Catalonia's hinterland, you'll see age-old mountain monasteries, wander through medieval quarters and take in picturesque, sun-dappled vineyards.

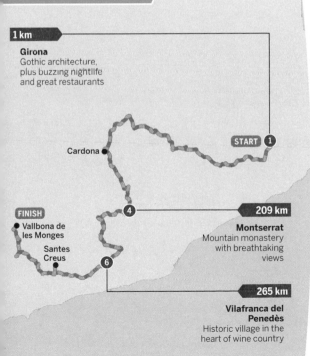

1 km

Girona
Gothic architecture, plus buzzing nightlife and great restaurants

Cardona

START 1

FINISH
Vallbona de les Monges

Santes Creus

4

6

209 km

Montserrat
Mountain monastery with breathtaking views

265 km

Vilafranca del Penedès
Historic village in the heart of wine country

2–4 DAYS
380 KM / 236 MILES

GREAT FOR...

BEST TIME TO GO
Any time, but March to November for warmer days.

ESSENTIAL PHOTO
Montserrat against its dramatic mountainous backdrop.

BEST FOR HISTORY
Strolling the medieval Jewish quarter in Girona.

16

Central Catalan's Wineries & Monasteries

You'll experience many of Catalonia's lesser-known charms on this memorable inland drive. The medieval town of Girona is crammed with historic sites, while a wander along Vic's cobblestone streets reveals architectural treasures. You'll find a photogenic castle in Cardona and atmospheric monasteries along the Cistercian route. The trip ends at the quaint village of Vilafranca del Penedès, in the heart of magnificent wine country.

TRIP HIGHLIGHT

❶ Girona

Northern Catalonia's largest city, Girona is a tight huddle of ancient arcaded houses, grand churches and climbing cobbled streets. It's home to Catalonia's most extensive and best-preserved medieval Jewish quarter, all enclosed by defensive walls, with the lazy Río Onyar meandering along the edge of town. The excellent **Museu d'Història dels Jueus de Girona** (www.girona.cat/call; Carrer

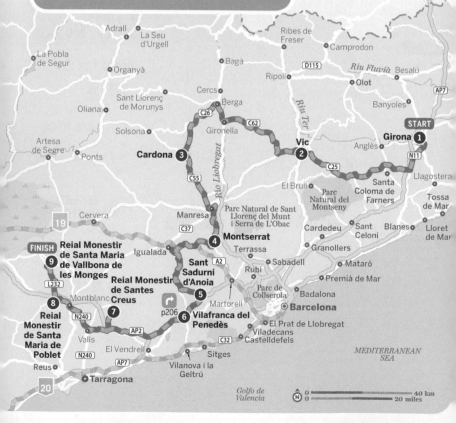

de la Força 8; adult/child €4/ free; ⊙10am-8pm Mon-Sat, to 2pm Sun) shows genuine pride in Girona's Jewish heritage. Nearby, the stunning 800-year-old **Catedral** (www.catedraldegirona.org; Plaça de la Catedral; adult/student incl Basílica de Sant Feliu €7/5, Sun free; ⊙10am-7.30pm Apr-Oct, 10am-6.30pm Nov-Mar) provides a window into medieval Christendom.

✕ 🛏 p209

The Drive » From Girona, it's about one hour (70km) to Vic. From Girona, take Carrer del Carme east out of town. At the roundabout (2.7km further), turn onto GIV6703. Merge onto the N11. Take exit 702 onto the C25. Follow this 50km through lush mountainous scenery, before taking exit 187 onto N141, which takes you into Vic.

LINK YOUR TRIP

19 Barcelona to Valencia

After finishing this trip, head 56km west to Lleida for historic villages and outdoor adventures.

20 Mediterranean Meander

From the last monastery, drive 64km south on C14 to Tarragona for a highlight-filled drive along Spain's south coast.

2 Vic

Vic is one of Catalonia's gems. Its enchanting old quarter is crammed with Roman remnants, medieval leftovers, a grand Gothic cloister, an excellent art museum, some hectic markets and a glut of superb restaurants.

Plaça Major, the largest of Catalonia's central squares, is lined with medieval, baroque and Modernista mansions. It's still the site of the huge twice-weekly market (Tuesday and Saturday mornings). Around it swirl the narrow serpentine streets of medieval Vic, lined by mansions, churches, chapels, a Roman temple and a welcoming atmosphere.

The **Museu Episcopal** (www.museuepiscopalvic. com; Plaça del Bisbe Oliba 3; adult/child over 10yr €7/3.50; ⊙10am-1pm & 3-6pm Tue-Fri, 10am-7pm Sat, 10am-2pm Sun) holds a marvellous collection of Romanesque and Gothic art, including works by key figures such as Lluís Borrassà and Jaume Huguet.

✕ 🛏 p209

The Drive » From Vic, take a northern, slightly longer, route to Cardona for stunning mountain scenery. Take C25 west from town. After about 6km, take exit 170 onto C651, then take C62, which merges onto C154. Around La Plana, take E9 north, then take the C26 southwest. Stay on this until the B420, and follow signs to Cardona.

3 Cardona

Long before arrival, you spy in the distance the outline of the impregnable 18th-century fortress high above Cardona, which itself lies next to the Muntanya de Sal (Salt Mountain). The castle – follow the signs uphill to the Parador Ducs de Cardona, a lovely place to stay overnight – was built over an older predecessor. The single-most remarkable element of the buildings is the lofty and spare Romanesque **Església de Sant Vicenç**.

The Drive » It's a one-hour drive south to Montserrat. The scenic route along C55 passes over forested slopes and around the old village of Manresa (a pilgrimage site). About 20km south of there, take BP1121 and follow the signs to Centre Urbà/Montserrat.

TRIP HIGHLIGHT

4 Montserrat

Montserrat is a spectacular 1236m-high mountain of strangely rounded rock pillars, shaped by wind, rain and frost. With the historic Benedictine Monestir de Montserrat, this is one of Catalonia's most important shrines. Its caves and many mountain paths offer spectacular rambles, reachable by funiculars.

You can explore the mountain above the monastery on a web of paths leading to some of the peaks and to 13 empty hermitages. The **Funicular de Sant Joan** (one way/return €2.40/3.70; ☺ every 20min 10am-6.50pm, closed mid-late Jan) will carry you up the first 250m from the monastery. To see the chapel on the spot where the holy image of the Virgin was discovered, you can drop down the **Funicular de Santa Cova** (one way/return €2.20/3.50; ☺ every 20min, closed mid-Jan–Feb), or else it's an easy walk down, followed by a stroll along a precipitous mountain path with fabulous views.

🛏 p209

The Drive » The drive from the monastery offers magnificent views from clifftop heights, particularly along BP1103, which merges onto B110. A few kilometres further, take the ramp onto A2 and stay on it for 9km. Take exit 559 toward Vilafranca del Penedès, then take C15 south, and BP2151 into Sant Sadurní d'Anoia.

↱ DETOUR: TORRES

Start: ❻ Vilafranca del Penedès

Just 2km northwest of Vilafranca del Penedès on the BP2121, **Torres** (☎ 93 817 74 87; www.torres.es; vineyard tour adult/child €6.70/4.70; ☺ 9am-5pm Mon-Sat, to 1pm Sun & holidays) is the area's premier winery, with a family winemaking tradition dating from the 17th century. It revolutionised Spanish winemaking in the 1960s by introducing temperature-controlled, stainless-steel technology and French grape varieties. Torres produces an array of reds and whites of all qualities, using many grape varieties.

❺ Sant Sadurní d'Anoia

Some of Spain's finest wines come from the Penedès plains southwest of Barcelona. Sant Sadurní d'Anoia, located about a half-hour west of Barcelona, is the capital of *cava*, a sparkling, champagne-style wine popular worldwide, and drunk in quantity in Spain over Christmas.

The headquarters of **Codorníu** (☎ 93 891 33 42; www.codorniu.es; Avinguda de Jaume Codorníu; adult/child €9/6; ☺ 9am-5pm Mon-Fri, to 1pm Sat & Sun) are in a beautiful Modernista cellar at the entry to Sant Sadurní d'Anoia. Next to the Sant Sadurní train station, **Freixenet** (☎ 93 891 70 96; www.freixenet.com; Carrer de Joan Sala 2; adult/child 9-17yr €7/4.20; ☺ 1½hr tours 10am-1pm & 3-4.30pm Mon-Thu, 10am-1pm Fri-Sun) is the biggest *cava*-producing

MICHAL KRAKOWIAK / GETTY IMAGES ©

company in Penedès. Visits include a tour of its 1920s cellar, a spin on the tourist train around the property and samples of its *cava*.

The Drive » It's a speedy 15km drive to the next stop. To avoid the AP7 toll road, take the Rambla de la Generalitat southwest and follow it onto C243a. Stay on this all the way to Vilafranca del Penedès.

TRIP HIGHLIGHT

❻ Vilafranca del Penedès

Vilafranca del Penedès is an attractive historical town and the heart of the Penedès Denominación

Girona Colourful buildings line the banks of the Río Onyar

de Origen (DO; Denomination of Origin) region, which produces noteworthy light white wines and some very tasty reds.

Vilafranca has appealing narrow streets lined with medieval mansions. The mainly Gothic **Basilica de Santa Maria** (Plaça de Jaume I) stands at the heart of the old town. The basilica faces the **Museu de les Cultures del Vi de Catalunya** (www. vinseum.cat; Plaça de Jaume I 5; adult/child €7/4; 10am-2pm & 4-7pm Tue-Sat, 10am-2pm Sun) across Plaça de Jaume I. Housed in a fine Gothic building, a combination of museums here

covers local archaeology, art, geology and bird life, and has an excellent section on wine.

✕ p209

The Drive » Leave town via Avinguda de Tarragona. Follow this onto the AP7. Take the E90/AP2 exit toward Lleida. After 17km on this road, take exit 11 and get onto TP2002, which leads up to Santes Creus. All told it's about a 45-minute drive.

- - - - - - - - -

❼ Reial Monestir de Santes Creus

Cistercian monks settled here in 1168 and from then on this **monastery** (Plaça de Jaume el Just, Santes

Creus; adult/senior & student €4.50/free; 10am-6.30pm Jun-Sep, 10am-5pm Oct-May) developed as a major centre of learning and a launch pad for the repopulation of the surrounding territory. Behind the Romanesque and Gothic facade lies a glorious 14th-century sandstone cloister, austere chapter house, cavernous dormitory and royal apartments where the count-kings often stayed when they popped by during Holy Week.

The Drive » Take TP2002 south and turn onto C51 about 7km south of Santa Creus. Stay on C51 for a few kilometres before taking N240. Fine views await as you cross the Tossal Gros mountain, part of Catalonia's precoastal range. Exit onto TV7001 toward L'Espluga de Francolí. You'll pass through this small town along T700 en route to the monastery.

⑧ Reial Monestir de Santa Maria de Poblet

A Unesco World Heritage site, the fortified **Reial Monestir de Santa Maria de Poblet** (www.poblet. cat; Vimbodí-Poblet; adult/ student €7/4; ☺10am-12.45pm & 3-6pm Mon-Sat, 10am-12.30pm & 3-5.30pm Sun) was founded in 1151. It became Catalonia's most powerful monastery and the burial place of many of its rulers. Poblet was sacked in 1835 by marauding peasants as

payback for the monks' abuse of their feudal powers, which included imprisonment and torture. High points include the mostly Gothic main cloister and the alabaster sculptural treasures of the Panteón de los Reyes (Kings' Pantheon). The raised alabaster sarcophagi contain eight Catalan kings, such greats as Jaume I (the conqueror of Mallorca and Valencia) and Pere III.

The Drive » The last stop is another 30km north. You'll take the T700 back through L'Espluga de Francolí, then hop onto the T232. You'll take the L220 as you reach Els Omells de na Gaia. Follow this north, about another 1km, then look for the signed right turn leading to Vallbona de les Monges.

⑨ Reial Monestir de Santa Maria de Vallbona de les Monges

The **Reial Monestir de Santa Maria de Vallbona de les Monges** (📞973 33 02 66; Carrer Major, Vallbona de les Monges; adult/child €4/1; ☺10.30am-1.30pm & 4.30-6.45pm Tue-Sat, noon-1.30pm & 4.30-6.45pm Sun Mar-Oct, closes 5.30pm rest of year) was founded in the 12th century and is where a dozen *monges* (nuns) still live and pray. The monastery has undergone years of restoration, which has finally cleared up most of the remaining scars of civil war damage.

SIQUI SANCHEZ / GETTY IMAGES ©

Torres The area's premier winery

Eating &Sleeping

Girona ❶

✗ Txalaka
Basque €€

(☏972 22 59 75; www.restaurant-txalaka.com; Carrer Bonastruc de Porta 4; mains €12-20, pintxos €2.50-4; ⏱1-4pm & 7.30-11.30pm;) For sensational Basque cooking and *pintxos* (tapas) washed down with *txakoli* (the fizzy white wine from the Basque coast) poured from a great height, don't miss this popular local spot. Just load up your plate with bar-top snacks, make sure to order some hot ones from the kitchen too and pay according to the number of *montadito* (bread) sticks/dishes.

✗ Nu
Catalan €€

(☏972 22 52 30; www.nurestaurant.cat; Carrer d'Abeuradors 4; mains €16-18, degustation menu €50; ⏱1.15-3.45pm & 8.15-10.45pm Tue-Sat, 1.15-3.45pm Mon;) Sleek and confident, this handsome contemporary old-town spot has innovative, top-notch plates prepared in view by the friendly team. There are always some very interesting flavour combinations, and they work. Great value for this quality.

🛏 Bells Oficis
B&B €€

(☏972 22 81 70; www.bellsoficis.com; Carrer dels Germans Busquets 2; r incl breakfast €55-85;) A lovingly restored, 19th-century flat just by the Rambla in the heart of Girona makes a stylish and ultrawelcoming place to stop. Period details combine with modern styling most effectively: the whole package is immaculate. There are just five beautiful, light rooms: some share bathrooms – those with en suite have no bathroom door – while the largest (€105) has ample room for four people.

Vic ❷

✗ El Jardinet
Catalan €€

(☏938 86 28 77; www.eljardinetdevic.com; Carrer de Corretgers 8; menus €19-27, mains €18-23;

⏱1-3.30pm daily, 8.30-11pm Fri & Sat;) An exceedingly good choice, whose fairly spare interior is enlivened by really warm-hearted service and beautifully prepared traditional dishes, presented with panache. It's the sort of place you'll head back to tomorrow, too.

🛏 Estació del Nord
Hotel €

(☏935 16 62 92; www.estaciodelnord.com; Plaça de l'Estació 4; s/d €48/61;) The 14 refurbished rooms of this smart little hotel, well located on the 1st floor of the 1910 train station, are decked out in soothing creams and whites and overseen by a friendly family. It's well soundproofed from the trains and busy road.

Montserrat ❹

🛏 Hotel Abat Cisneros
Hotel €€

(☏938 77 77 01; www.montserratvisita.com; s/d €63/108;) The only hotel in the monastery complex has a super location next to the basilica, and tasteful, spacious rooms, some of which look over Plaça de Santa Maria. There are also inexpensive basic apartments and family packages available. Its **restaurant** (mains €17-20) serves imaginative Catalonian dishes.

Vilafranca del Penedès ❻

✗ Cal Ton
Catalan €€€

(☏938 903 741; www.restaurantcalton.com; Carrer Casal 8; mains €16-24; ⏱1-4pm & 8.30-10.30pm Tue-Sat, 1-4pm Sun) Hidden away down a narrow side street, Cal Ton has a crisp, modern decor and offers inventive Mediterranean cuisine with a touch of oriental influence – all washed down with local wines.

Llavorsí Embark on a white-water rafting adventure down the Riu Noguera Pallaresa

Peaks & Valleys in Northwest Catalonia

17

Get off the beaten path in this jaw-dropping drive through Catalonia. Memorable hikes, white-water rafting and picturesque mountain villages are all part of the allure.

85 km

Espot
Gateway to hiking amid stunning glacially carved valleys

Vielha — Salardú
Arties

66 km

Llavorsí
Scenic setting for white-water rafting

Parc Nacional d'Aigüestortes i Estany de Sant Maurici ③

Erill la Vall

⑧ FINISH

②

La Seu d'Urgell

START

Taüll
Mountain village and setting for two historic Romanesque churches

196 km

2–4 DAYS
196 KM / 122 MILES

GREAT FOR...

BEST TIME TO GO
March to October for hiking and rafting.

ESSENTIAL PHOTO
Mountain-fringed Lake Sant Maurici in the unpronounceable Parc Nacional d'Aigüestortes i Estany de Sant Maurici.

BEST FOR OUTDOORS
White-water rafting from Llavorsí to Rialp.

211

Peaks & Valleys in Northwest Catalonia

17

This zig-zagging journey through northwest Catalonia takes you back through the centuries, as you roll through stone villages and past Romanesque churches sitting pretty against a backdrop of pine-covered peaks. This is also a major draw for adventure lovers, with white-water rafting through chiselled valleys along the Riu Noguera Pallaresa and scenic walks over wildflower-strewn valleys, past streams, waterfalls and lakes in an awe-inspiring national park.

❶ La Seu d'Urgell

The lively valley town of La Seu d'Urgell (la se-u dur-zhey) is Spain's gateway to Andorra, 10km to the north. La Seu has an attractive medieval centre, watched over by an admirable Romanesque cathedral. When the Franks evicted the Muslims from this part of the Pyrenees in the early 9th century, they made La Seu a bishopric and capital of the counts of Urgell; it remains an important market and cathedral town.

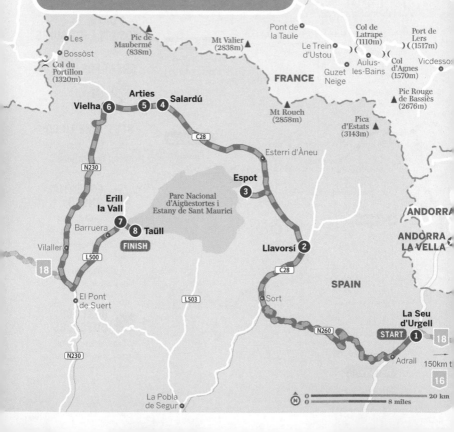

Much of town is dominated by the enormous 19th-century seminary above the cathedral. On the southern side of Plaça dels Oms, the 12th-century **Catedral de Santa Maria** (adult/child €3/free; ☉10am-1.30pm year-round, plus 4-6pm mid-Mar–May & mid-Sep–Oct, 4-7.30pm Jun–mid-Sep) is one of Catalonia's outstanding Romanesque buildings, with a gorgeous cloister full of characterful carved capitals.

🛏 p217

The Drive » Get ready for magnificent mountain scenery on this winding 66km drive. From La Seu take the N260 about 51km northwest to Sort. From there, switch to the C13 for

LINK YOUR TRIP

18 **The Pyrenees**
At trip's end in Taüll, drive 58km back to Vielha to intersect with the magnificent drive across the Pyrenees.

16 **Central Catalan's Wineries & Monasteries**
From Taüll it's about 185km south to Monestir de Santa Maria de Vallbona, where you can make this drive in reverse, visiting monasteries, historic villages and wineries.

the final 15km. It will take you straight into Llavorsí.

TRIP HIGHLIGHT

➋ Llavorsí

The Riu Noguera Pallaresa, running south through a dramatic valley about 50km west of La Seu d'Urgell, is Spain's best-known white-water river. The village of Llavorsí (along with Rialp and Sort) is a good place to organise a white-water trip.

The Riu Noguera Pallaresa's grade-IV drops attract a constant stream of white-water fans between mid-March and mid-October. It's usually at its best in May and June.

The best stretch is the 12km from Llavorsí to Rialp, on which the standard raft outing costs around €41 per person for two hours. In town, there are several rafting operators, including **Rafting Llavorsí** (🖉973 62 21 58; www.raftingllavorsi.com; Camí de Riberies). Longer rides to Sort and beyond will cost more, and Sort is the jumping-off point for the river's tougher grade-IV rapids. You can also arrange other summer activities including kayaking, canyoning, horse riding, rock climbing and canoeing.

🛏 p217

The Drive » More lush scenery including rolling pine-dappled hillsides spread beneath you on this easy 20km

drive. From Llavorsí go 12km north along C13. At the tiny stone village of Berrós Jussà, switch to LV5004 for the final 7.5km.

TRIP HIGHLIGHT

➌ Espot

Espot is a principal gateway to the stunning **Parc Nacional d'Aigüestortes i Estany de Sant Maurici**, Catalonia's only national park. Although small – just 20km east to west, and 9km from north to south – the rugged terrain positively sparkles with more than 400 lakes and countless streams and waterfalls. This combined with a backdrop of pine and fir forests, and open bush and grassland, bedecked with wildflowers in spring, creates a wilderness of rare splendour.

Created by glacial action over two million years, the park is essentially two east–west valleys at 1600m to 2000m altitudes lined by jagged 2600m to 2900m peaks of granite and slate. The park is crisscrossed by paths. Numerous good walks of three to five hours return will take you up into spectacular side valleys from Estany de Sant Maurici or Aigüestortes.

Espot is 4km east of the park's eastern boundary and 8km away from the huge Estany de Sant Maurici lake.

🍴 p217

The Drive » The scenery just keeps getting better as you travel through the mountains. From Espot, travel east along the LV5004 to C28, and take this north 37km, passing through to sleepy villages along the way.

- - - - - - - - - -

❹ Salardú

Salardú's nucleus of old houses and narrow streets has largely resisted the temptation to sprawl. In the apse of the village's 12th- and 13th-century Sant Andreu church, you can admire the 13th-century Crist de Salardú crucifixion carving. Refugi Rosta houses an entertaining private **PyrenMuseu** (www.pyrenmuseu.com; Plaça Major 3; adult €5; ⏰10.30am-1.30pm & 4.30-7pm) covering the history of tourism in Val d'Aran, with a glass of wine included in the price to enhance your enjoyment.

🛏 p217

The Drive » It's a quick hop (3.5km) west along C28, with green peaks looming above you.

- - - - - - - - - -

❺ Arties

This village on the southern side of the highway sits astride the confluence of the Garona and Valarties rivers. Among its cheerful stone houses is the Romanesque Església de Santa Maria, with its three-storey belfry and triple apse. Arties has cachet, and is packed with upmarket restaurants and bars.

EDUCATION IMAGES / GETTY IMAGES ©

🗨 LOCAL KNOWLEDGE: HIKING IN THE VALL DE BOÍ

There are some spectacular hikes in the Parc Nacional d'Aigüestortes i Estany de Sant Maurici, but one of my favourites is the **Marmot Trail** – a round trip of 3½ hours – which begins next to the impressive Cavallers dam and passes a series of waterfalls. The hike ends at **Estany Negré** (Black Lake), close to this trail's first *refugi* (mountain shelter), **Ventosa i Calvell**; you spend a half-day among the beautiful mountains with breathtaking views of the Vall de Boí. There is also a nice three-hour trail from Taüll that takes in the entire valley and passes through the four villages along the way – Boí, Durro, Barruerra, Boí again, and back to Taüll.

You can also plan longer multiday hikes and spend the night in a *refugi*. Keep in mind that these can get quite crowded in July and August, when there are 70 people sleeping in the same room. Things are much more comfortable in May, June, September and October.

People sometimes ask when is the best season to visit the park. It's difficult to choose a favourite time of year! In spring the valley is at its greenest, and the rivers are running the fastest from the snowmelt; in autumn the colours are at their best, and both spring and autumn are great times for hiking as there are not too many visitors. *By Tony Capanna, restaurateur and owner of Alberg Taüll in the Vall de Boí.*

Erill la Vall Discover quaint Romanesque churches dotting the landscape

The Drive » It's a brief 10-minute drive to Vielha, 7km west along C28. Despite the brevity, you'll want to take it slow to admire the fine vistas.

- - - - - - - - - - -

❻ Vielha

It wasn't all that long ago that the verdant Val d'Aran, Catalonia's northernmost outpost, was one of the remotest parts of Spain and its only connection to the outside world was via a small pass leading into France. All this changed with the opening of a tunnel connecting the valley's capital, Vielha, with the rest of the country in the 1950s, which led to a surge of tourism development. The valley is spectacular, like a secret world of cloud-scraping mountain peaks and tumbling valley slopes dotted with hill villages, many with exquisite Romanesque churches. From Aran's pretty side valleys, walkers can go over the mountains in any direction, notably southward to the Parc Nacional d'Aigüestortes i Estany de Sant Maurici. Vielha is Aran's junction capital and a handy base for exploring the valley.

✗ p217

The Drive » Start this hour-long drive by heading 38km south along N230, which skirts the boundary between Aragon and Catalonia. About 17km after passing the scenic Baserca Reservoir, you'll turn onto the L500 and follow signs to La Vall de Boí.

- - - - - - - - - - -

❼ Erill la Vall

The sublime Vall de Boí is dotted with some of Catalonia's loveliest little Romanesque churches – unadorned stone structures sitting in the crisp alpine air, constructed between the 11th and 14th centuries – which together were declared a Unesco

World Heritage site in 2000. Start off in the **Centre d'Interpretació del Romànic** (☏973 69 67 15; www.centreromanic. com; Carrer del Batalló 5; admission €2; ☉9am-2pm & 5-7pm Easter–mid-Oct) in the small village of Erill la Vall. Here you'll find a small Romanesque art collection; it's also where you can organise guided tours of the churches.

The Drive ⟫ It's a short (5.5km) but scenic drive, past pine forests and the odd stone cottage, to Taüll. Take L500 1km north and turn onto the L501 heading south. After about 3.5km you'll see Sant Climent de Taüll on the left.

TRIP HIGHLIGHT

❽ Taüll

Continue the journey back in time at **Sant Climent de Taüll** (admission €5; ☉10am-2pm & 4-7pm, closed Mon Nov). Located at the entrance to Taüll, this church, with its slender six-storey bell tower, is a gem, not only for its elegant, simple lines but also for the art that once graced its interior. The central apse contains a copy of a famous 1123 mural that now resides in Barcelona's Museu Nacional d'Art de Catalunya. At the church's centre is a Pantocrator (Christ figure), whose rich Mozarabic-influenced colours, and expressive but superhuman features, have become a virtual emblem of Catalan Romanesque art.

In the old village centre of Taüll you can see the **Santa Maria de Taüll** (☉10am-7pm), with its striking five-storey tower. The central fresco is reproduced here (again, the original is preserved in Barcelona).

✕ p217

Taüll Sant Climent de Taüll

Eating & Sleeping

La Seu d'Urgell ❶

🛏 Casa Rural
La Vall del Cadí　　　Casa Rural €

(☏973 35 03 90; www.valldelcadi.com; Carretera de Tuixén; s/d €45/55; 🅿❄🛜) Barely a 1km walk south of the centre and across the Segre Riu, you are in another, protected, bucolic world in this stone country house on a working family-run farm (and it smells as such!). Cosy rooms, with terracotta floors, iron bedsteads and, in some cases, timber ceiling beams, have a nice winter detail – underfloor heating. Some rooms share bathrooms. The extensive breakfast (€3 or €7.50) features famous Cadí butter and delicious regional cured meats and cheeses.

Llavorsí ❷

🛏 Hostal Noguera　　　Hostal €

(☏973 62 20 12; www.hostalnoguera.info; Carretera Vall d'Aran; s/d €30/58; 🅿🛜) This stone building, on the southern edge of the village, has pleasant rooms overlooking the river, whose cascading noise will lull you to sleep. The downstairs restaurant specialises in regional cuisine and the fresh local fish is particularly good.

Espot ❸

✖ Restaurant Juquim　　　Catalan €€

(☏973 62 40 09; Plaça San Martí 1; mains €11-20; ⊙1-3.30pm & 8-11pm, closed Tue mid-Oct–May) This classic on the main square has a varied menu concentrating largely on hearty country fare, with generous winter warmers such as *olla pallaresa* (steaming hotpot) or *civet*

de senglar (wild boar stew). The adjacent **bar** (⊙open 8am-11pm Thu-Tue) does simpler fare and sandwiches.

Salardú ❹

🛏 Hotel Seixes　　　Hotel €€

(☏973 64 54 06; www.seixes.com; Bagergue; s/d incl breakfast €60/80; 🅿@🛜) This hikers' favourite in the village of Bagergue, 2km north of Salardú, has spacious and comfortable rooms, some of which have huge views over the valley and surrounding peaks. While you're tucking into a hearty buffet breakfast with more great vistas the staff will fill you in on all the local trekking routes.

Vielha ❻

✖ El Moli　　　Catalan €€

(☏973 64 17 18; Carrer Sarriulera 26; mains €12-22; ⊙1.30-4.30pm & 8-11.30pm Tue-Sun, 8-11.30pm Mon Dec-Apr & Jun-Oct) In an attractive dining area overlooking the river, this does a great line in steaks cooked over a wood grill, and also excels in creative salads and seasonal set menus. Service is reliably excellent.

Taüll ❽

✖ Sedona　　　International €

(☏973 69 62 52; Les Feixes 2; menu €15; ⊙meals 1.30-4pm & 8.30-11pm; 🛜) A varied menu of Catalan and international dishes (which may change under prospective new ownership), longer opening hours than anywhere else in the village and use of locally grown organic produce puts this friendly spot ahead of the competition. The bar's a good place to haunt, après-ski or après-hiking, too.

Zugarramurdi Forest stairway
leading to the Cuevas de
Las Brujas caves

The Pyrenees

18

Great food, spectacular scenery and frozen-in-time villages perched high in the mountains are among the big draws of this exhilarating drive across the Pyrenees.

TRIP HIGHLIGHTS

88 km

Puerto de Izpegui
Dramatic mountain pass on the French border

835 km

Ribes de Freser
Departure point for a fantastic rack-and-pinion train up to Núria

San Sebastián

START 3

Zugarramurdi

6 9

Jaca

12 Besalú

FINISH Barcelona

Sos del Rey Católico
Beautiful medieval village and major historic site

298 km

Torla
Gateway to spectacular walks in nearby national park

484 km

5–7 DAYS
1040 KM /
646 MILES

GREAT FOR...

BEST TIME TO GO
May to October for warm weather and outdoor activities.

ESSENTIAL PHOTO
A mouthwatering plate of *pintxos* (tapas) at a San Sebastián eatery.

BEST FOR CULTURE
Peering through microscopes at incredible artwork in Besalú.

18 The Pyrenees

The rolling, mist-covered hills and snow-plastered mountains that make up the Pyrenees are a playground for outdoor enthusiasts. Aside from hiking, skiing and simply admiring the view, the Pyrenees are home to old-fashioned villages that are rich in history. Of course foodies will delight in the abundant Basque, Aragonese and Catalan produce – not to mention two world-class dining cities (San Sebastián and Barcelona) book-ending the drive.

❶ **San Sebastián**

San Sebastián (Basque: Donostia) is a stunning city that loves to indulge. With Michelin stars apparently falling from the heavens onto its restaurants and a *pintxo* (tapas) culture almost unmatched anywhere else in Spain, San Sebastián frequently tops lists of the world's best places to eat. But just as good as the food is the summer fun in the sun. For its setting, form and attitude, Playa de la Concha is the equal of

any city beach in Europe. Then there's Playa de Gros (also known as Playa de la Zurriola), with its surfers and sultry beach-goers.

About 700m from Playa de la Concha, the Isla de Santa Clara is accessible by boats that run every half-hour from the fishing port. At low tide the island gains its own tiny beach and you can climb its forested paths to a small lighthouse.

For great views over the city, head up to **Monte Igueldo**, just west of town. The best way to get there is via the old-world **funicular railway** (www.monteigueldo.es; Plaza del Funicular; return adult/child €3.15/2.35; ⊘ roughly 10am-9pm Jun-Aug, shorter hours rest of year) to the Parque de Atracciones.

✕ ⤶ p227

The Drive ›› Start this 50km journey by taking the GI20 east and continuing onto the AP8. Just before hitting France, take N121 south, then switch to the peaceful country road NA4410 near Bera. As it crosses into France, the road becomes D406. Cut back south and into Spain, before reaching Sare.

---

❷ Zugarramurdi

Just before the French border is the pretty village of Zugarramurdi, home to the decidedly less pretty Cuevas de Las Brujas. These caves were once, according to the Inquisition, the scene of evil debauchery. Having established this, the perverse masters of the Inquisition promptly tortured and burned scores of alleged witches. Playing on the flying-broomstick theme is the **Museo de las Brujas** (www.turismozugarramurdi. com; adult/child €4.50/2; ⊘11am-7.30pm mid-Jul–mid-Sep), a fascinating dip into the mysterious cauldron of witchcraft in the Pyrenees.

The Drive ›› Drive east of town then take the N121B south.

🅢 LINK YOUR TRIP

7 Northern Spain Pilgrimage

At Roncesvalles, join pilgrims on the Camino de Santiago for a drive through stunning scenery and history-rich villages.

17 Peaks & Valleys in Northwest Catalonia

You can add on to this trip by connecting in Vielha with a scenic drive around northwest Catalonia.

After 18km or so, take NA2600 east. The 56km drive takes about 75 minutes, and passes through stunning mountain scenery with great views lurking around every turn.

❸ Puerto de Izpegui

The road here meanders dreamily amid picturesque farms, villages and hills before climbing sharply to the French border pass of Puerto de Izpegui, where the world becomes a spectacular collision of crags, peaks and valleys. At the pass, you can stop for a short, sharp hike up to the top of Mt Izpegui. You'll find a good number of *casas rurales* (farmstead accommodation) throughout the area.

The Drive » To avoid lengthy backtracking, continue into France toward the pretty town of Saint-Jean Pied de Port. From there take the D933, which turns into the N135 as it crosses south back into Spain. The 48km drive takes a little over an hour.

❹ Roncesvalles

Roncesvalles (known in Basque as Orreaga) has a fascinating history. Legend has it that it was here that the armies of Charlemagne were defeated and Roland, commander of Charlemagne's rearguard, was killed by Basque tribes in 778. In addition to violence and bloodshed, though, Roncesvalles is also a pivotal stop on

the road to Santiago de Compostela, where Camino pilgrims visit the famous monastery before continuing the eastward journey. Don't miss the Real Colegiata de Santa María, an atmospheric monastery with an iconic statue of the Virgin Mary. For more on Roncesvalles, see p109.

🛏 p227

The Drive » It's a scenic 70km drive to the next stop. Head south out of Roncesvalles to get on the NA140 east. Follow this to the NA137 south, which takes you into Roncal.

❺ Roncal

Navarra's most spectacular mountain area is around Roncal, a charming village of cobblestone alleyways that twist and turn between dark stone houses and meander down to a river full of trout. Roncal is renowned for its Queso de Roncal, a sheep's-milk cheese that's sold in the village.

The Drive » Start this 70km drive by taking NA137 south, then turn onto A21 west, which offers fine views of the Yesa reservoir (the shoreline-hugging NA2420 is even more scenic). At Liédena, take NA127 south, which turns into A127.

❻ Sos del Rey Católico

If Sos del Rey Católico were in Tuscany, it would

be a world-famous hill town. It's one of Aragón's most beautiful villages and the old medieval town is a glorious maze of twisting, cobbled lanes that wriggle between dark stone houses with deeply overhung eaves.

Fernando II of Aragón is said to have been born in the **Casa Palacio de Seda** (Plaza de la Hispanidad; adult/child €2.60/1.50, incl tour of village €4/2; ☉10am-2pm & 4-8pm; 👫) in 1452. It's an impressive noble mansion, which now contains an interpretative centre, with fine exhibits on the history of Sos and the life of the

Roncesvalles A pivotal stop on the road to Santiago de Compostela

king. The Gothic **Iglesia de San Esteban** (admission €1; ⊙10am-1pm & 3.30-5.30pm), with a weathered Romanesque portal, has a deliciously gloomy crypt decorated with medieval frescos. Above the central Plaza de la Villa, the Renaissance-era **town hall** is one of the grandest public buildings in Sos. Duck inside to admire the magnificent central courtyard.

🛏 p227

The Drive » Retrace the drive back to N240 and continue east. At Puente de la Reina de Jaca, take the A176 north. Plan on 75 minutes or so to make the 90km drive.

❼ Echo

The verdant Echo valley is mountain magic at its best, beginning with gentle climbs through the valley and the accumulating charms of old stone villages punctuating slopes of dense mixed woods of beech, pine, rowan, elm and hazel. As the valleys narrow to the north, 2000m-plus peaks rise triumphantly at their heads.

Lovely Echo, the largest village in the valley, is an attractive warren of solid stone houses with steep roofs and flower-decked balconies. At the heart of Echo is the endearing **Museo Etnológico Casa Mazo** (www.hecho.es; Calle Aire; admission €1.50; ⊙10.30am-1.30pm & 5-8pm; 🚻), with a captivating display of photographs of villagers from the 1920s and 1930s.

The Drive » Take A176 back south, cross the bridge at Puente de la Reina de Jaca, and continue east along the N240. It takes about an hour to make the 54km drive, which takes in rolling green hillsides and wide open fields.

❽ Jaca

A gateway to the western valleys of the

LOCAL KNOWLEDGE: WHAT'S COOKING IN ARAGÓN?

The kitchens and tables of Aragón are dominated by meat. The region's cold harsh winds create the ideal conditions for curing *jamón* (ham), a top tapa here; some of the best can be found in no-frills bars. Likewise, another meaty favourite, *jarretes* (hock of ham or shanks), is available in simple village restaurants such as Torla's **La Brecha** (Calle Francia; mains €8-10; ⏰1.30-4pm & 8-10.30pm), while heartier *ternasco* (suckling lamb) is generally served as a steak or ribs with potatoes – try it at **Bodegas del Sobrarbe** (www.bodegasdelsobrarbe.com; Plaza Mayor 2; mains €15-22; ⏰noon-2pm & 7-11pm Apr-Dec) in Aínsa.

Other popular dishes include *conejo a la montañesa* (mountain-style rabbit) served with gusto (and sometimes with snails) at Echo's **Restaurante Gaby** (📞974 37 50 07; www.casablasquico.es; Plaza de la Fuente 1; mains €9-19; 🛜), while (phew!) vegetarians can seek out tasty *pochas viudas* (white-bean stew with peppers, tomatoes and onion), a popular starter at restaurants including **La Cocina del Principal** (📞948 88 83 48; www.lacocinadelprincipal.com; Calle Mayor 17; mains €14-17.50; ⏰1.30-3.30pm & 8.30-10.30pm Tue-Sat, noon-4pm Sun) in Sos del Rey Católico.

Aragonese Pyrenees, Jaca has a compact and attractive old town dotted with remnants of its past as the capital of the nascent 11th-century Aragón kingdom. These include an unusual fortress and a sturdy cathedral, while the town also has some great places to eat.

Jaca's 11th-century **Catedral de San Pedro** (Plaza de la Catedral; ⏰11.30am-1.30pm & 4.15-8pm) is a formidable building, its imposing facade typical of the sturdy stone architecture of northern Aragón.

There are some lovely old buildings in the streets of the *casco historico* (old town) that fan out south of the cathedral, including the 15th-century **Torre del**

Reloj (clock tower; Plaza del Marqués de la Cadena) and the charming little **Ermita de Sarsa** (Avenida Oroel).

The star-shaped, 16th-century **citadel** (www.ciudadeladejaca.es; Calle del Primer Viernes de Mayo; adult/concession/child under 8yr €10/5/free; ⏰11am-2pm & 5-8pm Tue-Sun; 🚗) is Spain's only extant pentagonal fortress. You can visit on a 40-minute multilingual guided tour.

🍴 p227

The Drive » Take the A7 east. At Sabiñánigo, take the N260 north. Keep following the N260 as it loops east around Biescas and continues toward Torla, with winding roads offering spectacular panoramas. The 72km drive takes about 1¾ hours.

TRIP HIGHLIGHT

❾ Torla

This is where the Spanish Pyrenees really take your breath away. At the heart of it all is a dragon's back of limestone peaks skirting the French border.

Torla is gateway to spectacular walking in the **Parque Nacional de Ordesa y Monte Perdido** (www.senderos.turismodearagon.com), located 3km northeast. This lovely alpine-style village has stone houses with slate roofs, and a delightful setting above Río Ara under a backdrop of the national park's mountains. In your ramblings around town, make for the 13th-century **Iglesia de San Salvador**; there are fine views from the small park on the church's northern side.

The Drive » It's a 45km drive to Aínsa along the N260. You'll pass beside sunlit streams with forested conical peaks on either side of you on this straightforward trip.

⑩ Aínsa

The beautiful hilltop village of medieval Aínsa, which stands above the modern town of the same name, is one of Aragón's gems, a stunning village hewn from uneven stone. From its perch, you'll have commanding panoramic views of the mountains.

The **castle** (ecomuseum admission €4; ☺ ecomuseum 11am-2pm Wed-Fri, 10am-2pm & 4-7pm Sat & Sun Easter-Oct) and fortifications off the western end of the Plaza de San Salvador contains a fascinating ecomuseum on Pyrenean fauna and an exhibition space covering the region's geology.

🛏 p227

The Drive » Take N260 east. Around Castarné, switch to the N230 north. Allow about 1¾ hours to cover the 105km drive.

⑪ Vielha

Vielha is Aran's junction capital, a sprawl of holiday housing and apartments straggled along the valley and creeping up the sides, crowded with skiers in winter. The tiny centre retains some charm in the form of the **Església de Sant Miquèu**,

which houses some notable medieval artwork, namely the 12th-century *Crist de Mijaran*. The **Muséu dera Val D'Aran** (Carrer Major 11; ☺ 5-8pm Tue, 10am-1pm & 5-8pm Wed-Sat, 10am-1pm Sun) covers Aranese history through a series of black-and-white photos and period furnishings. See p215 for more about Vielha.

The Drive » This 214km drive takes about four hours, owing to curving mountain roads. From Vielha take C28 down to Sort, continue east on N260 to Ribes de Freser.

TRIP HIGHLIGHT

⑫ Ribes de Freser

The famous pilgrimage site and ski resort of Núria lies nestled high in the mountains and is only accessible by foot or train. You can get here from Ribes de Freser in the valley. The narrow-gauge rack-and-pinion *cremallera* (railway) rises over 1000m on its 12km journey from Ribes de Freser, via the scenic village of Queralbs, up the green, rocky valley of the thundering Riu Núria. It's worth the trip for the scenery alone.

There are great marked trails throughout the valley, with one of the best leading down through the gorge from Núria to Queralbs (two hours).

The Drive » Take N260 south to Ripoll and east onto to Olot. The 60km drive takes about 90 minutes. You'll pass over forested hillsides, with fine views throughout the drive.

DETOUR: ANDORRA

Start: ⑪ Vielha

If you're on the lookout for great hiking or skiing, or just want to say you've been in a different country, then don't miss the curious nation of Andorra, just 10km north of La Seu d'Urgell – and a little over halfway along the drive from Vielha to Ribes de Freser. At only 468 sq km, it's one of Europe's smallest countries and, though it has a democratic parliament, the nominal heads of state are two co-princes: the bishop of Urgell in Spain and the President of France. Catalan is the official tongue, though Spanish, French and, due to a large immigrant workforce, Portuguese, are widely spoken. Make sure you fuel up in Andorra, as it's significantly cheaper. There's rarely any passport control, though you may be stopped by customs on the way back into Spain, so don't go over the duty-free limit.

⑬ Olot

Olot is the spread-out capital of La Garrotxa region, with wide, tree-lined walkways (with the exception of its serpentine medieval heart) and plenty of options for rambling in the surrounding countryside, shaped by the ancient activity of the well-dormant volcanoes of the nearby Parc Natural de la Zona Volcànica de la Garrotxa.

Found inside the pleasant Parc Nou, a botanical garden of Olot-area flora, the **Museu dels Volcans** (Parc Nou, Avinguda de Santa Coloma de Farners; adult/child €3/1.50; ⊗10am-2pm & 3-6pm Tue-Sat, 10am-2pm Sun) can teach you everything you ever wanted to know about volcanoes. The interactive section includes an earthquake simulator; other displays cover local flora, fauna and ecosystems.

✖ p227

The Drive ≫ It's a quick drive to the next stop, which is 22km east along the fast-moving A26. Take exit 67 to reach Besalú.

⑭ Besalú

The tall, crooked 11th-century Pont Fortificat (Fortified Bridge) over Riu Fluvià in medieval Besalú, with its two tower gates and heavy portcullis, is an arresting sight, leading you into the coiled maze of cobbled narrow streets that make up the core of this delightfully well-preserved town.

Besalú's thriving Jewish community fled the town in 1436 after relentless Christian persecution, leaving behind a **miqvé** (Baixada de Mikwe; guided tours €2.20) – a 12th-century ritual bath – the only survivor of its kind in Spain.

The curious **Micromundi** (www.museuminiaturesbesalu.com; Plaça Prat de Sant Pere 15; adult/child €4.90/2.50; ⊗10am-7pm daily May-Oct, to 3pm Tue-Fri, to 7pm Sat & Sun Nov-Apr; 🚻) is dedicated to painstakingly painted miniatures and microminiatures that you can peer at through microscopes. Don't miss an incredibly detailed Pinocchio and Gepetto's workshop (inside a pistachio nut).

The Drive ≫ The journey to Barcelona ends with a 132km drive (1¾ hours) from the mountains down to the sea. Take C66 south. At Montegut, take the AP7 and follow signs to Barcelona.

⑮ Barcelona

After rolling through remote mountain villages, the buzzing metropolis of Barcelona may come as a shock. But don't delay, dive in. One way into the city's heart is through its celebrated food scene. Start the culinary journey at **Mercat de la Boqueria** (☎93 318 25 84; www.boqueria.info; La Rambla 91; ⊗8am-8.30pm Mon-Sat, closed Sun; Ⓜ Liceu), the city's great produce market. Head to the back for a meal at one of the much-loved tapas bars. Afterwards, stop by the nearby **MACBA** (Museu d'Art Contemporani de Barcelona; ☎93 412 08 10; www.macba.cat; Plaça dels Àngels 1; adult/concession €10/8; ⊗11am-7.30pm Mon & Wed-Fri, 10am-9pm Sat, 10am-3pm Sun & holidays; Ⓜ Universitat) for a look at some of the city's best contemporary exhibitions. The building, designed by Richard Meier, is a work of art in itself. Barcelona is justly famous for its Modernista architecture. You can wander through a Gaudí-designed fairy tale in spacious **Park Güell** (☎93 409 18 31; www.parkguell.cat; Carrer d'Olot 7; admission to central area adult/child €7/4.50; ⊗8am-9.30pm daily; 🚌24 or 32, Ⓜ Lesseps or Vallcarca) located north of downtown. End the day with a meal in one of the atmospheric restaurants in the **Barri Gòtic**. For a walking tour of Barcelona, see p238.

Eating & Sleeping

San Sebastián ❶

✕ La Fábrica — Modern Basque €€

(☎943 98 05 81; www.restaurantelafabrica.es; Calle del Puerto 17; mains €15-20, menús from €25; ☺12.30-4pm & 7.30-11.30pm Mon-Fri, 1-4pm & 8-11pm Sat & Sun) The red-brick interior walls and white tablecloths lend an air of class to this restaurant, whose modern takes on Basque classics have been making waves with San Sebastián locals over the last couple of years. At just €25, the multidish tasting *menú* is about the best-value deal in the city. Advance reservations are essential.

⌸ Pensión Kursaal — Boutique Hotel €€

(☎943 29 26 66; www.pensionesconencanto. com; Calle de Peña y Goñi 2; d €85-91; ❈@☎) With a rattling 1930s-style lift and massive, wall-sized photos this excellent place, full of light and colour, is a real mix of the old and the new. The majestic rooms have a suitably refined edge, all of which help it feel more like a proper hotel than a *pensión* (small private hotel). It's virtually on Playa de Gros.

Roncesvalles ❹

⌸ Casa de Beneficiados — Hotel €€

(☎948 76 01 05; www.casadebeneficiados.com; Roncesvalles; apt €80; ☺mid-Mar–Dec; ☎) In a former life this was an 18th-century monks' residence. Today it's reborn as a far less pious hotel, which is comfortable and utterly modern.

Sos del Rey Católico ❻

⌸ Casa del Infanzón — Boutique Hotel €€

(☎605 940536; www.casadelinfanzon.com; Calle Coliseo 3; d/ste €59/68; ❈☎) In the heart of the Jewish quarter, this is a great deal with aesthetically furnished rooms sporting plush fabrics, a soothing colour scheme and spacious bathrooms. Several rooms have small terraces and the ample breakfast includes homemade breads, local *jamón* and eggs prepared to order. There is a cosy salon with a fireplace.

Jaca ❽

✕ La Tasca de Ana — Contemporary Tapas €

(Calle de Ramiro I 3; tapas from €3; ☺7-11.30pm Mon-Fri, 12.30-3.30pm & 7-11.30pm Sat & Sun; ☎) One of Aragón's best tapas bars, La Tasca de Ana has tempting options lined up along the bar, more choices cooked to order and a carefully chosen list of local wines. Check out its *tapas mas solicitados* (most popular orders) listed on the blackboard. Top contenders include the *tostada* (toast) topped with goat's cheese and blueberries.

Aínsa ❿

⌸ Hotel los Siete Reyes — Hotel €€

(☎974 50 06 81; www.lossietereyes.com; Plaza Mayor; d €70-120; ❈☎) Set in one of the most charming stone buildings overlooking Plaza Mayor, this temple of style has stunning bathrooms, polished floorboards, exposed stone walls and some lovely period detail wedded to a contemporary designer look. The rooms are all spacious and some have lovely mountain views, while others look out over the Plaza Mayor. Breakfast is served in the former wine cellar.

Olot ⓭

✕ La Quinta Justa — Cuina Volcànica €€

(☎972 27 12 09; www.laquintajusta.cat; Passeig de Barcelona 7; mains €11-20; ☺1-4pm & 8-11pm Mon-Sat, 1-4pm Sun; ☎) Central, stylish restaurant with excellent service serving plenty of volcanic delights. Anything with local mushrooms or beans in it is bound to be delicious, and the creations with *foie* (liver) are sensational. You might be better à la carte than off the various set menus. Very worthwhile.

Valencia *Stunning architecture, scenic parks and an embarrassing wealth of restaurants*

Barcelona to Valencia

19

On this memorable drive, you'll experience some of Eastern Spain's prettiest villages, explore lush natural scenery and enjoy the heady sights of two very vibrant cities.

TRIP HIGHLIGHTS

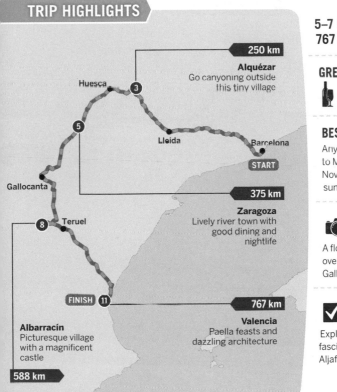

250 km

Alquézar
Go canyoning outside this tiny village

Huesca ③

Lleida

Barcelona

START

⑤

Gallocanta

375 km

Zaragoza
Lively river town with good dining and nightlife

⑧ Teruel

FINISH ⑪

Albarracín
Picturesque village with a magnificent castle

588 km

767 km

Valencia
Paella feasts and dazzling architecture

5–7 DAYS
767 KM / 477 MILES

GREAT FOR...

BEST TIME TO GO
Any time, but March to May and October to November to beat the summer crowds.

ESSENTIAL PHOTO
A flock of cranes flying over the Laguna de Gallocanta.

BEST FOR CULTURE
Exploring the fascinating Islamic-era Aljafería in Zaragoza.

229

19 | Barcelona to Valencia

Some of Spain's great unsung wonders are on display on this drive that travels between coast and mountain. You'll find architectural and culinary treasures in Valencia and Barcelona, Unesco World Heritage–listed gardens, Spain's largest lake (a birdwatcher's delight from autumn to spring) and adrenaline-fueled adventures along the canyons near Alquézar. There's also relics from the past, from Roman ruins and an Islamic-era palace to Gothic and Modernista masterpieces.

❶ Barcelona

Home to historical treasures, brilliantly inventive architecture, and a boundless dining and drinking scene, Barcelona is one of Europe's most enchanting cities. Start off with a visit to the **Barri Gòtic**, the old medieval quarter of Barcelona, which is packed with quaint squares, cobblestone lanes with old shops and looming churches. Delve into the past at the **Museu d'Història de Barcelona** (☎93 256 21 00; www.museuhistoria.bcn.cat; Plaça

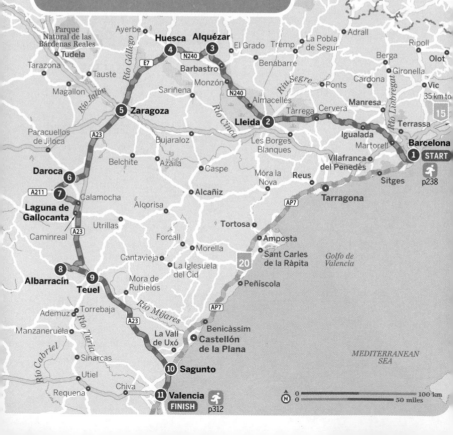

del Rei; adult/child €7/free, free 1st Sun of month & 3-8pm Sun; ⊙10am-7pm Tue-Sat, 10am-8pm Sun; M Jaume I). This fascinating museum takes you back through the centuries to the very foundations of Roman Barcino. Afterwards, stop in the palm-filled **Plaça Reial** (M Liceu), where you'll find eateries and bars with outdoor tables on the square. You can't leave Barcelona without touring at least one building designed by Antoni Gaudí. A good starting point is Casa Batlló; see p238 for a walking tour which takes in this strange and fantastical building.

✘ ⊨ p236

The Drive ⟫ In Barcelona take the waterfront Passeig de Colom southwest and get onto the D10. After 7km continue onto the A2. Stay on this for 165km

LINK YOUR TRIP

15 Artistic Inspiration on the Costa Brava

From Barcelona, go 90km up the coast for a drive past sunny beaches, rugged coves and Dalí theatrics.

20 Mediterranean Meander

Once you hit Valencia, keep going! Follow this sea-lover's drive all the way to Málaga.

then take exit 465 for Lleida. It's about two hours' drive total from Barcelona to Lleida.

- - - - - - - - - - - -

② Lleida

The mighty fortress-church on top of the hill in the town centre – Lleida's major historical landmark – is one of the most spectacular in Spain and is in itself reason enough to visit. Enclosed within a fortress complex, Lleida's 'old cathedral', **La Seu Vella** (www.turoseuvella.cat; adult/child €5/free; ⊙10am-1.30pm & 3-5.30pm Tue-Fri, 10am-5.30pm Sat, 10am-3pm Sun), towers above the city. The cathedral is a masterpiece with beautiful cloisters, the windows of which are laced with exceptional Gothic tracery. Lleida has several intriguing museums, including the **Museu d'Art Jaume Morera** (☎973 70 04 19; Carrer Major 31; ⊙5-8pm Tue-Fri, noon-2pm & 5-8pm Sat, 11am-2pm Sun). This impressive collection of Catalan art focuses particularly on work by Lleida-associated artists, such as the surrealist sculptures by Leandre Cristòfol.

✘ p236

The Drive ⟫ Take Av Alcalde Rovira Roure (just north of Plaça Cervantes) to the N240, which merges into the A22. Stay on this for 50km then take exit 51 onto the N240. From here you'll pass through the wine-making center of Somontano. Around Barbastro (the epicentre of this

winery region), follow signs to A1232 and follow this to Alquézar.

- - - - - - - - - - - -

TRIP HIGHLIGHT

③ Alquézar

Picturesque Alquézar is a handsome village that's famed for its canyoning (*descenso de barrancos*), which involves following canyons downstream by whatever means available – walking, abseiling, swimming, even diving. There are many local outfitters that lead tours, including **Vertientes** (☎974 31 83 54; www.vertientesaventura.com; Calle San Gregorio 5).

Alquézar is crowned by the large castle-monastery of the **Colegiata de Santa María** (admission €2.50; ⊙11am-1.30pm & 4.30-7.30pm Wed-Mon). Originally built as an *alcázar* (fortress) by the Arabs in the 9th century, it was subsequently conquered and replaced by an Augustinian monastery in 1099.

⊨ p236

The Drive ⟫ It's a short drive (50 minutes or so) to Huesca. From Alquézar take the A1233, then switch to the A1229 around Adahuesca. After 11km get onto the A22 toward Huesca.

- - - - - - - - - - - -

④ Huesca

Huesca is a provincial capital in more than name, a town that shutters down during the afternoon hours and stirs back into life in the evenings. That said, its old centre retains considerable appeal. The Gothic **Catedral de Santa María** (Plaza de la Catedral; cathedral free, museum & tower €4; ☺cathedral times vary, museum & tower 10.30am-2pm & 4-8pm Mon-Fri, 10.30am-2pm Sat) is one of Aragón's great surprises. The richly carved main portal dates from 1300, the attached Museo Diocesano contains some extraordinary frescos, and you can round off your visit by climbing the 180 steps of the bell tower for 360-degree views.

✕ p236

The Drive » Zaragoza is about an hour's drive (75km). From Huesca, take Av Martínez de Velasco west. Hop onto the E7 heading southwest. Stay on this for 59km, then take exit 298 onto N330 toward Zaragoza.

- - - - - - - - - - - - - -

TRIP HIGHLIGHT

⑤ Zaragoza

Zaragoza (Saragossa) is a vibrant, elegant and fascinating city located on the banks of the mighty Río Ebro. Its residents comprise over half of Aragón's population and enjoy a lifestyle that revolves around some of the best tapas bars in the province, as well as superb shopping and a vigorous nightlife. The restoration of the riverbank a few years back has created footpaths on either side of the Río Ebro, resulting in an 8km circular route. It's superb

birdwatching territory, with herons, kingfishers and many other species.

Brace yourself for the great baroque cavern of Catholicism known as the **Basílica de Nuestra Señora del Pilar** (Plaza del Pilar; lift admission €3; ☺7am-9.30pm, lift 10am-1.30pm & 4-6.30pm Tue-Sun). The faithful believe that it was here on 2 January AD 40 that Santiago saw the Virgin Mary descend atop a marble *pilar* (pillar). A lift whisks you most of the way up the north tower from where you climb to a superb viewpoint over the city.

The 11th-century **Aljafería** (Calle de los Diputados; admission €3, Sun free; ☺10am-2pm Sat-Wed, plus 4.30-8pm Mon-Wed, Fri & Sat Jul & Aug) is Spain's finest Islamic-era edifice outside Andalucía. Tours take place throughout the day.

✕ 🛏 p236

The Drive » From Zaragoza take Av Valencia west. Turn right onto Av Septimo Arte and follow this as it merges onto the A23. Follow the A23 for 68km and take exit 210 near Romanos onto the A1506. Just outside of town, get on the N234; follow this another 1.5km, then exit onto La Libertad which will take you into Daroca. The 87km drive takes just over an hour.

- - - - - - - - - - - - - -

⑥ Daroca

Daroca, a sleepy medieval town, was a one-time Islamic stronghold and, later, a Christian fortress town in the early medi-

ANGEL P.S / GETTY IMAGES ©

eval wars against Castilla. Its well-preserved old quarter is laden with historic references and the crumbling old city walls encircle the hilltops; the walls once boasted 114 military towers. The pretty **Plaza de España**, at the top of the village, is dominated by an ornate Romanesque Mudéjar Renaissance–style church, which boasts a lavish interior and organ.

The Drive » From Daroca, take Av Madrid southwest and merge onto the A211. Follow this 23km then follow signs to Gallocanta, another 1km south of the A211.

Zaragoza Basílica de Nuestra Señora del Pilar

7 Laguna de Gallocanta

This is Spain's largest natural lake, with an area of about 15 sq km (though it can almost dry up in summer). It's a winter home for tens of thousands of cranes, as well as many other waterfowl – more than 260 bird species have been recorded here. The cranes arrive in mid-October and leave for the return flight to their breeding grounds in Scandinavia in March. Unpaved tracks of 36km in total encircle the lake, passing a series of hides and observation points – the tracks can be driven in normal vehicles except after heavy rain. Take binoculars.

🛏 p237

The Drive ≫ Take the A1507 east. Around Calamocha, get on the N234, then merge onto the A23. Stay on this for 53km, before taking exit 131 onto TEV9021. Around Cella switch to the TEV9011, follow this a few kilometres, then right onto the A1512, which will take you into Albarracín. The drive takes about 90 minutes.

TRIP HIGHLIGHT

8 Albarracín

Built on a steep, rocky outcrop and surrounded by a deep valley carved out by the Río Guadalaviar, Albarracín is one of Spain's most beautiful villages. It's famous for its half-timbered houses with dusky-pink facades, reminiscent of southern Italy.

Crowning the old town (with stunning views) is a fascinating castle, with 11 towers and an area of 3600 sq metres. It dates from the 9th century when Albarracín was an

LOCAL KNOWLEDGE: THE LOVERS OF TERUEL

In the early 13th century, Juan Diego de Marcilla and Isabel de Segura fell in love, but, in the manner of other star-crossed historical lovers, there was a catch: Isabel was the only daughter of a wealthy family, while poor old Juan Diego was, well, poor. Juan Diego convinced Isabel's reluctant father to postpone plans for Isabel's marriage to someone more appropriate for five years, during which time Juan Diego would seek his fortune. Not waiting a second longer than the five years, Isabel's father married off his daughter in 1217, only for Juan Diego to return, triumphant, immediately after the wedding. He begged Isabel for a kiss, which she refused, condemning Juan Diego to die of a broken heart. A final twist saw Isabel attend the funeral in mourning, whereupon she gave Juan Diego the kiss he had craved in life. Isabel promptly died and the two lovers were buried together. You can see their tombs at the Mausoleum of the Lovers in Teruel.

important Islamic military post. Albarracín's highest point, the **Torre del Andador** (Walkway Tower), has enviable views over town.

✗ p237

The Drive » It's an easy 40-minute drive to your next stop. From Albarracín get back on the A1512, and follow it for 37km to Teruel. It's a scenic drive that takes in forest and rocky foothills, before descending into the wide open plains outside Teruel.

– – – – – – – – – – – –

❾ Teruel

Lovely, compact Teruel is an open-air museum of ornate Mudéjar monuments. But this is very much a living museum where the streets are filled with life – a reflection of a city with serious cultural attitude. Teruel's **Catedral de Santa María de Mediavilla** (Plaza de la Catedral; adult/child incl Museo de Arte Sacro €3/2; ⊙11am-2pm & 4-8pm) is a rich example of the Mudéjar imagination at work with its kaleidoscopic brickwork and colourful ceramic tiles.

The somewhat curious **Mausoleum of the Lovers** (www.amantesdeteruel.es; Calle Matías Abad 3; Mausoleo/ Iglesia de San Pedro & Torre de San Pedro €4/5, combined ticket €7; ⊙10am-2pm & 4-8pm Sep-Jul, 10am-8pm Aug) pulls out the stops on the city's famous legend of Isabel and Juan Diego. Here they lie in modern alabaster tombs with their heads tilted endearingly towards each other. Around this centrepiece has been shaped a predictably sentimental audiovisual exhibition, featuring music and theatre.

The most impressive of Teruel's Mudéjar towers is the **Torre de El Salvador** (www.teruelmudejar.com; Calle El Salvador; adult/concession €2.50/1.80; ⊙11am-2pm & 4.30-7.30pm), an early-14th-century extravaganza of brick and ceramics built around an older Islamic minaret. Climb up the narrow stairways for Teruel's best views.

🛏 p237

The Drive » It's 120km southeast to Sagunto, though just a 70-minute drive on the A23. From Teruel, take Av de Sagunto south. Just beyond the centre, you'll pass by Dinópolis, a dinosaur theme park that's a hit with families. From here, continue onto the N234 and onto the A23.

– – – – – – – – – – – –

❿ Sagunto

The port town of Sagunto offers spectacular panoramas of the coast, Balearics and sea of orange groves from its hilltop castle complex. Sagunto was once a thriving Iberian community (called – infelicitously, with hindsight – Arse) that traded with Greeks and Phoenicians. A highlight here is the restored

Roman theatre. Above it, the stone walls of the castle complex girdle the hilltop for almost 1km.

The Drive » It's about a 30-minute drive to Valencia. From Sagunto, take the N340 south, and merge onto the V23. Around Puçol, merge onto the V21, and enjoy the view along the coast as you near the city.

- - - - - - - - - - - -

TRIP HIGHLIGHT

⑪ Valencia

The vibrant city of Valencia has much going for it, from stunning architecture and scenic parks to an embarrassing wealth of restaurants.

Bright and spacious, the **Museo de Bellas Artes** (San Pío V; www. museobellasartesvalencia. gva.es; Calle de San Pío V 9; ⊙10am-7pm Tue-Sun, 11am-5pm Mon) ranks among Spain's best. Highlights include the grandiose Roman Mosaic of the Nine Muses, a collection of magnificent late-medieval altarpieces, and works by El Greco, Goya and Velázquez.

For a dose of greenery, stroll the **Jardines del Turia**. Stretching the length of Río Turia's former course, this 9km-long park is a fabulous mix of playing fields, walking paths, lawns and playgrounds. For more on Spain's third-largest city see p254 and p312.

✕ ⨯ 🛏 p237

KRZYSZTOF DYDYNSKI / GETTY IMAGES ©

Valencia Museo de Bellas Artes

Eating & Sleeping

Barcelona ❶

✗ La Vinateria del Call   Spanish €€

(☎93 302 60 92; www.lavinateriadelcall.com; Carrer de Sant Domènec del Call 9; small plates €7-12; ⏲7.30pm-1am; Ⓜ Jaume I) In a magical setting in the former Jewish quarter, this tiny jewelbox of a restaurant serves up tasty Iberian dishes including Galician octopus, cider-cooked chorizo and the Catalan *escalivada* (roasted peppers, aubergine and onions) with anchovies. Portions are small and made for sharing, and there's a good and affordable selection of wines.

⭐ Hotel Banys Orientals   Boutique Hotel €€

(☎93 268 84 60; www.hotelbanysorientals. com; Carrer de l'Argenteria 37; s €96, d €115-143; ❊ 🛜; Ⓜ Jaume I) Book well ahead to get into this magnetically popular designer haunt. Cool blues and aquamarines combine with dark-hued floors to lend this clean-lined, boutique hotel a quiet charm. All rooms, on the small side, look onto the street or back lanes. There are more spacious suites in two other nearby buildings.

Lleida ❷

✗ l'estel de la Mercè   Catalan €€€

(☎973 28 80 08; www.lesteldelamerce.com; Carrer Cardenal Cisneros 30; mains €16-25; ⏲1-4pm & 9-11.30pm Wed-Sat, 1-4pm Tue & Sun) A 10-minute walk from the centre, this prolific mother-and-son team has a new, sleek modern base. They continue to create beautiful fusion dishes using fresh seasonal produce. Feast on the likes of fig 'carpaccio' with foie gras, *risotto de bogavante* (lobster risotto) and cod loin with *butifarra negra* (black pudding) and finish off with strawberries flambéed with pepper.

Alquézar ❸

⭐ Hotel Villa de Alquézar   Hotel €€

(☎tel/fax 974 31 84 16; www.villadealquezar. com; Calle Pedro Arenal Cavero 12; d incl breakfast €69-110; 🅿 🛜) This is a lovely place

with plenty of style in its airy rooms; several sport great views and there are period touches throughout. The most expensive rooms on the top floor are large and have wonderful covered balconies – they're perfect for watching the sun set over town while nursing a bottle of Somontano wine.

Huesca ❹

✗ Tatau Bistro   Tapas €

(www.tatau.es; Calle San Lorenzo 4; tapas from €2.80, raciones from €3.80; ⏲noon-midnight Tue-Sat, to 4pm Sun) This place has a bright contemporary look with a whiff of a '50s diner about it (or is it the waitresses hair-dos?). Daily tapas and *raciones* (large tapas) are chalked up on a blackboard and range from more ambitious dishes such as steak tartare to the traditional standard *croquetas de jamón* (ham croquettes).

Zaragoza ❺

✗ El Ciclón   Contemporary Spanish €€

(Plaza del Pilar 10; raciones €7-8.50, set menus €15-20; ⏲11am-11.30pm) Opened in November 2013 by three acclaimed Spanish chefs (all with Michelin-star restaurant experience), the dishes here are superbly prepared. Choose between set menus and tapas and *raciones* such as the Canary Island favourite, *papas arrugadas* (new potatoes with a spicy coriander sauce), noodles with mussels, and artichokes with *migas* (crumbs) and cauliflower cream.

⭐ Hotel Sauce   Boutique Hotel €€

(☎976 20 50 50; www.hotelsauce.com; Calle de Espoz y Mina 33; s from €45, d €51-66; ❊ 🛜) This chic, small hotel has a great central location and a light and airy look, with white wicker, painted furniture, stripy fabrics and tasteful watercolours on the walls. The superior rooms are well worth the few euros extra. Breakfast (€8) includes homemade cakes and a much-lauded *tortilla de patatas* (potato omelette).

Laguna de Gallocanta ❼

🛏 Allucant
Hostal €

(www.allucant.com; Calle San Vicente; dm €13, d with shared/private bathroom from €30/45; 🅿🛜) Serious twitchers will feel right at home at this simple but well-run birdwatching base in the village of Gallocanta. Meals (€9 to €12) and picnic lunches (€7) can be arranged. The place also acts as an informal cultural centre with regular art exhibitions and courses available, ranging from photography to painting.

Albarracín ❽

✕ Tiempo de Ensueño
Contemporary Spanish €€

(📞978 70 40 70; www.tiempodeensuenyo. com; Calle Palacios 1B; mains €19-25; 🕑1-4pm & 7-11pm Tue-Sun) This restaurant has a sleek dining room, attentive but discreet service, and food that you'll remember long after you've left. Spanish nouvelle cuisine in all its innovative guises makes an appearance here with a changing menu, as well as a long wine list, mineral-water menu, choice of olive oils, welcome cocktail and exquisite tastes.

Teruel ❾

🛏 Hotel el Mudayyan
Boutique Hotel €€

(📞978 62 30 42; www.elmudayyan.com; Calle Nueva 18; s €55-70, d €70-90; ❄🛜) A delightful small hotel, El Mudayyan has just

eight rooms with polished wood floors, wooden beams and a charming interior design. It also has a *tetería* (Moroccan-style teahouse) and a fascinating subterranean passage that dates back to the 13th century. An adjacent Modernista building with an additional 20 rooms should be open by the time you read this.

Valencia ⓫

✕ Carosel
Valencian €

(📞961 13 28 73; www.carosel.es; Calle Taula de Canvis 6; mains €7-16, menu €15; 🕑1-4pm & 9-11pm Tue-Sat, 1-4pm Sun) Jordi and his partner, Carol, run this delightful small restaurant with outdoor seating on a square. The freshest of produce from the nearby market is blended with Alicante and Valencia traditions to create salads, cocas, rices and other delicious titbits. Top value and warmly recommended.

🛏 Hotel Atarazanas
Hotel €€

(📞963 20 30 10; www.hotelatarazanas.com; Plaza Tribunal de las Aguas 5; r €107; 🅿❄🛜) In an interesting, nontouristy zone handy for both beach and port, this has a breezy rooftop terrace with a magnificent wraparound view of sea and city. The cream walls and fabrics of each bedroom contrast with the dark, stained woodwork. Sybaritic bathrooms have deep tubs with hydromassage and the broad shower head is as big as a discus. It's an extra-good deal in the low season.

STRETCH YOUR LEGS
BARCELONA

Start: Parc de la Ciutadella

Finish: Casa Batlló

Distance: 3.5km

Duration: Three hours

Packed with historic treasures and jaw-dropping architecture, Barcelona is a wanderer's delight. This stroll takes you through atmospheric medieval lanes and along elegant boulevards, leading you past Gothic cathedrals, lively tapas bars and picturesque plazas.

Take this walk on Trips

Parc de la Ciutadella

The handsomely landscaped Parc de la Ciutadella is a local favourite for a leisurely promenade. Start in the northeast corner, and descend past the monumental **Cascada** (waterfall), then stroll south across the park, passing a small lake and Catalonia's regional parliament.

The Walk >> With your back to the park, cross Passeig de Picasso and walk along restaurant-lined Passeig del Born. According to legend, jousting matches were once held here.

Basílica de Santa Maria del Mar

Nothing prepares you for the singular beauty of **Basílica de Santa Maria del Mar** (☏93 310 23 90; Plaça de Santa Maria del Mar; ⏰9am-1.30pm & 4.30-8.30pm, from 10.30am Sun; Ⓜ Jaume I). Barcelona's most stirring Gothic structure, the 14th-century church was built in just 59 years. In contrast to the tight warren of neighbouring streets, a real sense of light and space pervades the entire sanctuary of the church.

The Walk >> Leave via the main entrance and follow Carrer de l'Argenteria up to busy Via Laietana. Turn left onto Baixada de la Llibreteria, then right onto Carrer de la Freneria. After a few blocks, you'll see the massive cathedral on your left.

La Catedral

For centuries the spiritual heart of Barcelona, **La Catedral** (☏93 342 82 62; www.catedralbcn.org; Plaça de la Seu; admission free, special visit €6, choir admission €2.80; ⏰8am-12.45pm & 5.15-7.30pm Mon-Sat, special visit 1-5pm Mon-Sat, 2-5pm Sun & holidays; Ⓜ Jaume I) is at once lavish and sombre, anchoring the city in its past. Begun in the late 13th century and not completed until six centuries later, the cathedral is Barcelona's history rendered in stone.

The Walk >> Turn left out of the main entrance and left again down Carrer del Bispe. Just before reaching Plaça Sant Jaume, turn right onto Carrer del Call. Follow this narrow lane a few blocks, then turn left onto Carrer d'en Quintana. After two blocks, you'll reach the plaza.

Plaça Reial

One of the most photogenic squares in Barcelona, the Plaça Reial is not to be missed. Numerous eateries, bars and nightspots lie beneath the arcades of 19th century neoclassical buildings, with a buzz of activity at all hours. The lamp posts by the central fountain are Antoni Gaudí's first known works in the city.

The Walk ›› Exit the square onto famous La Rambla, a bustling boulevard with a wide pedestrian-filled strip in the middle. Walk north a few blocks until you see the large cast-iron market off to your left.

Mercat de la Boqueria

This temple of temptation is one of Europe's greatest permanent **produce fairs** (☎93 318 25 84; www.boqueria.info; La Rambla 91; ☺8am-8.30pm Mon-Sat, closed Sun; MLiceu). Step inside for a seemingly endless bounty of glistening fruits and vegetables, smoked meats, pungent cheeses and chocolate truffles. In the back, a handful of popular tapas bars serve up delectable morsels.

The Walk ›› Get back on La Rambla and continue north. You'll soon reach the spacious Plaça de Catalunya. Walk diagonally across this plaza, and turn left onto the grand boutique-lined Passeig de Gràcia, and walk up four blocks to the architectural treasures looming just past Carrer del Consell de Cent.

Casa Batlló

Even Gaudí outdid himself with this fantastical **apartment block** (☎93 216 03 06; www.casabatllo.es; Passeig de Gràcia 43; adult/concessions/child under 7yr €21.50/€18.50/free; ☺9am-9pm daily; MPasseig de Gràcia): an astonishing confection of rippling balconies, optical illusions and twisted chimney pots along Barcelona's grandest boulevard. The facade, sprinkled with bits of blue, mauve and green tiles and studded with wave-shaped window frames and balconies, rises to an uneven blue-tiled roof with a solitary tower.

The Walk ›› Since it's a long walk back to the start, hop on the metro and head to Arc de Trionf station, a short stroll from Parc de la Ciutadella.

Andalucía & Southern Spain

WIND DOWN THE WINDOW, decide who's going to be the non-sherry-drinking driver and stick some flamenco on the sound system; the caminos of Andalucía are calling in the same way they once called Roman legionnaires, sighing Moors and 19th-century romantics dreaming of Carmen and Don Juan.

Immortalised in operas and depicted in Goya-era works of art, Andalucía often acts as a synonym for Spain, a land of troubadours, bull-fighters, operatic heroines, and Roma singers wailing sad laments.

While time may have eroded many of the clichés, the passion of Andalucía remains. Experience it driving between mountains, Moorish cities and hilltop villages on a network of well-maintained 21st-century roads.

Granada View over the rooftops of this historic city (Trip 22)

Andalucía & Southern Spain

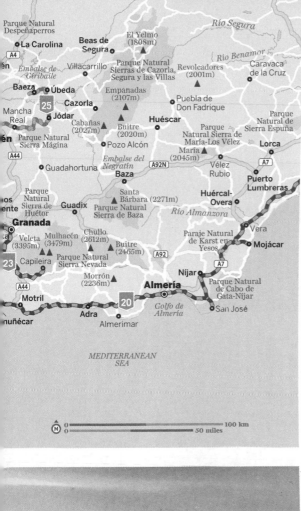

✓ DON'T MISS

Zuheros

A spectacular white village in Córdoba province that's off the *pueblo blanco* circuit. Visit it on Trip 22

Cabo de Gata

A slice of arid coastline that the developers forgot to dig up. Fortunately, it's now protected in a natural park and sports abundant flora and birdlife. Explore it on Trip 20

El Torcal

Craggy moonscape that characterises the uplands overlooking the town of Antequera; weird and wonderful even by Andalucian standards. Visit it on Trip 23

Orchidarium

Europe's largest orchid collection is protected in a glass dome in the Costa del Sol beach town of Estepona. Meander through it on Trip 21

Sendero del Acantilado

Cliff-top path linking tuna-fishing town of Barbate with the hip, beach town of Los Caños de Meca on the Costa de la Luz. Hike it on Trip 23

Cordoba River view looking out to the Mezquita (Trip 22)

Barcelona Visit Gaudí's Sagrada Familia – the city's ever-evolving symbol

Mediterranean Meander

20

Follow the Mediterranean coast northeast out of Málaga and you'll be contemplating far more than just beach umbrellas. Roman ruins, heavyweight art, and fabulous festivals also pepper this surprisingly cultural coastline.

TRIP HIGHLIGHTS

1095 km

La Rambla
Stretch your legs on one of Europe's finest boulevards

726 km

Ciudad de las Artes y las Ciencias
See Valencia's and Spain's new cutting edge in this futuristic complex

START

Museo Picasso Málaga
Admire the greatest 20th-century master in the city of his birth

1 km

Tarragona ⑫ **FINISH**

⑨

Xàtiva

Cartagena

Mojácar

①   ④

Cabo de Gata
Precious enclave of pure unblemished Mediterranean coastline

254 km

**7 DAYS
1095 KM /
680 MILES**

GREAT FOR...

BEST TIME TO GO

March to June is sunny, but not too hot, and there are plenty of festivals, including Las Fallas.

ESSENTIAL PHOTO

The chameleonic Sagrada Familia changes every time you visit.

BEST FOR OUTDOORS

Parque Natural de Cabo de Gata-Nijar.

Mediterranean Meander

20

From the Costa Daurada to the Costa del Sol, from Catalan pride in Sitges to Andalucian passion in Almería, from the Roman ruins of Tarragona to the Modernisme buildings of Barcelona: this drive proves that not all southern Spain is a beach bucket of cheesy tourist clichés. The full 1095km trajectory passes through four regions; two languages; Spain's second-, third- and sixth- largest cities; and beaches too numerous to count.

TRIP HIGHLIGHT

❶ Málaga

The Costa del Sol can seem wholly soulless until you fall gasping for a shred of culture into Málaga, an unmistakably Spanish metropolis curiously ignored by the lion's share of the millions of tourists who land annually at Pablo Ruíz Picasso International Airport.

Málaga is currently on the crest of a wave and is a great place to begin this epic 1000km-plus drive. The city that until 2003 lacked even a museum to its legendary native son, Picasso, is

becoming an art heavyweight to rival Madrid or Barcelona. Recent gallery openings include the modernist Centre Pompidou and the evocative **Museo Ruso de Málaga** (www.coleccionmuseoruso.es; Avenida de Sor Teresa Plat 15; adult/child €8/free; ⏰11am-10pm Tue-Sun; Ⓟ). They join over 20 established art nooks anchored by the distinguished **Museo Picasso Málaga** (www. museopicassomalaga.org; Calle San Agustín 8; admission €7; 10am-8pm Tue-Thu & Sun, to 9pm Fri & Sat) Moving with the times, Málaga is also developing its own arts district, Soho, transforming a former rundown

area near the port with giant murals and groovy cafes. See p308 for a walking tour of Málaga.

✖ 🛏 p258

The Drive ⟫ Head east out of Málaga on the A7 motorway towards Almería. This is southern Spain's epic coastal road (also known as European route 15 or E15) and will be your companion for much of

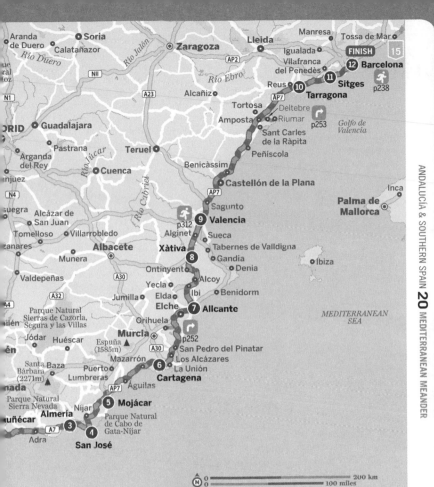

LINK YOUR TRIP

21 Costa del Sol Beyond the Beaches

Can't get enough of the Mediterranean? Jump onto this trip in Málaga and head all the way down the coast to Gibraltar.

15 Artistic Inspiration on the Costa Brava

You can also extend this trip at its Catalan nexus, heading north out of Barcelona along the Costa Brava.

this trip. The coast gets ever more precipitous as you enter Granada province. After 68km turn south on the N340 and follow it for 8km into Almuñécar.

------

2 Almuñécar

Granada province's cliff-lined, 80km-long coast has a hint of Italy's Amalfi about it, although it is definitively Spanish

Classic Trip

when you get down to the nitty-gritty. Its warm climate – there's no real winter to speak of – lends it the name, Costa Tropical. The region's unofficial capital is Almuñécar, a fiercely traditional town that's a little rough around the edges, but very relaxed.

Dedicated to beach fun, Almuñécar's seafront is divided by a rocky outcrop, the Peñón del Santo, with pebbly Playa de San Cristóbal stretching to its west, and Playa Puerta del Mar to the east backed by a strip of cool cafes. The **Museo Arque-ológico** (Calle San Joaquín; adult/child €2.35/1.60; ☺10am-1.30pm & 4-6.30pm Tue-Sat, 10.30am-1pm Sun) in the maze of the old town highlights Almuñécar's

ancient Phoenician roots. Tickets include entry to the **Castillo de San Miguel** (Santa Adela Explanada; adult/child €2.35/1.60; ☺10am-1.30pm & 4-6.30pm Tue-Sat, 10.30am-1pm Sun) at the top of a hill overlooking the sea, with fine views and another cleverly curated museum.

The Drive ›› After 20 years in the making, the final links of the A7 around Motril and Salobreña were established in 2015 after many delays. The *autopista* (toll way) takes drivers around the north of Motril, bypassing the older N340 in the south. As the landscape gets more arid you'll spy increasing numbers of commercial greenhouses punctuating the coastal landscape. Almería beckons. Distance from Almuñécar to Almería is 139km.

- - - - - - - - - - - - -

❸ Almería

Don't underestimate sun-baked Almería, a tough waterside city with an illustrious

history and a handful of important historical monuments to prove it. While the queues bulge outside Granada's Alhambra, mere trickles of savvy travellers head for Almería's equally hefty Alcazaba fortress, which lords it over a city that once served as chief sea outlet for the 10th-century Córdoba caliphate.

Almería's old Moorish quarter that lies in the skirts of the Alcazaba hill hasn't been spruced up for the tourist hordes, meaning it is scruffy, but very real. Get Moorishly acquainted with the **Alcazaba** (Calle Almanzor; ☺9am-7.30pm Tue-Sat Apr–mid-Jun, to 3.30pm Tue-Sat mid-Jun–mid-Sep, to 5.30pm Tue-Sat mid-Sep–Mar, to 3.30pm Sun all year), or the **Hammam Aire de Almería** (www.aire-dealmeria.com; Plaza de la Constitución 5; 1½hr session incl 15min aromatherapy €23; ☺10am-10pm), a sanitised modern-day version of a Arabic bathhouse. The city's latest sight is the fantastic **Museo de la Guitarra** (☎950 27 43 58; Ronda del Beato Diego Ventaja; admission €3; ☺10.30am-1.30pm Tue-Sun, 6-9pm Fri & Sat Jun-Sep, 10am-1pm Tue-Sun, 5-8pm Fri & Sat Oct-May), which documents Almería's understated role in the development of the iconic instrument.

✕ p258

The Drive ›› Head east out of Almería on the N344. Cross the

✕ p258

✓ TOP TIP: TOLL ROADS

The AP7 (also known as E15), is a toll-charging *autopista* (motorway) that parallels much of Spain's southern coastline. You will have to stop periodically to pay a toll at manned booths. The total cost for the route highlighted here will be in the vicinity of €57. The confusingly named A7 follows a similar route to the AP7, but is toll-free. The N340 is a third road paralleling Spain's southern coast, although these days much of it has merged with the A7. Some of the N340 follows the route of the Roman Vía Augustus.

THE PICASSO TRAIL

Málaga and Barcelona are linked by more than Mediterranean beaches – both cities have strong Picasso connections. The great Andalucían painter was born in Málaga in 1881 and lived there until he was 10, while Barcelona served as his inspiration and muse in the late 1890s and early 1900s when he intermittently resided in the Catalan capital. As a result, the start and finish points of this trip stand as important way-stations in Picasso's illustrious career and are loaded with plenty of art and artefacts to investigate.

Málaga guards the painter's birth house, the diminutive **Casa Natal de Picasso** (www.fundacionpicasso.malaga.eu; Plaza de la Merced 15; admission €3; ⏰9.30am-8pm), which includes a replica of his father's erstwhile studio. Nearby, and run by the same foundation, is the **Museo Picasso Málaga** (☑902 44 33 77; www.museopicassomalaga. org; Calle San Agustín 8; admission €7, incl temporary exhibition €10; ⏰10am-8pm Tue-Thu & Sun, to 9pm Fri & Sat), which opened in 2003. Barcelona hosts the **Museu Picasso** (☑93 256 30 00; www.museupicasso.bcn.cat; Carrer de Montcada 15-23; adult/child €14/free, temporary exhibitions adult/child €6.50/free, 3-8pm Sun & 1st Sun of month free; ⏰Tue, Wed & Fri-Sun 9am-7pm, to 9.30pm Thu; Ⓜ Jaume I), which, with over 4000 exhibits, has one of the most complete Picasso collections in the world.

On a more modest scale, but also worth perusing as you pass through, is Alicante's **Museo de Arte Contemporáneo** (MACA; www.maca-alicante.es; Plaza Santa María 3; ⏰10am-8pm Tue-Sat, to 2pm Sun) displaying Picasso's *Portrait d'Arthur Rimbaud* (1960); and the **Museu Cau Ferrat** (www.museusdesitges.cat; Carrer de Fonollar) in Sitges, encased in the house of Picasso's friend, the late artist Santiago Rusiñol.

Río Andarax and pass the airport on your right. Fork right onto the ALP202 and at a T-junction turn right. Follow the road (AL3108) through low hills into the village of San José (total distance 40km).

- - - - - - - - - - -

TRIP HIGHLIGHT

④ Cabo de Gata

If you can find anyone old enough to remember the Costa del Sol before the bulldozers arrived, they'd probably say it looked a bit like Cabo de Gata. Some of Spain's most beautiful and least-crowded beaches are strung between the grand cliffs and capes east of Almería City, where dark volcanic hills

tumble into a sparkling turquoise sea.

Though Cabo de Gata is not undiscovered, it still has a wild, elemental feel and its scattered fishing villages (remember them?) remain low-key.

A good nexus is San José, with its secluded beaches, including Playa de los Genoveses just southwest of the village. Footpaths run along the coast in either direction, criss-crossing the protected Parque Natural de Cabo de Gata-Nijar. They're good for a short tentative stroll or a full-blown multiday excursion. The area is also one of the best places

in Andalucía for diving. **Isub** (☑950 38 00 04; www. isubsanjose.com; Calle Babor 8; ⏰8.30am-2pm & 4-7.30pm Mon-Sat, to 2pm Sun Mar-Dec) in San José offers a full range of courses.

The Drive >> Follow the AL3108 inland from San José until you hit the A7 *autovía* (highway) just shy of Nijar. Head northeast towards Valencia for 43km until the exit for A370, signposted Mojácar.

- - - - - - - - - - -

⑤ Mojácar

Tucked away in an isolated corner of one of Spain's most traditional regions Mojácar was almost abandoned in the mid-20th century until a

Classic Trip

WHY THIS IS A CLASSIC TRIP
BRENDAN SAINSBURY, AUTHOR

Growing up, I always imagined Spain's southern coast to be full of raucous resorts plying 18 to 30 holidays. When I eventually visited, I found that, in between the 'Benidorms', there was as much culture as after-hours cacophony. Where else can you find a city more innately Spanish than Málaga, a coast more unsullied than Cabo de Gata, or a Roman amphitheater more thrillingly sited than Tarragona's?

Top: Outdoor dining in Málaga
Left: Tarragona's Roman amphitheatre
Right: Cabo de Gata

foresighted local mayor started luring artists and others with giveaway property offers. Although the tourists have arrived, Mojácar has retained its essence.

There are actually two towns here: old Mojácar Pueblo, a jumble of white, cube-shaped houses on a hilltop 2km inland, and Mojácar Playa, a modern beach resort.

Exploring Mojácar Pueblo is mainly a matter of wandering the mazelike streets, with their bougainvillea-swathed balconies, stopping off at craft shops, galleries and boutiques. **El Mirador del Castillo**, at the top-most point, has a cafe-bar and magnificent views. The fortress-style **Iglesia de Santa María** (Calle Iglesia) dates from 1560 and may have once been a mosque.

South of Mojácar Playa, the beaches are quieter, and once you get to the fringes of town, there are a number of more secluded areas.

🛏 p258

The Drive » Retrace your steps from Mojácar back to the A7 *autovia*. After 10km merge onto the AP7 near Vera. This is a toll road. Continue until the exit for Cartagena Oeste. At the roundabout take the N332 into the city. Mojácar to Cartagena is 134km.

❻ Cartagena

Cartagena's fabulous natural harbour has been used for thousands of years. Stand on the battlements of the castle that overlooks this city and you can literally see layer upon layer of history spread below you, from Phoenician traders through Roman legionaries, Islamic architects and the armies of the Christian Reconquista to the factories of the industrial age.

As archaeologists continue to reveal a long-buried, and fascinating, Roman and Carthaginian heritage, the city is finally starting to get the recognition it deserves. The **Museo Nacional de Arqueología Subacuática** (Arqua; http://museoarqua.mcu. es; Paseo del Muelle Alfonso XII 22; adult/child €3/free; ◷10am-8pm or 9pm Tue-Sat, to 3pm Sun) has lots of old pots, flashy lights, buttons to press, films to watch and a replica Phoenician trading ship, while the super **Museo del Teatro Romano** (www. teatroromanocartagena.org; Plaza del Ayuntamiento 9; adult/child €6/5; ◷10am-6pm or 8pm Tue-Sat, to 2pm Sun) transports visitors via escalators and an underground passage to a magnificent, recently restored Roman theatre dating from the 1st century BC.

✗ p258

The Drive » Get back on the AP7 towards Alicante (more tolls!). After 75km the *autovia* rejoins the (free) A7. Follow it for 32km before taking exit 17A signposted Alicante.

❼ Alicante

Of all Spain's mainland provincial capitals, Alicante is the most influenced by tourism, thanks to the nearby airport and resorts. Nevertheless, this is a dynamic, attractive Spanish city with a castle, old quarter and long waterfront. The eating scene is exciting

---

↱ DETOUR: ORIHUELA

Start: ❻ Cartagena

Beside the Río Segura and flush with the base of a barren mountain of rock, the historical heart of Orihuela, with superb Gothic, Renaissance and, especially, baroque buildings, well merits a detour. The old town is strung out between the river and a mountain topped by a ruined castle. The main sights are dotted along it, more or less in a line.

A few of the buildings are particularly worth looking out for. The **Convento de Santo Domingo** (Calle Adolfo Claravana; admission €2; ◷9.30am-1.30pm & 4-7pm or 5-8pm Tue-Sat, 10am-2pm Sun) is a 16th-century convent with two fine Renaissance cloisters and a refectory clad in 18th-century tilework. One of the town's splendid ecclesiastical buildings is the 14th-century Catalan Gothic **Catedral de San Salvador** (Calle Doctor Sarget; ◷10.30am-2pm & 4-6.30pm Tue-Fri, 10.30am-2pm Sat), with its three finely carved portals and a lovely little cloister. The Renaissance facade of **Iglesia de las Santas Justa y Rufina** (Plaza Salesas 1; ◷10am-1pm & 4-6pm Mon-Fri) is worth admiring, and its Gothic tower is graced with gargoyles.

Orihuela is between the Cartagena and Alicante stops on this trip. To reach it branch west off the AP7 onto the CV91 around 70km north of Cartagena.

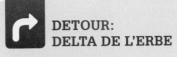

DETOUR:
DELTA DE L'ERBE

Start: ❾ Valencia

The delta of the Río Ebre, formed by silt brought down by the river, sticks out 20km into the Mediterranean near Catalonia's southern border. Dotted with reedy lagoons and fringed by dune-backed beaches, this completely flat and exposed wetland, with **Parc Natural Delta de l'Ebre** comprising 77 sq km, is northern Spain's most important waterbird habitat. The migration season (October and November) sees the bird population peak, but they are also numerous in winter and spring. Even if you're not a twitcher, a visit here is worthwhile for the surreal landscapes alone. Tiny whitewashed farmhouses seem to float on little islands among green and brown paddy fields which stretch to the horizon. It's completely unlike anywhere else in Catalonia.

The scruffy, sprawling town of **Deltebre** is at the centre of the delta but push on from here to smaller villages such as **Riumar**, the coastal village at the delta's easternmost point, or **Poblenou del Delta**.

To reach Deltebre, branch off AP7 at exit 41, 180km north of Valencia. The town lies 13km to the east along TV3454.

and the nightlife is absolutely legendary, whether you're chugging pints with the stag parties at 7pm or twirling on the dance floor with the locals seven hours later.

There are sweeping views over the city from the large 16th-century **Castillo de Santa Bárbara** (adult/child €3/1.50; ☉10am-10pm Apr-Sep, to 8pm Oct-Mar), which also houses a museum recounting the history of Alicante. If you're not up for the steep climb, the city has a couple of good free museums. The Museo de Arte Contemporáneo de Alicante (p249) displays Dalí, Miró and Picasso, among others. The **Museu de Fogueres** (Museo de las Hogueras; Rambla de Méndez Núñez 29; ☉10am-2pm & 5-8pm or 6-9pm Tue-Sat) has photos, costumes and an audiovisual presentation of the Fiesta de Sant Joan.

🍴 p258

The Drive » Leave Alicante on the A77 signposted Valencia. After 10km merge onto the A7. The *autovia* proceeds north, passing through a couple of tunnels and heading progressively downhill as it forges an inland route to Valencia. After 106km exit on the CV645 signposted Xàtiva. It's 5km to the town itself.

- - - - - - - - - - - - -

❽ Xàtiva

Xàtiva (Spanish: Játiva) is often visited on an easy and rewarding 50km day trip from Valencia or – in this case – as a stop on the way north from Alicante. It has a small historic quarter and a mighty castle strung along the crest of the Serra Vernissa, at whose base the town snuggles.

The Muslims established Europe's first paper manufacturing plant in Xàtiva, which is also famous as the birthplace of the Borgia Popes Calixtus III and Alexander VI. The town's glory days ended in 1707 when Felipe V's troops torched most of the town.

What's interesting in Xàtiva lies south and uphill from the Alameda, including the **castle** (adult/child €2.40/1.20; ☉10am-6pm or 7pm Tue-Sun), which clasps to the summit of a double-peaked hill overlooking the old

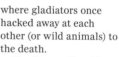

town. Today, behind its crumbling battlements you'll find a mixture of flower gardens (bring a picnic), tumbledown turrets and towers, and an excellent museum on medieval life. The walk up to the castle is a long one, but the views are sensational.

The Drive » Use N340 to rejoin the A7 and head north to Valencia. Just outside the city when the A7 merges with the AP7, take the V31, Valencia's main southern access road for the final 18km into the city centre.

TRIP HIGHLIGHT

⑨ Valencia

Spain's third-largest city is a magnificent place, content for Madrid and Barcelona to grab the headlines while it gets on with being a wonderfully liveable city with thriving cultural, eating and nightlife scenes. Never afraid to innovate, Valencia has diverted its flood-prone river to the outskirts of town and converted the former riverbed into a wonderful green ribbon of park winding right through the city. On it are the strikingly futuristic buildings of the **Ciudad de las Artes y las Ciencias** (City of

Arts & Sciences; www.cac. es; combined ticket for Oceanogràfic, Hemisfèric & Museo de las Ciencias Príncipe Felipe adult/child €36.25/27.55), designed by local-boy-made-good Santiago Calatrava. Other brilliant contemporary buildings grace the city, which also has a fistful of fabulous Modernista architecture, great museums and a large, characterful old quarter.

Valencia, surrounded by the fertile fruit-and-veg farmland La Huerta, is famous as the home of rice dishes such as paella, but its buzzy dining scene offers plenty more besides. Check out the highlights on our walking tour (p312).

✕ ⊨ p259

The Drive » Leave Valencia on the V21 signposted Puçol. After 23km you'll rejoin your reliable old friend, the AP7. Get your toll money ready! The AP7 is your route for the next 200km, taking you into Catalonia. Take exit 38 and get on the A7 for the final 35km of the route into Tarragona.

⑩ Tarragona

The eternally sunny port city of Tarragona is an improbable mix of Mediterranean beach life, Roman history and medieval alleyways. As Spain's second-most important Roman site, Tarragona has a wealth of ruins, including a seaside amphitheatre

where gladiators once hacked away at each other (or wild animals) to the death.

The Unesco-listed Roman sites are scattered around town. Entrance tickets can be acquired at the **Museu d'Historia de Tarragona** (MHT; www. museutgn.com; adult/child per site €3.30/free, all sites €11.05/free; ⊙ sites 9am-9pm Tue-Sat, 10am-3pm Sun

Sitges A seaside resort with great nightlife

Easter-Sep, 10am-7pm Tue-Sat, 10am-3pm Sun Oct-Easter).

The town's medieval heart is one of the most beautifully designed in Spain, its maze of narrow cobbled streets encircled by steep walls and crowned with a splendid **Catedral** (www.catedralde-tarragona.com; Plaça de la Seu; adult/child €5/3; ⏲10am-7pm Mon-Sat mid-Mar–Oct, 10am-5pm Mon-Fri, 10am-7pm Sat Nov–mid-Mar). A lively eating and drinking scene makes for an enticing stop.

🍴 🛏 p259

The Drive » From Tarragona use the N240 to get back onto AP7 and head east towards Barcelona. After 23km take exit 31 onto the C32. Follow this road for 31km, crossing one viaduct and burrowing through two tunnels, to Sitges.

⑪ Sitges

This lovely fishing-village-turned-pumping-beach-resort town has been a favourite with upper-class Catalans since the late 19th century, as well as a key location for the burgeoning Modernisme movement which paved the way for the likes of

Picasso. A famous gay destination, in July and August Sitges turns into one big beach party with a nightlife to rival Ibiza; the beaches are long and sandy, the tapas bars prolific and the Carnaval bacchanalian.

The main beach is flanked by the attractive seafront Passeig Maritim, dotted with *chiringuitos* (beachside bars) and divided into nine sections with different names by a series of breakwaters.

The art highlight is the recently refurbished Museu Cau Ferrat (p249), built in the 1890s as a house-cum-studio by artist Santiago Rusiñol – a pioneer of the Modernista movement. The whitewashed mansion is full of his own art and that of his contemporaries, including his friend Picasso, as well as a couple of El Grecos.

The Drive » It's only 40km to Barcelona! Get back onto the C32 and pay your last cursed toll. Fly through a multitude of tunnels. After 30km of driving, take exit 168 and follow the signs for Barcelona, Gran Via and Centre Ciutat.

TRIP HIGHLIGHT

🔟 Barcelona

Barcelona is a guidebook in itself and a cultural colossus to rival Paris or Rome, let alone Madrid.

Take our 'stretch your legs' walk (p238) to bag some of its many highlights. The city's ever-evolving symbol is Gaudí's one-of-a-kind **Sagrada Familia** (📞93 207 30 31; www.sagradafamilia. cat; Carrer de Mallorca 401; adult/child under 11yr/senior & student €14.80/free/12.80; 🕘9am-8pm Apr-Sep, to 6pm Oct-Mar; Ⓜ Sagrada Família), which rises like an unfinished symphony over L'Eixample district. The surrounding grid is well known for the whimsical waves of Modernisme architecture, a style expounded most eleoquently in **La Pedrera** (Casa Milà; 📞90 220 21 38; www.lapedrera. com; Carrer de Provença 261-265; adult/student/child €20.50/16.50/10.25; 🕘9am-8pm Mar-Oct, to 6.30pm

LEGACY OF THE ROMANS

What did the Romans ever do for us? Well, quite a lot actually, an assertion that rapidly gains validity as you drive northeast up the Mediterranean coast of Spain.

The Roman colonies in Hispania (their name for the Iberian peninsula) lasted from around 400BC to 200BC and reminders of their existence are spread all along the coast from Andalucía up to Catalonia. The three main stops for Romaphiles are Málaga, Cartagena and Tarragona, all once flourishing Roman cities whose pasts equal or outweigh their present profiles in modern Spain. Málaga's **Roman amphitheatre** (📞951 50 11 15; Calle Alcazabilla 8), nestled beneath its Alcazaba, was rediscovered in 1951 and dates from the 1st century AD when the settlement was called Malaca. An adjacent interpretive centre has touch screens and displays artefacts dug up from the site. Cartagena (Carthago Nova to the Romans) has multiple Roman sights including villas, a theatre and parts of an old wall. The history is all pulled together at the new-ish Museo del Teatro Romano (p252), where you can buy a museum pass for all the sights. Tarragona (Tarraco) was once capital of Rome's Spanish provinces and has ruins to prove it, including an amphitheatre, a forum, street foundations and the **Aqüeducte Romà** (Pont del Diable; admission free; 🕘9am-dusk), a glorious two-tiered aqueduct. Wonderful ocean-themed mosaics can be seen in the nearby **Museu Nacional Arqueològic de Tarragona** (www.mnat.cat; Plaça del Rei 5; adult/child €2.40/free; 🕘9.30am-6pm Tue-Sat, 10am-2pm Sun).

LOCAL KNOWLEDGE: FESTIVALS

If you're undertaking this trip in February, March or August, look out for the following festivals.

Feria de Malaga (⊙mid-Aug) Málaga's nine-day *feria* (fair), launched by a huge fireworks display, is the most ebullient of Andalucía's summer *ferias*. It resembles a mad Rio-style street party with plenty of flamenco and *fino* (sherry); head for the city centre to be in the thick of it. At night, festivities switch to large fairgrounds and nightly rock and flamenco shows at Cortijo de Torres, 3km southwest of the city centre; special buses run from all over the city.

Las Fallas de San José (www.fallas.es; ⊙March) The exuberant, anarchic swirl of Las Fallas de San José – fireworks, music, festive bonfires and all-night partying – is a must if you're visiting the city of Valencia in mid-March. The *fallas* themselves are huge sculptures of papier mâché on wood built by teams of local artists. Each neighbourhood sponsors its own *falla*.

Sitges Carnaval (www.sitges.com/carnaval) Carnaval in Sitges is a week-long booze-soaked riot made just for the extroverted and exhibitionist, complete with masked balls and capped by extravagant gay parades held on the Sunday and the Tuesday night, featuring flamboyantly dressed drag queens, giant sound systems and a wild all-night party with bars staying open until dawn. Held in February/March; dates change from year to year.

Nov-Feb; Ⓜ Diagonal) with its rooftop chimney pots and statues of medieval knights. History lurks in the Barri Gòtic, home to **La Catedral** (☎93 342 82 62; www.catedralbcn.org; Plaça de la Seu; admission free, special visit €6, choir admission €2.80; ⊙8am-12.45pm & 5.15-7.30pm Mon-Sat, special visit 1-5pm Mon-Sat, 2-5pm Sun & holidays; Ⓜ Jaume I), while the modern hip crowd congregate in the Born, a subneighbourhood of La Ribera quarter.

A good orientation point in this complex city is the legendary (and much copied) **La Rambla** (Ⓜ Catalunya, Liceu or Drassanes), a tree-lined pedestrian promenade which was made with the evening *paseo* (stroll) in mind. La Rambla divides the Barri Gòtic and La Ribera from El Raval. To the northeast lies the Modernisme-inspired L'Eixample quarter; to the south are the steep parks and gardens of Montjuïc, site of the 1992 Olympics.

✖ 🛏 p259

Eating & Sleeping

Málaga ❶

✖ El Mesón de
Cervantes   Tapas, Argentinian €€

(☏952 21 62 74; www.elmesondecervantes.com; Calle Álamos 11; mains €13-16; ⏱7pm-midnight Wed-Mon) Cervantes started as a humble tapas bar run by expat Argentinian Gabriel Spatz (the original bar is still operating around the corner), but has expanded into plush spacious digs with an open kitchen, fantastic family-style service and incredible meat dishes.

🛏 Molina Lario   Hotel €€

(☏952 06 20 02; www.hotelmolinalario.com; Calle Molina Lario 20-22; r €116-130; ❄🔊≋) Perfect for romancing couples, this hotel has a sophisticated contemporary feel with spacious rooms decorated in a cool palette of earthy colours. There are crisp white linens, marshmallow-soft pillows and tasteful paintings, plus a fabulous rooftop terrace and pool with views to the sea. Situated within confessional distance of the cathedral.

Almería ❸

✖ Casa Puga   Tapas €

(www.barcasapuga.es; Calle Jovellanos 7; wine & tapa €2.80; ⏱noon-4pm & 8pm-midnight Mon-Sat, closed Wed evening) The undisputed tapas champ (since it opened in 1870) is Casa Puga; make it an early stop, as it fills up fast. Shelves of ancient wine bottles, and walls plastered with everything from lottery tickets to ancient maps, are the backdrop for a tiny cooking station that churns out saucers of tasty stews and griddled meats, fish, mushrooms and shrimps.

Mojácar ❺

🛏 Hostal El Olívar   Hostal €

(☏950 47 20 02; www.hostalelolivar.es; Calle Estación Nueva 11, Mojácar Pueblo; s/d incl breakfast €38/59; ❄@🔊) A stylish and welcoming addition to the Mojácar Pueblo options, the Olívar has contemporary, pretty rooms with up-to-date bathrooms and tea/coffee sets. Some overlook a plaza, others the countryside. Breakfast is generous and you can take it on a panoramic terrace, when the weather is decent.

Cartagena ❻

✖ Techos Bajos   Seafood €€

(www.techosbajos.com; Calle Joaquín Madrid; dishes €7-16; ⏱9.30am-4pm Tue-Sun, plus 7pm-midnight Fri & Sat) Locals absolutely flood this large, no-frills kind of place at lunchtime for its well-priced portions of fresh fish and seafood. You'll find it down the hill from the bus station, right opposite the fishing port.

Alicante ❼

✖ Cervecería Sento   Tapas €

(Calle Teniente Coronel Chápuli 1; tapas €2-8; ⏱10am-5pm & 8pm-midnight Mon-Sat) Superb, quality *montaditos* (little rolls) and grilled things are the reason to squeeze into this brilliant little bar. Watching the nonstop staff in action is quite an experience too. They've got a bigger branch nearby, but this has the atmosphere.

Valencia ❾

✖ Delicat   Tapas, Fusion €€

(☎963 92 33 57; Calle Conde Almodóvar 4;
mains €9-14; ⊗1-4pm & 8.30-11.30pm Tue-
Sat, 1-4pm Sun) At this particularly friendly,
intimate option (there are only nine tables, plus
the terrace in summer), Catina, up front, and
her partner, Paco, on full view in the kitchen,
offer an unbeatable-value, five-course menu
of samplers for lunch and a range of truly
innovative tapas anytime.

🛏 Caro Hotel   Hotel €€€

(☎963 05 90 00; www.carohotel.com; Calle
Almirante 14; r €143-214; P ❄ 🛜) Housed in
a sumptuous 19th-century mansion, this sits
atop some 2000 years of Valencian history, with
restoration revealing a hefty hunk of the Arab
wall, Roman column bases and Gothic arches.
Each room is furnished in soothing dark shades,
has a great king-sized bed, and varnished
cement floors. Bathrooms are tops. For that
very special occasion, reserve the 1st-floor
grand suite, once the ballroom. Savour, too, its
excellent restaurant Alma del Temple.

Tarragona ❿

✖ AQ   Catalan €€

(☎977 21 59 54; www.aq-restaurant.com;
Carrer de les Coques 7; degustation €40-50;
⊗1.30-3.30pm & 8.30-11pm Tue-Sat) This is a
bubbly designer haunt alongside the cathedral
with stark colour contrasts (black, lemon and
cream linen), slick lines and intriguing plays on
traditional cooking. One of the two degustation
menus is the way to go here, or the weekday
lunch menú for €18.

🛏 Hotel Plaça de la Font   Hotel €€

(☎977 24 61 34; www.hotelpdelafont.com; Plaça
de la Font 26; s/d €55/75; ❄ 🛜) Comfortable
modern rooms, with photos of Tarragona
monuments above the bed, overlook a bustling
terrace in a you-can't-get-more-central-than-
this location, right on the popular Plaça de
la Font. The ones at the front are pretty well
soundproofed and have tiny balconies for
people-watching.

Barcelona ⓬

✖ Quimet i Quimet   Tapas €€

(☎93 442 31 42; Carrer del Poeta Cabanyes 25;
tapas €4-11; ⊗noon-4pm & 7-10.30pm Mon-Fri,
noon-4pm Sat & Sun; Ⓜ Paral·lel) Quimet i
Quimet is a family-run business that has been
passed down from generation to generation.
There's barely space to swing a *calamar* (squid)
in this bottle-lined, standing-room-only place,
but it is a treat for the palate, with *montaditos*
made to order. Let the folk behind the bar advise
you, and order a drop of fine wine to accompany
the food.

✖ Tapas 24   Tapas €€

(☎93 488 09 77; www.carlesabellan.com; Carrer
de la Diputació 269; tapas €4-9; ⊗9am-midnight
Mon-Sat; Ⓜ Passeig de Gràcia) Carles Abellan,
master of Comerç 24 in La Ribera, runs this
basement tapas haven known for its gourmet
versions of old faves. Specials include the *bikini*
(toasted ham and cheese sandwich – here
the ham is cured and the truffle makes all the
difference) and a thick black *arròs negre de sípia*
(squid-ink black rice).

🛏 Five Rooms   Boutique Hotel €€

(☎93 342 78 80; www.thefiverooms.com; Carrer
de Pau Claris 72; s/d from €155/165; ❄ @ 🛜;
Ⓜ Urquinaona) Like they say, there are five
rooms (standard rooms and suites) in this
1st-floor flat virtually on the border between
L'Eixample and the old centre of town. Each
is different and features include broad, firm
beds, stretches of exposed brick wall, mosaic
tiles and minimalist decor. There are also two
apartments.

🛏 DO   Boutique Hotel €€€

(☎93 481 36 66; www.hoteldoreial.com;
Plaça Reial 1; s/d from €230/280; ❄ 🛜 🛏;
Ⓜ Liceu) Overlooking the magnificent plaza for
which it is named, this 18-room property has
handsomely designed rooms, set with beamed
ceilings, wide plank floors and all-important
soundproofing. The service is excellent, and the
facilities extensive, with roof terrace (with bar
in summer), dipping pool, solarium and spa. Its
excellent market-to-table restaurants draw in
visiting foodies.

Málaga Check out the city's
increasingly sophisticated foodie scene

Classic Trip

Costa del Sol Beyond the Beaches

21

This coast-hugging trip travels via a sparkling tiara of holiday resorts, as well as some little known gems and a diamond of a capital: Málaga.

TRIP HIGHLIGHTS

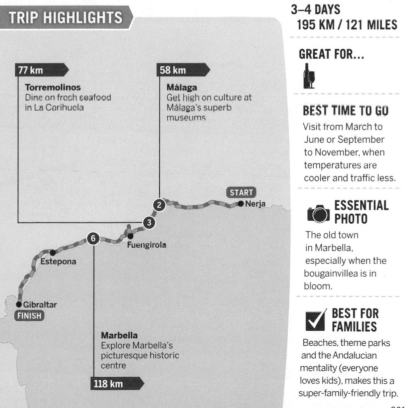

77 km
Torremolinos
Dine on fresh seafood in La Carihuela

58 km
Málaga
Get high on culture at Málaga's superb museums

2

3

6

START
● Nerja

Fuengirola

● Estepona

● Gibraltar
FINISH

Marbella
Explore Marbella's picturesque historic centre

118 km

3–4 DAYS
195 KM / 121 MILES

GREAT FOR...

BEST TIME TO GO
Visit from March to June or September to November, when temperatures are cooler and traffic less.

ESSENTIAL PHOTO
The old town in Marbella, especially when the bougainvillea is in bloom.

BEST FOR FAMILIES
Beaches, theme parks and the Andalucian mentality (everyone loves kids), makes this a super-family-friendly trip.

Classic Trip

Costa del Sol Beyond the Beaches

21

This drive, running from Nerja in the east to Gibraltar in the west, travels via a landscape that constantly shifts and changes: from orchards of subtropical fruit trees to shimmering white urbanisations; a culture-loving metropolis to the cobbled backstreets of a former fishing village. Be prepared for a journey that constantly challenges any preconceived ideas you may have about this, Spain's most famous, tourist-driven coast.

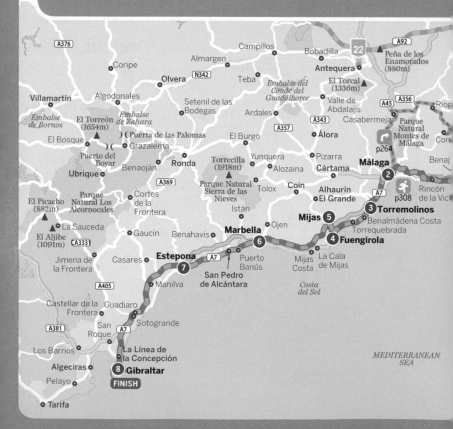

❶ Nerja

In a charmed spot sitting at the base of the Sierra Almijara peaks, this former fishing village has retained its low-rise village charm, despite the proliferation of souvenir shops and day trippers. At its heart is the Balcón de Europa, one of the most beautiful promenades on the Costa del Sol, built on the site of a Moorish castle. Grab a coffee at one of the terraced cafes before heading north of town to visit the extraordinary

DETOUR: FRIGILIANA

Start: ❶ Nerja

After the cavernous gloom of the Cueva de Nerja, consider heading inland to Frigiliana, a *pueblos blanco* voted as the prettiest in Andalucía by the Spanish tourism authority. It's well signposted: take the M5105 inland from Nerja, passing groves of mango and avocado trees and follow signs to the *casco historico* and car park. Frigiliana is famed for its sweet local wine and honey, which you can buy at small village shops. It is an enchanting place with a tangible Moroccan feel; read the plaques around town to learn why – the village stretches back to the time of the Moors.

Cueva de Nerja (www.cuevadenerja.es; adult/child €9/5; ⏰ unguided visit 10am-1pm & 4-5.30pm Sep-Jun, 10am-6pm Jul & Aug; guided visit 1-2pm & 5.30-6.30pm Sep-Jun, 11am-noon & 6.30-7.30pm Jul & Aug), dating back a cool five million years: it's a 4km long theatrical wonderland of extraordinary rock formations, subtle shifting colours and stalactites and stalagmites.

🍴 p269

The Drive » Consider taking the slightly slower, but more scenic, N340 to Rincón de la Victoria, then pick up the A7-E15 bypass to Málaga. This meandering coastal road passes through pretty agricultural land. Look for the centuries-old watchtowers from the days of Barbarian invaders. It's a total drive of 58km (1¼ hours).

TRIP HIGHLIGHT

❷ Málaga

Book a one- or two-night stay here to experience the city's buzzing bar life

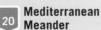

LINK YOUR TRIP

20 Mediterranean Meander

Málaga is the start of this east-coast ramble that takes in several of the most stunning cities in Spain, including its final destination: Barcelona.

22 Golden Triangle

Nerja is a speedy hour's drive from Granada, with its magnificent Alhambra; this winning drive also takes in Seville and Córdoba, two of the other great cities of Spain.

ANDALUCÍA & SOUTHERN SPAIN 21 COSTA DEL SOL BEYOND THE BEACHES

and increasingly sophisticated foodie scene. Málaga has also emerged as a serious cultural capital, with some 30 museums, including the **Museo Carmen Thyssen** (www.carmenthyssenmalaga.org; Calle Compañía 10; admission €4.50, incl temporary exhibition €9; 10am-7.30pm Tue-Sun), the **Museo Ruso** (951 92 61 50; www.coleccionmuseoruso.es; Avenida de Sor Teresa Plat 15; adult/child €8/free; 11am-10pm Tue-Sun; P), and the **Museo del Vidrio y Cristal** (Museum of Glass & Crystal; 952 22 02 71; www.museovidrioycristalmalaga.com; Plazuela Santísimo Cristo de la Sangre 2; admission €5; 11am-7pm Tue-Sun), a private collection that concentrates on glass and

crystal. Climb the tower for fabulous views from the landmark 16th-century **Catedral de Málaga** (952 21 59 17; Calle Molina Lario; cathedral & museum €5, tower €6; 10am-6pm Mon-Sat), then duck inside to admire the gorgeous retables and stash of 18th-century religious art. Travel further back in time by visiting the **Alcazaba** (Calle Alcazabilla; admission €2.20, incl Castillo de Gibralfaro €3.40; 9.30am-8pm Tue-Sun), a fascinating 11th-century Moorish palace-fortress. Across from the entrance – and **Roman Amphitheatre** (951 50 11 15; Calle Alcazabilla 8) – **Batik** (952 22 10 45; www.batikmalaga.com; Calle Alcazabilla 12; mains €12-20; 10am-midnight;) is an atmospheric place for a drink and innovative bite to eat. To see more of Málaga's sights, check

out our walking tour on p308.

p269

The Drive » Leaving Málaga, take the A7 in the direction of Algeciras, Torremolinos and Cádiz, then follow the MA20 signposted to Torremolinos. This is a busy stretch of *autovia* (highway) that passes the airport. It's a drive of 18.5km or 25 minutes.

TRIP HIGHLIGHT

❸ Torremolinos

Start your exploration in the centre of town with a meander down pedestrian **Calle San Miguel**, lined with shops, cafes and bars. Continue as the street winds down to steps which lead to Playamar, the main beach. Turn right for one of the most delightful walks on the Costa, round the rocky headland to **La Carihuela**; the former

---

↱ DETOUR: COMARÉS

Start: ❷ Málaga

Heading inland, northeast of Málaga, brings you to La Axarquía, a stunning rugged region, great for hiking, and stippled with pretty unspoiled *pueblos* (villages). A highlight of the area is, quite literally, Comarés which sits like a snowdrift upon a lofty mountain (739m) commanding spectacular views of the surrounding mountain range and coast. Wander the tangle of narrow lanes and don't miss the remarkable summit cemetery. There are also several walking trails that start from here; stop by the small *ayuntamiento* (town hall) on Plaza de la Axarquía for more information and maps. The village is home to several bars and a couple of restaurants, as well as a small supermarket for self-caterers. Get here via the A45 *autovia* (highway), direction Granada, Córdoba and Seville, take the Casabermeja exit and follow signs to Comarés via the A356 (through Riogordo) and the MA159. The journey totals 55km and should take you roughly one hour.

fishing *barrio* (neighbourhood) which is now, fittingly, home to some superb seafood restaurants such as **Casa Juan** (www.losmellizos.net; Calle San Ginés 20, La Carihuela; mains €13-20). This *paseo* (walk) continues to the **Puerto Deportivo de Benalmádena** (Benalmádena; [P]), striking for its Gaudí-cum-Asian-cum-Mr Whippy–style architecture, and large choice of bars, restaurants and shops overlooking the boats (one of which reputedly belongs to actor celeb and native *malagueño* Antonio Banderes).

✕ p269

The Drive » Continue on the N340, which hugs the coast and passes through the busy coastal resort of Benalmádena Costa. Note that there is a 50km speed limit on this scenic stretch.

- - - - - - - - - - - -

❹ Fuengirola

The appeal of Fuengirola lies in the fact that it is a genuine Spanish working town, as well as a popular resort. There is a large foreign resident population here as well, many of whom arrived here in the '60s and stayed after their ponytails went grey. Grab a (bar) chair in pretty flower-festooned Plaza de la Constitucíon, which is overlooked by the baroque facade of the church, then explore the surrounding narrow pedestrian streets flanked

TOP TIP: TOLL ROAD AP7

If you are travelling in July and August, consider taking the AP7 toll road, at least between Fuengirola and Marbella as the A7 can become dangerously congested. This particular A7 stretch (formerly part of the N340) used to be notorious for accidents; however, the situation has improved since the introduction of a 80km/h speed limit in former trouble spots.

by idiosyncratic small shops and tapas bars. The excellent **Bioparc** ([☎]952 66 63 01; www.bioparcfuengirola.es; Avenida Camilo José Cela; adult/child €18/13; ⏰10am-sunset; [P]), northwest of here, is the Costa's best zoo and treats its animals very well, with no cages or bars, but, rather, spacious enclosures and conservation and breeding programs.

✕ p269

The Drive » From Fuengirola's central Renfe train station, take Avenida Alcalde Clemente Díaz Ruiz inland. Cross the *autovía* A7 and continue on the Carretera de Mijas. In Mijas follow signs to the underground carpark (€1 for 24 hours). This 7km journey should take around 10 minutes.

- - - - - - - - - - - -

❺ Mijas

The *pueblo blanco* (white village) of Mijas has retained its sugar-cube cuteness despite being on the coach-tour circuit. Art buffs should check out the **Centro de Arte Contemporáneo de Mijas** (CAC; www.cacmijas.info; Calle Málaga 28;

admission €3; ⏰10am-7pm Tue-Sun) contemporary art museum, with its second-largest collection of Picasso ceramics in the world. Otherwise this village is all about strolling the narrow cobbled streets, dipping into the tapas bars and shopping for souvenirs. Be sure to walk up to the **Plaza de Toros** (museum €3; ⏰10am-8pm); an unusual square-shaped bullring at the top of the village, surrounded by lush ornamental gardens with spectacular views of the coast. Mijas also has a large foreign resident population and a vigorous calendar of events, including live flamenco shows in the main plaza every Wednesday at noon, an annual blues festival in July and regular concerts in the auditorium.

The Drive » Return to the A7 *autovía*. This double carriageway passes through the most densely built span of the entire Costa, with urbanisations such as Calahonda and Miraflores that date from the 1980s,

WHY THIS IS A CLASSIC TRIP
JOSEPHINE QUINTERO, AUTHOR

My home for two decades, the Costa del Sol is changing all the time and definitely for the better. Whatever you already know about this coast, one fact is for sure – it is extraordinary: both crazily diverse and supremely entertaining. In other words, I have ensured there's never a dull moment on this classic drive – and there shouldn't be dull weather either – it's called 'the sunshine coast' for good reason.

Top: Gibraltar ape perched high above the town
Left: Resort life in Marbella
Right: Estepona's pretty balconied houses

HOLGER LEUE / LOOK-FOTO / GETTY IMAGES ©

KEN WELSH / ALAMY ©

when the Costa was at its peak of popularity and expansion. Continue west along here until you reach the exit for Marbella; a total drive of 33km or 25 minutes.

- - - - - - - - - - - - - - -

TRIP HIGHLIGHT

⑥ Marbella

Marbella is the Costa del Sol's classiest 'rich and famous' resort and is a good choice for an overnight stop. This town has a magnificent natural setting, sheltered by the beautiful Sierra Blanca mountains, as well as a gorgeous old town with pristine white houses, narrow traffic-free streets and geranium-filled balconies. At its heart is picturesque **Plaza de los Naranjos**, dating back to 1485 with tropical plants, palms and orange trees. From here walk to the coastal promenade via the lush **Parque de la Alameda** gardens with its fountains and tiled seats. Next consider a gentle stroll east along the seafront towards the luxurious marina of Puerto Banús, past the five-star resorts of the Marbella Club and Puente Romano, the latter named after the still-standing Roman bridge, once part of the Via Augustus linking Càdiz to Rome. It's 6km in total to the port if you decide to stride out all the way.

✕ 🛏 p269

Classic Trip

The Drive » Continue due west on the A7 *autovía*, signposted to Algeciras and Cádiz. This stretch of highway is less built up and passes by San Pedro de la Alcántera, as well as five golf courses (they don't nickname this the Costa del Golf for nothing!). It's a snappy 20 minutes or just 24km to your next stop: Estepona.

❼ Estepona

This is the Costa del Sol resort which is most intrinsically Spanish, with a charming historic centre of narrow cobbled streets flanked by simple *pueblo* houses decorated by well-tended pots of geraniums. Make a beeline for the historic Plaza de las Flores square with its fountain centrepoint, orange trees and handy tourist office, where you can stop for a town map. Highlights here include the fabulous **Orchidarium** (www.orchidariumestepona.es; Calle Terraza 86; ⏰11am-2pm & 5-9pm Tue-Thu & Sun, to 11pm Fri & Sat), with the largest orchid collection in Europe, some 1500 species, plus subtropical plants, flowers and trees. A meandering path takes you through the exhibition space and past a dramatic 17m-high waterfall. Estepona's **Puerto Deportivo** is excellent for water sports, as well as bars and restaurants.

❌ p269

The Drive » For the final leg consider taking the AP7 toll road for the first 20km (12 minutes, €3.50) as the N340 coastal stretch here is very slow, with numerous roundabouts. At Guadiaro the AP7 merges with the A7 for the rest of the 34km journey. Consider a refreshment stop at swanky Sotogrande harbour; Sotogorande is also home to Spain's leading golf course, the Real Club Valderrama.

❽ Gibraltar

Red pillar boxes, fish-and-chips shops, bobbies on the beat and creaky seaside hotels. Stuck strategically at the jaws of Europe and Africa, Gibraltar's Palladian architecture and camera-hogging Barbary apes create an interesting contrast and finale to your journey. Highlights on 'the Rock' include the **Upper Rock Nature Reserve** (adult/child incl attractions £10/5, vehicle £2, pedestrian excl attractions £0.50; ⏰9am-6.15pm, last entry 5.45pm), one of the most dramatic landforms in southern Europe. Entry tickets include admission to the extraordinary **St Michael's Cave** (St Michael's Rd; ⏰9am-5.45pm, to 6.15pm Apr-Oct), the Apes' Den, the **Great Siege Tunnels** (⏰9.30am-6.15pm), the Moorish castle, the Military Heritage Centre, and the 100-tonne gun. The Rock's most famous inhabitants, however, are the tailless Barbary macaques. Some of the 200 apes hang around the top cable-car station while others are found at the Apes' Den. Most Gibraltar soujourns start in Grand Casemates Sq, a jolly place surrounded by bars and restaurants, but with a grim history as the site of public executions. Learn more about the Rock's history at the fine **Gibraltar Museum** (www.gibmuseum.gi; 18-20 Bomb House Lane; adult/child £2/1; ⏰10am-6pm Mon-Fri, to 2pm Sat); don't miss the well-preserved Muslim bathhouse and an intricately painted 7th-century-BC Egyptian mummy that washed up here in the late 1800s.

Eating & Sleeping

Nerja ❶

✕ Oliva   Modern European €€€

(☎952 52 29 88; www.restauranteoliva.com; Calle Pintada 7; mains €19-23; ☻1-4pm & 7-11pm) Impeccable service, single orchids, a drum-and-bass soundtrack and a charcoal-grey-and-green colour scheme; in short, this place has class. The menu is reassuringly brief and changes regularly according to what's in season. The inventive dishes combine unlikely ingredients such as pistachio falafel and mango panna cotta with black-olive caramel. Reservations recommended.

Málaga ❷

✕ Uvedoble Taberna   Tapas €

(www.uvedobletaberna.com; Calle Císter 15; tapas €2.70; ☻12.30-4pm & 8pm-midnight Mon-Sat; ☎) There's not much elbow room at this slick contemporary place, but this local tapas hotspot is planning to expand to meet the demand for their famously popular seafood-based tapas such as *fideos negro tostada con calamaritos* (toasted black noodles with baby squid), and grilled octopus with potatoes and chives.

⛱ El Hotel del Pintor Boutique Hotel €€

(☎952 06 09 81; www.hoteldelpintor.com; Calle Álamos 27; s/d €59/70; ✳@☎) The red, black and white colour scheme of this friendly, small hotel echoes the abstract artwork of *malagueño* artist Pepe Bornov, whose paintings are on permanent display throughout the public areas and rooms. Although convenient for most of the city's main sights, pack your earplugs, as the rooms in the front can be noisy, especially on a Saturday night.

Torremolinos ❸

✕ El Cordobes   Andalucian €€

(Playamar; mains €12-15; ☻) The best of the beachside *chiringuitos* (seafront restaurants), attracting a loyal Spanish clientele. Specialities include a delicious *salmorejo* (thick garlicky gazpacho), barbecued sardines, and *almejas* (clams) in a spicy paprika-based sauce. The terrace fronts onto the sand.

Fuengirola ❹

✕ La Cepa   Seafood €

(Plaza Yate 21; tapas €3, mains €7-10; ☻noon-4pm & 7-11pm Mon-Sat, to 3.30pm Sun) Hidden away on an attractive bar-and-restaurant-lined square, the menu concentrates on seafood, including such tentacle ticklers as fried squid, and prawns wrapped in bacon.

Marbella ❺

✕ El Estrecho   Tapas €

(Calle San Lázaro; tapas €2.50-3.50; ☻noon-midnight) It's always crammed, so elbow your way to a space in the small back dining room and order from a massive menu that includes tapas such as *salmorejo* (gazpacho) and seafood salad.

⛱ Hotel San Cristóbal   Hotel €€

(☎952 86 20 44; www.hotelsancristobal.com; Avenida Ramñon y Cajal 3; s/d incl breakfast €60/85; ☎) Dating back to the '60s, this solid midrange hotel has recently revamped rooms sporting tasteful pale-grey and cream decor contrasting with smart navy fabrics. Most rooms have balconies and a pool is being planned.

Estepona ❻

✕ La Esquina del Arte   Tapas €

(Calle Villa; tapas €2-3; ☻noon-midnight Mon-Sat; ☎) This place may be in the middle of the historic centre but there is nothing old fashioned about the creative tapas and *pintxos* (Basque tapas) here. Expect tasty bites such as prawns wrapped in flaky pastry, pâté with fig jam and peppers stuffed with salt cod. It has excellent wines by the glass.

Seville *Enjoy tapas and flamenco in this vibrant city*

Golden Triangle

22

This drive captures all of Andalucía's big-hitter sights in one succinct triangle, including a Gothic cathedral, a Moorish mosque, an illustrious Alhambra, and plenty of opportunities to sample tapas and flamenco.

TRIP HIGHLIGHTS

140 km

Córdoba's Mezquita
1000 years of history in this magnificent mosque turned church

214 km

Zuheros
White town overlooking Subbéticas Natural Park

START/FINISH
1

Écija

4

5

Osuna

6

Antequera

Seville's Alcázar
Seville's glorious mudéjar palace rivals the Alhambra for opulence

1 km

The Alhambra
The glittering highpoint of architectural design in medieval Europe

314 km

5–7 DAYS
576 KM / 358 MILES

GREAT FOR...

BEST TIME TO GO

April to June is good for spring festivals; plus September and October to avoid the heat of summer.

ESSENTIAL PHOTO

The Alhambra with the Sierra Nevada in the background.

BEST FOR TAPAS

Seville has the best stash of creative tapas bars in Andalucía.

22 | Golden Triangle

The three cities of Seville, Córdoba and Granada have taken it in turns to direct cultural and political life in Andalucía over the last 1000 years, and between them guard a truly golden legacy. This triangular drive links all three cities and their stories, but also enables you to see snippets of small-town beauty and quiet rural life in between.

TRIP HIGHLIGHT

① Seville

'He who has not at Seville been, has not, I trow, a wonder seen,' goes an old Arab proverb. Shaped by half a dozen civilisations and reborn in numerous incarnations since its founding over 2000 years ago, Seville has never lost its capacity to amaze. Drenched for most of the year in spirit-enriching sunlight, this is a city of feelings as much as sights, with different

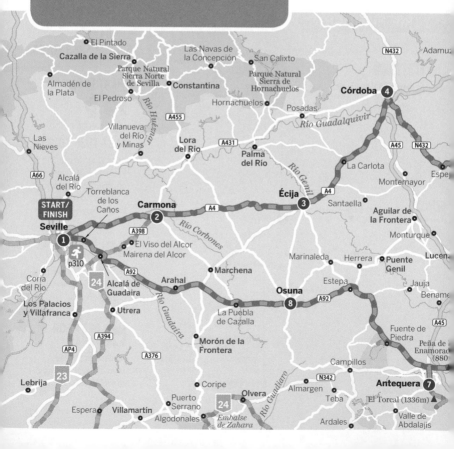

seasons prompting vastly contrasting moods.

Take our walking tour (p310) to see the main sights, including obligatory visits to the Alcázar and Catedral, handily located opposite each other in the city centre. You also shouldn't leave Seville without seeing at least one flamenco show and tasting as many creative (and traditional) tapas as time allows. Those on a slower itinerary might want to visit the old Jewish quarter of **Santa Cruz** and the former Roma quarter of **Triana**. Overnighters should take their marks at the starting point of Seville's best nightlife, the **Alameda de Hércules**.

 p278

The Drive » Leave Seville on the A4 (also known as the E5) heading northeast. Pass Seville airport on your right and follow signs towards Carmona on a four-lane carriageway. Take the first exit for Carmona after 33km.

- - - - - - - - - - - - -

❷ Carmona

Sitting atop a diminutive ridge overlooking the arid yet beautifully pastoral farmland of western Andalucía, Carmona is like a mini-Seville that never grew up. The easily walkable town centre is sprinkled with Roman remains, stately palaces and a church with a smaller version of Seville's Giralda. An interesting background to the town can be explored at the Museo de la Ciudad; see p294 for more.

Carmona's luxuriously equipped **parador** (954 14 10 10; www.parador. es; Calle Alcázar; r €188; P❋@☎☲) feels even more luxurious for the ruined Alcázar in its grounds. The beautiful **dining room** (menú del día €33) overlooks a jaw-dropping (and unexpected) view of the surrounding Vega roasting under the Sevillan sun.

 p278

LINK YOUR TRIP

23 The Great Outdoors

This vastly different rural take on Andalucía intersects with the Golden Triangle at either Antequera or Osuna.

24 Andalucía's White Villages

After finishing this trip in Seville, retrace the 35km to Carmona and hop onto this spectacular mountain drive around Cádiz and Málaga provinces.

The Drive » Get back on the A4 (E5) and follow it 53km due east to Écija. The agricultural landscapes around the Genil and Guadalquivir river valleys act as a heat-trap in summer earning Écija its nickname, '*El sartén de Andalucía*' (the frying pan of Andalucía).

---

❸ Écija

A city of baroque church towers, suffocating summer heat, and an unpronounceable name if you're a non-Spanish speaker, Écija (*eth*-ee-ha) is a hardworking Andalucian settlement where tourism is an afterthought and the history can be peeled off in layers, starting with the Romans. Archaeological treasures lie like discarded jewels all over (and under) the city centre, barely seen by the bulk of Andalucía's 7.5 million annual visitors.

Écija's spire-studded townscape hints at a prosperous past. One of the finest towers belongs to the **Iglesia de Santa María** (Plaza de Santa María; ◷9.30am-1.30pm & 5-8.30pm Mon-Sat, 9.30am-1.30pm Sun), just off Plaza de España.

The 18th-century Palacio de Benamejí puts things into historical context at the **Museo Histórico Municipal** (☏954 83 04 31; http://museo.ecija.es; Plaza de la Constitución 1; ◷10am-2pm Tue-Sun Jun-Sep, 10am-1.30pm & 4.30-6.30pm Tue-Sat, 10am-3pm Sun Oct-May).

Pride of place goes to the best Roman finds from the area, including a sculpture of an Amazon (legendary female warrior).

The Drive » Return to the A4 (E5) *autovía* (highway) and follow it for 55km in a northeasterly direction to the city of Córdoba. It's best to find parking on the south side of the Río Guadalquivir and walk across the Roman bridge into Córdoba's centre.

TRIP HIGHLIGHT

❹ Córdoba

Córdoba has easier road access than other Andalucian cities, although its labyrinthine centre is best explored on foot, by diving into old wine bars, and feeling millennia of history at every turn. Its centrepiece is the gigantic **Mezquita** (Mosque; ☏957 47 05 12; www.catedraldecordoba.es; Calle Cardenal Herrero; adult/child €8/4, 8.30-9.30am Mon-Sat free; ◷8.30-9.30am & 10am-7pm Mon-Sat, 8.30-11.30am & 3-7pm Sun Mar-Oct, to 6pm daily Nov-Feb), an architectural anomaly and one of the only places in the world where you can worship Mass in a mosque. Surrounding it is an intricate web of winding streets, geranium-sprouting flower boxes and cool intimate patios that are at their most beguiling in late spring.

The narrow streets of the old Judería (Jewish quarter) and Muslim quarter stretch out from the great mosque like capillaries, some clogged with tourist bric-a-brac, others delightfully peaceful.

✗ ➤ p278

The Drive » Leave Córdoba from the south on the N432, the main road to Granada. Soon after bypassing the town of Baena, branch west onto the A318 (Autovía del Olivar). Zuheros will appear as a white splash on the crags to the south. To reach it, fork south after 4km onto the CP85, which winds up to the town. Total distance from Córdoba is 77km.

TRIP HIGHLIGHT

❺ Zuheros

Rising above the low-lying *campiña* (country-side) south of the A318, Zuheros sits in a dramatic location, crouching in the lee of a craggy mountain. It's approached via a steep road through a series of hairpin bends and provides a beautiful base for exploring the northern portion of the Parque Natural Sierras Subbéticas. Zuheros is also renowned for its local organic cheeses.

The town has a delightfully relaxed atmosphere. All around the western escarpment on which it perches are miradors (lookouts) with exhilarating views of the dramatic limestone crags that tower over the village and create such a powerful backdrop for Zuheros' **castle** (Plaza de la Paz; admission or tours €2; ⊙10am-2pm & 5-7pm Tue-Fri, tours 11am, 12.30pm, 2pm, 5.30pm & 6.30pm Sat, Sun & holidays, all afternoon times 1hr earlier Oct-Mar). Admission to the castle is included when you buy a ticket for the **Museo Arqueológico** (📞957 69 45 45; Plaza de la Paz), located opposite.

✖ p278

The Drive » Retrace your tyre tracks via the CP85 and A318 back to the arterial N432 and head 100km in a southeasterly direction towards the looming Sierra Nevada and the city of Granada nestled beneath them.

TRIP HIGHLIGHT

❻ Granada

The last citadel of the Moors in Europe is a tempestuous place where Andalucía's complex history is laid out in ornate detail. The starting point for 99% of visitors is the **Alhambra** (📞902 44 12 21; www.alhambra-tickets. es; adult/under 12yr €14/free,

Generalife only €7; ⊙8.30am-8pm 15 Mar-14 Oct, to 6pm 15 Oct-14 Mar, night visits 10-11.30pm Tue-Sat Mar-Oct, 8-9.30pm Fri & Sat Oct-Mar), the Nasrid emirs' enduring gift to architecture, a building whose eerie beauty is better seen than described. Below it nestles a city where brilliance and shabbiness sit side by side in bohemian bars, shadowy *teterías* (teahouses), winding lanes studded with stately *cármenes* (large mansions with walled gardens), and backstreets splattered with street art.

If this is your first Granada trip, prioritise visiting the Alhambra. If ever a monument lived up to the hype, this is it. It's possible (and advisable) to buy Alhambra tickets beforehand. They're available up to three months in advance online or by phone from

Alhambra Advance Booking (☑902 88 80 01, for international calls +34 958 92 60 31; www.alhambra-tickets. es). All advance tickets incur a 13% surcharge, meaning most visitors end up paying €15.40 for a standard entry ticket. Equally haunting is the **Albayzin** (old Moorish quarter), where getting lost was never so attractive. Ask directions in a *tetería* and digest them over a pot of tea and a pastry. Old masters can be seen in the brilliant gold **Basilica San Juan de Dios** (Calle San Juan de Díos; admission €4; ⊙10am-1pm & 4-7pm). New masters can be found in the street art of the Realejo quarter.

✕ ⫞ p279

The Drive ≫ Head west out of Granada on the main Seville road, the A92, passing Federico Lorca International Airport. After 95km you'll cross the A45, the main north–south *autovia* between Málaga and Córdoba. A couple of kilometres further on, turn south on the A7281 to Antequera, which sits nestled beneath the rocky moonscapes of the Torcal uplands nearby.

– – – – – – – – – –

❼ Antequera

Antequera is a fascinating town, both architecturally and historically, yet has somehow managed to avoid being on the coach-tour circuit – which only serves to add to its charms. The three major influences in the region, Roman, Moorish and Spanish, have left the town with a rich tapestry of architectural gems.

The substantial remains of the Alcazaba are within easy (if uphill) walking distance of the town centre; see p284 for more information. Get an audioguide inside to set the historical scene.

VÍA VERDE DE LA SUBBÉTICA

Despite being one of Andalucía's least-visited parks, the Parque Natural Sierras Subbéticas is not lacking in trails, many of which emanate from the spectacular white town of Zuheros. The park's easiest and best-marked path is the Vía Verde de la Subbéticas that runs along a disused railway converted to a cycling and walking 'greenway'. It snakes for 65km across southern Córdoba province from Camporreal near Puente Genil to the Río Guadajoz on the Jaén border, skirting the western and northern fringes of the natural park.

With gentle gradients and utilising old bridges, tunnels and viaducts, the greenway makes for a fun outing for travellers of all ages. There are cafes and bike-hire outlets in old station buildings along the route, and informative map boards – it's impossible to get lost!

Subbética Bike's Friends (☑672 605088; www.subbeticabikesfriends.com; bikes per hour/half-day/day €3.50/9.50/14.50, child seats €2; ⊙10am-6pm Sat & Sun; 🚹) at Doña Mencía station, 4km west down the hill from Zuheros, rents a range of different bikes, including children's. Call ahead for availability.

Casa de la Memoria (954 56 06 70; www.casadelamemoria.es; Calle Cuna 6; €18; ⊗shows 7.30pm & 9pm) Cultural centre that holds *duende* (spirit) evoking shows often touted as the best in Seville.

Museo del Baile Flamenco (www.museoflamenco.com; Calle Manuel Rojas Marcos 3; adult/ seniors & students €10/8; ⊗10am-7pm) Although better known as a museum, this place also holds nightly flamenco performances in a lush patio with plenty of aficionados yelling encouragement.

El Palacio Andaluz (954 53 47 20; www.elpalacioandaluz.com; Calle de María Auxiliadora; admission with drink/dinner €38/76; ⊗shows 7pm & 9.30pm) A 400-seater theatre where top performers show off their amazing skills in slickly choreographed performances.

Casa Anselma (Calle Pagés del Corro 49; ⊗midnight-late Mon-Sat) Rambunctious cheek-by-jowl bar in Triana district where raw folkloric flamenco happens most nights. Don't bother arriving before midnight.

After you've drunk in the views of the city from the hilltop, descend to some of the best tapas bars this side of Granada.

🛏 p279

The Drive » Get back onto the A92, heading northwest in the direction of Seville. The *autopista* bypasses the towns of La Roda de Andalucía and Espeta before bringing into view the small but grandiose baroque town of Osuna after 76km.

- - - - - - - - - - - - -

❽ Osuna

Osuna is a small provincial town with a legacy that far outweighs its size. Many of its riches were bequeathed by the noble dukes of Osuna who lent the

town its name. Beautifully preserved baroque heirlooms include the impressive **Monasterio de la Encarnación** (Plaza de la Encarnación; admission €2.50; ⊗10am-1.30pm & 3.30-6.30pm), a Spanish baroque monastery filled with art treasures. The brilliant ensemble shimmers like a mirage above the hot, empty *vega*, tricking you into thinking you've entered a fantasy land. No small wonder the producers of TV show *Game of Thrones* chose to film parts of their fifth series here; Osuna's **Plaza de Toros** (bullring; adult/child €2/1; ⊗10am-2pm & 4-6pm

Sat, 10am-2pm Sun) featured in a key scene.

Among the most ornate of Osuna's 18th-century mansions is the **Palacio del Marqués de La Gomera** (Calle San Pedro 20), now a hotel. It features elaborate pillars on its facade, with the family shield at the top. Inside you'll find individually styled rooms of princely proportions and quiet luxury. For more about Osuna, see p285.

✖ p279

The Drive » It's a straightforward 87km drive along the main Seville–Granada road, the A92, back to Seville heading west and then northwest through increasingly populated outlying towns.

Eating & Sleeping

Seville ❶

✖ La Brunilda   Tapas, Fusion €€

(✆954 22 04 81; Calle Galera 5; tapas €3.50-
6.50; ⊙1-4pm & 8.30-11.30pm Tue-Sat, 1-4pm
Sun) Seville's crown as Andalucía's tapas capital
is regularly attacked by well-armed rivals from
the provinces, meaning it constantly has to
reinvent itself and offer up fresh competition.
Enter La Brunilda, a newish font of fusion tapas
sandwiched into an inconspicuous backstreet in
the Arenal quarter where everything – including
the food, staff and clientele – is pretty.

✖ La Pepona   Tapas €€

(✆954 21 50 26; Javier Lasso de la Vega 1; tapas
€3.50-6.50; ⊙1.30-4.30pm & 8pm-midnight
Mon-Sat) One of the best newcomer restaurants
of 2014, La Pepona gets all the basics right,
from the bread (doorstop-sized rustic slices),
to the service (fast but discreet), to the decor
(clean Ikea lines and lots of wood). Oscar status
is achieved with the food, which falls firmly into
the nouveau tapas camp.

⌂ Hotel Amadeus   Hotel €€

(✆954 50 14 43; www.hotelamadeussevilla.
com; Calle Farnesio 6; s/d €100/114; P ❋ 🛜)
Just when you thought you couldn't find hotels
with pianos in the rooms anymore, along came
Hotel Amadeus. It's run by an engaging musical
family in the old judería (Jewish quarter) –
several of the astutely decorated rooms come
complete with soundproof walls and upright
pianos, ensuring you don't miss out on your
daily practice.

⌂ Hotel Casa 1800   Luxury Hotel €€€

(✆954 56 18 00; www.hotelcasa1800sevilla.
com; Calle Rodrigo Caro 6; r from €195; ❋ @ 🛜)
Reigning as number one in Seville's 'favourite
hotel' charts is this positively regal Santa
Cruz pile where the word casa (house) is taken
seriously. This really is your home away from
home (albeit a posh one), with charming staff
catering to your every need. Historic highlights
include a complimentary afternoon-tea buffet,
plus a quartet of penthouse garden suites with
Giralda views.

Carmona ❷

✖ Bar Goya   Tapas, Raciones €€

(Calle Prim 2; raciones €5-12; ⊙8am-11pm
Sat-Mon & Thu, 8am-3pm Tue, noon-11pm Fri;
�) From the kitchens of this ever-crammed
bar on Plaza de San Fernando comes forth a
fabulous array of tasty tapas. Apart from such
carnivores' faves as carrillada (pigs' cheeks)
and menudo (tripe), chef Isabel offers pure
vegetarian treats such as alboronía (a delicious
veg stew) and an excellent Carmona spinach
(blended with chickpeas).

Córdoba ❹

✖ Garum 2.1   Contemporary
                                  Andalucian €€

(Calle San Fernando 122; tapas €3-7, raciones
€7-17; ⊙ noon-4pm & 8pm-midnight, to 2am Fri
& Sat) Garum serves up traditional meaty, fishy
and vegie ingredients in all sorts of creative,
tasty new concoctions. We recommend the
presa ibérica con herencia del maestro (Iberian
pork with potatoes, fried eggs and ham).
Service is helpful and friendly.

⌂ Bed and Be   Hostel €

(✆661 42 07 33; www.bedandbe.com; Calle Cruz
Conde 22; dm €17-20, d with shared bathroom
€50-80; ❋ 🛜) An exceptionally good hostel
option a bit north of Plaza de las Tendillas. Staff
are clued up about what's on and what's new
in Córdoba, and they offer a social event every
evening – anything from a bike tour to a sushi
dinner. The assortment of double and dorm
rooms are all super-clean and as gleaming white
as a pueblo blanco (white town).

Zuheros ❺

✖ Restaurante Zuhayra   Andalucian €€

(www.zercahoteles.com; Calle Mirador 10;
medias-raciones €3.50-7.50, raciones €6-14;
⊙1-4pm & 8-10.30pm; 🚶) The restaurant of
Hotel Zuhayra prepares excellent versions of
local and Andalucian favourites, such as its

homemade partridge pâté or lamb chops with thyme. There are good vegetarian options too; try the *ensalada Zuhayra* with baked vegetables, cress, almonds and caramelised local cheese.

Aside from the high standard of cleaning, bonuses include an afternoon bottle of water delivered to your room and a sleek downstairs bar-restaurant called Vitola Gastrobar – ideal for breakfast or tapas.

Granada ⑥

✗ Carmela Restaurante   Tapas, Andalucian €€

(📞958 22 57 94; www.restaurantecarmela. com; Calle Colcha 13; tapas €5-10; ⊙12.30pm-midnight) Long a bastion of traditional tapas, Granada has taken a leaf out of Seville's book and come up with something a little more out-of-the-box at this new streamlined restaurant, guarded by the statue of Jewish philosopher Yehuba ibn Tibon at the jaws of the Realejo quarter. The best of Carmela's creative offerings is the made-to-order tortilla and cured-ham croquettes the size of tennis balls.

⌸ Casa Morisca Hotel   Historic Hotel €€€

(📞958 22 11 00; www.hotelcasamorisca. com; Cuesta de la Victoria 9; d/ste €167/220; ❄@🛜) You can recline like a Nasrid emir in this late-15th-century mansion, which perfectly captures the spirit of the Albayzín and nearby Alhambra. Atmosphere and history are laid on thick without sacrificing home comforts, and beautiful architectural details abound from the silver candelabras to the tiled ornamental pool.

⌸ Hotel Párraga Siete   Hotel €€

(📞958 26 42 27; www.hotelparragasiete.com; Calle Párraga 7; s/d €65/85; ❄🛜) Seemingly furnished out of an Ikea-inspired style guide, the Párraga Seven has small modern rooms that feel as new as a freshly starched shirt.

Antequera ⑦

⌸ Hotel San Sebastían   Hotel €

(📞952 84 42 39; www.hotelplazasansebastian. com; Plaza de San Sebastián 4; s/d €25/40; 🅿❄🛜) You can't get much more central than this smartly refurbished hotel situated on a pretty square across from the magnificent Iglesia de San Sebastián. Its terrace is the best perch on the plaza to watch the evening *paseo* (street). The rooms are plain with dated decor but have welcome perks, such as fridges and small balconies. Breakfast is not included but there are plenty of bars nearby. Parking costs an extra €7 per day.

Osuna ⑧

✗ Casa Curro   Tapas €

(📞955 82 07 58; www.facebook.com/restaurantecasacurro; Plazuela Salitre 5; tapas €2, mains €6-12; ⊙noon-4pm & 8pm-midnight Tue-Sun; 🍴) Welcome to the tapas bar of your dreams, a fabulous blend of tradition and nouvelle cuisine. Plate after plate issues from the corner kitchen at this popular hall: crunchy grilled wild mushrooms, cheese-and-ham-stuffed courgette, Iberian 'secret' in a quince sauce. And yes, that's a dedicated *Game of Thrones* menu – the avocado, spinach and pomegranate Khaleesi salad is delicious. It's 500m west of Plaza Mayor.

Tarifa *Take to the skies at this beach-lovers' paradise*

The Great Outdoors

23

From summiting mainland Spain's highest peak to getting lost in wild, ethereal Doñana, this epic outdoor adventure throws you straight into the endlessly varied open-air playground that is Andalucía.

TRIP HIGHLIGHTS

400 km

Parque Nacional de Doñana
Raw, natural world brimming with wildlife

1 km

Capileira
Quiet, rural walks and the Sierra Nevada's highest peaks

Seville

Osuna

6

Antequera

Granada

2

1 START

Los Caños de Meca

9 FINISH

Tarifa
A Moroccan-flavoured, white-sand haven of outdoor fun

792 km

El Torcal
Eerily beautiful limestone rock formations

160 km

7 DAYS
792- KM / 492 MILES

GREAT FOR...

BEST TIME TO GO
April to June and September to October for ideal weather.

ESSENTIAL PHOTO

Tarifa, beaches and kitesurfers backed by Morocco, from Punta Paloma dune.

BEST FOR WILDLIFE

Huelva's majestic World Heritage–listed Parque Nacional de Doñana.

Classic Trip

23 The Great Outdoors

Starting up high in the Sierra Nevada, this outdoorsy itinerary swings west and south through a mesmerising patchwork of dramatically contrasting Andalucian landscapes. First you'll tackle Las Alpujarras' twisting mountain roads, then you'll fly across the Sevillan campiña (countryside) into Parc Nacional de Doñana national park and cruise past Tarifa's white-sand surfer beaches. It's all packed into an adventure-filled drive that uncovers a stash of history, architecture and cuisine as richly varied as its natural backdrop.

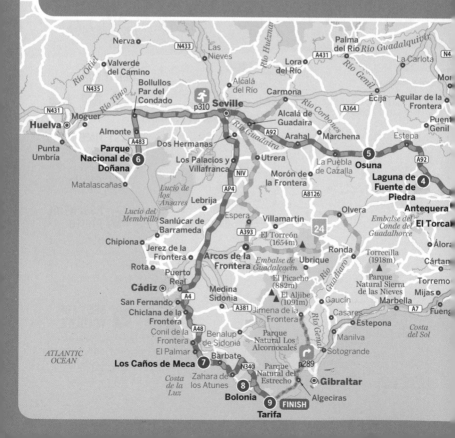

TRIP HIGHLIGHT

1 Capileira

Kick things off in pretty Capileira, perched above Pampaneira and Bubión in Las Alpujarras' Barranco de Poqueira, on the south side of the 75km-long Sierra Nevada. At 1436m, it's the highest of the Barranco's three whitewashed villages, and just an hour's drive northeast through dramatic mountainscapes from the Salobreña-Granada A44 (via the A348, A4132 and A4129).

Two nights here allows a full day of blissful walking trails, authentic mountain cooking and fine leatherwork such as at **J Brown** (www.jbrown-tallerdepiel.com; Calle Doctor Castilla 7; ⌚10am-1.30pm & 5-8pm Mon-Fri, to 1.30pm Sat).

A national-park minibus (July to October) runs from Capileira up to the Mirador de Trevélez (2700m), three hours' walk (6km) from the summit of Mulhacén (3479m), the tallest peak in the Sierra Nevada and mainland Spain.

Plenty more beautiful walks depart from the minibus drop-off point and from Capileira itself into the Poqueira gorge, many doable in a day. You'll probably spot ibex bounding around. The best Alpujarras walking months are April to mid-June and mid-September to October, but July to early September for the high peaks.

✕ 🛏 p290

The Drive » From Capileira, wind 36km downhill past Bubión, Pampaneira, Órgiva and Lanjarón (A4129, A4132 and A348). Drive 50km north on the A44, bypassing Granada onto the A92. Go 92km west; take exit 149 into Antequera. From the three-arch roundabout, 'El Torcal' signs lead to the A7075.

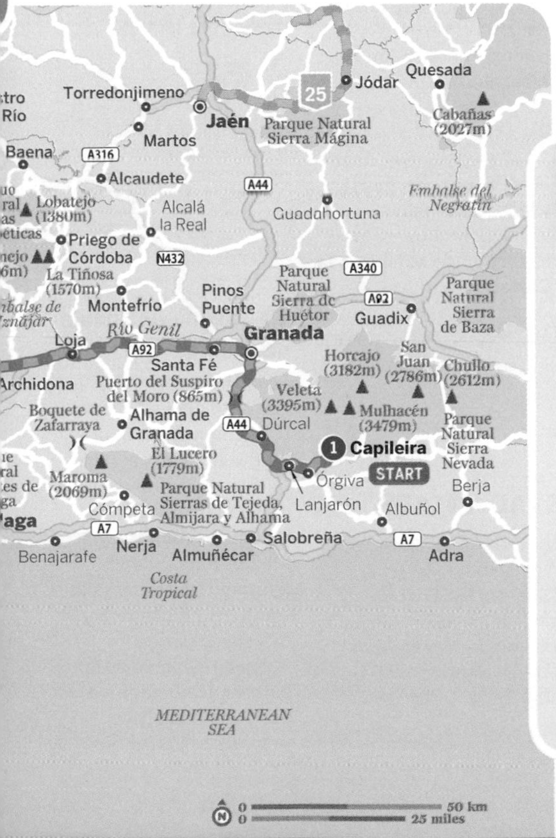

LINK YOUR TRIP

24 Andalucía's White Villages

From Osuna, it's a 61km spin northwest to Carmona to pick up our trip through Andalucía's classic white villages.

25 Olive Oil & the Renaissance in Jaén

Whiz 90km north on the A44 from Granada to Jaén to explore architectural Renaissance gems scattered across olive-covered countryside.

Classic Trip

After 11km, turn uphill to El Torcal (4km). As you climb, the Mediterranean sparkles just south.

- - - - - - - - - - - -

TRIP HIGHLIGHT

② El Torcal

What a stop. Making up the eerily wild, rugged and otherworldly 12-sq-km Paraje Natural Torcal de Antequera are some of the most bizarre and beautiful rock formations you'll ever see. Rising to 1336m, south of Antequera, this gnarled, jagged and deeply fissured limestone complex came to life as a seabed 150 million years ago. The vistas down soft green hills, past splashes of white villages, to the Mediterranean are exquisite.

From the excellent **Centro de Visitantes** (☎952 24 33 24; www.visitasfuentepiedra.es; ⊙10am-9pm), the marked

1.5km Ruta Verde (Green Route) and the 3km Ruta Amarilla (Yellow Route) lead you through the rocks. You can prebook guided walks.

The Drive » Drive back into Antequera, where there's convenient underground parking on Calle Diego Ponce (north of Plaza de San Sebastián).

- - - - - - - - - - - -

③ Antequera

Despite its impressive collection of prehistoric, Roman, Islamic and Spanish-baroque sights and lively tapas bars, Antequera gets refreshingly little tourist traffic.

The impressive hilltop remains of the 14th-century Moorish-built **Alcazaba** (adult/child incl Colegiata de Santa María la Mayor €6/3; ⊙10am-7pm Mon-Sat, 10.30am-3pm Sun) loom over the historic quarter, which is a delight to wander. Swot up on local history at the **Museo de la Ciudad** (www.antequera.es; Plaza del Coso Viejo; compulsory guided tour €3; ⊙9.30am-2pm & 4.30-6.30pm Tue-Fri, 9.30am-

2pm Sat, 10am-2pm Sun), where the 1.4m bronze *Efebe* is quite possibly the finest Roman sculpture unearthed in Spain.

Go further back in time at Antequera's **dolmens** (Cerro Romeral; ⊙9am-7.30pm Tue-Sat, to 3.30pm Sun), 1km from the centre, on the road leading northeast to the A45. Built using huge slabs of rock, the Dolmen de Veira (2500 BC) and Dolmen de Menga (3790 BC) are two of Europe's most ancient burial chambers. The **Dolmen del Romeral** (Cerro Romeral; ⊙9am-6pm Tue-Sat, 9.30am-2.30pm Sun), another 3km northeast, dates from 1800 BC.

🍴 🛏 p290

The Drive » Continue 16km northwest on the A92 to the signposted Laguna de Fuente de Piedra turn-off. 'Laguna' signs lead you through Fuente de Piedra village to the lagoon's visitors centre (2km).

- - - - - - - - - - - -

④ Laguna de Fuente de Piedra

From January or February until about August, this shimmering 6km-long lagoon just outside Fuente de Piedra is one of Europe's two prime breeding grounds for the hot-pink greater flamingo (the other is the southern French region of Camargue).

Each year up to 20,000 pairs of flamingos breed here, accompanied by thousands of other birds of

---

✓ **TOP TIP:**
SIERRA NEVADA MAPS

The best maps for hiking in the Sierra Nevada and Las Alpujarras are Editorial Alpina's *Sierra Nevada, La Alpujarra* (1:40,000) and Editorial Penibética's *Sierra Nevada* (1:40,000), with route booklets. Stock up on these and other maps/advice at Pampaneira's **Nevadensis** (☎958 76 31 27; www.nevadensis.com; Plaza de la Libertad; ⊙10am-2pm & 5-7pm Tue-Sat, to 3pm Sun & Mon) office.

THE WORLD'S MOST ENDANGERED FELINE

Doñana's most famous inhabitant is the beautiful, elusive Iberian lynx. It's also the world's most endangered cat. Almost all of Spain's wild lynxes prowl around Andalucía, split between Doñana national and natural parks (about 100) and the Sierra Morena (200 to 220).

The Iberian lynx has battled for survival against disastrous slumps in its main prey, the rabbit, since the 1950s, but also against hunters, developers, habitat loss and even tourism. Roads are a major threat; 20 Spanish lynxes were run over in 2014, seven on roads around Doñana.

But there's good news: Andalucía's lynx numbers are up from under 100 in the early 2000s to over 300 in 2014. Most of the credit goes to an increasingly successful program of in-captivity breeding and release into the wild, along with topping up of local rabbit populations: in 2015 Doñana authorities introduced 10,000 new rabbits. In June 2015 the Iberian lynx was taken off the International Union for Conservation of Nature's 'critically endangered' list. For now, at least, the future looks brighter for Andalucía's lynxes.

Catch live videos of lynxes at Doñana's breeding centre at the Centro de Visitantes El Acebuche (p287).

about 170 different species, including grey herons and white-headed ducks. Spot just-hatched flamingo chicks in April and May.

For maps, binoculars and bird-spotting tips, swing by the **Centro de Información Fuente de Piedra** (☑952 71 25 54; www. visitasfuentepiedra.es; Laguna de Fuente de Piedra; ☉10am-2pm & 5-7pm) above the car park, where you can also book guided one-/three-hour walks (per person €3/6) to otherwise off-limits observation points.

The Drive » From Fuente de Piedra, it's a 54km spin west on the A92 past low-lying hills, endless olive groves and the hillside town of Estepa to Osuna.

⑤ Osuna

Unassuming Osuna sparkles with architectural and artistic treasures courtesy of the once-wealthy Duques de Osuna.

A steep climb from Plaza Mayor leads you to the magnificent, top-of-town Renaissance **Colegiata de Santa María de la Asunción** (☑954 81 04 44; Plaza de la Encarnación; guided tours €3; ☉10am-1.30pm & 4-6.30pm Tue-Sun) – actually two superposed churches above the 1548 family crypt of the Duques de Osuna. Its impressive art collection includes Juan de Mesa sculptures and paintings by José de Ribera (El Españoleto).

Stroll the triangle of streets west off Plaza Mayor to uncover Osuna's other stars: its preserved baroque mansions, including the late-18th-century **Palacio de los Cepeda** (Calle de la Huerta 10).

✗ p290

The Drive » Hop back on the A92 west across Sevilla province's flat, dry *campiña* (82km). Follow 'Huelva' signs to bypass Seville onto the A49 to Portugal. Drive 49km west, into Huelva province, then take the A483 27km south to El Rocío. Please heed lynx warning signs as you enter the Doñana area.

TRIP HIGHLIGHT

⑥ Parque Nacional de Doñana

Welcome to Spain's most celebrated national park, a hauntingly beautiful 542-sq-km roadless expanse protecting 360 bird species and 37 types of mammal, including wild boar, deer and the endangered Iberian lynx. It's buffered by the 538-sq-km **Parque Natural de Doñana**.

The obvious Doñana base is tiny, sultry El Rocío, host of Spain's

DIEGO LOPEZ ALVAREZ / NIS / GETTY IMAGES ©

KEN WELSH / GETTY IMAGES ©

WHY THIS IS A CLASSIC TRIP
ISABELLA NOBLE, AUTHOR

This drive whisks you off through Andalucía's amazingly multifaceted landscapes, from the Iberian peninsula's highest mountain range to low-lying coastal wetlands teeming with wildlife. Nothing beats exploring the magical, unspoilt wilderness of the Parque Nacional de Doñana. Surprisingly, you're completely free to walk/cycle its exquisite 28km Atlantic beach between Matalascañas and the mouth of the Río Guadalquivir.

Top: Birdwatching at Parque Natural de Doñana
Left: Los Caños de Meca beaches
Right: Ancient limestone stacks, El Torcal

JOSÉ ANTONIO JIMÉNEZ / GETTY IMAGES ©

largest religious pilgrimage, the **Romería del Rocío** (Pentecost weekend). El Rocío's 115 *hermandades* (brotherhoods) bring festive fervour to its famous **Ermita del Rocío** (⊙8am-9pm Apr-Sep, to 7pm Oct-Mar) and sand-blown streets on most weekends. Two nights here gives you a full day for Doñana.

El Rocío's gleaming wetlands offer some of Doñana's finest beast-and bird-watching. Spot horses, deer, spoonbills and bright-pink flamingos from the waterfront promenade and the **Francisco Bernis Birdwatching Centre** (☎959 44 23 72; www.seo.org; ⊙9am-2pm & 4-6pm Tue-Sun).

You can't enter Doñana *national* park in your own car, so you'll be jumping on a fun four-hour, land-based trip through dunes, marshes and forest in all-terrain vehicles. The two licensed outfits are **Cooperativa Marismas del Rocío** (☎959 43 04 32; www.donana-visitas.es; Centro de Visitantes El Acebuche; tours €29.50) and **Doñana Reservas** (☎959 44 24 74; www.donanareservas.com; Avenida de la Canaliega, El Rocío; tours per person €28). Book at least a month ahead in spring/summer. Other operators run worthwhile trips and horse rides into the *natural* park.

The **Centro de Visitantes El Acebuche** (☎959 43 96 29; ⊙8am-9pm

Classic Trip

Apr–mid-Sep, to 7pm mid-Sep–Mar), **12km south of El Rocío**, is the main visitors centre.

🍴 🛏 p290

The Drive » Rev up for a 245km drive. Backtrack to the A49 from El Rocío and head east. Follow 'A4 Cádiz' signs to circumnavigate Seville onto the AP4 tollway (€7.25) and whiz 85km south. Continue 48km south on the A4 then the A48. Turn off towards Conil (A2232) and travel 15km southeast along the A2233 to Los Caños de Meca.

---

❼ Los Caños de Meca

Once a favourite hippie hang-out on Cádiz province's wind-battered Costa de la Luz, Los Caños de Meca still retains its lazy, bohemian vibe and hedonistic summer scene. Stop by for its coastal walks, laid-back beach bars, and spectacular wide-open beaches – popular with nudists and ideal for kitesurfing, windsurfing, board-surfing or good old beach lazing.

Follow a tiny side-road (often covered in sand) at the western end of town to the famed **Cabo de Trafalgar**, off which the Spanish navy was brutally defeated by the British and Admiral Nelson in 1805. Along the cape access road, swing by ultimate surfer-relaxation spot **Las Dunas** (www.barlasdunas.es; Ctra del Faro de Trafalgar; dishes €6-11; ⏱10.30am-11.30pm Sep-Jun, to 3am Jul & Aug; 🛜), for Bob Marley tunes, great *bocadillos* (filled rolls), and a laid-back, beach-shack vibe.

From the eastern end of Caños, pick up the spectacular 7.2km **Sendero del Acantilado** to Barbate through the protected pine forests and marshlands of the 50-sq-km **Parque Natural de la Breña y Marismas del Barbate**. These clifftops rival Cabo de Gata in their beauty. Then retrace your steps or jump on a bus back to Caños (Monday to Friday).

🛏 p291

The Drive » This is classic Costa de la Luz driving. From Caños, travel 10km east to Barbate on the A2233. Take the A2231 10km southeast to Zahara de los Atunes. Head inland on the CA2227, past towering wind turbines, then zip 15km southeast on the N340 to the signposted CA8202 Bolonia turn-off. From here, it's a lovely, hilly 7km drive to Bolonia.

---

❽ Bolonia

With its gorgeous white-sand dune, broad beach and wind-bashed *chiringuitos* (beach bars) nestled beneath rolling green hills, sleepy Bolonia makes a wonderfully low-key stop on your trip down the Costa de la Luz.

Sands aside, you're here for the magnificent seaside ruins of **Baelo Claudia** (📞956 10 67 96; www.museosdeandalucia.es; admission €1.50, EU citizens free; ⏱9am-5.30pm Tue-Sat Jan-Mar & mid-Sep–Dec, to 7.30pm Apr–mid-Jun, to 3.30pm mid-Jun–mid-Sep & Sun year-round), one of Andalucía's most important Roman archaeological sites. Famous in Roman times for its *garum* (spicy seasoning made from leftover fish parts), Baelo Claudia peaked during the reign of Emperor Claudius (AD 41–54). Still standing today are the well-preserved open-air remains of thermal

---

✅ **TOP TIP:**
SURFING EL PALMAR

Cádiz' Costa de la Luz is famous for windsurfing/kitesurfing, but **El Palmar** (5km northwest of Caños) gets Andalucía's best board-surfing waves (October to May). For classes and boards, contact **Escuela de Surf 9 Pies** (📞620 104241; www.escueladesurf9pies.com; Avenida de la Playa, El Palmar; board & wetsuit rental per 2/4hr €13/20, classes €28).

DETOUR:
PARQUE NATURAL LOS ALCORNOCALES

Start: ❾ Tarifa

A gorgeous 1677 sq km of crinkled hills cloaked in Spain's most extensive cork-oak woodlands, the Parque Natural Los Alcornocales sprawls 75km from almost the Strait of Gibraltar to the Parque Natural Sierra de Grazalema. Packed full of historical, architectural and natural riches, it's particularly rewarding to explore with your own wheels – and still off Andalucía's beaten tourist trails.

Your best base is bucolic sun-bleached Jimena, about an hour's drive (68km) northeast from Tarifa. Its crumbling, 13th-century Nasrid **castle** (⊘24hr) perches atop town, with hypnotic views of Gibraltar and Africa. Several excellent hikes start from Jimena, such as the 3km riverside **Sendero Río Hozgarganta** past old mills.

Other walking paths and outdoor activities abound. For five particular walks, including the 3.3km climb up the park's second-highest peak, **El Picacho** (882m), you'll need pre-booked permits from the **Oficina del Parque Natural Los Alcornocales** (☏856 58 75 08; pn.alcornocales.cmaot@juntadeandalucia.es; Ctra Alcalá-Benalup Km 1 , Alcalá de los Gazules; ⊘9am-2pm Mon-Fri). There's detailed English-language walking info on www.ventanadelvisitante.es.

baths, workshops, a theatre, a paved forum and the basilica. Enjoy views across the crashing Atlantic to Africa, and do make time to explore the detailed museum.

The Drive ❯❯ Backtrack along the CA8202, turn right onto the N340 and drive 15km southeast into Tarifa. Parking in Tarifa can be tricky, but there's metered space on Avenida de la Constitución beside the Alameda.

TRIP HIGHLIGHT

❾ Tarifa

Wrap up your outdoors Andalucía adventure in Tarifa, on the southernmost tip of Spain, where the Mediterranean meets the Atlantic. Full of North African flavour, it's a haven of outdoor activities with a laid-back,

surf-inspired buzz, long history and international-focused culinary scene.

Walk under the Mudéjar **Puerta de Jerez** to the old town's Islamic-era streets. The one must-see monument is the restored 10th-century **Castillo de Guzmán** (Calle Guzmán El Bueno; adult/child €2/0.60; ⊘11am-2.30pm & 4-9pm May–mid-Sep, to 6.30pm mid-Sep–Apr), where Reconquista hero Guzmán El Bueno legendarily sacrificed his own son in 1294 to save Tarifa from Moroccan Merenid attackers. Stroll a little east to the **miramar** for fantastic views of Morocco – just 14km away.

Don't miss the surf-style boutiques packed with quirky Tarifa-born brands on Calle Batalla del Salado. Then hit the white sand stretching

10km northwest to **Punta Paloma** dune.

Kitesurfing and windsurfing are Tarifa's favourite pastimes. Link up with local operators such as **Gisela Pulido Pro Center** (☏608 577711; www.giselapulidoprocenter.com; Calle Mar Adriático 22; 3hr group courses per person €70) for equipment rental and classes. May, June and September are best conditions-wise. Aventura Ecuestre, 5km northwest of Tarifa, runs fabulous beach horse rides.

Other outdoor fun includes hiking, diving, biking and whale-watching. The **tourist office** (☏956 68 09 93; Paseo de la Alameda; ⊘10am-1.30pm & 4-6pm Mon-Fri, 10am-1.30pm Sat & Sun) has details.

✕ ⊨ p291

Classic Trip

Eating & Sleeping

Capileira ❶

✖ Taberna Restaurante
La Tapa   Spanish, Moroccan €
(☏618 30 70 30; Calle Cubo 6; mains €9-12; ⊙noon-4pm & 8pm-midnight; ☞) Las Alpujarras is a culinary microregion with its own distinct flavours and, at La Tapa, they're skilfully melded with the area's Moorish past, creating dishes such as wild boar casserole and couscous in earthenware dishes. The place is tiny but textbook Alpujarran.

⛏ Hotel Real de Poqueira   Hotel €€
(☏958 76 39 02; www.hotelpoqueira.com; Doctor Castillas 11; s/d €50/70; ❄☎☒) Located in an old house next to Capileira's lily-white church, this place is one of several Poqueira accommodations in the village all run by the same family. However, with its expansive lobby, flop-down couches and smart, boutique-like rooms, this one has the edge. It's not what you expect in a small Alpujarra village, which makes it all the more epiphanic.

Antequera ❸

✖ Arte de Cozina   Andalucian €€
(www.artedecozina.com; Calle Calzada 27-29; mains €12-15, tapas €2; ⊙1-11pm) The *simpática* (friendly) owner of this hotel-restaurant has her own garden that provides fresh ingredients for her dishes. Traditional dishes are reinterpreted, such as gazpacho made with green asparagus or *porra* (cold soup) with oranges, plus meat, fish, and Antequeran specialities. On Thursday and Friday evenings classical musicians provide entertainment.

⛏ Hotel Coso Viejo   Hotel €
(☏952 70 50 45; www.hotelcosoviejo.es; Calle Encarnación 9; s/d incl breakfast €44/54; ❄❄☎) This converted 17th-century palace is right in the heart of Antequera, opposite Plaza Coso Viejo and the town museum. The simply furnished rooms are set around a patio with a fountain, and there's a tapas bar and restaurant. No TVs.

Osuna ❺

✖ Casa Curro   Tapas €
(☏955 82 07 58; www.facebook.com/ restaurantecasacurro; Plazuela Salitre 5; tapas €2, mains €6-12; ⊙noon-4pm & 8pm-midnight Tue-Sun; ☞) Welcome to the tapas bar of your dreams, a blend of tradition and nouvelle cuisine. Crunchy grilled wild mushrooms, cheese-and-ham-stuffed courgette, Iberian 'secret' in a quince sauce. And yes, that's a dedicated *Game of Thrones* menu – the avocado, spinach and pomegranate Khaleesi salad is delicious. It's 500m west of Plaza Mayor.

Parque Nacional de Doñana ❻

✖ Restaurante Toruño   Andalucian €€
(☏959 44 24 22; www.toruno.es; Plaza Acebuchal 22; mains €12-20; ⊙8am-midnight) With its traditional Andalucian atmosphere and good food, this is El Rocío's one must-try restaurant. A highlight on the menu is the free-range *mostrenca* calf, unique to Doñana; for noncarnivores, the huge grilled veg *parrillada* (barbecue) is fantastic. On warm evenings dine in front of the restaurant by the 1000-year-old *acebuche* (wild olive) tree.

⛏ Hotel Toruño   Hotel €€
(☏959 44 23 23; www.toruno.es; Plaza Acebuchal 22; s/d incl breakfast €48/67; ℗❄☎) About 350m east of the Ermita in El Rocío, this brilliantly white villa stands right by the *marismas* (wetlands), where you can spot flamingos going through their morning beauty routine. Inside, tile murals continue the ornithological theme – even in the shower!

Rooms are bright and cosy, but only a few actually overlook the marshes.

Los Caños de Meca ➐

🛏 Casas Karen   Hotel €€

(📞956 43 70 67, 649 780834; www.casaskaren. com; Camino del Monte 6; d €85-125, q €155-190; 🅿🛜) This eccentric, Dutch-owned hideaway has characterful rustic rooms and apartments across a flower-covered plot. Options range from a converted farmhouse to thatched *chozas* (traditional huts) and two recently remodelled split-level 'studios'. Decor is casual Andalucian-Moroccan, full of throws, hammocks and colour. It's 1km east of the Cabo de Trafalgar turn-off.

Tarifa ➒

✕ Café Azul   Breakfast €

(www.facebook.com/cafeazultarifa; Calle Batalla del Salado 8; breakfasts €3.50-7.50; 🕑9am-3pm) This Italian-run place with eye-catching blue-and-white Moroccan-inspired decor whips up the best breakfasts in town, if not Andalucía. You'll want to eat everything. It does a wonderfully fresh fruit salad topped with muesli and yoghurt, plus good coffee, smoothies, juices, *bocadillos* (filled rolls) and cooked breakfasts. The fruit-and yoghurt-stuffed crêpe is a work of art.

🛏 Hostal África   Hostal €

(📞956 68 02 20; www.hostalafrica.com; Calle María Antonia Toledo 12; s/d €50/65, with shared bathroom €35/50; 🕑Mar-Nov; 🛜) This revamped 19th-century house just southwest of the Puerta de Jerez is one of the Costa de la Luz' best *hostales* (budget hotels). Full of plant pots and sky-blue-and-white arches, it's run by hospitable owners, and the 13 all-different rooms sparkle with bright colours. Enjoy the lovely, big roof terrace, with exotic cabana and views of Africa.

🛏 Hotel Dos Mares   Hotel €€€

(📞956 68 40 35; www.dosmareshotel.com; Ctra N340 Km 79.5; r incl breakfast €195-225; ❄🛜🏊) Tarifa is all about the beach, and inviting accommodation options line the coast to its northwest. Opening on to the sand, 5km northwest of town, Moroccan-flavoured Dos Mares has comfy, bright, tile-floored rooms and bungalows in yellows, blues and burnt oranges, some with sea-facing balconies. Other perks: a sleepy cafe, a gym, a pool, and an on-site **horse-riding school** (📞956 23 66 32; www. aventuraecuestre.com).

Grazalema *A whitewashed gateway to exploring the Parque Natural Sierra de Grazalema*

Andalucía's White Villages

24

Discover a world of blanched beauty, hilltop history, crag-top castles, peaceful walks and mysterious mazelike streets on this mountain-flavoured drive that weaves together Andalucía's classic white towns.

TRIP HIGHLIGHTS

START
Carmona

145 km

Grazalema
Rugged mountain beauty and gorgeous natural park walks

Torre Alháquime

Algodonales

El Bosque

2

3

7 FINISH

Benamahoma

Arcos de la Frontera
The white town of your dreams

105 km

Ronda
A spectacular cliff-top mountain town steeped in historical drama

200 km

4 DAYS
200 KM / 124 MILES

GREAT FOR...

BEST TIME TO GO
Perfect temperatures: May, June, September and October.

ESSENTIAL PHOTO
Arcos de la Frontera's cliff-top panoramas.

BEST FOR OUTDOORS
Beautiful Sierra de Grazalema mountain walks.

293

Andalucía's White Villages

Eons-old fortifications atop lofty crags soar above whitewashed homes tucked into green-cloaked country: a visual spectacle that threads right through this tour of Andalucía's prettiest *pueblos blancos*. You'll discover the historical lure of Cádiz' white towns – Grazalema, Arcos de la Frontera, Zahara de la Sierra – but you'll also loop in pastoral hikes and mountain passes. Kick off with Carmona's Sevillan twist; end with Ronda's mountain magic.

❶ Carmona

Crowning a low-rise *campiña* hill, 32km east of Seville, Carmona is like a living snapshot of Andalucian history. Its old town is a maze of centuries-old monu-ments, majestic Mudéjar and Christian palaces, churches and convents, and buzzy tapas bars – the perfect introduction to your white-towns tour.

Dig back to Paleolithic times at the excellent **Museo de la Ciudad** (☏954 14 01 28; www.museo ciudad.carmona.org; Calle

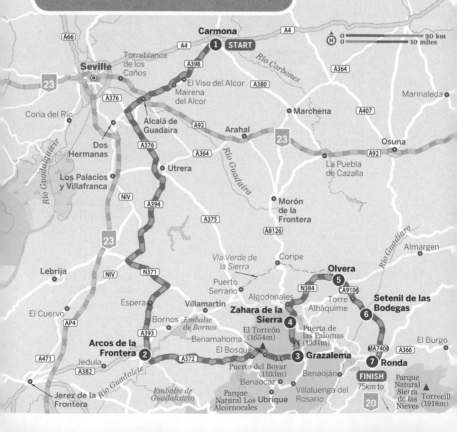

San Ildefonso 1; adult/child €3/1, free Tue; ⊙10am-2pm Mon-Sun & 6.30-8.30pm Mon-Fri mid-Jun–Aug, 11am-7pm Tue-Sun & 11am-2pm Mon Sep–mid-Jun); free Tuesdays. Right beside it is the splendidly over-the-top 15th- and 16th-century **Iglesia Prioral de Santa María de la Asunción** (☑954 19 14 82; Plaza Marqués de las Torres; admission €3; ⊙9.30am-2pm & 5.30-6.30pm Tue-Fri, to 2pm Sat), its gorgeous columned Patio de los Naranjos sporting a Visigothic calendar. Don't miss the exquisite Roman Gorgon Medusa mosaic inside the **town hall** (☑954 14 00 11; Calle El Salvador; admission free; ⊙8am-3pm Mon-Fri), just south.

On Carmona's southwestern fringe stands the eerily fascinating 1st- and 2nd-century **Necrópolis**

LINK YOUR TRIP

20 Mediterranean Meander

From Ronda, travel southeast to Málaga then up along the twinkling Mediterranean to Barcelona.

23 The Great Outdoors

Cruise 61km southeast from Carmona to Osuna to join an epic Andalucian outdoors adventure.

Romana (Roman cemetery; ☑600 143632; www.muse-osdeandalucia.es; Avenida de Jorge Bonsor 9; ⊙9am-7pm Tue-Sat & 9am-3.30pm Sun Apr-May, 9am-3.30pm Tue-Sun Jun–mid-Sep, 9am-5.30pm Tue-Sat & 9am-3.30pm Sun mid-Sep–Mar).

🛏 p299

The Drive » Take the A398, A392 and A376 southwest from Carmona to Utrera (54km). Pick up the A394 and NIV south (26km), then the A371 southeast towards Villamartín. Drive 12.5km, turn onto the narrow A393 towards Espera, and after 20km you'll reach Arcos de la Frontera. Park up in the underground parking below Paseo de Andalucía, west of the old town.

- - - - - - - - - - -

TRIP HIGHLIGHT
② Arcos de la Frontera

If there's one Cádiz province white town that outshines them all, it's Arcos de la Frontera. A sea of red-tile-roofed, whitewashed houses tumbles down from a sheer-sided crag, atop which huddles a soporific old-town labyrinth full of historical mystery. Over two centuries between the Christian conquest of Seville (1248) and the final Muslim emirate, Granada (1492), Arcos and its 'on the frontier' companions straddled the unstable Christian–Moorish border.

The main attraction is **Plaza del Cabildo** for spectacular vistas

over the Río Guadalete from its vertical-edged **mirador** (lookout). But the knockout view is the dramatic cliff-top panorama from the swanky adjacent **Parador** (☑956 70 05 00; www.parador.es; Plaza del Cabildo; r €100-170; ❄ @ 🛜) – best drunk in over a reinvigorating *café con leche* (milky coffee).

As you get lost down old Arcos' twisting narrow streets, step into the ornate Gothic-baroque **Basílica Menor de Santa María de la Asunción** (Plaza del Cabildo; admission €2; ⊙10am-1pm & 4-6.30pm Mon-Fri, 10am-2pm Sat Mar-Dec); its gold-leaf altarpiece is a miniature of the one in Seville cathedral.

✗ 🛏 p299

The Drive » It's a tame 32km east on the A372 from Arcos to El Bosque, then suddenly you're on a thrilling, winding 18km mountain climb to Grazalema. Stop at signposted Puerto del Boyar (1103m) for glorious mountainscapes.

- - - - - - - - - - -

TRIP HIGHLIGHT
③ Grazalema

Craving some physical activity? Clinging to green-clad rocky slopes, rust-roofed Grazalema is an idyllic white mountain town, but it's also your best stopover for exploring the rugged, 534-sq-km Parque Natural Sierra de Grazalema. Welcome to the rainiest spot in Spain (yes, really) – and all the more picturesque for it.

Hike the **El Calvario** trail to a ruined chapel (500m above the A372), or choose from numerous gorgeous Sierra walking paths (p298) starting near Grazalema. **Horizon** (☏956 13 23 63; www.horizonaventura.com; Calle Las Piedras 1; ☺10am-2pm & 5-8pm Mon-Sat) organises all kinds of adventure activities: hiking, kayaking, canyoning, paragliding.

Back in town, the **Museo de Artesanía Textil** (www.mantasdegrazalema.com; Ctra de Ronda; ☺8am-2pm & 3-6.30pm Mon-Thu, 8am-2pm Fri; P) reveals the age-old techniques behind Grazalema's famous wool blankets. Dotted around, including on the main **Plaza de España**, are several multispouted **Visigothic fountains**. Pick up Grazalema's honey and cheeses for picnics.

🛏 p299

The Drive » What a fantastic 17km. Full of sharp switchbacks, the steep CA9104 snakes north from Grazalema over the 1331m Puerto de las Palomas to Zahara de la Sierra. The views are fabulous: Zahara's reservoir twinkles turquoise, jagged mountains melt into the distance.

- - - - - - - - - - - - -

❹ Zahara de la Sierra

Ridiculously pretty Zahara de la Sierra is laced around a castle-topped spur at the foot of the Grazalema mountains, its white-village perfection enhanced by palm-studded, bougainvillea-draped streets and the sparkling reservoir below. Once a Moorish stronghold, today Zahara is a popular base/stop-off for Garganta Verde (p298) hikers.

It's a steepish 10- to 15-minute climb, starting opposite Hotel Arco de la Villa, to the 12th-century **castle** (admission free; ☺24hr). In 1481 Abu al-Hasan of Granada recaptured it overnight, triggering a Christian backlash that ended in the definitive reconquest of all that remained of Moorish Spain.

For more adventure, paddle off across the reservoir; **Zahara Catur** (☏657 926394; www.zaharacatur.com; Plaza del Rey 3) rents canoes (per hour €18).

The Drive » Skirt Zahara's reservoir onto the A2300 for 6km. Whiz 23km east on the A384, past hang-gliding-obsessed Algodonales, to Olvera, which you'll spot from miles away across sun-drenched, olive-carpeted countryside. The road passes the Peñón de Zaframagón, an important griffon vulture refuge.

- - - - - - - - - - - - -

❺ Olvera

Gutsier that its neighbours, Olvera is as much famed for its olive oil as for the wonderful, 36km

JOSE PERAL / GETTY IMAGES ©

Vía Verde de la Sierra (www.fundacionviaverdedelasierra.com), considered the finest of Andalucía's 23 *vías verdes* (hiking/cycling greenways made from disused railway lines). Rent bikes (per day €12) at **Hotel/Restaurante Estación Verde** (☏661 463207; Calle Pasadera 4; s/d/tr €25/40/60) and spin west to Puerto Serrano along four spectacular viaducts and 30 tunnels.

With an enthralling history swinging from 19th-century bandit hideout back to the Romans, Olvera itself is well worth exploring.

Ronda Magnificent white town perched above Tajo gorge

Climb past lime-washed walls and red roofs to the top-of-town late-12th-century **Castillo Árabe** (Plaza de la Iglesia; adult/child €2/1; ⊙10.30am-2pm & 4-7pm Tue-Sun), neoclassical **church** (Plaza de la Iglesia; admission €2; ⊙11am-1pm Tue-Sun) and Museo de La Frontera y Los Castillos inside **La Cilla** (Plaza de la Iglesia; adult/child €2/1; ⊙10.30am-2pm & 4-7pm Tue-Sun).

The Drive ≫ Follow the CA9106 and CA9120 south from Olvera past rolling hills, through Torre Alháquime, to Setenil de las Bodegas (14km).

⑥ Setenil de las Bodegas

Deep in untouristed territory, Setenil's entirely unique urban framework is a white-town anomaly. Instead of retreating inside cliff-top castles, people here burrowed into dark caves beneath the steep walls of the Río Trejo. The tactic was such a success that it took a 15-day siege for the Christians to expel the Moors from Setenil in 1484. Swing by to explore original cave-houses, the 12th-century **castle** (⊙hours vary) and rustic tapas bars on Plaza de Andalucía.

The Drive ≫ Zip 15km south into Málaga province to Ronda (CA9122, MA7403 and MA7400).

TRIP HIGHLIGHT

⑦ Ronda

End your road trip on a literal high. Spectacularly carved in half by the 100m-wide Tajo gorge, rugged Ronda revels in mountain drama. It's Málaga's most striking white town, one of Spain's oldest settlements, and the (alleged) birthplace of bullfighting. Stay overnight to beat (some) crowds.

LOCAL KNOWLEDGE:
SIERRA DE GRAZALEMA WALKS

Lovely marked walking trails fan out across the Sierra de Grazalema. Pick up maps and info at the **Centro de Visitantes el Bosque** (☎956 70 97 33; cv_elbosque@ agenciamedioambienteyagua.es; Calle Federico García Lorca 1; ☺9.30am-2pm Sun-Tue, 9.30am-2pm & 4-6pm Wed-Sat), **Punto de Información Zahara de la Sierra** (☎956 12 31 14; Plaza del Rey 3; ☺9am-2.30pm & 4-6pm Tue-Fri, 11am-3pm & 4-6pm Sat & Sun) and **Grazalema tourist office** (www.grazalema.es; Plaza de Asomaderos; ☺10am-2pm & 4-7pm Mon-Sat), and at www.ventanadelvisitante.es. These three highlights require free pre-booked permits from the Centro.

Garganta Verde Starting 3.5km south of Zahara de la Sierra (off the CA9104), this 2.5km (one hour) path meanders down into the precipitous Garganta Verde (Green Throat) with huge griffon vultures whooshing past at eye level. It's one of the Sierra's most spectacular walks.

El Torreón (☺Nov-May) Climb Cádiz province's highest peak (1654m) for unbeatable Gibraltar, Sierra Nevada and Morocco views. The 3km trail (2½ hours) begins 8km west of Grazalema on the A372.

El Pinsapar This 12km (six-hour) walk winds past rare dark-green *pinsapos* (Spanish firs) to Benamahoma. It starts 2km uphill from Grazalema off the CA9104.

Ronda's towering 18th-century Puente Nuevo straddles the gorge between new (north) and old towns (La Ciudad, south). Savour La Ciudad's ancient soul as you wander its walled, Islamic-era tangle of narrow streets, flavoured by fine Renaissance mansions and intriguing museums. The **Museo Lara** (www.museolara.org; Calle de Armiñán 29; adult/child €4/2; ☺11am-8pm; 👬) hosts the impressive, eclectic private collection of Juan Antonio Lara Jurado.

Across the chasm, **Plaza de España** and its grisly Spanish Civil War history were immortalised in Hemingway's *For Whom the Bell Tolls*. Just north, Ronda's 66m-wide, 200-year-old **Plaza de Toros** (Calle Virgen de la Paz; admission €7, €8.50 incl audioguide; ☺10am-8pm) is one of Spain's most illustrious bullrings.

 p299

Eating & Sleeping

Carmona ❶

🛏 Parador de Carmona
Historic Hotel €€€

(📞954 14 10 10; www.parador.es; Calle Alcázar; r €188; P ❄ @ 🗢 🏊) With jaw-dropping, unexpected views of the surrounding valley roasting under the Sevillan sun, Carmona's luxuriously equipped *parador* (top-end state-owned hotel) feels even more sumptuous for the ruined Alcázar in its grounds. Most of the smart, shiny-terracotta-floored rooms overlook the plains. The beautiful dining room serves a three-course €33 *menú*, or just pop in for coffee: the terrace is divine. Best rates online.

Arcos de la Frontera ❷

🍴 Taberna Jóvenes Flamencos
Andalucian, Tapas €

(📞657 133552; www.tabernajovenesflamencos. blogspot.com; Calle Deán Espinosa 11; tapas €2-3, raciones €6-10; ☺noon-midnight Thu-Tue; 📓) You've got to hand it to this popular place, which successfully opened up midrecession in 2012. Along with wonderful flamenco/bullfighting decor and brilliantly red tables, it has an easy-to-navigate menu of meat, fish, vegetarian and scramble dishes – including a delicious chunky courgette and Parmesan omelette. Service is impeccable and music and dance break out regularly.

🛏 La Casa Grande
Historic Hotel €€

(📞956 70 39 30; www.lacasagrande.net; Calle Maldonado 10; r €79-105, ste €94-105; ❄ @ 🗢) This gorgeous, rambling, cliffside mansion dating back to 1729 once belonged to the great flamenco dancer Antonio Ruiz Soler. With each of the seven rooms done in different but wonderfully tasteful design (all with divine views), it feels more like a home-cum-artists

retreat than a hotel. Great breakfasts, a well-stocked library, a fabulous rooftop terrace, and massage and yoga top off the perfect package.

Grazalema ❸

🛏 La Mejorana
Casa Rural €

(📞956 13 23 27, 649 613272; www.lamejorana. net; Calle Santa Clara 6; s/d incl breakfast €45/58; ❄ @ 🗢 🏊) A beautiful, welcoming house towards the upper end of Grazalema, La Mejorana has smartened up its six colourful, comfy rooms. Some have private lounges and bright blue Moroccan-style arches; others have balconies, huge mirrors or wrought-iron bedsteads. There's a big country-style sitting room plus a terrace with gorgeous village views – and a leafy garden that even includes a pool.

Ronda ❼

🍴 Casa María
Andalucian €

(📞951 08 36 63; Plaza Ruedo Alameda 27; menú €20; ☺noon-3.30pm & 7.30-10.30pm Thu-Tue; 🍴) This no-frills restaurant has a kitchen run by a passionate cook who prepares dishes strictly according to what is fresh in the market. There is no menu. The selection is not huge but most diners opt for the five-course *poco de todo* (little bit of everything) tasting *menú* reflecting Maria's delicious homestyle cooking.

🛏 Hotel San Gabriel
Hotel €€

(📞952 19 03 92; www.hotelsangabriel.com; Calle José M Holgado 19; s/d incl breakfast €72/100; ❄ 🗢) This charming hotel is filled with antiques and photographs that offer an insight into Ronda's history – bullfighting, celebrities and all. Ferns hang down the huge mahogany staircase and there is a billiard room, a cosy living room stacked with books, as well as a DVD-screening room with 10 velvet-covered seats rescued from Ronda's theatre.

Jaén Provincial town dwarfed by the Renaissance Catedral de la Asunción

Olive Oil & the Renaissance in Jaén

25

North of Granada and its Moorish masterpiece the Alhambra, travel through an ocean of olive trees to charming country towns blessed with exquisite architecture of quite a different kind.

TRIP HIGHLIGHTS

91 km

Úbeda Old Town
An architectural and culinary feast

120 km

Baeza
Winding streets lined by gorgeous stone-built mansions and churches

6 **FINISH**

4

Jódar

Mancha Real

Torres

Albánchez de Mágina

1 **START**

Castillo de Santa Catalina
Magnificent panoramas over Jaén and countryside

1 km

3–4 DAYS
120 KM / 75 MILES

GREAT FOR...

BEST TIME TO GO
April, May, June, September or October for perfect weather.

ESSENTIAL PHOTO

The panorama of mountains and olive groves from the Castillo de Albánchez.

BEST FOR AESTHETICS

Úbeda's Plaza Vázquez de Molina is a harmonious architectural composition.

Olive Oil & the Renaissance in Jaén

The 16th-century grandees of this region beautified their towns with elegant buildings just as the Classical lines of the Renaissance were reaching Spain from Italy – a legacy that makes World Heritage–listed Úbeda and Baeza, especially, a delight to the senses. Today the landscape between the towns is an unending pale-green carpet of millions of olive trees – a hard-to-believe spectacle that will thrill Extra Virgin fans with the high-quality oils it yields.

TRIP HIGHLIGHT

1 Jaén

Everything in the appealing historic centre of this provincial capital is dwarfed by the **Catedral de la Asunción** (Plaza de Santa María; adult/child incl audioguide €5/1.50; ☺10am-2pm & 4-8pm Mon-Fri, 10am-2pm & 4-7pm Sat, 10am-noon & 4-7pm Sun), designed by Andrés de Vandelvira, the master Renaissance architect whose work you'll see more of in Úbeda and Baeza. The cathedral's huge, round

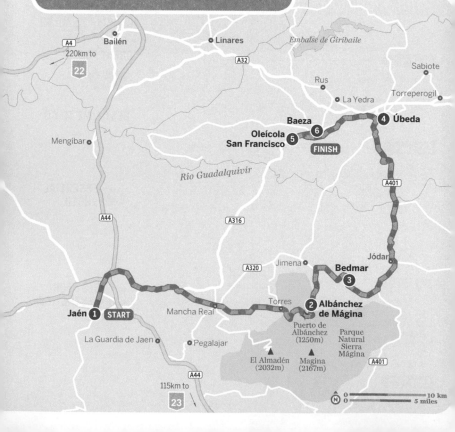

arches, clustered Corinthian columns, beautifully carved stone ceilings and great circular dome are all part and parcel of its Renaissance aesthetic.

Avoid the aggravation of Jaén's traffic system by taking a taxi (€7) up to the Cerro de Santa Catalina, the hill towering above the city. The views from the large cross at the end of the castle ridge are magnificent. The castle itself, the **Castillo de Santa Catalina** (Cerro de Santa Catalina; adult/child €3/1.50; ☺10am-2pm & 3.30-7.30pm Tue-Sat, to 3pm Sun; P), was built by the conquering Christians to replace the Muslim fortress they captured in 1246. Two-thirds of the old castle site is now occupied by the **Parador Castillo de Santa Catalina** (☏953 23 00 00;

LINK YOUR TRIP

22 **Golden Triangle**
Zip 90km down the A44 from Jaén to Granada to start this drive connecting Andalucía's three most splendid cities.

23 **The Great Outdoors**
Travel beyond Granada to the Sierra Nevada to start an adventurous trip around Andalucía's wild, wide-open spaces.

www.parador.es; Cerro de Santa Catalina; r €169; P ✲ @ ⬗ ✻), a luxurious hotel built in the 1960s (which is a fine place to stay if your budget will stretch to it). If you're not staying at the *parador*, drop in for a drink to see the extraordinary vaulted, decorative ceilings in the main salon and dining room.

Back down in the centre, get a taste of Jaén's atmosphere with an evening tour of some of the ancient and atmospheric tapas bars in the narrow streets just north of the cathedral.

🍴 p307

The Drive » Jaén's Avenida de Madrid feeds into the A316, which runs quickly across rolling, olive-covered country east to Úbeda. For a more scenic route totalling about four hours, we're turning off at Km 41.3 and following 'Torres' signs through Mancha Real to the pretty village of Torres. From here the narrow, dramatic JA3107 winds up over the 1250m-high Puerto de Albánchez pass and down to Albánchez de Mágina.

- - - - - - - - - - - -

② **Albánchez de Mágina**

This classic white Andalucían village nestled beneath a towering rocky cliff is the best place to halt on this leg of your drive for one reason: the **Castillo de Albánchez** (admission free; ☺24hr), whose 14th-century leaning tower perches atop a single rock high on the

sheer cliff rising above the village. You can, amazingly enough, walk up to it in about 20 steep minutes (ask the way from the central Plaza de la Constitución), and you'll be rewarded for the effort by stunning bird's-eye views over the whitewashed village and surrounding mountains. There are a few cafes and bars in Albánchez' centre if you'd like refreshments.

The Drive » From Albánchez, head north down the JA3105 and turn right along the A320 as you enter Jimena. It's 8km to Bedmar.

- - - - - - - - - - - -

③ **Bedmar**

Stop at this sizeable white village, with a backdrop of rugged crags, for a wander through its winding streets up to the picturesque remains of its 15th-century castle, set on a panoramic rocky outcrop at the top of the village.

The Drive » Continue along the A320 to meet the A401, where you turn left for Jódar and Úbeda. Parking in Úbeda's old town can be difficult, but the underground Parking Plaza in Plaza de Andalucía, on the edge of the old town, is reasonably convenient.

- - - - - - - - - - - -

TRIP HIGHLIGHT

④ **Úbeda**

The narrow streets and broad plazas of Úbeda's old town, lined with lovely, stone-built mansions and churches, are a feast for the eyes. You'll feast your taste buds here too in some deliciously creative eateries.

Make first for Plaza Vázquez de Molina, a wonderful composition of Renaissance architecture and cypress and orange trees that takes on an especially magical aura after dark. At its east end stands the **Sacra Capilla de El Salvador** (Sacred Chapel of the Saviour; www. fundacionmedinaceli.org; Plaza Vázquez de Molina; adult/child incl audioguide €5/2.50; ⊙9.30am-2pm & 5-7pm Mon-Sat, 11.30am-2pm & 5-8pm Sun, afternoon hours 30min earlier Apr-May, 1hr earlier Oct-Mar), built between 1536 and 1559 by Andrés de Vandelvira for Úbeda aristocrat Francisco de los Cobos. The main facade is a superb example of the early Renaissance style called plateresque, alive with sculpture depicting Greek myths and Cobos family shields

as well as the Christian transfiguration.

Along the plaza is the **Palacio de Vázquez de Molina** (Plaza Vázquez de Molina; ⊙8am-2.30pm Mon-Fri), a perfectly proportioned Italianate mansion built by Vandelvira for Francisco de los Cobos' nephew, Juan Vázquez de Molina.

As you explore old Úbeda's many other fascinating old buildings and museums, don't miss the **Casa Museo Arte Andalusí** (☑953 75 40 14; Calle Narváez 11; admission €2; ⊙11am-2pm & 5.30-8pm), a private museum in a 16th-century house with a huge, diverse collection of antiques assembled by owner Paco Castro. The informal guided tours make it all come alive.

✗ ⌂ p307

The Drive » Head west out of Úbeda onto the A316. Follow 'Jaén' signs, passing Baeza on a ring-road, and at Km 14 turn right onto the JA4107,

BORGESE MAURIZIO / HEMIS.FR / GETTY IMAGES ©

signposted 'Begíjar'. Turn right immediately past a petrol station after 1.4km: Oleícola San Francisco is 200m along the street.

JAÉN'S RENAISSANCE MASTERMIND

Most of the finest buildings you see in Úbeda, Baeza and Jaén are the creations of one man: Andrés de Vandelvira, born in Alcaraz, Castilla-La Mancha, in 1509. Under the patronage of Úbeda's powerful Cobos and Molina families, Vandelvira almost single-handedly brought the Renaissance to Jaén province. Little is known about his life but his oeuvre is a jewel of Spanish culture, spanning all main phases of Spanish Renaissance architecture, as shown by three exemplary buildings in Úbeda – the ornamental early phase called plateresque, on the Sacra Capilla de El Salvador; the purer line and classical proportions of the later Palacio de Vázquez de Molina; and the sober late-Renaissance style of the **Hospital de Santiago** (Calle Obispo Cobos; ⊙10am-2pm & 5-9pm, closed Sun Jul, closed Sat & Sun Aug), completed the year he died, 1575.

Úbeda Hospital de Santiago

⑤ Oleícola San Francisco

As you've guessed from all those olive trees out there, Jaén province produces a *lot* of olive oil. One-sixth of all the olive oil in the world, in fact. For the first-hand low-down on the olive oil business, and what distinguishes Extra Virgin from the rest, you can't beat the excellent tours at the modern oil mill **Oleícola San Francisco** (☏953 76 34 15; www.oleoturismojaen.com; Calle Pedro Pérez, Begíjar; 1½hr tours €5; ⊙ tours 11am

& 5pm). You'll learn all you could want to know about turning olives into oil and the technological revolution that has transformed the industry in recent decades. At the end you'll get to taste a few oils and be surprised at the diversity of their flavours. Tours can be given in English (ring ahead to ensure availability).

The Drive » Return to the A316 and head east, following signs into Baeza, where the underground car park on Calle Compañía is the easiest place to park.

TRIP HIGHLIGHT

⑥ Baeza

Baeza life today focuses on the lively plaza-cum-park Paseo de la Constitución, lined with cafes and bars. The oldest part of town and most of the monuments are in the zone just south of here. The number-one monument is the **Catedral de Baeza** (Plaza de Santa María; admission incl audioguide €5; ⊙10.30am-2pm & 4-7pm Mon-Fri, 10am-7pm Sat, 10am-6pm Sun), a fascinating stylistic melange begun in the 13th century – but with the 16th-century

Renaissance work of Andrés de Vandelvira predominant. Climb the tower for great views over the town and countryside.

Baeza's other finest architecture includes **Plaza del Pópulo** (Plaza de los Leones), a square surrounded by a variety of elegant 16th-century structures, and the **Pala-cio de Jabalquinto** (Plaza de Santa Cruz; ⊘9am-2pm Mon-Fri), whose flamboyant 15th-century Gothic facade features a bizarre array of naked humans clambering along the moulding over the doorway.

For a post-sightseeing breather, stroll along the **Paseo de las Murallas**, where the superb views stretch to the distant mountains of the Sierra Mágina (south) and Sierra de Cazorla (east). And do drop into **Café Teatro Central** (www.cafeteatrocentral.com; Calle Obispo Narváez 19; ⊘4pm-4am Tue-Sun, 9pm-4am Mon) for a drink of any kind and to wow at its amazingly eclectic contemporary decor!

✕ ⊨ p307

ANTONIO LUIS MARTINEZ CANO / GETTY IMAGES ©

Jaén The magnificent interior of the Catedral de la Asunción

Eating & Sleeping

Jaén ❶

🛏 Hotel Xauen
Hotel €€

(📞953 24 07 89; www.hotelxauenjaen.com; Plaza del Deán Mazas; s/d incl breakfast €55/65; 🅿️❄️📶) The Xauen has a superb location in the centre of town. Communal areas are decorated with large photos of colourful local scenes, while the rooms are a study in brown and moderately sized, but comfy and well cared-for. The rooftop sun terrace has stunning cathedral views. Parking nearby is €12.

Úbeda ❹

🍴 Misa de 12
Andalucian €€

(www.misade12.com; Plaza Primero de Mayo 7; raciónes €9-20; ⏱noon-midnight Wed-Sun) From the tiny cooking station in this little corner bar, a succession of truly succulent platters magically emerges – slices of *presa ibérica* (a tender cut of Iberian pork) grilled to perfection, juicy fillets of *bacalao* (cod), or *revuelto de pulpo y gambas* (eggs scrambled with octopus and shrimp).

🍴 Cantina de la Estación
Contemporary Andalucian €€

(📞687 777230; www.cantinalaestacion.com; Cuesta Corredera 1; mains €15-19; ⏱1.30-4pm & 8.15pm-midnight Thu-Sun, to 4pm Mon-Tue) The charming originality here starts with the design – three rooms with railway themes (the main dining room being the deluxe carriage). It continues with the seasonal array of inspired fusion dishes based on locally available ingredients, such as wild boar in red-wine sauce on vegetable couscous, or millefeuille of smoked salmon, parmesan and béchamel.

🛏 Afán de Rivera
Heritage Hotel €€

(📞953 79 19 87; www.hotelafanderivera.com; Calle Afán de Rivera 4; r €70-85; ❄️📶) This incredible small hotel lies inside one of Úbeda's oldest buildings, predating the

Renaissance. Expertly run by the amiable Jorge, it has beautifully historic common areas, and comfortable rooms that offer far more than is usual at this price: shaving kits, fancy shampoos and tastefully eclectic decor combining the traditional and the contemporary.

🛏 Palacio de la Rambla
Historic Hotel €€

(📞953 75 01 96; www.palaciodelarambla.com; Plaza del Marqués de la Rambla 1; incl breakfast s €70-96, d €100-130; ⏱closed Jul-Aug; ❄️📶) The lovely Palacio de la Rambla gives you the full aristocratic mansion experience. The ivy-clad patio is wonderfully romantic, there's a beautiful salon opening on to a garden-patio, and each room is clad in precious antiques, so that it feels like you're staying with aristocratic friends rather than in a hotel.

Baeza ❻

🍴 El Nanchoas
Andalucian €€

(www.elnanchoas.com; Calle Comendadores 6; mains €7-15; ⏱11.30am-4.30pm & 8pm-1am Mon & Wed-Sat, to 4.30pm Sun) Relaxed and friendly Nanchoas serves up well-prepared home-style Jaén favourites in a sunny little courtyard and stone-walled dining room. Try the tasty *lomo de orza* (pork loin slow-fried with spices then conserved in a clay vessel called an *orza*) with garlicky eggs, or some sheep's cheese with honey and raisins.

🛏 Hotel Puerta de la Luna
Heritage Hotel €€

(📞953 74 70 19; www.hotelpuertadelaluna.com; Calle Canónigo Melgares Raya 7; s €70-99, d €70-111, buffet breakfast €15; 🅿️❄️@📶♨️) There is no doubt where Baeza's Renaissance-era nobility would stay if they were to return today. This luxurious hotel in a 17th-century mansion sports orange trees and a pool in its elegant patio, and beautifully furnished salons with welcoming fireplaces. The spacious rooms are enhanced by classical furnishings and art, and good big bathrooms.

STRETCH YOUR LEGS MÁLAGA

Start/Finish: Muelle Uno

Distance: 3.2km

Duration: Three to four hours

This walk touches on the very best of Málaga, including a sophisticated shopping street, a bustling market, two iconic museums and a historic tapas bar with views of both a Roman amphitheatre and Moorish fortress.

Take this walk on Trips

Muelle Uno

Located on Muelle Uno and opened in 2015, the **Centre Pompidou Málaga** (☎951 92 62 00; www.centrepompidou.es; Pasaje Doctor Carrillo Casaux, Muelle Uno; admission €7, incl temporary exhibition €9; ☺9.30am-8pm Wed-Mon) is housed in a low-slung modern building crowned by a multicoloured cube. The permanent exhibition includes the extraordinary *Ghost* by Kader Attia depicting rows of Muslim women bowed in prayer created from domestic aluminum foil, plus works by such contemporary masters as Frieda Kahlo, Francis Bacon and Antoni Tàpies.

The Walk » Walk westwards beside the port until you reach the Plaza de la Marina, cross to the major thoroughfare Alameda Principal and continue west until you reach the corner of Calle Tómas Heredia.

Soho

The former rundown grid of streets between the Alameda and the port (known as Soho) has been transformed into an open art gallery with vast murals covering whole sides of buildings; including right here on the corner with the eye-catching painting of birds by renowned Chinese muralist DaLeast. This *barrio* (neighbourhood) is also attracting hip cafes, idiosyncratic shops and ethnic restaurants; it is well worth a wander.

The Walk » Cross the Alameda Principal and continue straight down Calle Torregordo, past a beautiful frescoed building and across Calle Atarazanas, following the shopping baskets to the market.

Mercado Atarazanas

The striking 19th-century **Mercado Atarazanas** (Calle Atarazanas; P) incorporates the original Moorish gate that once connected the city with the port. Choose from swaying legs of ham, cheese, fish and endless varieties of olives and nuts. The fruit and veg stalls are the most colourful, selling everything that is in season, ranging from big misshapen tomatoes to large purple onions, mild flavoured and sweet.

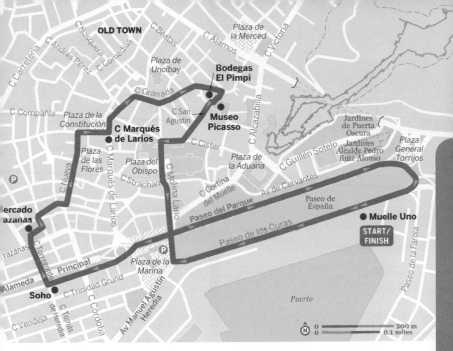

The Walk >> Exit due east, pass Casa Aranda (selling the best churros in town), and turn left onto pedestrian Calle Nueva from gracious Plaza de Felix Sáenz, with its lofty palms and pavement cafes. At the end of Calle Nueva, turn right onto Plaza de la Constitución.

Calle Marqués de Larios

The city's most famous shopping street leads from Plaza de la Constitución and is magnificent with glossy marble-clad paving, elegant balconied buildings and a compelling combination of designer boutiques, national chains, historic cafes and *farmàcias* (pharmacies).

The Walk >> From Plaza de la Constitucíon follow pedestrian Calle Granada. Look for the cathedral to your east and continue until the street narrows and you come to number 62 and your next stop.

Bodegas El Pimpi

Relax with a tapa and drink at the stunning **Bodegas El Pimpi** (www. bodegabarelpimpi.com; Calle Granada 62; ☺11am-2am; 🛜), encompassing a warren of atmospheric rooms with a terrace overlooking the Roman amphitheatre

and Gibralfaro. Walls are decorated with magnificent and historic *feria* (fair) posters; El Pimpi is an institution in this city, don't miss it.

The Walk >> Exit on Calle Granada and take the street just to your east, Calle San Agustín; the Picasso Museum is on your left.

Museo Picasso

The superb **Museo Picasso** (☎902 44 33 77; www.museopicassomalaga.org; Calle San Agustín 8; admission €7, incl temporary exhibition €10; ☺10am-8pm Tue-Thu & Sun, to 9pm Fri & Sat) has an enviable collection of 204 works, many on loan from Christine Ruiz-Picasso (wife of Paul, Picasso's eldest son) and Bernard Ruiz-Picasso (his grandson), including the heartfelt *Paulo con gorro blanco* (Paulo with a white cap), a portrait of Picasso's eldest son painted in the 1920s.

The Walk >> Carry on along Calle San Agustín, turn right past the cathedral and left on Molina Lario to the entrance to the port. End your walk with an amble through the delightful Alameda gardens, crossing over Paseo de Los Curas to your start point.

STRETCH YOUR LEGS
SEVILLE

Start/Finish: Jardines de Murillo

Distance: 3.75km

Duration: Three hours

Seville's historic core is no place for frustrated drivers. This stroll through some of the greatest monuments in colonial Spain kicks off from a central car park and provides enough shady diversions to pause, recuperate and escape the flaming summer heat.

Take this walk on Trip

22

Jardines de Murillo

Seville's most central underground car park at the Jardines de Murillo sits on the cusp of Santa Cruz, the former Jewish quarter, an antediluvian labyrinth of car-free streets that breaks occasionally into shady flower-embellished plazas. Tapas bars, hotels and flamenco venues crowd its historic entrails.

The Walk >> The most direct way through the Santa Cruz labyrinth is via Calle Ximénez de Enciso, but it's more fun if you get temporarily lost.

Alcázar

If you're short on time, visit the **Alcázar** (📞tours 954 50 23 24; www.alcazarsevilla. org; adult/child €9.50/free; ⊘9.30am-7pm Apr-Sep, to 5pm Oct-Mar) over the cathedral. While the latter can be enjoyed from the outside, 95% of the Alcázar's beauty lies within, behind walls first raised by the Almohads. The centrepiece is the Palacio de Don Pedro, one of the highpoints of Mudéjar architecture in Spain. Equally riveting are the Eden-like gardens with their mazes and statues.

The Walk >> Exit the Alcázar and you'll see Seville's cathedral on the other side of Plaza del Triunfo. From Mudéjar to Gothic in a few steps!

Catedral

Welcome to one of the greatest and largest cathedrals in the world, encased in a building that pretty much defines the word Gothic. Seville's immense **Catedral** (www.catedraldesevilla.es; adult/ child €9/free; ⊘11am-3.30pm Mon, 11am-5pm Tue-Sat, 2.30-6pm Sun) and its attached Giralda bell tower is famous for its Golden Age art, massive gilded altarpiece, Moorish courtyard, and tomb of Christopher Columbus. If you haven't got time to explore its dark, humongous interior, circumnavigate the walls and drink in its ethereal beauty.

The Walk >> Exit the cathedral via the Patio de los Naranjos, turn left, cross Av de la Constitución and follow Calle García de Vinuesa into the compact Arenal quarter. At a major five-point junction, take Calle Antonia Díaz towards the river.

Plaza de Toros de la Real Maestranza

Seville's **bullring** (☎954 22 45 77; www.realmaestranza.com; Paseo de Cristóbal Colón 12; tours adult/child €7/4; ☺tours half-hourly 9.30am-8pm, to 3pm bullfight days) is one of the most important in Spain and also the oldest (completed in 1765). It was established by the Real Maestranza de Caballería de Sevilla, a cavalry guild with origins in the 17th century. Visits to the bullring and its museum are by guided tour only. Among the exhibits inside you'll see numerous paintings (including prints by Goya), the historic stables and the altar where matadors pray before a fight.

The Walk » Cross Paseo de Cristóbal Colón and take the pleasant path alongside the Río Guadalquivir towards the Torre del Oro.

Torre del Oro

As much a symbol of Seville as the Giralda and almost as old, this distinctive **tower** (Paseo de Cristóbal Colón; admission €3, Mon free; ☺9.30am-6.45pm Mon-Fri, 10.30am-6.45pm Sat & Sun) beside the Río Guadalquivir River was built around 1220 by the Almohads, a couple of decades before Seville fell to the Christians. It was once used to store New World gold, hence its name: 'tower of gold'. These days it hosts a modest maritime museum.

The Walk » Cross the Paseo again and cut along Calle Almirante Lobo to the Puerta de Jerez. Follow Calle San Fernando past the neo-Mudéjar Hotel Alfonso XIII and you'll see the unmissable university on the right.

Antigua Fábrica de Tabacos

Thanks to French composer Bizet, Seville's sprawling **university campus** (Calle San Fernando; ☺8am-9.30pm Mon-Fri, to 2pm Sat, free tours 11am Mon-Thu) will always be better remembered for its former incarnation – as a tobacco factory and the fictional setting for the opera *Carmen*. The graceful classical building served as a tobacco factory from the 18th century until the 1950s.

The Walk » Cut along the path through the lush Jardines del Murillo back to the start.

STRETCH YOUR LEGS
VALENCIA

Start/Finish: Mercado Central

Distance: 2.25km

Duration: Two hours

Valencia is a legendary port and industrial city that recently rediscovered its cultural mojo. It's also the spiritual home of Spain's great gastro-invention, paella. The peripheral Ciudad de las Artes y las Ciencias is its big modern draw and deserves a separate visit, but the highlights of historic Valencia can be strung together in this short walking tour.

Take this walk on Trips

Mercado Central

Situated less than 200m from an underground car park on the corner of Avenida Barón de Cárcer and Calle del Hospital, Valencia's vast Modernista covered **market** (www.mercadocentralvalencia. es; Plaza del Mercado; ⊙8am-2.30pm Mon-Sat), constructed in 1928, is a swirl of smells, movement and colour. Don't miss the fish, seafood and offal annexe. A tapas bar in the middle of the market lets you sip a wine and enjoy the atmosphere.

The Walk » Exit the market and walk around the back into Plaza del Mercado, where you'll see the distinctive crenelated walls and tower of La Lonja opposite.

La Lonja

The splendid late-15th-century **La Lonja** (Calle de la Lonja; adult/child €2/1; ⊙10am-6pm or 7pm Tue-Sat, to 3pm Sun), a Unesco World Heritage site, was originally Valencia's silk and commodity exchange. Highlights are the colonnaded hall with its twisted Gothic pillars and the 1st-floor Consulado del Mar with its stunning coffered ceiling.

The Walk » Take narrow Calle de las Mantes off the Plaza del Mercado. Turn right into Calle de los Derechos. The Plaza Rodonda is on the left through a covered arcade just before the street bends to the left.

Plaza Redonda

Trim and smart, though over-tourist-oriented after an elaborate makeover, this small, circular 19th-century space – once the abattoir of Valencia's Mercado Central – is ringed by stalls.

The Walk » Exit the plaza via the opposite street arch and turn left into Calle de Jofrens. At the T-junction turn right into busy Plaza de la Reina. The cathedral sits at the other end, its facade tilted slightly to the left.

Catedral

Valencia's **Catedral** (Plaza de la Virgen; adult/child incl audioguide €5/3.50; ⊙10am-5.30pm or 6.30pm Mon-Sat, 2-5.30pm Sun, closed Sun Nov-Feb) was built over the mosque after the 1238 reconquest. Its low, wide, brick-

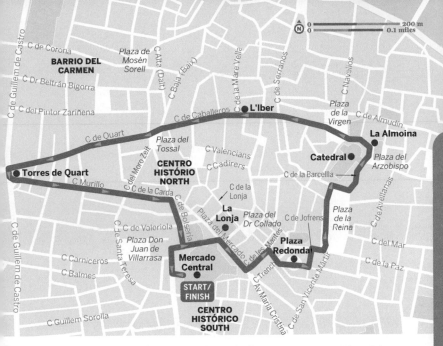

vaulted triple nave is mostly Gothic, with neoclassical side chapels. Highlights are rich Italianate frescoes above the altarpiece, a pair of Goyas in the Chapel of San Francisco de Borja, and what's claimed to be the Holy Grail, a Roman-era agate cup that was later modified.

The Walk » Take Calle de la Barcella on the east side of the cathedral and follow it around until it opens out into another plaza.

La Almoina

Beneath the square just to the east of Valencia's cathedral, the archaeological remains of the kernel of Roman, Visigoth and Islamic Valencia shimmer through a water-covered glass canopy. Guided tours available for a little extra.

The Walk » Continue around the back of the cathedral, cross Plaza de la Virgen and enter Calle de Caballeros. L'Iber is on the right.

L'Iber

With more than 85,000 pieces, **L'Iber** (Museo de Soldaditos de Plomo; www.museoliber. org; Calle de Caballeros 22; adult/under 27yr

€5/3; ☺11am-2pm & 4-7pm Wed-Sun) claims to be the world's largest collection of toy soldiers. The 4.7m-by-2.8m set piece of the Battle of Almansa (1707) has 9000 combatants, while cases teem with battalions and regiments of toy soldiers.

The Walk » Continue along Calle de Caballeros as it becomes Calle de Quart. Follow the narrow street until the unmistakable gateway of Torres de Quart appears before you.

Torres de Quart

Spain's most magnificent city **gate** (Calle de Guillem de Castro; adult/child €2/1, Sun free; ☺10am-6pm or 7pm Tue-Sat, 10am-3pm Sun) is quite a sight from the new town. You can clamber to the top of the 15th-century structure, which faces towards Madrid and the setting sun. Up high, notice the pockmarks caused by French cannonballs during the 19th-century Napoleonic invasion.

The Walk » From the gate's southern tower double-back along Calle Murillo and Calle de la Carda to Plaza del Mercado.

Portugal

PORTUGAL'S MIX OF THE MEDIEVAL AND THE MARITIME makes it a superb place to visit. A turbulent history involving the Moors, Spain and Napoleon has left the interior scattered with walled medieval towns topped by castles, while the pounding Atlantic has sculpted a coast of glorious sand beaches.

The nation's days of exploration and seafaring have created an introspective yet open culture with wide-ranging artistic influences. The eating and drinking scene here is a highlight, with several wine regions, and restaurants that are redolent with aromas of grilling pork or the freshest of fish.

Comparatively short distances mean that you get full value for road trips here: less time behind the wheel means you can take more time to absorb the atmosphere of the places you visit.

Nazaré Scenic coastal views of the surf beach near Nazaré (Trip 26)
ELINA MANNINEN / GETTY IMAGES ©

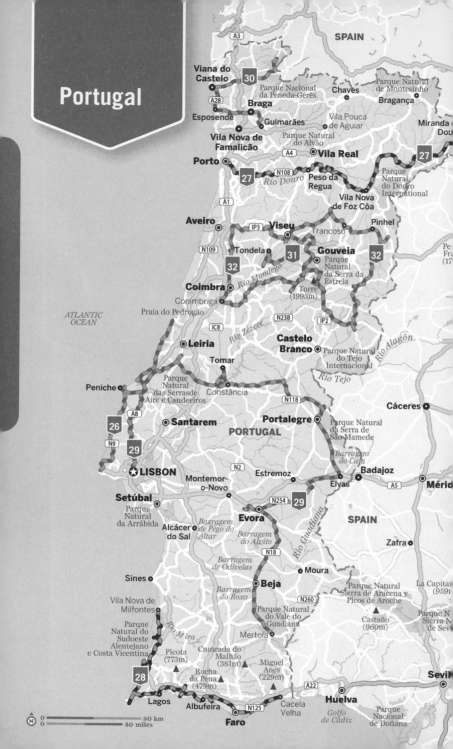

26 **Atlantic Coast Surf Trip 5–7 Days**
Lively towns, great seafood, and top beaches with monster waves. (p319)

Classic Trip
27 **Douro Valley Vineyard Trails 5–7 Days**
Heart-breakingly beautiful river valley laced with vines producing sensational ports and reds. (p329)

Classic Trip
28 **Alentejo & Algarve Beaches 4–6 Days**
Some of the world's great beaches and towns with Moorish heritage. (p339)

29 **Medieval Jewels in the Southern Interior 6–9 Days**
Understand Portugal's turbulent history through castles, monasteries and standing stones. (p351)

30 **The Minho's Lyrical Landscapes 2–4 Days**
Green Portugal, green wine and handsome historic cities. (p361)

31 **Tasting the Dão 2–4 Days**
Explore the wineries that produce the nation's silkiest reds. (p369)

32 **Highlands & History in the Central Interior 5–7 Days**
Student life, evocative villages and spectacular mountain scenery in Portugal's heartland. (p377)

Lagos Heading to the surf at a beach near Lagos

DON'T MISS

Wine Tasting
Often underrated, Portugal's wines are one of the region's great pleasures. Visit wineries and taste wines and ports on Trips **27** **31**

Castles
Love thy neighbour? Not in Iberia: Portugal is studded with castles staring defiantly towards Spain. See the best of them on Trips **27** **29** **32**

Surfing
Portugal is one of Europe's surfing hotspots: despite the Mediterranean vibe, this is the Atlantic, and those are serious waves on Trips **26** **28**

Music
Fado can encapsulate the stirrings of Portugal's sometimes melancholy soul. The two centres to hear it are Lisbon and Coimbra, on Trips **29** **32**

Hiking
Jump out of the car for some picturesque hill walking on Trips **27** **28** **30** **32** **32**

Nazaré Bask in the sun at Extremadura's most picturesque beach resort

Atlantic Coast Surf Trip 26

Get ready to ride the big ones on Portugal's wild, wave-lashed west coast – an alluring mix of sunshine, terrific surf, dune-backed beaches and nicely chilled towns.

TRIP HIGHLIGHTS

FINISH
● Pedrógão

181 km

Nazaré
Great surf, party spirit and a pretty, whitewashed centre

● São Pedro de Moel

São Martinho do Porto

8

6

150 km

4

109 km

Peniche
Cracking beaches, charming fortress-topped old town and epic waves

● Lourinhã

Foz do Arelho
Little-developed resort, with soft-sand beaches and great windsurfing

2

51 km

Erlceira
World Surfing Reserve with reliable swells and excellent surf camps

Praia do Guincho ●

START

5–7 DAYS
223 KM / 139 MILES

GREAT FOR...

BEST TIME TO GO
Spring to early autumn for the best surf and sunshine.

ESSENTIAL PHOTO
Snap the surf rolling in at sunset anywhere on the Atlantic Coast.

BEST TWO DAYS
The 129km from stops 4 to 8 pack the biggest surfing punch.

26 Atlantic Coast Surf Trip

If endless crashing surf sounds like your idea of heaven, you've come to the right country. Surfers and kitesurfers of all levels are in their element on Portugal's sparkling Atlantic coast, which is thrashed by some of Europe's biggest rollers. First-rate (and inexpensive) surf camps, gleaming white towns with authentic seafood restaurants, golden beaches fringed by dunes and pines, and memorable sunsets wrap up this little road trip nicely.

❶ Praia do Guincho

Just half an hour's drive west of Lisbon, Praia do Guincho is hammered by some terrific Atlantic waves. The site of previous World Surfing Championships, this long, wild, dune-backed beach holds plenty of pulling power for surfers, windsurfers and kitesurfers with its massive crashing rollers. Beware of the strong undertow which can be dangerous for swimmers and novice surfers. If you're keen to ride the waves, check out the surfing course available at the highly rated **Moana Surf School** (📞964 449 436; www.moanasurfschool.com; private surf class €40, group lesson €25, 4-lesson course €85), which arranges private lessons and group courses for all levels. It also rents out boards (€15/25 per half-/full day) and wetsuits (€10/15 per half-/full day).

The Drive >> From Guincho, the scenic N247 swings north through the rippling, forest-cloaked mountains of the Parque Natural de Sintra-Cascais, at its most atmospheric when veiled in early-morning mist. Roll down the window and breathe in that fresh air as you cruise north on the hour-long (51km) drive to Ericeira.

TRIP HIGHLIGHT

❷ Ericeira

Picturesquely draped across sandstone cliffs

with grandstand Atlantic views, sunny, white-washed Ericeira has a string of golden beaches that have surfers itching to grab their boards and jump in. This is one of just four World Surfing Reserves, starring alongside Malibu and Santa Cruz in California and Manly Beach in Australia. The swells are reliable and the mightiest waves roll in to cliff-backed Praia da Ribeira d'Ilhas. A World Qualifying Series (WQS) site and frequent host to Portuguese national surfing championships, the beach is famous for having one of the best reef breaks in Europe. The other biggie is Coxos, a right-hand point break

LINK YOUR TRIP

31 **Tasting the Dão**

Wine after the waves? Detour inland 120km from Praia de Pedrogão to Santa Comba Dão for tastings and cellar tours in a deliciously rural setting.

32 **Highlands & History in the Central Interior**

Why not tag on a road trip of Portugal's culture-loaded interior? The soulful university town of Coimbra is just a 77km drive northeast of Praia do Pedrógão.

producing incredible barrels. Most amateurs will find the waves at the nearby Praia de São Sebastião challenging enough. Standing out among the surf camps in Ericeira, **Rapture** (☏0919 586 722; www.rapturecamps. com; Foz do Lizandro 6; surf lessons €30, board & wetsuit rental per day €10, dm incl half-board €29-39) offers nicely chilled digs right on the beach and lessons with proficient instructors. For a post-surf beer or cocktail, stop by **Sunset Bamboo** (Travessa Jogo da Bola; ⊙noon-8pm Sun-Tue & Thu, to 2am Fri & Sat; 🛜).

✗ 🛏 p327

The Drive ≫ From Ericeira, the N247 veers north close to the contours of the coast, taking you through gently rolling farmland and past sun-bleached *aldeas* (hamlets), orchards and pinewoods. After a pleasant

hour (40km) behind the wheel, you emerge in Lourinhã.

- - - - - - - - - - -

❸ Lourinhã

Lourinhã is lesser-known than other west-coast surfing hotspots, yet it deserves more than just a cursory glance. In the peaceful shoulder seasons, you'll practically have its waves all to yourself on dune-fringed Praia Areal and Praia da Areia Branca. The former hosts national surfing events, while the latter is perfect for beginners and bodyboarders.

The Drive ≫ It's an easy 18km drive north on the countrified N247 and N114 to Peniche. The road takes you through softly undulating farmland, past bone-white hamlets and the odd ruin and windmill. To the west, you can often glimpse the hazy blue outline of the Atlantic.

RUI ALMEIDA FOTOGRAFIA / GETTY IMAGES ©

↱ DETOUR: BERLENGA GRANDE

Start: ❹ Peniche

Sitting about 10km offshore from Peniche, Berlenga Grande is a spectacular, rocky and remote island, with twisting, shocked-rock formations and gaping caverns. It's the only island of the Berlenga archipelago you can visit – the group consists of three tiny islands surrounded by clear, calm, dark-blue waters full of shipwrecks that are great for snorkelling and diving, for instance with **Acuasuboeste** (☏918 393 444; www.acuasuboeste.com; Porto de Pesca; diving intro course €80, single dive €30-35).

In the 16th century Berlenga Grande was home to a monastery, but now the most famous inhabitants are thousands of nesting seabirds, especially guillemots. The birds take priority over visitors and development has been confined to housing for a small fishing community and a lighthouse.

A number of boats make the short hop between Peniche and the island in the summer months.

Lourinhã Sunset over the beach

④ Peniche

Ask a local to rattle off Portugal's top surfing spots and Peniche invariably makes the grade. Straddling a headland with the sea on all sides, it is popular for its long fabulous town beach and nearby surf strands, with the added charm of a pretty walled historic centre and a 16th-century fortress. But it's the waves you are here for – and what epic waves they are! Long a favourite of clued-up surfers, Peniche shot to celebrity status when Supertubos beach, south of town, was selected as a stop on the ASP World Tour. Supertubos has some of Europe's best beach and reef breaks. Conditions are great year-round. Kitesurfing is also big. On the far side of high dunes about 500m east of the old town, **Peniche Kite & Surf Center** (☎919 424 951; www.penichekitecenter.com; Av Monsenhor Bastos, Praia de Peniche de Cima; ☺surf & kitesurf lesson €30) offers surfing and kitesurfing lessons.

✖ 🛏 p327

The Drive ❯❯ About 5km to the northeast of Peniche is the scenic island-village of Baleal, connected to the mainland village of Casais do Baleal by a causeway.

⑤ Baleal

A fine swoop of pale golden sand protected by dunes, Baleal is a paradise of challenging but, above all, consistent waves that make it an ideal learners' beach. Depending on the season, surf camps here charge between €240 to €550 for a week of classes, including equipment and

323

CULTURE FIX

If you can tear yourself away from the surf for a minute, factor in a detour to some of the hinterland's cultural treasures. Here are three worth the drive.

Óbidos

A 25km drive east of Peniche, this fortified wonder conceals a historic centre that is a maze of cobbled streets and flower-bedecked, whitewashed houses livened up with dashes of vivid yellow and blue paint. A hill lifts a medieval castle high above town.

Batalha

A detour off the road between Nazaré and São Pedro de Moel, Batalha's crowning glory is its Manueline monastery, a riot of flying buttresses and pinnacles, with gold stone carved into forms as delicate as snowflakes and as pliable as twisted rope.

Alcobaça

A 17km drive east of Nazaré, Alcobaça conceals a charming centre that is dwarfed by the magnificence of the 12th-century Mosteiro de Santa Maria de Alcobaça, one of Portugal's most memorable Unesco World Heritage sites.

self-catering lodging. Well-established picks include **Baleal Surfcamp** (☎262 769 277; www.baleal-surfcamp.com; Rua Amigos do Baleal 2; 1-/3-/5-day course €60/95/145) and **Peniche Surfcamp** (☎962 336 295; www.penichesurfcamp. com; Av do Mar 162, Casais do Baleal; ☺1/2/10 surf classes €30/50/225). You can also rent boards and wetsuits (€30/175 per day/week).

The Drive » From Baleal, connect up with the N114, taking you onto the A8 north, before veering west onto the N360. The road makes a sweeping arc, leading through pine forest and past farmland and low-rise hills. It skirts the impressive fortified city of Óbidos, where you might want to factor in a pitstop. It's around a 38km drive.

TRIP HIGHLIGHT

⑥ Foz do Arelho

With a vast, gorgeous swoop of sandy beach backed by a river-mouth estuary ideal for windsurfing, Foz do Arelho remains remarkably undeveloped. It makes a fine place to laze in the sun, and outside July and August it'll often be just you and the local fishermen. The beach has a row of relaxed bars and restaurants.

Escola de Vela da Lagoa (☎962 568 005, 262 978 592; www.esco-ladeveladalagoa.com; Rua do Penedo Furado; ☺10am-sunset daily Jun-Sep, shorter hrs in low season) hires out sailboats (€16 per hour), canoes (€10), windsurf boards (from €15) and catamarans (from €20). The school also provides

windsurfing and sailing lessons (two hours, €60 for one, €90 for two) and kayak lessons (€14 per person for a three-hour session). From Foz do Arelho village, it's a 2.8km drive: turn left on the road that follows the lagoon's inland edge past the rock called Penedo Furado and continue.

The Drive » A minor road, the Estrada Atlântica, hugs the coastline as it threads north to Santo Martinho do Porto, a drive of around 16km.

⑦ Santo Martinho do Porto

Fancy some time to hang out on the beach? Unlike nearby Nazaré, Santo Martinho do Porto is no party town, but it's a cheery place with a half-moon bay, perfect for swimming and just slowing the pace a notch or two.

The Drive » Back behind the wheel, you'll be edging your way north on the N242 through pine woods and farmland before crossing the Río Alcobaça and arriving in Nazaré, 14.5km away.

TRIP HIGHLIGHT

8 Nazaré

With a warren of narrow, cobbled lanes running down to a wide, cliff-backed beach, Nazaré is Estremadura's most scenic coastal resort. The sands are packed with multicoloured umbrellas in July and August and the town centre is jammed with

LOCAL KNOWLEDGE: THE INSIDE SCOOP ON SURFING

Read on for the lowdown on when to surf, what to take, surf tuition and rentals.

WHEN TO SURF

Spring and autumn tend to be the best for surfing action. Waves at this time range from 2m to 4.5m high. This is also the low season, meaning you'll pay less for accommodation, and the beaches will be far less crowded. Even during the summer, however, the coast gets good waves (1m to 1.5m on average) and, despite the crowds, it's fairly easy to head off and find your own spots (you can often be on your own stretch of beach just by driving a few minutes up the road).

WHAT TO TAKE

The water temperature here is colder than it is in most other southern European countries, and even in the summer you'll probably want a wetsuit. Board and wetsuit hire are widely available at surf shops and surf camps: you can usually score a discount if you rent long-term, otherwise, you'll be paying around €20 to €30 per day for a board and wetsuit, or €15 to €25 per day for the board alone.

TUITION

There are dozens of schools that run lessons and courses for surfers of all levels. Surf camps mostly offer weekly packages including simple accommodation (dorms, bungalows or camping), meals and transport to the beach.

SURF SITES

www.magicseaweed.com International site with English-language surf reports for many Portuguese beaches.

www.wannasurf.com Global site with the lowdown on surfing hotspots along Portugal's coast. Navigate by interactive map.

www.surfingportugal.com Official site of the Portuguese Surfing Federation.

www.surftotal.com/pt Portuguese-language site with news about the national surf scene and webcams showing conditions at a dozen popular beaches around Portugal.

seafood restaurants and bars with a party vibe.

Nazaré hit headlines in recent years for the monster waves that roll in just north of town at Praia do Norte and the record-breaking feats of the gutsy surfers that ride them. We're talking seriously big waves and steep, hollow peaks and strong currents here. Given the right conditions, they can be over 30m high – think an eight-storey office building. The official world record of 23.77m for the biggest wave surfed was set here in 2011 by Garrett McNamara, who nearly bettered the feat with another giant in 2013.

Storms and winds in the Atlantic can generate mighty waves, but Nazaré has a peculiarity that multiplies this potential: an offshore underwater canyon some 5km deep pointing right at Praia do Norte beach, which produces the massive rollers.

Smaller and less intimidating are the waves on the main beach in town, which is less exposed.

To get an entirely different perspective of Nazaré, take the funicular up to **Promontório do Sítio**, where picture-postcard coastal views unfold from the 110m-high cliffs, gazing down to the thrashing waves on one side and the village on the other. From Rua do Elevador, an **ascensor** (Funicular; adult/child €1.20/0.90; ⊙ every 15min 7.15am-9.30pm, every 30min 9.30pm-midnight) climbs up the hill. It's nice to walk back down, escaping the crowds of trinket sellers.

✗ 🛏 p327

The Drive 》 From Nazaré, the small, coast-hugging Estrada Atlântica heads 21km north through pockets of pine forest and past high sand dunes, affording the occasional tantalising glimpse of ocean. Wind down those windows for delicious breezes.

- - - - - - - - - - - - -

⑨ São Pedro de Moel

For a more offbeat experience than Nazaré, turn your gaze north to São Pedro de Moel, which sees some pretty good waves (both lefts and rights) but receives just a trickle of surfers by comparison. The surf here is fairly consistent year-round, though bear the rocks in mind. The village itself is a pretty whitewashed number, with a low-key vibe and some knockout sunsets.

Spreading immediately north of São Pedro de Moel is the Pinhal de Leiria. First planted by a forward-looking monarch some 700 years ago, this vast forest of towering pines backs one of the loveliest stretches of Portugal's Atlantic coast. Dom Dinis expanded it significantly as a barrier against encroaching dunes and also as a source of timber for the maritime industry – a great boon during the Age of Discovery.

The Drive 》 Continue north on the pretty Estrada Atlântica for the 15km drive to Praia da Vieira. The narrow road cuts through the pine woods of Pinhal de Leiria and scrubby dunes, with the occasional glimpse of ocean.

- - - - - - - - - - - - -

⑩ Praia da Vieira

Backed by the sun-dappled Pinhal de Leiria, Praia da Vieira entices with broad golden sands and consistent surf with beach breaks. Come during the week rather than at the weekend to experience it at its tranquil best.

The Drive 》 From Praia da Vieira, it's a cruisy 5km drive north to Praia do Pedrógão, taking you once again through lush green coastal pinewoods.

- - - - - - - - - - - - -

⑪ Praia do Pedrógão

Your final stop on this road trip is Pedrógão, which has lovely broad, dune-backed sands, few surfers and some pretty impressive beach breaks (both to the left and right). After all those big waves, you might want to take the chance just to kick back and watch in wonder as the Atlantic rolls in before you.

Eating & Sleeping

Ericeira ❷

✕ Mar d'Areia   Seafood €€

(☎261 862 222; Rua Fonte do Cabo 48; mains €9-13; ☺noon-4pm & 7-11pm Tue-Sun; 👪) They keep the decor simple – blue-and-white checked tablecloths and tile designs of fish in nets – and let the excellent grilled fish do the talking at this locally popular, family-friendly seafood eatery adjacent to the Mercado Municipal.

⌂ Blue Buddha   Hostel €

(☎910 658 849; www.bluebuddhahostel.com; Moinhos do Mar; dm €25, d with private/shared bathroom €69/60; P @ ☎) Like your very own beach house, this hostel has a bright, spacious living room with couches, cable TV, DVD player and free internet, plus a guest kitchen and barbecue area. Multilingual proprietress Luzia is generous in sharing her knowledge of the area, and her attention to detail really shows, including comfortable mattresses and bold happy colours on the walls. Surf lessons available.

Peniche ❹

✕ Restaurante A Sardinha   Seafood €

(☎262 781 820; Rua Vasco da Gama 81; mains €6-14; ☺11.30am-4pm & 6.30-10.30pm) This no-frills place on a narrow street parallel to Largo da Ribeira does a roaring trade in mains like simply grilled fish and *caldeirada* (fish stew) done well.

⌂ Peniche Hostel   Hostel €

(☎969 008 689; www.penichehostel.com; Rua Arquitecto Paulino Montês 6; dm/d €20/50; @ ☎) This cosy little hostel, only steps from the tourist office and a five-minute walk from the bus station, has colourfully decorated and breezy rooms. Surfboards and bikes are available for hire, and there's an attached surf school. The friendly owners make you feel at home immediately, as do the comfortable common areas and small sundeck.

Nazaré ❽

✕ A Tasquinha   Seafood €

(☎262 551 945; Rua Adrião Batalha 54; mains €6-10; ☺noon-3pm & 7-10.30pm Tue-Sun) This exceptionally friendly family affair serves high quality seafood in a pair of snug but pretty tiled dining rooms. Expect queues on summer nights. However many people there are, the delightful owners always try and squeeze you in, even if it's at someone else's table! Top value.

⌂ Magic Art Hotel   Hotel € €

(☎262 569 040; http://hotelmagic.pt; Rua Mouzinho de Albuquerque 58; s €70-85, d €75-90; P ✳ ☎) Close to the action, this breezy, newish hotel has gone for the chic modern look. Clean-lined, well-equipped white rooms with artily presented photos of oldtime Nazaré contrast with appealing black slate bathrooms.

Douro Valley The staggering view of the Douro vineyards on undulating terraced hillsides

Classic Trip

Douro Valley Vineyard Trails

27

The Douro is a little drop of heaven. Uncork this region on Porto's doorstep and you'll soon fall head over heels in love with its terraced vineyards, wine estates and soul-stirring vistas.

TRIP HIGHLIGHTS

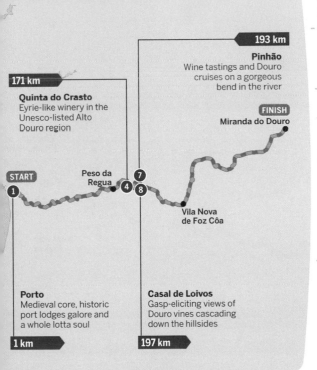

193 km

Pinhão
Wine tastings and Douro cruises on a gorgeous bend in the river

171 km

Quinta do Crasto
Eyrie-like winery in the Unesco-listed Alto Douro region

FINISH
Miranda do Douro

START
1

Peso da Regua

7
4
8

Vila Nova de Foz Côa

Porto
Medieval core, historic port lodges galore and a whole lotta soul

1 km

Casal de Loivos
Gasp-eliciting views of Douro vines cascading down the hillsides

197 km

5–7 DAYS
358KM / 222 MILES

GREAT FOR...

BEST TIME TO GO
Spring for wildflowers, early autumn for the grape harvest.

ESSENTIAL PHOTO
The staggering view of the Douro vineyards from Casal de Loivos miradouro.

BEST FOR FOODIES
Chef Rui Paula keeps it regional at DOC, with vineyard and river views from its terrace.

27 Douro Valley Vineyard Trails

You're in for a treat. This Unesco World Heritage region is hands down one of Portugal's most evocative landscapes, with mile after swoon-worthy mile of vineyards spooling along the contours of its namesake river and marching up terraced hillsides. Go for the food, the fabulous wines, the palatial *quintas,* the medieval stone villages and the postcard views on almost every corner.

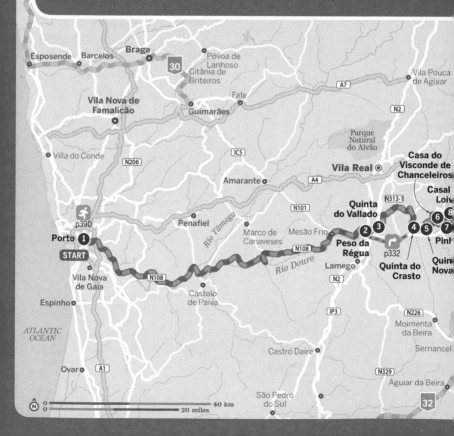

TRIP HIGHLIGHT

❶ Porto

Before kick-starting your road trip, devote a day or two to Porto, snuggled on banks of the Río Douro, where life is played out in the mazy lanes of the medieval Ribeira district (see p390 for our walking tour through here). From here, the double-decker **Ponte de Dom Luís I**, built by an apprentice of Gustav Eiffel in 1877, takes the river in its stride. Cross it to reach Vila Nova de Gaia, where grand 17th-century port lodges march up the hillside. Many open their barrel-lined cellars for guided tours and tastings – usually of three different ports – that will soon help you tell your tawny from your late-bottled vintage. Top billing goes to British-run **Taylor's** (223 742 800; www.taylor. pt; Rua do Choupelo 250; tour €5; 10am-6pm Mon-Fri, to

LINK YOUR TRIP

30 **The Minho's Landscapes**

Porto is a 55km drive from Guimarães, Portugal's birthplace and a starting point to explore the Minho's medieval cities, pilgrimage sites and Atlantic beaches.

32 **Highlands & History in the Central Interior**

Dip south of Porto 120km to Coimbra for a foray into Portugal's historic interior, weaving your way east to the Serra da Estrela mountains.

5pm Sat & Sun) (don't miss the immense 100,000L barrel), **Graham's** (☏223 776 484; www.grahams-port. com; Rua do Agro 141; tour €5-20; ⏰9.30am-6pm Apr-Oct, to 5.30pm Nov-Mar) and **Calém** (☏223 746 672; www. calem.pt; Avenida Diogo Leite 344; Cellar visit & tasting adult/ reduced/under 12 €5/2.50/ free; ⏰10am-6.30pm).

The Drive » There are quicker ways of getting from A to B, sure, but for immersion in Douro wine country, you can't beat this three-hour (137km) drive east on the N108. The serpentine road shadows the Río Douro from Porto to Peso da Régua, with views of hillsides combed with vines, little chapels and woodlands spilling down to the sparkling river.

❷ Peso da Régua

Terraced hills scaled with vines like a dragon's backbone rise around riverside Peso da Régua. The sun-bleached town is the region's largest, abutting the Río Douro at the western end of the demarcated port-wine area. It grew into a major port-wine *entrepôt* in the 18th century. While not as charming as its setting, the town is worth visiting for its **Museu do Douro** (www.museudodouro. pt; Rua Marqués de Pombal; adult/concession €6/3; ⏰10am-6pm daily May-Oct, Tue-Sun Nov-Apr). Housed in a beautifully converted riverside warehouse, the museum whisks you through the entire wine spectrum, from impressionist landscapes to the remains of an old flat-bottomed port hauler. Down at the pier, you'll find frequent 50-minute boat trips to Pinhão, offered by **Tomaz do Douro** (☏222 081 935; www.viadouro-cruzeiros. com; cruises from €10), for instance.

✕ ⛺ p337

The Drive » From Peso da Régua, take the first exit onto the N2 at the roundabout at the end of Rua Dr Manuel de Arriaga, then the third exit at the next roundabout to join the N313. Turn right onto the N313-1 when you see the yellow sign to Quinta do Vallado. It's around a 5km drive.

❸ Quinta do Vallado

Ah, what views! The vineyards spread picturesquely before you from **Quinta do Vallado** (☏254 318 081, 254 323 147; www.quintadovallado. com; Vilarinho dos Freires; r €120-180; P❋🛜🏊), a glorious 70-hectare winery. It brings together five rooms in an old stone manor and eight swank rooms in an ultra-modern slate building, decked out with chestnut and teak wood, each complete with a balcony. They all share a gorgeous pool. Guests get a free tour of the winery, with a tasting. Have a fine wine-paired meal and stay the night. The staff can also help arrange activities like cycling, hiking, fishing or canoeing – just ask.

DETOUR: DOC

Start: ❷ Peso da Régua

Architect Miguel Saraiva's ode to clean-lined, glass-walled minimalism, **DOC** (☏254 858 123; www.ruipaula. com; Folgosa; mains €27.50-29; ⏰12.30-3.30pm & 7.30-11pm) is headed up by Portuguese star chef Rui Paula. Its terrace peering out across the river is a stunning backdrop. Dishes give a pinch of imagination to seasonal, regional flavours, from fish *açordas* (stews) to game and wild mushrooms – all of which are paired with carefully selected wines from the cellar. It's in Folgosa, midway between Peso da Régua and Pinhão, on the south side of the river. Take the N2 south of Peso da Régua, then hook onto the N222 heading east.

The Drive » From Quinta do Vallado, the N313-2, CM1258 and N322-2 take you on a 29km drive east through the curvaceous wine terraces of the Alto Douro, past immaculately tended rows of vines and chalk-white hamlets, with tantalising glimpses of the river below. After Gouvinhas, the wiggling road takes you south to Quinta do Crasto.

❹ Quinta do Crasto

Perched like an eyric on a promontory above the Río Douro and a spectacular ripple of terraced vineyards, **Quinta do Crasto** (📞934 920 024, 254 920 020; www.quintadocrasto. pt; Sabrosa, Gouvinhas; tours €18; ⏰9am-6pm Mon-Fri) quite literally takes your breath away. The winery is beautifully set amid the lyrical landscapes of the Alto Douro, a Unesco World Heritage site. Stop by for a tour and tasting or lunch. It produces some of the country's best drops – reds that are complex, spicy and smooth, with wild berry aromas, and whites that are fresh, with a mineral nose and tang of citrus and apples. Designed by Portuguese architect Eduardo Souto Moura, the plunge pool here appears to nosedive directly into the valley below.

The Drive » From Quinta do Crasto it's an easy 4km drive east along the mellow banks of the Río Douro to Quinta Nova via the N322-2 and CM1268.

❺ Quinta Nova

Set on a ridge, surrounded by 120 hectares of ancient vineyards, overlooking the Douro river with mountains layered in the distance, **Quinta Nova** (📞254 730 420, 254 730 430; www.quintanova. com; s €134-152, d €152-173; 📶❄) is simply stunning. Besides plush lodgings in a beautifully restored 19th-century manor, it offers romantic grounds, a pool gazing out across vines rolling into the distance, a restaurant, wine tours, tastings and some of the region's top walking trails – the longest of which is 2½ hours.

The Drive » It's a 10km drive east from Quinta Nova to Casa do Visconde de Chanceleiros on the CM1268, tracing the contours of the emerald-green vines unfurling around you

❻ Casa do Visconde de Chanceleiros

Fancy staying the night up in the hills of the sublime Alto Douro? **Casa do Visconde de Chanceleiros** (📞254 730 190; www. chanceleiros.com; s €130-140, d €135-170; 🅿📶❄) is a gorgeous 250-year-old manor house, with spacious standard and superior rooms featuring classic decor and patios. The expansive views of the valley and lush terraced gardens steal the show, but so does the outdoor pool, tennis court, Jacuzzi, and sauna in a wine barrel. Delicious dinners (€38) are served on request.

The Drive » A gentle 7.5km drive east along the M590, with spirit-lifting views across the terraced vineyards, the deep-green Douro and family-run *quintas*, brings you to Pinhão.

❼ Pinhão

Encircled by terraced hillsides that yield some of the world's best port – and some damn good table wines too – little Pinhão sits on a particularly lovely bend of the Río Douro. Wineries and their competing signs dominate the scene and even the delightful train station has *azulejos* (tiles) depicting the grape harvest. The town, though cute, holds little of interest, but makes a fine base for exploring the surrounding vineyards. From here, you can also cruise upriver into the heart of the Alto Douro aboard a traditional flat-bottomed port boat with **Douro-a-Vela** (📞918 793 792; www. douro-a-vela.pt; 1hr cruise €25). Catch the boat from the Folgosa do Douro pier. Or rewind to the early days of viniculture on a guided tour followed by a tasting at **Quinta Nova Wine Museum & Shop** (Aris Douro; 📞254 730 030; www.quintanova.com; Largo da Estação 14; tours & tastings €5; ⏰tours 11am,

WHY THIS IS A CLASSIC TRIP
KERRY CHRISTIANI, AUTHOR

Step down a gear and enjoy the sweet life. Shadowing the bends in the river from Porto to the Spanish border, the Douro plays up romance, with its steeply climbing vines, giddy views and meandering roads leading to chalk-white hamlets, barrel-lined cellars and historic *quintas*, where fine meals and Portugal's best wines are served to the backbeat of cicadas.

Top: A boat cruises past the Douro's terraced vineyards
Left: Decorative tiles at Pinhão's train station
Right: The Río Douro framed by surrounding hills

MICHAEL MELFORD / GETTY IMAGES ©

3pm & 5pm Mon-Sat, 11am & 3pm Sun Apr-Oct).

✗ ⊨ p337

The Drive » Veer slightly west of Pinhão on the N323 and turn right onto the M585, following the sign for Casal de Loivos, 4.5km away. The country road that weaves up through the vines, with the river below, later becomes the cobbled Rua da Calçada, passing *socalcos* (stone-walled terraced vineyards).

- - - - - - - - - - - -

TRIP HIGHLIGHT

⑧ Casal de Loivos

It's a tough call, but Casal de Loivos has hands down one of the most staggeringly beautiful views in the region. From the *miradouro* (viewpoint), the uplifting vista reduces the Douro to postcard format, taking in the full sweep of its stone-walled terraced vineyards, stitched into the hillsides and fringing the sweeping contours of the valley, and the river scything through them. To maximise on these dreamy views, stay the night at **Casa de Casal de Loivros** (☎254 732 149; www.casadecasaldeloivos.com; s/d €90/110; @ ☀). The elegant house has been in this winemaking family for nearly 350 years. The halls are enlivened by museum-level displays of folkloric dresses, and the perch – high above the Alto Douro – is spectacular. Swim laps in the pool while peering down

across the vines spreading in all directions.

The Drive » Backtrack on the N323, then pick up the N222 south of the river for the 64km drive southeast to Vila Nova de Foz Côa. The winding road takes you through some picture-book scenery, with whitewashed hamlets and *quintas* punctuating vines, orchards and olive groves.

⑨ Vila Nova de Foz Côa

Welcome to the heart of the Douro's *terra quente* (hot land). This once-remote, whitewashed town has been on the map since the 1990s, when researchers, during a proposed project for a dam, stumbled across an astounding stash of Paleolithic art. Thousands of these mysterious rock engravings speckle the Río Côa valley. Come to see its world-famous gallery of rock art at the **Parque Arqueológico do Vale do Côa** (www.arte-coa. pt; Av Gago Coutinho 19 A, Foz Côa; park €10, museum €5

(N-S, afternoons €1), park & museum €12; ⊘ museum 10am-1.30pm & 2-5.30pm Tue-Sun, park 9am-12.30pm & 2-5.30pm Tue-Sun). The three sites open to the public include Canada do Inferno, with departures at around 9.30am from the park museum in Vila Nova de Foz Côa, which is the ideal place to understand just how close these aeons-old drawings came to disappearing.

The Drive » Wrap up your road trip by driving 120km northeast to Miranda do Douro via the N102, IP2 and IC5. The closer the Spanish border, the more you'll notice the shift in scenery, with lushness giving way to more arid, rugged terrain, speckled with vineyards and olive groves.

⑩ Miranda do Douro

A fortified frontier town hunkering down on the precipice of the Río Douro canyon, Miranda do Douro was long a bulwark of Portugal's 'wild east'. While its crumbling castle and handsomely severe 16th-century cathedral still lend an air of medieval charm, modern-day Miranda now receives weekend Span-

ish tourists, as opposed to repelling Castillian attacks. For an insight on the region's border culture, including ancient rites such as the 'stick dancing' of the *pauliteiros*, visit the **Museu da Terra de Miranda** (Praça de Dom João III; admission €2, Sun morning free; ⊘9am-1pm & 2-6pm Wed-Sun, 2-6pm Tue). If you'd rather get a taste of the rugged nature on Miranda's doorstep, **Europarques** (⌂273 432 396; www.europarques. com; adult/child under 10yr €16/8; ⊘trips 4pm daily, plus 11am Sat & Sun) runs 1½-hour river boat trips along a dramatic gorge. Boats leave from beside the dam on the Portuguese side. Stop by the **Parque Natural do Douro Internacional Office** (⌂273 431 457; Largo do Castelo; ⊘9.30am-12.30pm & 2-5.30pm Mon-Fri) for the inside scoop on hiking among the woods and towering granite cliffs of the 832-sq-km park, home to bird species including black storks, Egyptian vultures, peregrine falcons, golden eagles and Bonelli's eagles.

Eating & Sleeping

Peso da Régua ❷

✖ Castas e Pratos   Portuguese €€€

(☏254 323 290; www.castaspratos.com; Av José Vasques Osório; mains €19.50-22.50; ⏱10.30am-11pm) The coolest dining room in town is set in a restored wood-and-stone railyard warehouse with exposed original timbers. You can order grilled *alheira* sausage or octopus salad from the tapas bar downstairs or have the seabass on seafood fumet with saffron filaments, or kid goat in port with fava beans in the mezzanine.

🛏 Hotel Régua Douro   Hotel €€

(☏254 320 700; www.hotelreguadouro.pt; Largo da Estação; s €91-96, d €112.50-152.50; P❄@🛰🏊) This industrial-sized hotel sits by the river and is steps from the train station. It has plush, carpeted rooms in ruby (or is that tawny?) colour schemes and windows overlooking the Douro. The pool is much appreciated on hot days.

Pinhão ❼

✖ Veladouro   Portuguese €

(☏254 738 166; Rua de Praia 3; mains €6-8, ⏱10am-11pm Mon-Sat) Simple Portuguese food, such as wood-grilled meats, is served inside this quaint schist building or outside under a canopy of vines. From the train station, turn left and go along the main road for 150m, then left again under a railway bridge, and right at the river.

🛏 Quinta de la Rosa   B&B €€

(☏254 732 254; www.quintadelarosa.com; d €80-120, ste €120-140, villa per week €750-1800) Sitting on the banks of the Douro, 2km west of Pinhão, this charming vineyard and winery runs hour-long tours (€3) followed by tastings at 11am daily. The bright, appealing rooms straddle different buildings and private villas are available for weekly rental. Three-course dinners (€25) are perfectly matched with wines, and during the autumn harvest you can even join in with grape-treading traditions.

🛏 Vintage House   Boutique Hotel €€€

(☏254 730 230; www.csvintagehouse.com; Lugar da Ponte; s €140-210, d €180-285; P❄@🛰🏊) Occupying a string of 19th-century buildings right on the river, this luxurious sleep is actually very modern once you get past the distinctly English facade (a reminder of the key role Brits played in the port trade). This is where BB King stayed when he rocked the Douro. All rooms have terraces or balconies with river views.

Miranda do Douro ❿

✖ São Pedro   Portuguese €€

(☏273 431 321; Rua Mouzinho de Albuquerque; mains €7.50-12.50; ⏱noon-3pm daily, 7-10pm Tue-Sun) This spacious restaurant, just in from the main old-town gate, serves up a fine *posta á São Pedro* (grilled veal steak dressed with garlic and olive oil). The €11 tourist menu comes with soup, main, dessert, wine and coffee.

🛏 Hotel Parador Santa Catarina   Hotel €€

(☏273 431 005; www.hotelparadorsantacatarina.pt; Largo da Pousada; s/d/tr/q €50/80/85/100; P❄🛰) Every guest gets a private veranda with spectacular views of the gorge at this luxurious hotel perched on the canyon's edge. Rooms are a handsome mix of traditional and contemporary, with hardwood floors, flat-screen TVs and large marble bathrooms. The attached restaurant is the most upmarket in town.

Carvoeiro Stunning arch rock formations at Praia da Marinha

Classic Trip

Alentejo & Algarve Beaches

28

On this sunny coastal drive you'll experience some of Europe's finest beaches and explore the picturesque, formerly Moorish towns of Portugal's south.

TRIP HIGHLIGHTS

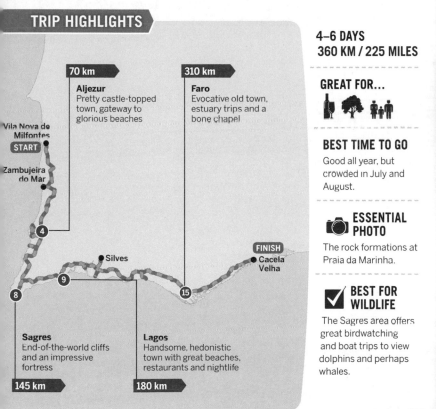

70 km

Aljezur
Pretty castle-topped town, gateway to glorious beaches

310 km

Faro
Evocative old town, estuary trips and a bone chapel

Vila Nova de Milfontes
START

Zambujeira do Mar

4

8

9

Silves

15

FINISH
Cacela Velha

Sagres
End-of-the-world cliffs and an impressive fortress

145 km

Lagos
Handsome, hedonistic town with great beaches, restaurants and nightlife

180 km

4–6 DAYS
360 KM / 225 MILES

GREAT FOR...

BEST TIME TO GO

Good all year, but crowded in July and August.

ESSENTIAL PHOTO

The rock formations at Praia da Marinha.

BEST FOR WILDLIFE

The Sagres area offers great birdwatching and boat trips to view dolphins and perhaps whales.

28 Alentejo & Algarve Beaches

Portugal's southern coasts offer a Mediterranean ideal, with fragrances of pine, rosemary, wine and grilling fish drifting over some absolutely stunning beaches. Only this isn't the Med, it's the Atlantic, so add serious surfable waves, important maritime history and great wildlife-watching opportunities to the mix. This drive takes in some of the finest beaches in the region, and explores the intriguing towns, which conserve their tight-knit Moorish street plans.

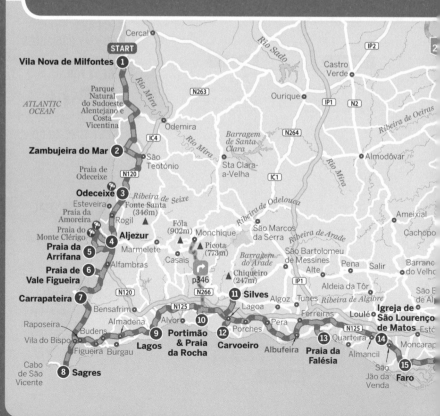

❶ Vila Nova de Milfontes

One of the loveliest towns along this stretch of the coast, Vila Nova de Milfontes has an attractive, whitewashed centre, sparkling beaches nearby and a laid-back population who couldn't imagine living anywhere else. Milfontes remains much more low-key than most resort towns, except in August when it's packed to the hilt with surfers and sun-seekers. It's located in the middle of the beautiful Parque Natural do Sudoeste Alentejano e Costa Vicentina and is still a port (Hannibal is said to have sheltered here) alongside a lovely, sand-edged limb of estuary.

Milfontes's narrow lanes, tiny plazas and beach harbour varied eating and drinking options. The town beach is sheltered but can get busy; the best strand in the vicinity is fantastic **Praia do Malhão**, backed by rocky dunes and covered in fragrant scrub, around 7km to the north.

The Drive » It's a 30km drive through protected parkland on the N393 south to Zambujeira.

❷ Zambujeira do Mar

Enchantingly wild beaches backed by rugged cliffs form the setting of this sleepy seaside village. The main street terminates at the cliff; paths lead to the attractive sands below. Quieter than Vila Nova, Zambujeira attracts a backpacker, surfy crowd, though in August the town is a party place and hosts the massive music fest, **Festa do Sudoeste**. The high-season crowds obscure Zambujeira's out-of-season charms: fresh fish in family-run restaurants, blustering cliff-top walks and a dramatic, empty coast.

🛏 p349

The Drive » Cutting back to the main road, you then head south on the N120. It's about 25km to Odeceixe through beautiful coastal woodland.

❸ Odeceixe

Located just as you cross into the Algarve from the Alentejo, Odeceixe is an endearing whitewashed village cascading down a hill below a picture-perfect windmill on the southern side of the Ribeira de Seixe valley. It's a sleepy town, except in summer, when it fills with people keen on its nearby beach. This tongue of sand is winningly set at a rivermouth and flanked

Parque
ural do Vale
Guadiana

São
Domingos

Moreanes

*Embalse
del Chanza*

SPAIN

El Granado

Pomarão

RTUGAL Alcoutim

ira da Foupana
queiros Foz de
ira de Odeleite Odeleite

Odeleite 192km to

Azinhal **24**

uel Anes
(229m) Vila Real de
Santo António

E01 **17 Cacela
Velha**

16 Tavira **FINISH**

Santa
Luzia

zeta

— 20 km
— 10 miles

LINK YOUR TRIP

24 Andalucía's White Villages

From the end of this trip it's an easy 192km on the A22 and A49 motorways, skirting Sevilla, to Carmona, the starting point of this route.

29 Medieval Jewels in the Southern Interior

From the end of this trip, head 75km north to Mértola, the finishing point of this route, and do it in reverse.

by imposing schist cliffs (try saying that with a mouthful of porridge...). It's a particularly good option for families, as smaller children can paddle on the peaceful river side of the strand while older kids tackle the waves on the ocean side. The beach is 3.5km from Odeceixe itself along a charming country road. At the beach, a small village has eating and surfing options. The Rota Vicentina, a long-distance walking path that leads right to the southwestern tip of Portugal, passes through Odeceixe, and there are great day walks in the vicinity.

The Drive » It's an easy 15km down the N120 to Aljezur, through woodland and open shrubland patched with heather and gorse.

TRIP HIGHLIGHT

❹ Aljezur

The old part of Aljezur is an attractive village with a Moorish feel. A collection of cottages winds down the hill below a ruined 10th-century hilltop **castle** (⏱24hr). Aljezur is close to some fantastic beaches, edged by black rocks that reach into the white-tipped, bracing sea – surfing hot spots. The handsomest beach in the Aljezur area, on the north side of the picturesque rivermouth and backed by wild dunes, is **Praia da Amoreira**. It's 9km by road from Aljezur, signposted off the main road north of town.

The Drive » A couple of kilometres south of Aljezur, the beaches of Monte Clérigo and Arrifana are signposted off to the right. At the top of the hill, head right (towards Monte Clérigo) for the full coastal panorama before winding your way south to Arrifana.

❺ Praia da Arrifana

Arrifana is a seductive fingernail-shaped cove embraced by cliffs. Just to add to the picturesqueness, it also sports an offshore pinnacle and a petite traditional fishing harbour. The beach is wildly popular with surfers of all abilities and there are several surf schools in the area. The beach break is reliable, but there's also a right-hand reef break that can offer some of the Algarve's best surfing when there's a big swell. There's a small, very popular beachside restaurant, and clifftop eateries near the ruined fortress up above, which offers breathtaking vistas. Good diving is also possible here.

The Drive » Praia de Vale Figueira is reached by a rough road that runs some 5km from the main road at a point 10km south of Aljezur. Before reaching the turnoff, you must turn right off the N120 on to the N268

❻ Praia de Vale Figueira

One of the remoter west coast beaches, this is a long, wide and magnificent stretch of whitish sand with an ethereal beauty, backed by stratified cliffs hazy in the ocean spray. It's reached by a rough, partly paved road. The beach, which

---

✔ **TOP TIP:**
FAMILY ATTRACTIONS

This central section of the Algarve coast is great for families, with numerous water parks and other attractions in the area. Two of the most popular are **Slide & Splash** (☎282 340 800; www.slidesplash.com; Estrada Nacional 125; adult/child 5-10yr €26/19; ⏱10am-5pm, 6pm or 6.30pm daily May-Sep, Mon-Sat Apr & Oct) and **Aqualand** (☎282 320 230; www.aqualand.pt; N125, Sítio das Areias, Alcantarilha; adult/child €22.50/16.50; ⏱10am-6pm Jul & Aug, to 5pm late Jun & early Sep).

has no facilities, faces due west and has pretty reliable surf, especially when a southeaster is blowing. It's one of those lonely, romantic beaches that's great to stroll on even when the weather's nasty.

The Drive » Head back to the main road and turn right onto it. It's about 10km from here to Carrapateira.

- - - - - - - - - - - -

❼ Carrapateira

Surf-central Carrapateira is a tranquil, pretty, spread-out village offering two fabulous beaches with spectacular settings and turquoise seas. Bordeira is a mammoth swath of sand merging into dunes 2km from the north side of town. Amado, with even better surf, is at the southern end. The circuit of both from Carrapateira (9km) is a visually stunning hike (or drive), with lookouts over the beaches and rocky coves and cliffs between them. In town, the **Museu do Mar e da Terra** (📞282 970 000; Rua de Pescador; adult/child €2.70/1.10; ⏰10am-5pm Tue Sat) is an intriguing place to visit, with great views.

The Drive » The N268 barrels on right down to Portugal's tip at Sagres (22km), via the regional centre of Vila do Bispo.

TRIP HIGHLIGHT

❽ Sagres

The small, elongated village of Sagres, with a rich nautical history, has an appealingly out-of-the-way feel. It sits on a remote peninsula amid picturesque seaside scenery with a sculpted coastline and stern **fortress** (📞282 620 140; http://www.monumentosdoalgarve.pt/pt/monumentos-do-algarve/fortaleza-de-sagres; adult/child €3/1.50; ⏰9.30am-8pm May-Sep, to 5.30pm Oct-Apr) giving access to a stunning clifftop walk. It also appeals for its access to fine beaches and water-based activities; it's especially popular with surfers. Outside town, the striking cliffs of **Cabo de São Vicente** (⏰lighthouse complex 10am-6pm Tue-Sun Apr-Sep, to 5pm Oct-Mar), the southwesternmost point of Europe, make for an enchanting visit, especially at sunset. Make sure you pop into the small **museum** (adult/child €1.50/1; ⏰10am-6pm Tue-Sun Apr-Sep, to 5pm Oct-Mar) here, which has interesting background on the Algarve's starring role in the Age of Discoveries. From Sagres' harbour, worthwhile excursions head out to observe dolphins and seabirds. **Mar Ilimitado** (📞916 832 625; www.marilimitado.com; Porto da Baleeira) is a recommended operator.

🍴 🛏 p349

The Drive » Head back to Vila do Bispo and turn right onto the N125 that will take you to Lagos, a total drive of 34km. Promising beach detours include Zavial and Salema.

- - - - - - - - - - -

TRIP HIGHLIGHT

❾ Lagos

Touristy, likeable Lagos lies on a riverbank, with 16th-century walls enclosing the old town's pretty, cobbled streets and picturesque plazas. A huge range of restaurants and pumping nightlife add to the allure provided by fabulous beaches and numerous

---

**TOP TIP:
THE SAGRES EAT
SCENE**

A closely packed string of surfer-oriented places on Rua Comandante Matoso offer a bit of everything, whether it's a coffee or a caipirinha you're after: they are cafes by day, restaurants serving international favourites whatever time hunger drags you away from the beach, and lively bars by night. Further down the same street, near the port, is a cluster of more traditional Portuguese restaurants.

WHY THIS IS A CLASSIC TRIP
ANDY SYMINGTON, AUTHOR

I can't think of a more impressive series of beaches than those of Portugal's south; they are simply magical. There's a wild and unspoiled romance to the seasprayed west-coast strands, while a succession of sun-baked golden sands in the south includes intriguing island beaches only reachable by boat. I love wandering the region's tight-knit old towns too, trying to detect which lane that delicious aroma of grilling fish is coming from...

Top: Sagres at sunset
Left: Faro's cobbled old town
Right: Sunbathers at Praia da Rocha

CHAD EHLERS / GETTY IMAGES ©

watery activities. Aside from the hedonism, there's plenty of history here: start by visiting the lovably higgledy-piggledy **Museu Municipal** (📞282 762 301; Rua General Alberto da Silveira; adult/concession €3/1.50; ⏱10am-12.30pm & 2-5.30pm Tue-Sun), which incorporates the fabulous baroque church **Igreja de Santo António** (Rua General Alberto da Silveira; adult/child incl museum €3/1.50; ⏱10am-12.30pm & 2-5.30pm Tue-Sun). Heading out on to the water is a must, perhaps cetacean-spotting with **Algarve Dolphins** (📞282 788 513; www.algarve-dolphins.com; adult/child from €35/25), kayaking with **Axessextreme** (📞919 114 649; www.axessextreme.com; 3hr tour €25) or learning to surf with **Lagos Surf Center** (📞282 764 734; www.lagossurfcenter.com; Rua da Silva Lopes 31; 1-/3-/5-day courses €55/150/225). East of town stretch the long, golden sands of Meia Praia, backed by worth-while beach restaurants.

✖ p349

The Drive » Portimão is really just along the coast from Lagos, but it's a 24km detour inland via the N125 in a car.

- - - - - - - - - -

❿ **Portimão & Praia da Rocha**

The Algarve's second-largest town, Portimão's history dates back to the Phoenicians before it became the region's fish-ing and canning hub in

Classic Trip

the 19th century. Though that industry has since declined, it's still an intriguing port with plenty of maritime atmosphere. Learn all about the town's fishing heritage in the excellent **Museu de Portimão** (☎282 405 230; www.museudeportimao. pt; Rua Dom Carlos I; adult/ child €3/free; ☺2.30-6pm Tue, 10am-6pm Wed-Sun Sep-Jul, 7.30-11pm Tue, 3-11pm Wed-Sun Aug), before strolling through the no-frills sardine restaurants of the fishermen's quarter of Largo da Barca near the road bridge. At the southern end of Portimão stretches the impressive resort beach of Praia da Rocha, backed

by numerous restaurants and nightlife options.

The Drive » The N125 leads you east to the junction with the N124-1, that takes you north to Silves. It's a drive of only 20km.

⓫ Silves

Silves is one of the Algarve's prettiest towns and replete with history: it was an important trading city in Moorish times and preserves a tightly woven medieval centre. At the top of the town, its sizeable **castle** (☎282 445 624; adult/concession/under 10yr €2.80/1.40/ free, joint ticket with Museu Municipal de Arqueologia €3.90; ☺9am-8pm Jun-Aug, to 6.30pm Mar-May & Sep-Nov, to 5pm Dec-Feb) offers great views from the ramparts. Originally occupied in the Visigothic period, what you see today dates mostly from the Moorish

era, though the castle was heavily restored in the 20th century. Below this, the atmospheric **cathedral** (Rua da Sé; admission €1; ☺9am-12.30pm & 2-5pm Mon-Fri, plus 9am-1pm Sat Jun-Aug) is the region's best-preserved Gothic church. The **Museu Municipal** (☎282 444 838; Rua das Portas de Loulé; adult/under 10yr €2.10/ free, joint ticket with Castelo €3.90; ☺10am-6pm) gives good background on the city's history and is built around a fascinating Moorish-era well, complete with spiral staircase. The old-town streets are great for strolling.

The Drive » Cruise 14km straight down the N124-1 to the beach at Carvoeiro.

⓬ Carvoeiro

Carvoeiro is a cluster of whitewashed buildings rising up from tawny, gold and green cliffs and backed by hills. This diminutive seaside resort is prettier and more laid-back than many of the bigger resorts. The town beach is pretty but small and crowded, however, there are lots of other excellent options in the area. The most picturesque of all, with stunning rock formations, is **Praia da Marinha**, best reached by the **Percurso dos Sete Vales Suspensos** clifftop walk, beginning

---

DETOUR: MONCHIQUE

Start: ⓾ Portimão & Praia da Rocha

High above the coast, in cooler mountainous woodlands, the picturesque little town of Monchique makes a lovely detour, with some excellent options for day hikes, including climbing the Algarve's highest hills, Picota and Fóia, for super views over the coast. Monchique and the surrounding area have some excellent eating choices and nearby Caldas de Monchique is a sweet little spa hamlet in a narrow wooded valley.

The N266 heads north from the N124 north of Portimão; it's a 27km drive from Lagos to Monchique, then another 30km on to Silves.

at Praia Vale Centianes, 2.3km east of town.

📑 p349

The Drive » Head back to Lagoa to join the N125 eastwards. After 25km, turn right and head towards the coast, emerging atop the long beach. It's a 37km total drive.

---

⑬ Praia da Falésia

This long straight strip of sand offers one of the region's most impressive first glimpses of coast as you arrive from above. It's backed by stunning cliffs in white and several shades of ochre, gouged by weather into intriguing shapes and topped by typical pines. The areas near the car parks get packed in summer (especially as high tides cover much of the beach), but as the strip is over 3km long, it's easy enough to walk and find plenty of breathing room. It's a good beach for strolling, as the cliffscape constantly changes colours and shapes, and there's a surprising range of hardy seaside plants in the cracks and crevices.

The Drive » Head back to the N125 and continue eastwards. Just after bypassing the town of Almancil, there's an exit to 'Almancil, São Lourenço, praias'. The church is signposted from here.

LOCAL KNOWLEDGE: MERCADO MUNICIPAL

Faro's impressive modern **market building** (📞289 897 250; www.mercadomunicipaldefaro.pt; Largo Dr Francisco Sá Carneiro; ⏰stalls 7am-3pm Mon-Sat; 📶) makes a great place to wander, to people-watch, to buy fresh produce, to sit down on a terrace with a coffee, or to lunch at one of the several worthwhile eateries.

---

⑭ Igreja de São Lourenço de Matos

It's worth stopping here to visit the marvellous interior of this small **church** (Church of St Lawrence; Rua da Igreja; admission €2; ⏰10am-1pm & 3-5pm Mon-Sat), built over a ruined chapel after local people, while digging a well, had implored the saint for help and then struck water. The resulting baroque masterpiece, built by fraternal master-team Antão and Manuel Borges, is wall-to-wall *azulejos* (painted tiles) inside, with beautiful panels depicting the life of the Roman-era saint, and his death by barbecue. In the 1755 earthquake, only five tiles fell from the roof.

The Drive » Back on the N125, head eastwards and after 12km you're in Faro.

TRIP HIGHLIGHT

⑮ Faro

The capital of the Algarve has a distinctly Portuguese feel and plenty to see. Its evocative waterside old town is very scenic and has several interesting sights, including the excellent **Museu Municipal** (📞289 897 400; Praça Dom Afonso III 14; adult/student €2/1; ⏰10am-7pm Tue-Fri, 11.30am-6pm Sat & Sun Jun-Sep, 10am-6pm Tue-Fri, 10.30am-5pm Sat & Sun Oct-May), set in a former convent. The area is centred around Faro's **cathedral** (📞289 823 018; www.paroquiasedefaro.org; Largo da Sé; adult/child €3/free; ⏰10am-6.30pm Mon-Fri, to 1pm Sat Jun-Aug, to 5pm Mon-Fri, to 1pm Sat Sep-May), built in the 13th century but heavily damaged in the 1755 earthquake. What you see now is a variety of Renaissance, Gothic and Baroque features. Climb the tower for lovely views across the walled town and estuary islands. These islands are part of the Parque Natural da Ria Formosa and can be explored on excellent boat trips run by **Formosamar** (📞918 720 002; www.formosamar.com; Clube Naval, Faro Marina). The cathedral has a small bone chapel,

but much spookier is the one at the **Igreja de Nossa Senhora do Carmo** (Largo do Carmo; chapel €2; ☺9am-1pm & 3-5pm or 6pm Mon-Fri, 9am-1pm Sat, mass 9am Sun), built from the mortal remains of over a thousand monks.

🍴 p349

The Drive ≫ It's 35km east along the N125 to Tavira. Despite the road's proximity to the coast, you won't see much unless you turn off: Fuzeta is a pleasant waterside village to investigate, with boat connections to island beaches.

🕛 Tavira

Set on either side of the meandering Río Gilão, Tavira is a charming town. The ruins of a hilltop **castle** (Largo Abu-Otmane; ☺8am-5pm Mon-Fri, 9am-7pm Sat & Sun, to 5pm winter), now housing a pleasant little botanic garden, the Renaissance **Igreja da Misericórdia** (Rua da Galeria; ☺9am-1pm & 2-6pm Mon-Sat), and the **Núcleo Islâmico** (Praça da República 5; adult/child €2/1, joint admission with Palácio da Galeria €3/1.50; ☺10am-12.30pm & 3-6pm mid-Jun–mid-Sep, 10am-4.30pm Tue-Sat mid-Sep–mid-Jun) museum of Moorish history are among the attractions. It's ideal for wandering; the warren of cobblestone streets hides pretty, historic gardens and shady plazas. Tavira is the launching point for the stunning, unspoilt beaches of the Ilha de Tavira, a sandy island that's another part of the Ria Formosa park.

🛏 p349

The Drive ≫ Cacela Velha is 14km east of Tavira: head along the N125 and you'll see it signposted; it's 1km off the road.

🕛 Cacela Velha

Enchanting, small and cobbled, Cacela Velha is a huddle of white-washed cottages edged with bright borders, and has a pocket-sized fort, orange and olive groves, and gardens blazing with colour. It sits above a gorgeous stretch of sea, with a character-ful local bar, plus other restaurants, a church and heart-lifting views. From nearby Fábrica, you can get a boat across to the splendid Cacela Velha beach, which has a low-key LGBT scene in summer.

MANFRED GOTTSCHALK / GETTY IMAGES ©

Tavira Saturday street bazaar

Eating & Sleeping

Zambujeira do Mar ②

🛏 Herdade do Touril   Rural Inn €€

(📞937 811 627; www.herdadedotouril.pt; r from €90; @ 🐾) Four kilometres north of Zambujeira do Mar is this upmarket *quinta* building with rooms and apartments of the fluffy-pillow variety. Some are located within the original building (built in 1826), others are converted farm cottages. The rustic and contemporary design of this tranquil place has an African safari-lodge feel – without the lions. Instead, storks nest in nearby cliffs (note, this area is not safe for children). There's a seawater pool, a buffet breakfast and free bikes. Good taste, good choice.

Sagres ⑧

🍴 A Casínha   Portuguese €€

(📞917 768 917; www.facebook.com/acasinha.restaurantesagres; Rua de São Vicente; mains €12-18; ⊘dinner Mon, lunch & dinner Tue-Sat) This cosy terracotta-and-white spot – built on the site of the owner's grandparents' house – serves up some fabulous Portuguese cuisine, including standout barbecued fish, a good variety of *cataplanas* for two (€34) and *arroz de polvo* (octopus rice). High quality and a pleasant atmosphere.

🛏 Pousada do Infante   Luxury Hotel €€€

(📞218 442 001, 282 620 240; www.pousadas.pt; Rua Patrão António Faustino; s/d €215/225, superior €260/270; P 🐾 @ 🛜 🐾) This modern *pousada* has large rooms in a great setting near the clifftop. Count on green or orange interiors, handsome public areas and picture-perfect views from the terraces. A well priced, quality pick.

Lagos ⑨

🍴 A Forja   Portuguese €€

(📞282 768 588; Rua dos Ferreiros 17; mains €8-15; ⊘noon-3pm & 6.30-10pm Sun-Fri) The

secret is out. This buzzing place pulls in the crowds – locals, tourists and expats – for its hearty, top-quality traditional food served in a bustling environment at great prices. Plates of the day are always reliable, as are the fish dishes.

Carvoeiro ⑫

🛏 O Castelo   Guesthouse €€

(📞919 729 259; www.ocastelo.net; Rua do Casino 59; d without view €65, with view €90-110; 🐾🛜) To the west of the bay, behind the *turismo*, this standout guesthouse with a welcoming and justifiably proud owner is recently renovated and gleamingly well-maintained. Rooms are most inviting; some share a large terrace and sea views (with sunrises), while one has a private balcony. They get all the details right; it's a stunning outlook and a lovely, lovely place.

Faro ⑮

🍴 Faz Gostos   Portuguese, French €€

(📞289 878 422; www.fazgostos.com; Rua do Castelo 13; mains €14-20; ⊘lunch & dinner Mon-Fri, dinner Sat, 🛜) Elegantly housed in the old town, this offers high-class French-influenced Portuguese cuisine in a spacious, comfortably handsome dining area. There's plenty of game, fish and meat on offer with rich and seductive sauces, and a few set menus are available.

Tavira ⑯

🛏 Casa Beleza do Sul   Apartment €€

(📞960 060 906; www.casabelezadosul.com; Rua Dr Parreira 43; apt €90-120; 🛜) A gorgeous historic house in central Tavira is showcased to full advantage in this beautiful conversion. The result is a cute studio and three marvellous suites of rooms, all different with original tiled floors and modern bathrooms. All have a kitchenette and there are numerous decorative and thoughtful touches that put this well above the ordinary. Minimum stays apply. Breakfast available for an extra charge.

Évora Delve into the past with enchanting medieval architecture at every turn

Medieval Jewels in the Southern Interior

29

A stunning assemblage of walled towns and sturdy castles take their place alongside some of the peninsula's most arresting monasteries in this drive, a goldmine of medieval architecture.

TRIP HIGHLIGHTS

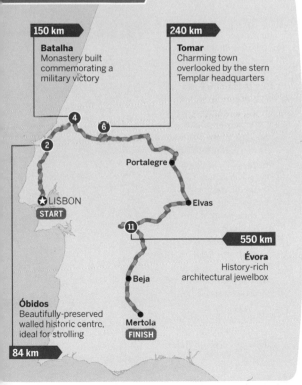

150 km

Batalha
Monastery built commemorating a military victory

240 km

Tomar
Charming town overlooked by the stern Templar headquarters

Portalegre

LISBON
START

Elvas

550 km

Évora
History-rich architectural jewelbox

Beja

Óbidos
Beautifully-preserved walled historic centre, ideal for strolling

84 km

Mertola
FINISH

6–9 DAYS
720 KM / 450 MILES

GREAT FOR...

BEST TIME TO GO

March to June and September to October for pleasant weather without extreme heat.

ESSENTIAL PHOTO

Any of the medieval town walls at sunset.

✓ BEST TWO DAYS

From Alcobaça to Tomar, with a dash to Évora if you have time.

29 Medieval Jewels in the Southern Interior

War defined medieval Portugal. Towns were fortified with sturdy walls, castles defended them, and when you won a victory, you built a monastery in thanks to the powers that be. That turbulent history has left a region studded in architectural jewels. This drive takes you from Portugal's romantic capital around a stunning selection of them, through typical hill landscapes softened by cork-oaks and pine. Hearty inland cuisine adds to the authentically Portuguese experience.

❶ Lisbon

Spread across steep hillsides overlooking the Río Tejo (Tagus), Portugal's capital offers real enchantment in its narrow cobbled streets, centenarian cafes and local *bairro* life; explore it on our walking tour, p388. On either side of the low central district, Baixo, rise hills. Bairro Alto is a bohemian district of restaurants and bars, while facing it, Alfama is Lisbon's Moorish time capsule: a medina-like district of tangled alleys, hidden palm-shaded squares and narrow terracotta-roofed houses that tumble down to the glittering Tejo. It is the birthplace of fado, the melancholic Portuguese singing that you can investigate at the excellent **Museu do Fado** (www.museudofado.pt; Largo do Chafariz de Dentro; admission €5; ⏰10am-6pm Tue-Sun). Atop the district is the dramatic **Castelo de São Jorge** (http://castelodesaojorge.pt; adult/child €8.50/5; ⏰9am-9pm Mar-Oct, to 6pm Nov-Feb), which still conserves a residential district within its outer walls. Farther afield, in the district of Belém, the spectacular Manueline **Mosteiro dos Jerónimos** (www.mosteirojeronimos.pt; Praça do Império; adult/child €10/5; ⏰10am-6.30pm Tue-Sun, free 10am-2pm Sun) and **Torre de Belém**

(www.torrebelem.pt; adult/child
€6/3, free 1st Sun of month)
fortress jutting out onto
the river, are World
Heritage–listed sights.

✕ 🛏 p359

The Drive » It's a fairly dull
84km run north up the A8
motorway to Óbidos.

- - - - - - - - - - - - - - - -

TRIP HIGHLIGHT

② Óbidos

Surrounded by a classic
crenellated wall, Óbidos'
gorgeous historic centre
is a labyrinth of cob-
blestoned streets and
flower-bedecked, white-
washed houses livened
up with dashes of vivid
yellow and blue paint.
The main gate, Porta
da Vila, leads directly
into the main street,
Rua Direita, lined with
chocolate and cherry-
liqueur shops. It's quite

🔗 LINK YOUR TRIP

6 Ancient Extremadura

From Évora, it's a direct
160km northeast on
motorways A6 and A5 to
Mérida in Spain, starting
point for this trip.

28 Alentejo & Algarve Beaches

After all the inland scenery,
time to hit the coast! You
can do this route in reverse
by hitting Cacela Velha,
75km south of Mértola.

touristy, so wind your way away from it and you'll soon capture some of the town's atmosphere in more peace. There are pretty bits outside the walls, too.

You can walk around the wall for uplifting views over the town and surrounding countryside. The walls date from Moorish times (later restored), but the *castelo* (castle) itself is one of Dom Dinis' 13th-century creations. It's a stern edifice, with lots of towers, battlements and big gates. Converted into a palace in the 16th century (some Manueline touches add levity), it's now a deluxe hotel.

The town's elegant main church, **Igreja de Santa Maria** (Praça de Santa Maria; 🕘9.30am-12.30pm & 2.30-7pm), stands out for its interior, with a wonderful painted ceiling and tiled walls.

The aqueduct, southeast of the main gate, dates from the 16th century and is 3km long.

The Drive » It's an unexciting 42km drive north up the IC1/ A8. Take exit 22, signposted to Alcobaça among other places.

---

❸ Alcobaça

The little town of Alcobaça has a charming if touristy centre with a little river and bijou bridges. All, however, yield centre stage to the magnificent 12th-century **Mosteiro de Santa Maria de Alcobaça** (📞262 505 126; www.mosteiroalcobaca. pt; church free, monastery adult/child €6/free, with Tomar & Batalha €15; 🕘9am-7pm Apr-Sep, 9am-5pm Oct-Mar). One of Iberia's great monasteries, it utterly dominates the town. Hiding behind the imposing baroque facade lies a high, austere, monkish church with a forest of unadorned 12th-century arches. But make sure you visit the rest too: the beautiful cloisters, atmospheric refectory, vast dormitory and other spaces bring back the Cistercian life, which, according to sources, wasn't quite as austere here as it should have been.

STUART FORSTER / GETTY IMAGES ©

The monastery was founded in 1153 by Afonso Henriques, first king of Portugal. The monastery estate became one of the richest and most powerful in the country, apparently housing 999 monks, who held Mass nonstop in shifts. In the 18th century, however, it was the monks' growing decadence that became famous. The party ended in 1834 with the dissolution of the religious orders.

The Drive » It's a short drive eastwards on the IC9, then northwards on the IC2 to Batalha, 23km away.

TOP TIP: COMBINED MONASTERY TICKET

If you're planning to visit the monasteries at Alcobaça and Batalha, as well as the Convento de Cristo in Tomar, you can get (from any one of them) a combined ticket for €15 (a saving of €3) that will let you in to all three and is valid for a week.

Batalha Nuno Álvares Pereira statue in front of the Mosteiro de Santa Maria da Vitória

TRIP HIGHLIGHT

④ Batalha

The 1385 Battle of Aljubarrota fought here put the Castilians from Spain in their place and set the foundations for Portugal's golden age. An extraordinary abbey, the **Mosteiro de Santa Maria da Vitória** (☏244 765 497; www.mosteirobatalha. pt; church free, rest adult/child €6/free, with Alcobaça & Tomar €15; ◔9am-6.30pm Apr-Sep, to 5.30pm Oct-Mar), was built to commemorate it. Most of the monument was completed by 1434 in Flamboyant Gothic, but Manueline exuberance steals the show, thanks to additions made in the 15th and 16th centuries. The Claustro Real is a masterpiece, as are the unfinished Capelas Imperfeitas.

The battlefield itself is on the southern edge of town. Here, the **Batalha de Aljubarrota Centro de Interpretação** (www. fundacao-aljubarrota.pt; adult/teen/child €7/5/3.50; ◔10am-5.30pm Tue-Sun Oct-Apr, to 7pm May-Sep) is a museum whose crowning glory is a blood-and-thunder 30-minute film depicting the battle.

🛏 p359

The Drive » This picturesque drive takes you south on the N362 to castle-topped Porto de Mós. The N243 then takes you across the lonely landscapes of the Serra de Aire before the A23 brings you to Constância, near the next stop.

⑤ Castelo de Almourol

Like the stuff of legend, 10-towered **Castelo de Almourol** (◔10am-1pm & 2.30-7.30pm Mar-Oct, 10am-1pm & 2.30-5.30pm Nov-Feb) stands tantalisingly close to shore but just out of reach in the Río Tejo. The castle is 5km from Constância. Boats (€2.20,

DETOUR:
MONUMENTO NATURAL DAS PEGADAS
DOS DINOSSÁURIOS

Start: ❹ **Batalha**

On your way between stops 4 and 5, turn off onto the N360 at Minde, head north for 7km, then another 5km east. On the N357, 10km south of Fátima in a village called Bairro, the **Monumento Natural das Pegadas dos Dinossáurios** (☑249 530 160; www.pegadasdedinosaurios.org; adult/child €3/1.50; ⊙10am-12.30pm & 2-6pm Tue-Sun, to 8pm Sat & Sun Apr-Sep; ♿) is one of the most important locations for sauropod prints in the world.

The visit starts with a 20-minute video in Portuguese, then you take a 1.5km walk around the quarry, first seeing the prints from above then walking among them. These, the oldest and longest sauropod tracks in the world, record walks in the mud 175 million years ago. As you walk across the slope you can clearly see the large elliptical prints made by the hind feet and the smaller, half-moon prints made by the forefeet.

five minutes) leave regularly from a riverside landing directly opposite the castle. Once on the island, a short walk leads up to the ramparts, where you're free to linger as long as you like.

The island, almost jumping distance from land, was once the site of a Roman fort; the castle was built by Gualdim Pais, Grand Master of the Order of the Knights Templar, in 1171. It's no surprise that Almourol has long caught the imagination of excitable poets longing for the Age of Chivalry.

The Drive » The next stop lies around 30km north, easily accomplished by following the N358 through typical central Portuguese farmland.

TRIP HIGHLIGHT

❻ Tomar

Tomar is one of central Portugal's most appealing small towns, with a pedestrian-friendly historic centre and pretty riverside park in a charming natural setting adjacent to the lush Mata Nacional dos Sete Montes (Seven Hills National Forest).

But to understand what makes Tomar truly extraordinary, cast your gaze skywards. Wrapped in splendour and mystery, the Knights Templar held enormous power in Portugal from the 12th to 16th centuries, and largely bankrolled the Age of Discoveries. The **Convento de Cristo** (www. conventocristo.pt; Rua Castelo dos Templários; adult/child €6/free; ⊙9am-6.30pm),

their headquarters, sits on wooded slopes above the town and enclosed within 12th-century walls. It's a stony expression of magnificence, with chapels, cloisters and choirs in diverging styles, added over the centuries by successive kings and Grand Masters.

The **charola**, an extraordinary 16-sided church, dominates the complex. Its eastern influences give it a very different feel to most Portuguese churches; the interior is otherworldly in its vast heights – an awesome combination of simple forms and rich embellishment. It's said that the circular design enabled knights to attend Mass on horseback.

The Drive » It's time to head deep into Portugal, first south on the A13, then eastwards along the A23. Take exit 15 on to the IP2 towards Portalegre, then slip onto the N246 heading east. It's a total drive of 125km through increasingly wild inland landscapes.

---

7 Castelo de Vide

High above lush, rolling countryside, Castelo de Vide is one of Portugal's most attractive and underrated villages. Its fine hilltop vantage point, dazzlingly white houses, flower-lined lanes and proud locals are reason alone to visit. Originally inhabitants lived within the walls of the **castle** (⊗9.30am-1pm & 2-5.30pm Sep-May, to 6pm Jun-Aug), which preserves a small inner village. Nearby is a Jewish quarter with a **synagogue and museum** (⊗9.30am-1pm & 2-5pm Tue-Sun Sep-May, to 6pm Jun-Aug). Castelo de Vide is famous for its crystal-clear mineral water, which spouts out of numerous pretty public fountains.

🛏 p359

The Drive » Marvão is just 10km east of Castelo de Vide, signposted off the N246.

---

8 Marvão

On a jutting crag high above the surrounding countryside, the narrow lanes of Marvão feel like a retreat far removed from the settlements below. The whitewashed village of picturesque tiled roofs and bright flowers has marvellous views, a splendid **castle** (⊗9am-9pm summer, 10am-7pm winter) built into the rock at the western end of the village, and a handful of low-key guesthouses and restaurants.

The Drive » Take the N359 to Portalegre, then continue south on the N246 through typical Alentejan landscape of shrubs and cork-oaks to Elvas, 78km from your starting point.

---

9 Elvas

The impressive Unesco-listed fortifications zig-zagging around this pleasant little town reflect an extraordinarily sophisticated military technology. Its moats, fort and heavy walls would indicate a certain paranoia if it weren't for Elvas' position, near the Spanish border. Inside the stout, buttressed **fortifications** (📞268 628 357), you'll find a lovely town plaza, some quaint museums, narrow medina-like streets and a few excellent eateries. Outside, a magnificently ambitious **aqueduct** brings water from a point 7km west of town.

The Drive » Head west and a little south from Elvas to reach Vila Viçosa, some 40km away via the N4.

---

10 Vila Viçosa

Once home to the Bragança dynasty, this is the most rewarding of several 'marble towns' hereabouts. One of Portugal's largest palaces dominates the centre of town. The **Paço Ducal** (📞268 980 659; www.fcbraganca.pt; adult/under 10yr €6/ free; ⊗2-5pm Tue, 10am-1pm & 2-5pm Wed-Fri, 9.30am-1pm & 2-5pm Sat & Sun, closes 5.30pm or 6pm Apr-Sep), built in the 16th century, is imposingly enormous. The palace's best furniture went to Lisbon after Dom João IV ascended the throne, and some went on to Brazil after the royal family fled there in 1807, but there are still some stunning pieces on display, such as a huge 16th-century Persian rug in the Dukes Hall. Lots of royal portraits put into context the interesting background on the royal family.

The Drive » The more scenic of the routes to Évora is the N254 running southwest. It's around 60km between stops via the handsome little town of Redondo.

TRIP HIGHLIGHT

11 Évora

One of Portugal's most beautifully preserved medieval towns, Évora is an enchanting place to delve into the past. Inside the 14th-century walls, Évora's narrow, winding lanes lead to striking architectural works. Guarded by a pair of rose granite towers, the fortress-like medieval

cathedral (Largo do Marquês de Marialva; admission €1.50, with cloister €2.50; ⊙9am-5pm) has fabulous cloisters and a museum jam-packed with ecclesiastical treasures.

Once part of the Roman Forum, the cinematic columns of the **Templo Romano** (Temple of Diana; Largo do Conde de Vila Flor), dating from the 2nd or early 3rd century, are a heady slice of drama right in town. The city's main square, **Praça do Giraldo**, has seen some potent moments in Portuguese history, including the 1483 execution of Fernando, Duke of Bragança; the public burning of victims of the Inquisition in the 16th century; and fiery debates on agrarian reform in the 1970s. The narrow lanes to the southwest were once the *judiaria* (Jewish quarter).

Aside from its historic and aesthetic virtues, Évora is also a lively university town, and its many attractive restaurants serve up hearty Alentejan cuisine.

✗ ⊨ p359

The Drive » Head west of Évora on the N114, then after 11km take a left turn signposted to Guadalupe and the Cromeleque dos Almendres. Follow signs to reach the monument, some 17km in total from Évora.

‑ ‑ ‑ ‑ ‑ ‑ ‑ ‑ ‑ ‑ ‑ ‑

⑫ Cromeleque dos Almendres

Set within a beautiful landscape of olive and cork trees stands the Cromeleque dos Almendres. This huge, spectacular oval of standing stones is the Iberian Peninsula's most important megalithic group and an extraordinary place to visit.

The site consists of a huge oval of some 95 rounded granite monoliths – some of which are engraved with symbolic markings – spread down a rough slope. They were erected over different periods, it seems, with basic astronomic orientations, and were probably used for social gatherings or sacred rituals back in the dawn of the Neolithic period.

Two and a half kilometres before Cromeleque dos Almendres stands **Menir dos Almendres**, a single stone about 4m high, with some very faint carvings near the top. Look for the sign; to reach the menhir you must walk a few hundred metres from the road.

The Drive » Backtrack through the Évora ringroad and on to the N256 southeast. When you hit the IP2, head south across the Alentejan hills and plains, skirting the city of Beja before continuing on the IC27/N122 to Mértola, a total drive of 150km.

‑ ‑ ‑ ‑ ‑ ‑ ‑ ‑ ‑ ‑ ‑ ‑

⑬ Mértola

Spectacularly set on a rocky spur, high above the peaceful Río Guadiana, the cobbled streets of medieval Mértola are a delightful place to roam. A small but imposing castle stands high, overlooking the jumble of dazzlingly white houses and a picturesque church that was once a mosque. A long bout of economic stagnation at this remote town has left many traces of Islamic occupation intact, so much so that Mértola is considered a *vila museu* (open-air museum). There's a lot to see here, from the parish church, formerly a mosque, to the castle and a group of museums covering various aspects of the town's history.

Eating & Sleeping

Lisbon ❶

✕ 100 Maneiras   Fusion €€€

(📞910 307 575; www.restaurante100maneiras.
com; Rua do Teixeira 35; tasting menu €55,
with wine pairing €90; ⏰7.30pm-2am) How
do we love 100 Maneiras? Let us count the
hundred ways... The 10-course tasting menu
changes daily and features imaginative,
delicately prepared dishes. The courses are
all a surprise – part of the charm – though the
chef will take special diets and food allergies
into consideration. There's a lively buzz to the
elegant and small space. Reservations essential.

⛏ Casa Amora   Guesthouse €€

(📞919 300 317; casaamora.com; Rua João
Penha 13; d €105-170; ❈📶) Casa Amora has
10 beautifully designed guestrooms, with
eye-catching art and iPod docks. There's
a lovely garden patio where the first-rate
breakfast is served. It's located in the peaceful
neighbourhood of Amoreiras, a few steps
from one of Lisbon's prettiest squares. Rooms
are bright, elegantly furnished and uniquely
designed, and each pays homage to a different
Portuguese persona (such as poet Fernando
Pessoa, fadista Amália Rodrigues and painter
Amadeo Souza Cardoso).

Batalha ❹

⛏ Casa do Outeiro   Boutique Hotel €€

(📞244 765 806; www.casadoouteiro.com;
Largo Carvalho do Outeiro 4; s/d/tr €59/64/75;
P ❈ @ 📶 ≋) One of our favourite hotels in
central Portugal, this excellent place would be
worth a detour even if there wasn't a monastery
looming in plain view of some of the rooms. This
place feels in parts like a casual contemporary

gallery – stylish and colourful, with the owners'
original artworks decorating the rooms and
passageways. Rooms are modern, commodious
and attractive, and all a little different.

Castelo de Vide ❼

⛏ Casa de Hóspedes Melanie   Guesthouse €

(📞245 901 632; Largo do Paça Novo 3; s/d/tr
€25/35/45; ❈) Situated near a leafy square,
this clean spot is up there with Portugal's best-
value accommodation. It has five neat and light
rooms with cork-tile floors. Longer stayers are
invited to enjoy the roof terrace.

Évora ⓫

✕ Dom Joaquim   Portuguese €€

(📞266 731 105; Rua dos Penedos 6; mains
€12-15; ⏰noon-3pm & 7-10.45pm Tue-Sat,
noon-3pm Sun) Amid stone walls and modern
artwork, Dom Joaquim serves excellent
traditional cuisine including meats (game and
succulent, fall-off-the-bone lamb) and seafood
dishes, such as *cação* (dogfish).

⛏ Albergaria do Calvario   Boutique Hotel €€€

(📞266 745 930; www.albergariadocalvario.com;
Travessa dos Lagares 3; s €98-110, d €108-120;
P 📶) Unpretentiously elegant, discreetly
attentive and comfortable (but not can't-put-
your-feet-up-uber-luxurious), this place has an
ambience that travellers adore. The delightful
staff leave no service stone unturned and
breakfasts are among the region's best, with
locally sourced organic produce, homemade
cakes and egg dishes.

Guimarães
Birthplace of Afonso
Henrique

The Minho's Lyrical Landscapes

30

Portugal's northwestern corner is made for road-tripping, with its trilogy of medieval cities, pilgrimage sites and dune-flanked Atlantic beaches. Brace yourself for lyrical landscapes and cultural highs.

TRIP HIGHLIGHTS

217 km

Peneda
Mountain gateway to Parque Nacional da Peneda-Gerês

9 FINISH

Ponte da Barca

Ponte de Lima

6

32 km

Braga
Church bells chime in the country's most devout city

Esposende
Barcelos
3

Citânia de Briteiros

1

1 km

Viana do Castelo
A double hit of medieval charm and gorgeous, dune-flanked beaches

START

Guimarães
Alluring medieval centre topped by a 1000-year-old castle

99 km

2–4 DAYS
217 KM / 135 MILES

GREAT FOR...

BEST TIME TO GO
Year-round in the cities; spring to autumn on the coast.

ESSENTIAL PHOTO
Escadaria do Bom Jesus – a real baroque stunner of a staircase.

BEST FOR OUTDOORS
Hit the trail in the granite wilds of Parque Nacional da Peneda-Gerês.

361

30

The Minho's Lyrical Landscapes

Sidling up to Spain on Portugal's northwestern tip, the Minho is the birthplace of the Portuguese kingdom and the home of its emblematic cockerel – and you feel it. The region has a pinch of everything that makes this country special – fortified villages and vineyards, gorgeous dune-backed beaches and lush river valleys, high meadows patrolled by shepherds, granite peaks, and cities with both medieval looks and personality.

TRIP HIGHLIGHT

❶ Guimarães

Proudly waving the flag as the birthplace of Afonso Henrique in 1110 and, thus, the Portuguese Kingdom, Guimarães hides one of the most exquisitely preserved medieval centres in the country – a warren of cafe-filled plazas and labyrinthine lanes. Unesco duly noted this and made its alley-woven heart a World Heritage site. It is crowned by a 1000-year-old bird's nest

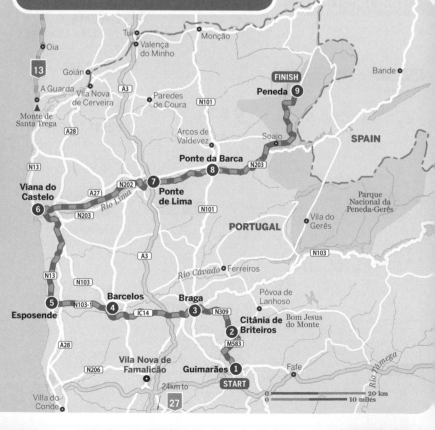

of a **castle** (🕐10am-6pm), which commands sweeping views over town to a ripple of hills beyond. Looming over the city on Guimarães' hilltop, with its crenulated towers and cylindrical brick chimneys, **Paço dos Duques de Bragança** (Rua Conde D Henrique; adult/child €5/free; 🕐9.30am-6.15pm) was first built in 1401 and later pompously restored as a presidential residence for Salazar. Its rooms now house Flemish tapestries, medieval weapons and a chapel with glittering stained-glass windows.

Some 7km southeast of Guimarães up a twisting, cobbled road is Penha (617m), whose cool woods make it a

LINK YOUR TRIP

27 Douro Valley Vineyard Trails

From Guimarães, it's just a 55km drive to Porto, from where you can easily dip into the terraced vineyards and outstanding wineries of the Unesco World Heritage Douro.

13 Coast of Galicia

Head just across the border to A Guarda, for a drive along Galicia's wild, storm-buffeted coast, past quaint fishing villages and coves steeped in legend.

wonderful escape from the summer heat. If you'd rather leave the car in town, hitch a ride on the Teleférico da Penha, 600m east of Guimarães' old centre.

🍴 🛏 p367

The Drive » Head on the N101 northwest of Guimarães, then the M583 (direction Prazins), which leads through gentle countryside and takes you onto the N309 to Citânia de Briteiros. It's a 16km drive.

---

❷ Citânia de Briteiros

Factor in at least an hour or so for a ramble around one of Portugal's most evocative archaeological sites, **Citânia de Briteiros** (admission incl museum adult/student €3/1.50; 🕐9.30am-6pm May-Sep, to 5pm Oct-Apr). This is the largest of a liberal scattering of northern Celtic hill settlements, or *citânias* (fortified villages), which date back at least 2500 years. It's likely that this sprawling 3.8 hectare site, inhabited from 300 BC to AD 300, was the last stronghold against the invading Romans.

The Drive » It's a 16km drive from Citânia de Briteiros to Braga. The N309 heads northwest through undulating countryside sprinkled with orchards, woods and church-topped villages. Before reaching Braga, allow time to visit Bom Jesus do Monte.

TRIP HIGHLIGHT

❸ Braga

Stay the night in Braga and your wake-up call will be the alarm of some three dozen church bells. *Bemvindo* (welcome) to Portugal's most devout city. Highest on your list should be the Romanesque **Sé** (www.se-braga. pt; Rua Dom Paio Mendes; 🕐8am-7pm high season, 9am-6pm low season), Portugal's oldest cathedral dating to 1070. Don't miss the intricate west portal, carved with scenes from Reynard the Fox, the filigree Manueline towers and the cloister lined with Gothic chapels. But Braga is more than the sum of its prayers – students and a vibrant cafe scene inject it with youthful spirit. Start or finish your evening in one of the cafes lining the **Praça da República**.

Lying around 5km east of central Braga, Bom Jesus do Monte is the goal of legions of penitent pilgrims every year. One of Portugal's most recognisable icons, the sober neoclassical church stands atop a forested hill that affords grand sunset views across the city. But most come for the extraordinary tiered baroque staircase, **Escadaria do Bom Jesus**. The lowest staircase is lined with chapels representing the Stations of the Cross. The area is chocked with tourists on summer weekends – best avoided if you want to experience the place at its peaceful best.

 p367

The Drive » On the IC14 it's a 23km drive west to Barcelos. A slightly slower alternative is to take the prettier, more relaxed N103 through pinewoods, cultivated fields and low-rise hills.

- - - - - - - - - - - - -

❹ Barcelos

Sitting on the Rio Cávado and hiding a pretty medieval core, dinky Barcelos is worth more than a cursory glance. This town is famous for its roosters (adorning every souvenir stall), pottery and, above all, its massive **Feira de Barcelos** (Campo da República; ⊙7am-7pm Thu) market, still a largely rural affair, with villagers hawking everything from scrawny chickens to hand-embroidered linen and carved ox yokes.

The Drive » The N103-1 takes you through west through countryside and small settlements for the 16km drive to Esposende.

- - - - - - - - - - - - -

❺ Esposende

After immersing yourself in the rural delights of the hinterland, it's time to hit the coast for a restorative blast of Atlantic air. Consistent swells and breezes attract surfers and kitesurfers to Esposende's broad golden beaches flanked by low dunes.

The Drive » Trace the contours of the coast north on the N13 past fields, little farms and villages on the 28km drive to Viana do Castelo. Or hop on the A13 instead to carve 15 minutes off your journey.

JAPATINO / GETTY IMAGES ©

🗨 LOCAL KNOWLEDGE: PARQUE NACIONAL DA PENEDA-GERÊS

Spread across four impressive granite massifs in Portugal's northernmost reach, this 703-sq-km park encompasses boulder-strewn peaks, precipitous valleys, and lush forests of oak and fragrant pine. It shelters more than 100 granite villages and hamlets that have changed little over the centuries. Many of the oldest villages are found in the Serra da Peneda and remain in a time warp, with oxen being trundled along cobbled streets by black-clad widows, distinctive *espigueiros* (stone granaries) and shepherds herding livestock up to high pastures for five months each year.

This is a wild landscape and in its remotest parts, a few wolves roam, as do wild boar, badgers and otters. With luck, you may catch a glimpse of roe deer and wild ponies. Hiking trails ranging from 1km to 30km abound in all sections of the park and mountain-bike rental is easy to source. For the lowdown on the park, including marked trail descriptions and an accommodation booking service, visit www. adere-pg.pt.

Ponte de Lima Wander through the town's winding streets

6 Viana do Castelo

The Costa Verde's biggest stunner, Viana do Castelo is a double shot of medieval centre and gorgeous beaches. Narrow lanes lined with Manueline manors and rococo palaces unfurl to **Praça da República**, with its Renaissance fountain and fortress-like town hall. For wondrous views down the coast and up the Lima Valley, hop on the funicular up to the eucalyptus-cloaked **Monte de Santa Luzia** and linger to glimpse the fabulously over-the-top, neo-Byzantine **Templo do Sagrado Coração de Jesus** (Temple of the Sacred Heart of Jesus; ⊙11am-1pm & 3-8pm). A five-minute ferry trip across the river brings you to **Praia do Cabedelo** (⊙ferry 9am-6pm), one of the Minho's best beaches, where powder-soft sands fold into grassy dunes and wind-blown pines.

✕ ⊨ p367

The Drive » The 28.5km drive east along the N202 to Ponte de Lima weaves past orchards, fields and a succession of low-key, whitewashed villages.

7 Ponte de Lima

The name is a giveaway – Ponte de Lima's showstopper is its 31-arched **Ponte Romana** loping across the Rio Lima – the finest medieval bridge in all Portugal. Most of it dates from the 14th century, though the segment on the north bank is bona fide Roman. The town itself is mellow and photogenic, with **ecovia** trails for cycling along the river, two crenulated 14th-century towers and a cute old town for a mosey. The town cranks to life at weekends and every other Monday, when a vast market spreads along the river bank.

🛏 p367

The Drive ≫ It's a 19km drive east of Ponte de Lima on the quaint and countrified N203 to Ponte da Barca.

- - - - - - - - - -

❽ Ponte da Barca

Serene Ponte da Barca takes its name from the barge (*barca*) that once ferried pilgrims and others across the Río Lima. Slow the pace here with a stroll along the willow-shaded riverfront or a bike ride into a wooded valley. **ADERE Peneda-**

Gerês (🖪258 452 250; www. adere-pg.pt; Rua Dom Manuel I; ☺9am-12.30pm & 2.30-6pm Mon-Fri) is a great source of information on the national park.

The Drive ≫ From Ponte da Barca, the N203 swings northeast, with snapshot views initially of the Río Lima, then twists and turns through the verdant, mountainous heart of the Parque National da Peneda-Gerês, affording fabulous views on almost every corner. It's around an hour and a half's drive (60km) to Peneda.

- - - - - - - - - -

TRIP HIGHLIGHT

❾ Peneda

There are many bases for striking out into the

Parque Nacional da Peneda-Gerês, but few rival Peneda for sheer beauty. This is one of the park's most stunning mountain villages and the *serra*'s namesake. It straddles both sides of a deep ravine and is backed by a domed mountain and gushing waterfall. Come for a quiet slice of village life and terrific hiking opportunities. A short 1km trail takes you to a lake high in the hills where wild horses graze.

🛏 p367

PAULO LOPES / ALAMY ©

Parc Nacional da Peneda-Gerês Waterfall cascading over red granite boulders

Eating & Sleeping

Guimarães ❶

✕ Manifestis Probatum   Tapas €

(Rua Egas Moniz 57-63; tapas €3-7.50; ⊗6pm-midnight Tue-Thu & Sun, 6pm-2am Fri & Sat) This stylish wine and tapas bar serves creative tapas and Portuguese *petiscos* that focus on canned fish – from trout in white wine to smoked mackerel. Pick between many Portuguese wines by the glass or sip a Sovina craft beer on the wooden bar or the clean-lined airy back room with leafy views.

⸝ Pousada de Santa Marinha   Rural Inn €€€

(⌨253 511 249; www.pousadas.pt; Largo Domingos Leite de Castro, Lugar da Costa; r €140-290; P✳🛜🏊) This former monastery overlooking the city from the slopes of Penha is a magnificent, sprawling structure. The gardens are stunning and you'll want to wander around the cloister, past dribbling fountains and masterful *azulejos*. The rooms inside the former monks' cells feel cramped, so book a room in the modern wing.

Braga ❸

✕ Cozinha da Sé   Portuguese €€

(Rua Dom Frei Caetano Brandão 95; mains €10-14; ⊗noon-3pm & 7-11pm Wed-Sun, 7-11pm Tue) Contemporary artwork hangs from the exposed stone walls at this intimate cheery Braga pick. Traditional standouts include baked *bacalhau* (dried salt-cod) and *açorda de marisco* (seafood stew in a bread bowl).

⸝ Pop Hostel   Hostel €

(⌨253 058 806; http://bragapophostel. blogspot.co.uk; Rua do Carmo 61; dm/d from €17/42; @🛜) This small cosy hostel in a top-floor apartment is a great recent addition to Braga, with a colourfully decked lounge, a hammock on the balcony and a friendly owner who knows all the great eating and drinking spots in town. Bike hire and tours available.

Viana do Castelo ❻

✕ O Pescador   Seafood €€

(⌨258 826 039; Largo de São Domingos 35; mains €9.50-15.50; ⊗noon-3pm & 7-10pm Mon-Sat, noon-3pm Sun) A simple, friendly, family-run restaurant admired by locals for its good seafood and tasty lunch specials (from €6.50).

⸝ Margarida da Praça   Guesthouse €€

(⌨258 809 630; www.margaridadapraca.com; Largo 5 de Outubro 58; s €60-75, d €78-88; @🛜) Fantastically whimsical, this boutique inn offers thematic rooms in striking pinks, sea greens and whites, accented by stylish floral wallpaper, candelabra lanterns and lush duvets. The equally stylish lobby glows with candlelight in the evening.

Ponte de Lima ❼

⸝ Carmo's Boutique Hotel   Boutique Hotel €€€

(⌨258 938 743; www.carmosboutiquehotel. com; Estrada Nacional 203, Gemeira; d/ste €220/320; P✳🛜🏊) The area's best hotel, this boutique hideaway in the village of Gemeira en route to Ponte da Barca has 15 stunning rooms, two pools and a small basement spa inside a contemporary two-wing structure. Inside is all about casual and cosy chic, breakfast is served till noon and rates include dinner at the restaurant, which whips up great regional dishes. Worth a splurge.

Peneda ❾

⸝ Peneda Hotel   Hotel €€

(⌨251 460 040; www.penedahotel.pt; Lugar da Peneda, Arcos de Valdevez; s/d €70/75; P🛜) Once a nest for Igreja Senhora de Peneda's pilgrims, this mountain lodge features a waterfall backdrop, a gushing creek beneath and ultra cosy rooms with blonde-wood floors, French windows and views of quaint Peneda village across the ravine. There's also a decent restaurant.

Carregal do Sal *Sample boutique wines at Quinta de Cabriz in Portugal's rural heartland*

Tasting the Dão

31

Dip into one of Portugal's little-frequented regions and you'll have its vineyards, woods, authentic villages and mountain trails pretty much to yourself.

TRIP HIGHLIGHTS

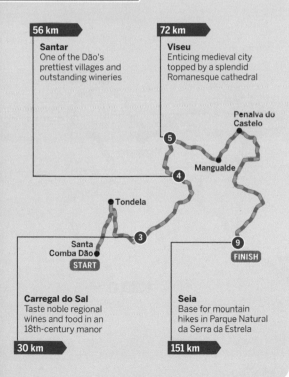

56 km

Santar
One of the Dão's prettiest villages and outstanding wineries

72 km

Viseu
Enticing medieval city topped by a splendid Romanesque cathedral

Penalva do Castelo

5

Mangualde

4

Tondela

3

Santa Comba Dão
START

9

FINISH

Carregal do Sal
Taste noble regional wines and food in an 18th-century manor

30 km

Seia
Base for mountain hikes in Parque Natural da Serra da Estrela

151 km

2–4 DAYS
151 KM / 94 MILES

GREAT FOR...

BEST TIME TO GO
Spring to autumn for mild weather and seasonal colour.

ESSENTIAL PHOTO
The countryside rippling far and wide from the top of Caramulinho.

BEST FOR FOODIES

Head to Tres Pipos for regional food cooked to a T and paired with superb Dão wines.

31 Tasting the Dão

The Dão is off-the-beaten track Portugal in a nutshell. Get ready to slow tour the country's rural heartland, an enticing ensemble of vineyards, pine and eucalyptus woods, family-run wineries and whitewashed villages full of sleepy charisma. Cellar tours, manor house sleeps, hearty meals with beefy red wines and hikes in the wilds of the country's highest peaks in Serra da Estrela all await. Wind down the window. Hear that? Silence.

❶ Santa Comba Dão

With its cluster of whitewashed, red-roofed houses tucked among low hills, *miradouros* (lookouts) gazing across the Río Dão and fine, twin-towered baroque church, this market town makes an appealing stop for an hour or so. Santa Comba Dão is the start of the wine region proper and used to be the terminus of the narrow-gauge Dão railway line to/from Viseu. Most Portuguese recognise the name as the birthplace of the

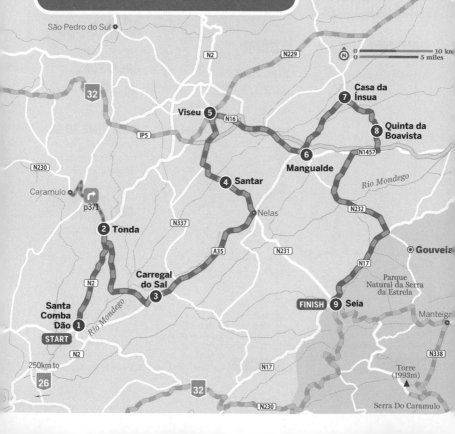

notorious dictator and former prime minister António de Oliveira Salazar, who was born and buried in the nearby village of Vimieiro.

The Drive » From Santa Comba Dão, the N2 blazes 15km north past arable countryside, woodlands of pine and eucalyptus, and small settlements, with Serra do Caramulo rippling northwest in the distance. Before reaching Tondela, exit right following the signs to Tonda, Couço and Mouraz.

- - - - - - - - - -

❷ Tonda

For a hearty meal while on the wine trail, head straight to **Tres Pipos** (☎232 816 851; www.3pipos.

LINK YOUR TRIP

26 Atlantic Coast Surf Trip

Craving breezy ocean views? Swing over to the wave-battered Atlantic Coast for a sun and surf fix. Praia de Pedrogão is 120km southwest from Santa Comba Dão.

32 Highlands & History in the Central Interior

Detour 52km southwest of Santa Comba Dão to erudite Coimbra, the start of a drive with historic cities and evocative fortress towns on every turn.

DETOUR: SERRA DO CARAMULO

Start: ❷ Tonda

From Tonda, the N230 wiggles up through little hamlets and spruce and eucalyptus woods to Caramulo, a good base for striking out into the surrounding Serra do Caramulo. Here fields flanked by woods of oak, pine and chestnut rise to granite, boulder-speckled heights, where small waterfalls and brooks run swift and clear. The mountains are loveliest when wildflowers like heather, oleander and broom bloom in spring and early summer. The range tops off at the 1076m peak of Caramulinho, worth climbing if it is a clear day for far-reaching views stretching all the way to the Serra da Estrela in the south and Aveiro and the Atlantic to the west. The trail begins close to Hotel Caramulo – ask locals to point you in the right direction.

- - - - - - - - - - -

pt; Rua de Santo Amaro 966; mains €9-16; ☺noon-3pm Tue-Sun, 7-10pm Tue-Sat) in the small village of Tonda. It's a convivial, family-run affair, dishing up spot-on regional dishes like *cabrito* (roast kid) and *polvo à lagareiro* (octopus cooked with potatoes, garlic and olive oil) in atmospheric dining rooms that have old wooden ceilings and thick stone walls. There's a good selection of Dão wines on the list and also a shop where you can stock up on local *vinho* as well as regional honeys, preserves, sausages, oils and black earthenware from nearby Molelos.

🛏 p375

The Drive » From Tonda, a minor road threads 14.5km

south through pine and eucalyptus woodlands and past tiny orchards and vineyards and unassuming villages like Nagozela, before crossing the Rio Dão. As you approach Carregal do Sal, turn right at the roundabout to reach Quinta de Cabriz.

- - - - - - - - -

`TRIP HIGHLIGHT`

❸ Carregal do Sal

The main attraction in Carregal do Sal is **Quinta de Cabriz** (☎232 960 140, 232 961 222; www.quintadecabriz.pt; Carregal do Sal; ☺9am-10pm Mon-Sat, to 6pm Sun), the headquarters of Dão Sul, one of the region's foremost wine producers, where 38 hectares of vines fan out from an 18th-century manor house. Here you can stock up at the wine boutique, savour regional dishes expertly paired with wines in the restaurant, enjoy a tasting or hook onto a guided tour of the vineyards (no booking required, just turn up). Fine wines produced here include the Quinta de Cabriz Touriga Nacional, a spicy, dark-fruit number, and Quinta de Cabriz Encruzado, a crisp, lemony white.

The Drive » The A35 and N234 and N231 take you northeast from Quinta de Cabriz to Santar, 26km away. The second half of the route is more attractive, leading past pockets of pine woodland, neat rows of vines and cultivated fields.

TRIP HIGHLIGHT

❹ Santar

Santar is a dinky little village and one of the Dão's prettiest, with narrow lanes twisting past baroque villas. The biggest draw, however, is its standout wineries. Top billing goes to the centrally located **Paço dos Cunos de Santar** (☎232 945 452; Largo do Paço de Santar ; ⏰10am-10pm Tue-Sun), a 17th-century estate, where you can tour the vineyard before a tasting of its noble wines and olive oils, which go nicely with the

CEPHAS PICTURE LIBRARY / ALAMY ©

LOCAL KNOWLEDGE: WINES OF THE DÃO

The Dão rivals the Douro and Alentejo when it comes to the quality of its wines, some of Portugal's best. The conditions are ideal for wine-growing, with granitic soils, a temperate climate and shelter provided by the Serra da Estrela, Serra do Caramulo and Serra da Nave.

If the region has sidestepped the global spotlight until recently, it is because viticulture here still tends to be small scale, with vineyards still often little bigger than your average backyard, tucked between cultivated fields, orchards and mountains wreathed with pine and eucalyptus woods. These little wineries work hand in hand with large cooperatives.

Most wine lovers rave about the region's smooth reds, made from grapes like the Touriga Nacional, Tinta Roriz, Jaen and Alfrocheiro. These are ruby-hued, velvety and full-bodied, with aromas of spices, black cherry and other dark fruits.

The region also produces some very decent whites – keep an eye out, particularly, from those made from the tangy Encruzado grape, which are fresh and citrusy, with flavours of apple, lemon and melon.

seasonal, creative takes on regional cuisine in the contemporary restaurant. Close by is the **Casa de Santar** (☎232 942 937; http://casadesantar. com; Santar; ⏰guided visits 11am & 3pm Tue-Sat, shop 10am-noon & 2-6pm Tue-Sat), a family-owned winery with attractive grounds and baroque architecture. A guided visit takes you deep into its granite cellars, where robust reds are aged in oak barrels. There is also a gourmet shop where you can pick up some nice bottles and regional specialities.

The Drive » The N231 swings north from Santar to Viseu, a

Viseu Sweeping view over the vineyards

16km drive away. It's a relaxed country road, taking you past small vineyards and stands of olive and pine.

TRIP HIGHLIGHT

❺ Viseu

Viseu merits at least half a day of your time, or stay overnight to really absorb the atmosphere of the alley-woven medieval city (see p384 for more). After a culture dose, you may well be in the mood for a glass of Dão wine at slinky bar **Palato** (☎232 435 081; www.noitebiba.pt/palato; Praça de Dom Duarte 1; ⏰8pm-4am Mon-Sat).

 p375

The Drive >> Take the meandering N16 east of town through pinewoods, with views of low mountains and past stone-walled vineyards before crossing a bridge over the Río Dão. Then follow the A25, taking exit 22 onto the N329-1 to Mangualde. It's a 17km drive.

❻ Mangualde

Mangualde is an elegant town, crowned by a hilltop neoclassical church, **Igreja de Nossa Senhora do Castelo**, which is reached by a long flight of steps. Climb up here for sweeping views over the surrounding countryside.

The Drive >> From Mangualde, the N329-1 swings 12km north past hamlets and hills thickly cloaked in pines and eucalyptus. As you enter Penalva do Castelo, head straight at the second roundabout for Casa da Ínsua.

❼ Casa da Ínsua

Tiptoe away from civilisation for a night at the sublime **Casa da Ínsua** (☎232 642 222, 232 640 110; www.casadainsua. pt; Penalva do Castelo; r €95-150, q apt €145-200). This 18th-century manor and winery has been lovingly converted into a five-star hotel, complete with manicured landscape gardens, chandelier-lit salons, high-ceilinged rooms brimming with historic charm, a wine-tasting room and highly regarded restaurant. Staff arrange activities including afternoons in the vineyards and cheese- and preserve-making workshops.

The Drive » Veer southeast from Casa da Ínsua, heading straight at the roundabout onto a minor road that takes you east through undulating countryside. Continue on this road southeast to Quinta da Boavista, roughly 7km away.

⑧ Quinta da Boavista

A shining example of enotourism, **Quinta da Boavista** (☎919 858 340; www.quintadaboavista.eu; Penalva do Castelo; s/d €50/80; P🛜🏊) in Penalva do Castelo is a winery run with a passion by João

Tavares de Pina and his family. The eco-aware farmhouse sits in a secluded spot and offers well-equipped apartments, wine tastings of its full-bodied reds and delicious home-cooked meals. There's also a swimming pool and the chance to go horse riding should you so wish. It's a chilled spot to wind out your road trip of the Dão wine region.

The Drive » It's a 43km drive south to Seia on the N1457, N232 and N17. The drive takes you through tranquil countryside streaked with olive trees and vines and backed by low, forested hills.

TRIP HIGHLIGHT

⑨ Seia

Besides sweeping views over the surrounding lowlands, Seia's big draw is its cluster of museums, including the **Centro de Interpretação da Serra**

da Estrela (CISE; ☎238 320 300; www.cise.pt; Rua Visconde Molelos; adult/ child €4/2.50; ⏰10am-6pm Tue-Sun), providing an excellent introduction to the mountainous region. This is the best place for information on hiking routes, maps and arranging guided hikes. From here you can easily strike out into the **Parque Natural da Serra da Estrela**, the country's largest protected area at 1011 sq km. It's a wilderness of rugged boulder-strewn meadows and icy lakes, crowned by mainland Portugal's highest peak, 1993m Torre. Crisp air and immense vistas make this a trekking paradise. As surprisingly few people get off the main roads, you'll often feel as though you have the park all to yourself.

🛏 p375

CRO MAGNON / ALAMY ©

Seia Rock formations in the mountainous Serra da Estrela

Eating & Sleeping

Tonda ②

🛏 Quinta dos Três Rios   Hotel €€

(📞232 959 189; www.minola.co.uk; Rua Padre
Francisco de Oliveira 239, Parada de Gonta;
2-/4-person apt from €100/150, 3-course dinner
€20; P 🛜) At this remarkable getaway 10km
southwest of Viseu, every room is a suite with
5m-high ceilings and 4m French doors opening
onto a symphony of frogs and nightingales by
night, and vistas of the surrounding olive trees,
vineyards and river by day. The hosts make
fabulous dinners with homemade olive oil and
wine. They also lead impromptu tours of the
surrounding area that encompass everything
from wineries to traditional fishing and barrel-
making to grape stomping during the harvest
season. When you get to Parada de Gonta, go
through the village and down the hill towards
the river – you'll see the *quinta* on your right.

Viseu ⑤

✕ O Hilário   Portuguese €

(Rua Augusto Hilário 35; mains €5-9; ⏱10am-
10pm Mon-Sat) Fantastically friendly and
welcoming, this slice of old Portugal is named
for the 19th-century fado star who once lived
down the street. Great value *doses* (portions)
will feed one hungry person, but halves are
available for lighter appetites. If your favourite
grandparents owned a restaurant this would
be it.

🛏 Casa da Sé   Boutique Hotel €€

(📞232 468 032; www.casadase.net; Rua
Augusta Cruz 12; s/ste €69/140, d €75-113;
✳🛜) Right in the heart of old Viseu, this
handsome boutique hotel is owned by an

antique dealer, so the historic building is full of
period furniture and objets d'art, all for sale, so
you can take the bed with you when you check
out. All rooms are different and exceedingly
well-decorated. Staff are helpful, and there's a
warm, hospitable feel to the place.

🛏 Pousada de Viseu   Hotel €€€

(📞210 114 433, 210 407 610; www.pousadas.
pt; Rua do Hospital; s €85-116, d €95-157;
P ✳ @ 🛜 ⚐) This superbly refashioned
pousada is set in a monumental 19th-century
hospital and is a top luxury option. The original
three floors, all with ridiculously high ceilings
and spacious rooms, have been enhanced with
a 4th floor dedicated to special suites with
panoramic terraces. The enormous central
courtyard, complete with bar, is a neoclassical
delight, while the elegant former pharmacy has
been converted into a cosy lounge. Indoor and
outdoor pools, plus spa complex complete the
picture. Excellent value.

Seia ⑨

🛏 Casas da Ribeira   Cottage €

(📞919 660 354, 238 311 221; www.
casasdaribeira.com; Póvoa Velha; 2-person
cottages €50-70, 4-person €100; 🛜) Close
to Seia's services but feeling a million miles
away, this charming collection of vine-draped
stone cottages sits in the hills above town. The
six houses are similar, rustic and beautifully
restored with kitchens and fireplaces (firewood
included). A delicious breakfast with home-
baked bread is provided. There's normally a
two-night minimum stay; prices drop with extra
nights. From Seia, climb the Sabugueiro road for
about 5km, then turn left 1km to Póvoa Velha.
Call ahead. Wi-fi at reception only.

Conímbriga Extraordinarily preserved Roman mosaics in Portugal's most extensive ruins

Highlands & History in the Central Interior

32

This wide-ranging trip takes in many Portuguese historic highlights, from the university town of Coimbra to borderland fortresses, intermingled with picturesque villages and the majesty of the Serra da Estrela.

TRIP HIGHLIGHTS

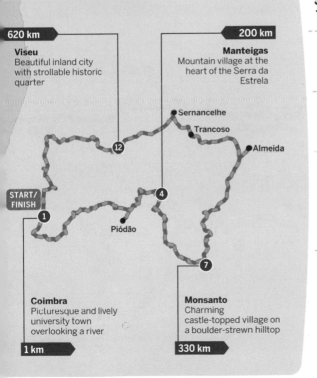

620 km

Viseu
Beautiful inland city with strollable historic quarter

200 km

Manteigas
Mountain village at the heart of the Serra da Estrela

Sernancelhe

Trancoso

Almeida

12

START/ FINISH

4

1

Piódão

7

Coimbra
Picturesque and lively university town overlooking a river

1 km

Monsanto
Charming castle-topped village on a boulder-strewn hilltop

330 km

5–7 DAYS
770 KM / 480 MILES

GREAT FOR...

BEST TIME TO GO
May to October for best temperatures.

 ESSENTIAL PHOTO

The sweeping mountaintop view from Fragão de Covão above Manteigas.

 BEST FOR OUTDOORS

Hiking the Serra da Estrela around Manteigas.

32

Highlands & History in the Central Interior

History is tangible at every turn in Portugal's interior, and this route combines some of the nation's most evocative historic sights, from the venerable university library of Coimbra or Viseu's cathedral to picture-perfect traditional villages like Piódão or Idanha-a-Velha. Sturdy fortress towns like Almeida and Trancoso shore up the border with Spain, while the Serra da Estrela mountains offer superb vistas and glorious hiking opportunities.

TRIP HIGHLIGHT

❶ Coimbra

While Porto and Lisbon take the headlines, the university town of Coimbra, between the two, is one of Portugal's highlights. Its atmospheric historic centre cascades down a hillside above the river Mondego: a multicoloured assemblage of buildings covering a millennium of architectural endeavour.

The spiritual heart of the old town is the **Velha Universidade**

COIMBRA FADO

If Lisbon represents the heart of Portuguese fado music, Coimbra is its head. The 19th-century university was male-only, so the town's womenfolk were of great interest to the student body. Coimbra fado developed partly as a way of communicating with these heavily chaperoned females, usually in the form of serenades sung under the bedroom window. For this reason, fado is traditionally sung only by men, who must be students or ex-students.

The Coimbra style ranges from hauntingly beautiful serenades and lullabies to more boisterous students-out-on-the-piss type of songs. The singer is normally accompanied by a 12-string *guitarra* (Portuguese guitar) and perhaps a Spanish (classical) guitar too. Due to the clandestine nature of these bedroom-window concerts, audience appreciation is traditionally indicated by softly coughing rather than clapping.

There are several excellent venues in Coimbra to hear fado, including **À Capella** (📞239 833 985; www.acapella.com.pt; Rua Corpo de Deus; admission incl one drink €10; 🕐9pm-2am).

(Old University; www.uc.pt; adult/child €9/free, tower €1/ free; 🕐9am-7.30pm daily mid-Mar–mid-Oct, 9.30am-1pm & 2-5.30pm mid-Oct–mid-Mar), whose stunning 16th- to 18th-century buildings surround the Patio des Escolas square. The

LINK YOUR TRIP

29 **Medieval Jewels in the Southern Interior**

Head down to Lisbon from Coimbra to explore more of the interior, or connect part-way along in Tomar, 80km south of Coimbra.

31 **Tasting the Dão**

From Viseu you can access this pleasure-trip around Portugal's silkiest reds.

Biblioteca Joanina (João V Library; 📞239 859 818) library is the sumptuous highlight. Within a short stroll are two other Coimbra masterpieces: the **Sé Velha** (Old Cathedral; 📞239 825 273; www.sevelha-coimbra.org; Largo da Sé Velha; admission €2; 🕐10am-6pm Mon-Sat, 1-6pm Sun) is one of Portugal's finest Romanesque buildings, while the altogether more modern **Museu Nacional de Machado de Castro** (📞239 853 070; www.museumachadocastro.pt; Largo Dr José Rodrigues; adult/child €6/free, crypto-portico only €3; 🕐2-6pm Tue, 10am-1pm & 2-6pm Wed-Sun Oct-Mar, 2-6pm Tue, 10am-7pm Wed-Sun Apr-Sep) presents an excellent collection of art as well as taking you down to the city's Roman origins.

🍴 🛏 p386

The Drive » It's a short drive southeast along the IC3/N1 some 16km to Condeixa-a-Nova, on whose outskirts sit the Roman ruins of Conímbriga.

- - - - - - - - - - -

❷ Conímbriga

Hidden amid humble olive orchards in the rolling country southwest of Coimbra, Conímbriga boasts Portugal's most extensive and best-preserved Roman ruins, and ranks with the best-preserved sites on the entire Iberian Peninsula.

To get your head around the history, begin at the small, somewhat old-fashioned **museum** (www.conimbriga.pt; adult/child incl Roman Ruins €4.50/free; 🕐10am-7pm). Displays present every aspect of Roman life from mosaics to medallions. Then, head out to the **ruins** (🕐10am-7pm) themselves. A massive defensive wall

379

running right through the site speaks of times of sudden crisis; in contrast, the extraordinary mosaics of the Casa dos Repuxos speak of times of peaceful domesticity.

The Drive » It's a couple of hours in the car to the next stop. The most interesting route is to take the N342 east, turning north onto the N236, then taking the N17 and IC6 northeast. The last stretch on the N230 is a spectacular if occasionally nerve-racking drive, following valleys with breathtaking views, sheer drops and tight curves.

❸ Piódão

Remote Piódão offers a chance to see rural Portugal at its most pristine. This tiny traditional village clings to a terraced valley in a beautiful, surprisingly remote range of vertiginous ridges, deeply cut valleys, rushing rivers and virgin woodland called the Serra de Açor (Goshawk Mountains).

Until the 1970s you could only reach Piódão

on horseback or by foot, and it still feels as though you've slipped into a time warp. The village is a serene, picturesque composition in schist and slate; note the many doorways with crosses over them, said to offer protection against curses and thunderstorms.

Houses descend in terraces to the square, where you'll find the fairy-tale parish church, the **Igreja Nossa Senhora Conceição**, and a low-key touristy scene selling local liqueurs and souvenirs.

The Drive » It's only 66km to the next stop, but with the winding roads, spectacular scenery and intriguing villages en route, it may take you some time. Retrace your steps, then head northeast on the N338. The N231 takes you to Seia; from there the N339 then N232 is one of Portugal's great drives, through typical landscapes of the Serra da Estrela and down a vertiginous descent into Manteigas.

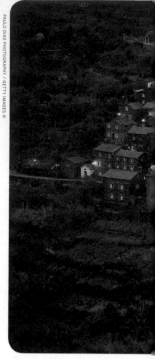

`TRIP HIGHLIGHT`

❹ Manteigas

In the heart of the Serra da Estrela, Portugal's loftiest and most spectacular highland region, this is the most atmospheric of the mountain towns hereabouts. Cradled at the foot of the beautiful Vale do Zêzere, with high peaks and forest-draped slopes dominating the horizon in all directions, Manteigas enjoys a spectacular natural setting. There are lots of good marked walks in the surrounding area, so you may want to

LOCAL KNOWLEDGE: WALKS FROM MANTEIGAS

The **Trilhos Verdes** (www.manteigastrilhosverdes.com) are an excellent network of marked trails in the Manteigas area. Each route is viewable online and has its own leaflet available at the park information office in town.

The relatively easy ramble (11km one way) through the magnificent, glacier-scoured **Vale do Zêzere**, one of the park's most beautiful and noteworthy natural features, is a highlight. It's quite exposed in summer.

Piódão Traditional Portuguese village set in the hillside

set aside a day to explore the Serra landscapes on foot. Walk through the glacial valley above town and you'll still encounter terraced meadows, stone shepherds' huts and tinkling goat-bells, while in Manteigas itself cobblestone streets and older homes still hold their own against the high-rise development that has taken root on the Serra's fringes.

🛏 p386

The Drive » The drive from Manteigas to Torre (22km, around 35 minutes) is especially breathtaking, first following the N338 along the Vale do Zêzere. After turning

right onto the N339 towards Torre, you pass through the Nave de Santo António – a traditional high country sheep grazing meadow – before climbing through a surreal moonscape of crags and gorges. Visible near the turn-off for Torre is Cántaro Magro, a notable rock formation, rising 500m straight from the valley below.

❺ Torre

In winter, Torre's road signs are so blasted by freezing winds that horizontal icicles barb their edges. Portugal's highest peak, at 1993m, Torre ('Tower') produces a winter freeze so reliable that it's got a small ski

TOP TIP: VIEWPOINT

At Penhas Douradas, at the top of the hill before the long descent into Manteigas, don't miss the stunning view from a stub of rock called Fragão de Covão; just follow the signs.

DETOUR: PARQUE NATURAL DO TEJO INTERNACIONAL

Start: ⑥ Idanha-a-Velha

Still one of Portugal's wildest landscapes, this 230-sq-km park shadows the Río Tejo (Tagus), the border between Portugal and Spain. It shelters some of the country's rarest bird species, including black storks, Bonelli's eagles, royal eagles, Egyptian vultures, black vultures and griffon vultures.

The best-marked hiking trail, the **Rota dos Abutres** (Route of the Vultures), descends from Salvaterra do Extremo (34km southeast of Idanha-a-Velha) into the dramatic canyon of the Río Erges. It's an 11km circuit that includes a vulture colony viewing point, and great views of a castle over in Spain.

resort with mainly beginners' slopes.

Outside the snow season (mid-December to mid-April), Portugal's pinnacle is rather depressing, though a park visitor centre with displays about the region's natural and cultural history is worthwhile.

Even if you decide to give Torre itself a miss, it is worth the drive here to survey the astoundingly dramatic surroundings.

The Drive » Retrace your steps from Torre and continue straight on along the N339 to eventually descend steeply into Covilhã. Take the IP2/A23 motorway south, then the N18 and N239 roughly eastwards, finally reaching the N332 which takes you the last stretch to Idanha-a-Velha. It's a drive of around 90km.

⑥ Idanha-a-Velha

Extraordinary Idanha-a-Velha is a very traditional small village with a huge history. Nestled in a remote valley of patchwork farms and olive orchards, it was founded as the Roman city of Igaeditânia (Egitania). Roman ramparts still define the town, though it reached its apogee under Visigothic rule: they built a **cathedral** (⊙24hr) and made Idanha their regional capital. It's also believed that their legendary King Wamba was born here.

Moors were next on the scene, and the cathedral was turned into a mosque during their tenure. They, in turn, were driven out by the Knights Templar in the 12th

century. It's believed that a 15th-century plague virtually wiped out the town's population. Today a small population of shepherds and farmers live amid the Roman, Visigothic and medieval ruins.

Wandering this picturesque village is an enchanting trip back in time.

The Drive » Head north up the N332 again, then turn right at the N239. The turn-off to Monsanto is clearly marked. It's only a 15km drive. Passengers who want to stretch their legs could walk the pretty 7km trail from Idanha to Monsanto.

TRIP HIGHLIGHT

⑦ Monsanto

Like an island in the sky, the stunning village of Monsanto towers high above the surrounding plains. A stroll through its steeply cobbled streets, lined with stone houses that seem to merge with the boulder-strewn landscape, is reason enough to come. But to fully appreciate Monsanto's rugged isolation, climb the shepherds' paths above town to the abandoned and crumbling hilltop **castle** (⊙24hr). This formidable stone fortress seems almost to have grown out of the boulder-littered hillside that supports it. It's a beautiful site, windswept and populated by lizards and wildflowers. Immense vistas include

Spain to the east and the Barragem da Idanha dam to the southwest. Walkers will also appreciate the network of hiking trails threading through the vast cork-oak-dominated expanses below.

✗ ⊨ p386

The Drive » Sortelha is about 60km north of Monsanto across a variety of hilly landscapes. Head due north from Monsanto, eventually linking up with the N233. Turn off in the village of Terreiro, following the brown signs for Sortelha.

- - - - - - - - - - - -

⑧ Sortelha

Perched on a rocky promontory, Sortelha is the oldest of a string of fortresses guarding the frontier in this region. Its fortified 12th-century castle teeters on the brink of a steep cliff, while immense walls encircle a village of great charm. Laid out in Moorish times, it remains a winning combination of stout stone cottages, sloping cobblestone streets and diminutive orchards.

'New' Sortelha lines the Santo Amaro–Sabugal road. The medieval hilltop fortress is a short drive, or a 10-minute walk, up one of two lanes signposted *castelo*.

The entrance to the fortified old village is a grand, stone Gothic gate. From here, a cobbled lane leads up to the heart of the village, with a *pelourinho* (pillory) in

front of the remains of a small castle and the parish church. Higher still is the bell tower – climb it for a view of the entire village. For a more adventurous and scenic climb, tackle the ramparts around the village (beware precarious stairways and big steps).

✗ p387

The Drive » Head east to Sabugal, then turn north, following the N324 north before joining the N340 for the final run northeast to Almeida. It's a drive of around 65km.

- - - - - - - - - - - -

⑨ Almeida

After Portugal regained independence from Spain in the 1640s, the country's border regions were on constant high alert. Almeida's vast, star-shaped fortress is the handsomest of the defensive structures built during this period.

The fortified old village is a place of great charm, with enough history and muscular grandeur to set the imagination humming.

Most visitors arrive at the fortress via the handsome **Portas de São Francisco**, two long tunnel-gates separated by an enormous dry moat.

The long arcaded building just inside is the 18th-century **Quartel das Esquadras**, the former infantry barracks.

Not far away, the interesting **Museu Histórico**

Militar de Almeida (adult/child €3/free, with Sala de Armas & CEAMA €3.50/free; ⊙9am-5.30pm Tue-Sun Oct-Jun, 10am-6.30pm Tue-Sun Jul-Sep) is built into the *casamatas* (casemates or bunkers), a labyrinth of 20 underground rooms used for storage, barracks and shelter for troops in times of siege. Piles of cannonballs fill a central courtyard of the museum, with British and Portuguese cannons strewn about nearby.

Make sure you also see the attractive **Picadero d'el Rey**, once the artillery headquarters, and what's left of the **castle**, blown to smithereens during a French siege in 1810.

⊨ p387

The Drive » Retrace your steps down the N340, then head northwest on the N324. At Pinhel, turn westwards onto the N221/N226, all the way to Trancoso, around 60km in total.

- - - - - - - - - - - -

⑩ Trancoso

A warren of cobbled lanes squeezed within Dom Dinis' mighty 13th-century walls makes peaceful Trancoso a delightful retreat from the modern world. The walls run intact for over 1km around the medieval core, which is centred on the main square, Largo Padre Francisco Ferreira. The square, in turn, is anchored by an octagonal *pelourinho* dating from 1510. The Portas d'El

Rei (King's Gate), surmounted by the ancient coat of arms, was always the principal entrance, its guillotine-like door sealed out unwelcome visitors. On a hill in the northeast corner of town is the tranquil **castle** (☺9am-12.30pm & 2-5.30pm Tue-Sun Jun-Sep, 9am-12.30pm, 2-5.30pm Tue-Fri, 10am-12.30pm, 2-5pm Sat, 10am-12.30pm, 2-4.30pm Sun Oct-May), with its crenellated towers and the distinctively slanted walls of the squat, Moorish Torre de Menagem, which you can climb for views.

The Drive >> Head 30km northwest along the N226 to reach the next stop, Sernancelhe.

⓫ Sernancelhe

Located 30km northwest of Trancoso, Sernancelhe has a wonderfully preserved centre fashioned out of warm, beige-coloured stone. Sights include a 13th-century church that boasts Portugal's only free-standing Romanesque sculpture; an old Jewish quarter with crosses to mark the homes of the converted; several grand 17th- and 18th-century town houses, one of which is believed to be the birthplace of the Marquês de Pombal; and hills that bloom with what are considered to be Portugal's best chestnuts.

The Drive >> The N229 leads you 55km southwest through increasingly fertile countryside to Viseu.

TRIP HIGHLIGHT

⓬ Viseu

One of central Portugal's most appealing cities, Viseu has a well-preserved historical centre that offers numerous enticements to pedestrians: cobbled streets, meandering alleys, leafy public gardens and a central square – Praça da República, aka the 'Rossio' – graced with bright flowers and fountains. Sweeping vistas over the surrounding plains unfold from the town's highest point, the square fronting the 13th-century granite **cathedral** (☺8am-noon & 2-7pm Mon-Wed & Fri, 2-7pm Thu & Sat, 9am-noon & 2-7pm Sun), whose gloomy Renaissance facade conceals a splendid 16th-century interior, including an impressive Manueline ceiling. On show next door in the **Museu Grão Vasco** (www.imc-ip.pt; Adro da Sé; admission €4, Sun morning free; ☺2-5.30pm Tue, 10am-6pm Wed-Sun) is some standout Portuguese art, in particular paintings by local boy Vasco Fernandes, known as Grão Vasco (the Great Vasco; 1480–1543) – one of the nation's seminal Renaissance painters.

✗ ⏅ p387

The Drive >> It's a drive of 90km to the next stop. The quickest way is to take the A25

motorway west, turning south onto the IC2.

⓭ Sangalhos

In the village of Sangalhos, in the Bairrada wine-producing region between Aveiro and Coimbra, the extraordinary **Aliança Underground Museum** (☎234 732 045, 916 482 226; www.alianca.pt; Rua do Comercio 444; admission €3; ☺90min visits 10am, 11.30am, 2.30pm, 4pm daily) is part wine *adega*, part repository of an eclectic, enormous, and top-quality art and artefact collection. Under the winery, vast vaulted chambers hold sparkling wine, barrels of maturing aguardente, and a series of galleries displaying a huge range of objects. The highlight is at the beginning: a superb collection of African sculpture, ancient ceramics and masks, but you'll also be impressed by the spectacular mineral and fossil collection and the beauty of some of the spaces. Other pieces include *azulejos* (tiles), a rather hideous collection of ceramic and faience animals, and an upstairs gallery devoted to India. The only complaint is that there's no information on individual pieces, and you don't have time to linger over a particular piece. Phone ahead to book your visit, which can be conducted in English and includes a glass of sparkling wine.

The Drive >> It's an easy 20km drive down the N235 to the town of Luso and on up the hill to the Buçaco forest.

----

⑭ Mata Nacional do Buçaco

This famous, historic national **forest** (www.fmb.pt; car/cyclist/pedestrian €5/free/free; ☺8am-8pm Apr-Sep, to 6pm Oct-Mar) is encircled by high stone walls that for centuries have reinforced a sense of mystery. The aromatic forest is criss-crossed with trails, dotted with crumbling chapels and graced with ponds, fountains and exotic trees. In the middle, like in a fairytale, stands a royal palace. Now a luxury hotel, it was built in 1907 as a royal summer retreat on the site of a 17th-century Carmelite monastery. This wedding cake of a building is over-the-top in every way: outside, its conglomeration of turrets and spires is surrounded by rose gardens and swirling box hedges in geometrical patterns; inside (non-guests are more or less prohibited entry) are neo-Manueline carvings, suits of armour on the grand staircases and *azulejos*.

Nearby, **Santa Cruz do Bussaco** (www.fmb.pt; adult/child €2/1; ☺10am-1pm & 2-5pm Oct-Mar, to 6pm Apr-Sep) is what remains of a convent where the future Duke of Wellington rested after the Battle of Bussaco in 1810. The atmospheric interior has decaying religious paintings, an unusual passageway right around the chapel, some guns from the battle, and the much-venerated image of Nossa Senhora do Leite (Our Lady of Milk), with ex-voto offerings.

Outside the forest walls lies the old-fashioned little spa town of Luso.

✖ 🛏 p387

The Drive >> Heading back to Coimbra, ignore your GPS and make sure to take the lovely foresty N235, which later joins the IP3. It's a picturesque drive.

SERGIO AZENHA / ALAMY ©

Sangalhos Wine ageing in barrels at the Aliança Underground Museum

Eating & Sleeping

Coimbra ①

✗ Fangas Mercearia Bar — Petiscos €€

(☎934 093 636; http://fangas.pt; Rua Fernandes Tomás 45; petiscos €4-7; ⏰noon-4pm & 7pm-1am Tue-Sun; 🛜🍴) Top-quality deli produce is used to produce delightful *petiscos* (tapas) in this bright, cheery dining room, the best place to eat in the old town. Service is slow but friendly and will help you choose from a delicious array of tasty platters – sausages, stuffed vegetables, conserves – and interesting wines. Book ahead as this small space always fills quickly.

🛏 Casa Pombal — Guesthouse €€

(☎239 835 175; www.casapombal.com; Rua das Flores 18; d with/without bathroom €65/54; @🛜) In a lovely old-town location, this winning, Dutch-run guesthouse squeezes tons of charm into a small space. A delicious breakfast is served in the gorgeous blue-tiled breakfast room.

🛏 Quinta das Lágrimas — Hotel €€€

(☎239 802 380; www.quintadaslagrimas.pt; Rua António Augusto Gonçalves; r €160-260; 🅿❄🛜🛗) This splendid historical palace is now one of Portugal's most enchanting upper-crust hotels. Choose between richly furnished rooms in the old palace, or Scandinavian-style minimalist in the modern annexe – complete with jacuzzi. A few rooms look out onto the garden where Dona Inês de Castro reputedly met her tragic end. Significant discounts are sometimes available online, even in high season, and it's cheaper midweek. Other facilities include a pitch 'n' putt course and driving range.

Manteigas ④

🛏 Casa das Obras — Hotel €€

(☎275 981 155; www.casadasobras.pt; Rua Teles de Vasconcelos; r summer/winter €68/80; 🛜🛗) Elegant and friendly, Manteigas's nicest in-town lodging is a lovely 18th-century town house that has been carefully renovated to preserve its original grandeur and stone-walled charm. It's all historic feel and noble elegance but it's no shrine, rather a relaxed spot with a top welcome from the family who has owned this place for centuries.

🛏 Casa das Penhas Douradas — Hotel €€€

(☎275 981 045; www.casadaspenhasdouradas. pt; Penhas Douradas; s €120-145, d €135-160; 🅿❄@🛜🛗) On its mountaintop perch between Manteigas and Seia, this hotel gets everything right. The rooms all have great natural light, views, and some come with sloping ceilings or appealing terraces. An enlightened attitude to guest comfort means all sorts of welcome details, such as a heated pool, bikes and kayaks, books, DVDs and spa and massage treatments are available.

Monsanto ⑦

✗ Adega Típica O Cruzeiro — Portuguese €€

(☎277 314 528; Rua Fernando Namora 4; mains €10-12; ⏰12.30-3pm Thu-Tue, 7-9pm Thu-Mon) Just below the old town, this likeable place is a rather surprising find as you descend into the bowels of a modern municipal building. The attractive dining area boasts spectacular views over the plains below, and the super-friendly staff serve very tasty meals from a seasonal menu – if you spot a dish with wild mushrooms *(cogumelos silvestres),* go for it.

🛏 Casa da Tia Piedade — Guesthouse €

(☎966 910 599; www.casadatiapiedade.com; Rua da Azinheira 21; d/q without breakfast €50/70; ❄🛜) You've just about got your own house attached to this warmly welcoming spot in Monsanto's heart, with separate entrance, terrace and kitchen/lounge. There are two lovely bedrooms (the smaller one has a view) but only one is let at a time unless you're a group, so the exterior bathroom is private. The owners are helpful and kind but also respect privacy.

Sortelha ⑧

✗ Dom Sancho I Portuguese €€

(☎271 388 267; Largo do Corro; mains €10-16; ⊘lunch & dinner Tue-Sat, lunch Sun) **Sortelha's** favourite eatery sits just inside the main Gothic gates. Prices for the regional cuisine – with several game options – are high, but the food is renowned and the dining room rustically elegant. For lighter snacks and drinks, head to the beamed, stone-walled bar (with cosy fireplace in winter) downstairs.

Almeida ⑨

🛏 Hotel Fortaleza de Almeida Hotel €€

(☎271 574 250; www.hotelfortalezadealmeida. com; s €73-98, d €85-110; [P][✳][@][📶]) This ageing but likeable hotel sits on the site of former cavalry quarters near the north bastion. A genuine personal welcome is offered and rooms are large and comfortable, all with giant windows and/or balconies; some have great views over the walls. Natural light and plenty of space is key to the relaxing feel, and there's a lovely restaurant area and terrace.

Viseu ⑫

✗ O Cortiço Portuguese €€

(☎232 423 853; Rua Augusto Hilário 45; mains €11-17; ⊘lunch & dinner) This heartily recommended stone-walled eatery specialises in traditional recipes collected from surrounding villages. Generous portions are served in heavy tureens, and the good house wine comes in medieval-style wooden pitchers. Finish your meal with a glass of the local firewater made from olives.

🛏 Casa da Sé Boutique Hotel €€

(☎232 468 032; www.casadase.net; Rua Augusta Cruz 12; s/ste €69/140, d €75-113; [✳][📶]) Right in the heart of old Viseu, this handsome boutique hotel is owned by an antique dealer, so the historic building is full of period furniture and objets d'art, all for sale, so you can take the bed with you when you check out. All rooms are different and exceedingly well-decorated. Staff are helpful, and there's a warm, hospitable feel to the place.

Mata Nacional do Buçaco ⑭

✗ Pedra de Sal Portuguese €€

(☎231 939 405; www.restaurantepedradesal. com; Rua Francisco António Dinis 33; mains €10-16; ⊘lunch & dinner) Winningly done out in dark wood, this is the best restaurant in Luso by quite a distance. It specialises in succulent cuts of pork from the Iberian pig, has some excellent wines to wash them down with and top service to boot. Book ahead at weekends.

🛏 Alegre Hotel Boutique Hotel €€

(☎231 930 256; www.alegrehotels.com; Rua Emídio Navarro 2, s/d €45/55; [P][📶][♿]) This grand, atmospheric, pinkish-coloured 19th-century town house has large doubles with plush drapes, decorative plaster ceilings and polished period furniture. Its appeal is enhanced by an elegant entryway, formal parlour and pretty vine-draped garden with pool.

STRETCH YOUR LEGS
LISBON

Start/Finish: Praça do Comércio

Distance: 2.4km

Duration: Three to four hours

Regal plazas, old-school shops in Baixa, Wonka-like elevators and *miradouros* (viewpoints) with knockout views over the cityscape – it's all packed into this 'greatest hits' walk of downtown Lisbon. Wear flat, comfy shoes to pound these steep, cobbled streets.

Take this walk on Trip

29

Praça do Comércio

With its grand 18th-century arcades, lemon facades and mosaic cobbles, the riverfront **Praça do Comércio** (Terreiro do Paço) is a square to out-pomp them all. Everyone arriving by boat used to disembark here, and it still feels like the gateway to Lisbon, thronging with activity and rattling trams. At its centre rises the dashing equestrian statue of **Dom José I**. For the inside scoop on Portuguese wine, nip into **ViniPortugal** (www.viniportugal.pt; Praça do Comércio; ⊙11am-7pm Tue-Sat).

The Walk » Cross the square heading north to reach the Arco da Vitória and Rua Augusta.

Rua Augusta

As you approach Rua Augusta you'll pass under the monumental **Arco da Vitória** (Rua Augusta 2-10; admission €2.50), a triumphal arch built in the wake of the 1755 earthquake. A lift whisks you to the top, where fine views of Praça do Comércio, the river and the castle await. The arch leads through to pedestrianised, mosaic-cobbled Rua Augusta, which buzzes with street entertainers and shoppers.

The Walk » Swing a left onto Rua de Santa Justa to reach the Elevador de Santa Justa.

Elevador de Santa Justa

If the lanky, wrought-iron **Elevador de Santa Justa** (cnr Rua de Santa Justa & Largo do Carmo; return trip €5; ⊙7am-10.45pm) seems uncannily familiar, it's probably because the neo-Gothic marvel is the handiwork of Raul Mésnier, Gustave Eiffel's apprentice. It's Lisbon's only vertical street lift. Zoom to the top for 360-degree views over the city's skyline.

The Walk » Back at ground level, saunter east along Rua de Santa Justa then turn left to head up Rua Augusta to reach Praça da Figueira.

Praça da Figueira

Praça da Figueira is framed by Pombaline town houses, old-school stores and alfresco cafes with stellar views of hilltop Castelo de São Jorge. At its centre rises gallant **King João I**, once

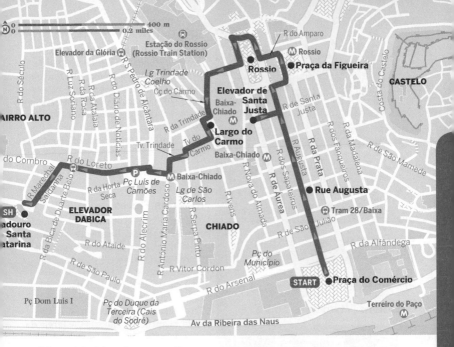

celebrated for his 15th-century discoveries in Africa, now targeted by pigeons and gravity-defying skateboarders.

The Walk » Bear left onto Rua do Amparo to reach Rossio.

Rossio

Simply **Rossio** (Praça Dom Pedro IV) to locals, Praça Dom Pedro IV throngs around the clock. Shoe-shiners and lottery-ticket sellers, buskers and office workers drift across its wavelike cobbles, gazing up to its ornate fountains and **Dom Pedro IV** (Brazil's first emperor), perched on a marble pedestal. Don't miss **Estação do Rossio**, a frothy neo-Manueline train station with horseshoe-shaped arches and swirly turrets.

The Walk » Behind the train station, Calçada do Carmo climbs to Chiado's Largo do Carmo.

Largo do Carmo

Jacaranda trees shade pavement cafes and the 18th-century **Chafariz do Carmo** fountain on this pretty plaza. Rising above it all are the arches of **Convento do Carmo** (adult/child €3.50/free; ☉10am-7pm Mon-Sat), which was all but devoured by the 1755 earthquake. That's what makes it so captivating. Its shattered pillars and wishbone-like arches are completely exposed to the elements.

The Walk » Edge west along Travessa do Carmo and Travessa da Trindade to Praça Luís de Camões, with a statue of its namesake 16th century poet. Head straight onto Rua do Loreto, turning left onto Rua Marechal Saldanha to reach Miradouro de Santa Catarina.

Miradouro de Santa Catarina

Students bashing out rhythms, hippies, stroller-pushing parents and loved-up couples all meet at the precipitous **Miradouro de Santa Catarina** (Rua de Santa Catarina; ☉24hr). The views are fantastic, stretching from the river to the Ponte 25 de Abril and Cristo Rei. Pause for coffee at **Noobai** (Miradouro de Santa Catarina; ☉noon-midnight).

The Walk » It's around a 15-minute walk east back to the starting point, Praça do Comércio.

STRETCH YOUR LEGS
PORTO

Start/Finish: São Bento train station

Distance: 2.1km

Duration: Two to three hours

This laid-back walk takes you through Porto's Unesco World Heritage heart, Ribeira. The alley-woven neighbourhood rises in a helter-skelter of chalk-coloured houses, soaring bell towers and Gothic and baroque churches. Every so often the cityscape cracks open to reveal spectacular *miradouros* (viewpoints).

Take this walk on Trip

27

São Bento

One of the world's most beautiful train stations, Beaux Arts–style **São Bento** (⏱5am-1am) evokes a more graceful age of rail travel. The *azulejo* (tile) panels in the front hall are the real attraction. Designed by Jorge Colaço in 1930, some 20,000 tiles depict historic battles (including Henry the Navigator's conquest of Ceuta).

The Walk » Cross the street to duck down the Rua das Flores opposite.

Rua das Flores

Rua das Flores is one of Ribeira's most charming streets, lined with cafes, delis like the rustic-cool **Mercearia das Flores** (Rua das Flores 110; petiscos €2.50-5.50; ⏱10am-7.30pm Mon-Thu, to 9pm Fri & Sat, 1-7pm Sun), boutiques and speciality shops. Check out the vibrant street-art-splashed electricity boxes. To the right near the bottom sits the **Igreja da Misericórdia** (Rua das Flores 5; ⏱8am-noon & 2-5.30pm Tue-Fri, 8.30am-12.30pm Sat & Sun), a baroque beauty designed by Nicolau Nasoni, with an interior replete with blue and white *azulejos*.

The Walk » Veer right on Rua de Belmonte, then immediately left down Rua Ferreira Borges, to reach Jardim do Infante Dom Henrique. Here Henry the Navigator sits high on a pedestal in front of the 19th-century Mercado Ferreira Borges.

Palácio da Bolsa

Presiding over Jardim do Infante D Henrique is **Palácio da Bolsa** (Stock Exchange; Rua Ferreira Borges; tours adult/child €7/4; ⏱9am-6.30pm Apr-Oct, 9am-12.30pm & 2-5.30pm Nov-Mar). Built from 1842 to 1910, this splendid neoclassical monument honours Porto's past and present money merchants. No expense was spared on its mosaic- and mural-lined halls, sweeping granite staircase, Escadaria Noble, and kaleidoscopic Salão Árabe.

The Walk » Swinging a right brings you to the the Igreja de São Francisco, Porto's most striking church.

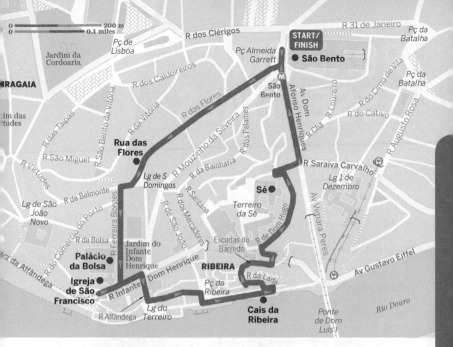

Igreja de São Francisco

Igreja de São Francisco (Praça Infante
Dom Henrique; adult/child €3.50/1.75; ⊙9am-
8pm Jul-Sep, to 7pm Mar-Jun & Oct, to 6pm
Nov-Feb) looks austerely Gothic from
the outside, but inside it hides one of
Portugal's most dazzling displays of
baroque finery. Hardly an inch escapes
unsmothered, as otherworldly cherubs
and sober monks are drowned by
nearly 100kg of gold leaf.

The Walk » As you exit, bear left on Rua do
Infante D Henrique, then right onto Rua Alfândega,
passing Casa do Infante, the medieval town house
where Henry the Navigator was born in 1394. Turn
left onto Rua da Fonte Taurina, then right to reach
Cais da Ribeira.

Cais da Ribeira

Strolling along Cais da Ribeira is your
golden ticket to the city's soul, with
the Ribeira's pastel houses daubing
the hillside behind you and the Douro
unfurling before you. Colourful *barcos
rabelos* (flat-bottomed boats once
used to ship port wine along the river)

bob in front of pavement cafes and
restaurants, and the graceful swoop of
the double-decker Ponte de Dom Luís I
frames the picture neatly.

The Walk » Climb up Rua da Lada, turning right
then right again onto Escadas do Barredo, a steep,
narrow flight of steps, wedged between brightly
painted houses. At the top, Rua de Dom Hugo
sweeps up to the cathedral.

Sé

Gazing proudly over the city from
its hilltop perch, the fortress-like **Sé**
(Terreiro da Sé; cloisters adult/student €3/2;
⊙9am-12.30pm & 2.30-7pm Apr-Oct, to 6pm
Nov-Mar) is where Henry the Navigator
was baptised and King John I married.
History reverberates in its Roman-
esque-meets-baroque nave and *azulejo*
cloister, and the terrace commands
photogenic views over Porto's higgledy-
piggledy lanes and rooftops.

The Walk » From the Sé, bear left on Avenida
Dom Afonso Henriques for a five-minute stroll
back to your starting point at São Bento.

ROAD TRIP ESSENTIALS

Spain & Portugal Driving Guide

With picturesque scenery, good-quality roads and an extensive highway network, Spain and Portugal are excellent places for a road trip – no matter where you roam.

DRIVING LICENCE & DOCUMENTS

Drivers must carry the following at all times:

➡ passport or an EU national ID card
➡ valid driving licence
➡ car-ownership papers
➡ proof of third-party liability assurance

An International Driving Permit (IDP) is not required when renting a car but it can be useful in the event of an accident or police stop, as it translates and vouches for the authenticity of your home licence.

INSURANCE

Third-party motor insurance is a minimum requirement in Spain, Portugal and throughout Europe. Ask your insurer for a European Accident Statement form, which can simplify matters in the event of an accident. A European breakdown-assistance policy such as the AA Five Star Service or RAC Eurocover Motoring Assistance is a good investment. Car-hire companies also provide this minimum insurance, but be careful to understand what your liabilities and excess are, and what waivers you are entitled to in case of accident or damage to the hire vehicle.

Driving Fast Facts

➡ **Right or left?** Drive on the right
➡ **Manual or automatic?** Manual
➡ **Legal driving age** 18
➡ **Top speed limit** In Portugal and Spain 120km/h on major autoways (though some Spanish toll roads now have 130km/h limits)
➡ **Signature car** SEAT Léon Mk3

Road Trip Websites

AUTOMOBILE ASSOCIATIONS

RAC (www.rac.co.uk/travel/driving-abroad/spain and www.rac.co.uk/travel/driving-abroad/portugal) Info for British drivers on driving in Spain and Portugal.

ROUTE MAPPING

Mappy (www.mappy.es)
Michelin (www.viamichelin.com)

HIRING A CAR

To rent a car in Spain or Portugal you have to have a licence, be aged 21 or over and, for the major companies at least, have a credit or debit card. Smaller firms in areas where car hire is particularly common (such as the Balearic Islands) can sometimes live without this last requirement. Although those with a non-EU licence should also have an IDP, you will find that national licences from countries such as Australia,

Local Expert: Driving Tips

Driving tips from Bert Morris, Research Consultant for IAM (www.iam.org.uk) and former Motoring Policy Director for the AA:

➡ First thing if you're British: watch your instinct to drive on the left. Once I was leaving a supermarket using the left-turn exit lane. I turned by instinct into the left lane of the street and nearly had a head-on collision. My golden rule: when leaving a parking lot, petrol station or motorway off-ramp, do it on the right and your instinct to stay right will kick in.

➡ The law says to give way to traffic on the right, even when you're on a main road. So I advise people to ease off on the foot whenever you get to a junction.

➡ Never go below a third of a tank, even if you think there's cheaper petrol further down the road; sometimes the next station's a long way off. My approach is, don't fret about cost; you're on holiday!

Canada, New Zealand and the USA are usually accepted without question.

Most car-hire companies do not charge extra if you plan to drive between Spain and Portugal, but you should inform them of your travel plans. Smaller companies may charge an additional fee.

Rental cars with automatic transmission are rare in Spain and Portugal; book well ahead for these.

Car-hire companies include the following:

Atesa (www.atesa.es)

Autojardim (www.auto-jardim.com) Offers some of the best rates in Portugal.

Auto Europe (www.autoeurope.com) US-based clearing house for deals with major car-rental agencies.

Autos Abroad (www.autosabroad.com) UK-based company offering deals from major car-rental agencies.

Avis (www.avis.es)

Europcar (www.europcar.es)

Hertz (www.hertz.es)

Holiday Autos (www.holidayautos.es) A clearing house for major international companies.

Ideamerge (www.ideamerge.com) Renault's car-leasing plan, motor-home rental and more.

Pepecar (www.pepecar.com) Local low-cost company, but beware of 'extras' that aren't quoted in initial prices.

SixT (www.sixt.es)

BRINGING YOUR OWN VEHICLE

Any foreign motor vehicle entering Spain or Portugal must display a sticker or licence plate identifying its country of registration. Right-hand-drive vehicles brought from the UK or Ireland must have deflectors affixed to the headlights to avoid dazzling oncoming traffic.

MAPS

We recommend you purchase detailed regional driving maps as a companion to this book, as they will help you navigate back roads and explore alternative routes. Michelin publishes a 234-page spiral-bound road atlas of Spain and Portugal. For walking and hiking, maps by IGN/CNIG, Spain's civilian survey organisation, are among the best. You can purchase maps from vendors like Stanfords (www.stanfords.co.uk).

Centro Nacional de Información Geográfica (CNIG; www.cnig.es) Publishes a range of 1:200,000 provincial road maps and 1:25,000-scale hiking maps of national parks as well as some city maps.

Michelin (www.travel.michelin.co.uk) Sells tear-proof yellow-orange 1:400,000-scale regional maps tailor-made for cross-country driving. It also sells detailed city maps to places like Madrid, Barcelona and Granada.

ROADS & CONDITIONS

Spain and Portugal have an extensive network of roads and highways. Here's a breakdown of various types of inter-city roads in Spain.

➡ Autovías/auto-estradas (highway names beginning with A) are multilane divided highways. In Spain, toll roads are further designated AP (*autopistas*). Toll-road signage is usually in blue and indicate tolls (*peajes* in Spanish), *portagens* in Portuguese).

➡ National highways (Carreteras Nacionales) are marked with N or CN.

➡ Regional highways (Carreteras Comaracales) are designated with C and the road number.

Driving Problem-Solver

I can't speak the language; will that be a problem? While it's preferable to learn some Spanish or Portuguese before travelling, road signs are mostly of the 'international symbol' variety, and English is increasingly spoken among the younger generation. Our Language chapter can help you navigate some common roadside emergency situations. In a worst-case scenario, a good attitude and sign language can go a long way.

What should I do if my car breaks down? Safety first: turn on your flashers, put on a safety vest (compulsory in rental cars, usually in glove compartments) and place a reflective triangle (also compulsory) 30m to 100m behind your car to warn approaching motorists. Call for emergency assistance (☑112) or walk to the nearest roadside call box (stationed at 2km intervals on motorways). If renting a vehicle, your car-hire company's service number may help expedite matters. If travelling in your own car, verify before leaving home whether your local auto club has reciprocal roadside-assistance arrangements in Spain and Portugal.

What if I have an accident? For minor accidents you'll need to fill out a *constat amiable d'accident* (accident statement, typically provided in rental-car glove compartments) and report the accident to your insurance and/or rental-car company. If necessary, contact the police (☑112).

What should I do if I get stopped by the police? Show your passport (or EU national ID card), licence and proof of insurance. See our Language chapter for some handy phrases.

What's the speed limit and how is it enforced? Speed limits (indicated by a black-on-white number inside a red circle) range from 30km/h in small towns to 130km/h on the fastest autoroutes. If the police pull you over, they'll fine you on the spot or direct you to the nearest police station to pay. If you're caught by a speed camera (placed at random intervals along highways), the ticket will be sent to your rental-car agency, which will bill your credit card, or to your home address if you're driving your own vehicle. Fines depend on how much you're over the limit.

How do Iberian tolls work? Some Spanish and Portuguese autoroutes charge tolls. Take a ticket from the machine upon entering the highway and pay as you exit. Some exit booths are staffed by people; others are automated and will accept only chip-and-PIN credit cards or coins.

What if I can't find anywhere to stay? During summer and holiday periods, book accommodation in advance whenever possible. Local tourist offices can sometimes help find you a bed during normal business hours. Otherwise, try your luck at chain hotels, which are typically clustered at autoroute exits outside urban areas.

Spain Road Distances (km)

	Alicante	Badajoz	Barcelona	Bilbao	Córdoba	Granada	León	Madrid	Málaga	Oviedo	Pamplona	San Sebastián	Seville	Toledo	Valencia	Valladolid
Badajoz	696															
Barcelona	515	1022														
Bilbao	817	649	620													
Córdoba	525	272	908	795												
Granada	353	438	868	829	166											
León	755	496	784	359	733	761										
Madrid	422	401	621	395	400	434	333									
Málaga	482	436	997	939	187	129	877	544								
Oviedo	873	614	902	304	851	885	118	451	995							
Pamplona	673	755	437	159	807	841	404	407	951	463						
San Sebastián	766	768	529	119	869	903	433	469	13	423	92					
Seville	609	217	1046	933	138	256	671	538	219	789	945	1007				
Toledo	411	368	692	466	320	397	392	71	507	510	478	540	458			
Valencia	166	716	349	633	545	519	685	352	648	803	501	594	697	372		
Valladolid	615	414	663	280	578	627	134	193	737	252	325	354	589	258	545	
Zaragoza	498	726	296	324	725	759	488	325	869	604	175	268	863	396	326	367

Portugal, meanwhile, uses a slightly different nomenclature for its roads. Top of the range are *auto-estradas* (motorways):

➡ A prefixes indicate Portugal's toll roads.

➡ IP (*itinerário principal*) indicates main highways in the country's network.

➡ IC (*itinerário complementar*) indicates subsidiary highways.

Numbers for the main two-lane *estradas nacionais* (national roads) have no prefix letter on some road maps, whereas on other maps they're prefixed by N.

Roads are generally in good shape in Spain and Portugal. A growing number of cars on the road can lead to heavy congestion in developed areas, both in cities and in resort areas along the coast. Keep in mind that Spain, owing to the siesta, has four rush hours: typically 8am to 9.30am, 1pm to 2.30pm, 3.30pm to 5pm and 6.30pm to 8.30pm.

ROAD RULES

Despite the sometimes chaotic relations between drivers, there are rules. To begin with, driving is on the right, overtaking is on the left and most signs use international symbols. An important rule to remember is that traffic from the right usually has priority.

By law, car safety belts must be worn in the front and back seats, and children under 12 years may not ride in the front. The police can impose steep on-the-spot fines for speeding and parking offences, so save yourself a big hassle and remember to toe the line.

Key points to keep in mind:

➡ Blood-alcohol limit: 0.05%. Breath tests are common, and if found to be over the limit, you can be judged, condemned, fined and deprived of your licence within 24 hours. Fines range up to around €600 for serious offences. Non-resident foreigners may be required to pay up on the spot (at 30% off the full fine). Pleading linguistic ignorance will not help – the police

Portugal Road Distances (km)

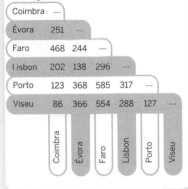

	Coimbra	Évora	Faro	Lisbon	Porto	Viseu
Coimbra	---					
Évora	251	---				
Faro	468	244	---			
Lisbon	202	138	296	---		
Porto	123	368	585	317	---	
Viseu	86	366	554	288	127	---

officer will produce a list of infringements and fines in as many languages as you like. If you don't pay, or don't have a Spanish resident to act as guarantor for you, your vehicle could be impounded, although this is rare.

➡ Motorcyclists: must use headlights at all times and wear a helmet if riding a bike of 125cc or more.

➡ Overtaking: Spanish truck drivers often have the courtesy to turn on their right indicator to show that the way ahead of them is clear for overtaking (and the left one if it is not and you are attempting this manoeuvre).

➡ Roundabouts (traffic circles): vehicles already in the circle have the right of way.

➡ Speed limits: unless otherwise marked, in built-up areas 50km/h (and in some cases, such as inner-city Barcelona, 30km/h), which increases to 100km/h on major roads and up to 120km/h on *autovías* and *autopistas* (toll-free and tolled dual-lane highways, respectively). Cars towing caravans are restricted to a maximum speed of 80km/h.

PARKING

In city centres, most on-the-street parking places are metered from 9am to 7pm Monday to Saturday. Buy a ticket at the nearest coin-fed ticket machine and place it on your dashboard with the time stamp clearly visible. Bigger cities also have public parking garages.

In Spain, if you've parked in a street parking spot and return to find that a parking inspector has left you a parking ticket, don't despair. If you arrive back within a reasonable time after the ticket was issued (what constitutes a reasonable time varies from place to place, but it is rarely more than a couple of hours), don't go looking for the inspector, but instead head for the nearest parking machine. Most machines in most cities allow you to pay a small penalty (usually around €5) to cancel the fine (keep both pieces of paper just in case). If you're unable to work out what to do, ask a local for help.

FUEL

Gasolina (petrol) in Spain is pricey, but generally slightly cheaper than in its major EU neighbours (including France, Germany, Italy and the UK). It's even more expensive in Portugal (by about 20%).

Petrol is about 10% cheaper in Gibraltar than in Spain and 15% cheaper in Andorra.

There are plenty of service stations, and credit cards are accepted at most.

SAFETY

Rental cars are especially at risk of break-ins or petty theft in larger towns, so don't leave anything of value visible in the car. The ultracautious unscrew the radio antenna and leave it inside the car at night; they might also put the wheel covers (hubcaps) in the boot (trunk) for the duration of the trip.

RADIO

Radio Nacional de España (RNE) has Radio 1, with general-interest and current-affairs programs; Radio 5, with sport and entertainment; and Radio 3 (Radio d'Espop). Stations covering current affairs include the left-leaning Cadena Ser, or the right-wing COPE. The most popular commercial pop and rock stations are 40 Principales, Kiss FM, Cadena 100 and Onda Cero.

Portugal's national radio stations consist of state-owned Rádiodifusão Portuguesa (RDP; www.rtp.pt), which runs Antena 1, 2 and 3 and plays Portuguese broadcasts and evening music (Lisbon frequencies 95.7, 94.4 and 100.3). For English-language radio there's the BBC World Service (Lisbon 90.2) and Voice of America (VOA), or a few Algarve-based stations, such as Kiss (95.8 and 101.2).

Spain & Portugal Travel Guide

GETTING THERE & AWAY

Spain is one of Europe's top holiday destinations and is well linked to other European countries by air, rail and road. There are ferry links to the UK, Italy, France, Morocco and the Canary Islands, among other places. Unless visiting on a cruise, those coming to Portugal usually arrive by air.

Flights, tours and rail tickets can be booked online at lonelyplanet.com/bookings.

AIR

All of Spain's airports share the user-friendly website and flight information telephone number of **Aena** (☑902 404704; www.aena.es), the national airports authority. Rental cars are available at all of the major airports.

Madrid's Aeropuerto de Barajas is Spain's busiest (and Europe's fourth- or fifth-busiest) airport. Other major airports include Barcelona's Aeroport del Prat and the airports of Palma de Mallorca,

Málaga, Alicante, Girona, Valencia, Ibiza, Seville and Bilbao. There are also airports at Almería, Asturias, Jerez de la Frontera, Murcia, Reus, Santander, Santiago de Compostela and Seville.

In Portugal, Lisbon, Porto and Faro are the main international gateways. For more information, including live flight arrival and departure schedules, see www.ana.pt.

CAR & MOTORCYCLE

Entering Spain or Portugal from other parts of the EU is usually a breeze – no border checkpoints and no customs – thanks to the Schengen Agreement. Things are a little different in Andorra, where old-fashioned document and customs checks are still the norm when passing through – many border guards, however, will simply wave you through.

SEA

In 2014 **LD Lines** (www.ldlines.co.uk) inaugurated a new year-round route between Gijón and Poole (25 hours, weekly).

Brittany Ferries (☑0871 244 0744; www.brittany-ferries.co.uk) runs the following services:

➡ Plymouth to Santander (20 hours, weekly, mid-March to October only)

➡ Portsmouth to Santander (24 hours, twice weekly)

➡ Portsmouth to Bilbao (24 hours, twice weekly)

An alternative is to catch a ferry across the Channel (or the Eurotunnel vehicle train beneath it) to France and motor down the coast. The fastest sea crossings travel between Dover and Calais, and are operated by **P&O Ferries** (www.poferries.com). For travel through the Channel Tunnel, visit Eurotunnel (www.eurotunnel.com).

Practicalities

➡ **Time** Central European time zone, GMT/UTC plus one hour.

➡ **TV & DVD** Like the UK, Portugal and Spain use the PAL system – incompatible with US and French systems.

➡ **Weights & Measures** Metric.

➡ **Smoking** In Spain, smoking is banned in indoor spaces. In Portugal, it's allowed in some restaurants and bars with separate smoking sections.

TRAIN

Rail services link Spain (and Portugal via Spain) with France and beyond.

Renfe (☏902 243402; www.renfe.com) is the excellent national train system that runs most of the services in Spain. Portugal has a good rail railroad network as well, operated by Caminhos de Ferro Portugueses (www.cp.pt).

DIRECTORY A–Z

ACCOMMODATION

Spain and Portugal have a wide range of accommodation, and it's generally of good value. You'll find everything from hostels and small, family-run guesthouses to boutique hotels and the old-world opulence of *paradores/pousadas* (state-owned hotels in heritage buildings).

Categories

At the lower end of the budget category there are dorm beds (from €18 per person) in youth hostels or private rooms with shared bathrooms in the corridor. If you're willing to pay a few euros more, there are many budget places, with good, comfortable rooms and private bathrooms.

Spain and Portugal generally have excellent midrange hotels. You should always have your own private bathroom, and breakfast is sometimes included in the room price. Boutique hotels, including many that occupy artistically converted historical buildings, largely fall into this category and are usually good choices.

At the top end you'll find a raft of cutting-edge, hip design hotels with stylish lounges in the big cities and major resort areas. Wherever you stay, expect to pay more for a room with a view – especially sea views or with a balcony.

Guesthouses

There are various types of guesthouses; prices typically range from €50 to €90 for a double room with private bathroom (and as little as €35 for the simplest lodgings with shared bathrooms).

➡ The *hostal* (Spain)/*residencial* (Portugal) is generally the most comfortable type of guesthouse, with breakfast usually included.

➡ The *pensión/pensão* is a slight step down in comfort and quality. These typically offer some rooms with shared bathrooms or rooms with only a shower or sink.

➡ The *hospedaria* or *casa de huéspedes/casa de hóspedes* is at the bottom of the heap, with low prices and very basic rooms, usually with shared bathrooms; breakfast is rarely served.

Paradores/Pousadas

One of the best places to stay in Spain or Portugal is at a *parador/pousada* (Spain: www.parador.es; Portugal: www.pousadas.pt). These are former castles, monasteries and palaces that have been turned into luxurious hotels, roughly divided into rural and historic options. In Portugal the prices range from €90 to €200. In Spain prices run from €70 to €230. Prices are lower during the week; and there are often discounts and deals.

Rural Tourism in Spain

Rural tourism has become quite popular in Spain, with accommodation available in many new and often charming *casas rurales*. These are usually comfortably renovated village houses or farmhouses with a handful of rooms. Lower-end prices typically hover around €30/50 for a single/double per night, but classy boutique establishments can easily charge €100 or more for a double. Many are rented out by the week.

Agencies include the following:

Apartments-Spain (www.apartments-spain.com)

Atlas Rural (www.atlasrural.com)

Casas Cantabricas (www.casas.co.uk)

Cases Rurals de Catalunya (www.casesrurals.com)

Escapada Rural (www.escapadarural.com)

Fincas 4 You (www.fincas4you.com)

Guías Casas Rurales (www.guiascasasrurales.com)

Holiday Serviced Apartments (www.holidayapartments.co.uk)

Owners Direct (www.ownersdirect.co.uk)

Ruralka (www.ruralka.com)

Rustic Rent (www.rusticrent.com)

Rusticae (www.rusticae.es)

Secret Destinations (www.secretdestinations.com)

Secret Places (www.secretplaces.com)

Top Rural (www.toprural.com)

Traum Ferienwohnungen (www.traumferienwohnungen.de)

Villas 4 You (www.villas4you.co.uk)

Vintage (www.vintagetravel.co.uk)

Turihab Properties in Portugal

These charming properties offer accommodation in a farmhouse, manor house, country estate or rustic cottage. High-season rates for two people, either in a double room or a cottage, range from €70 to €140. Some properties have swimming pools, and most include breakfast (often with fresh local produce).

There are three types of Turihab lodgings:

Solares de Portugal (www.solaresdeportugal.pt) Grand manor houses, some of which date from the 17th or 18th centuries.

Aldeias de Portugal (www.aldeiasdeportugal.pt) Lodging in rural villages in the north, often in beautifully converted stone cottages.

Casas no Campo (www.casasnocampo.net) Country houses, cottages and luxury villas.

Camping

Camping is popular in Spain and Portugal, though Spain has a greater selection – with around 1000 *campings* (camping grounds). Some of these are well located in woodland or near beaches or rivers, but others are on the outskirts of towns or along highways. Few of them are near city centres. Facilities generally range from reasonable to very good, although any camping ground can be crowded and noisy at busy times (especially July and August). The best sites have swimming pools, supermarkets, restaurants, laundry service, children's playgrounds and tennis courts.

Camping grounds usually charge per person, per tent and per vehicle – typically €4.50 to €9 for each. Children usually pay a bit less than adults. Many camping grounds close from around October to Easter.

Spain:

Guía Camping (www.guiacampingfecc.com) Online version of the annual Guía Camping (€13.60), which is available in bookshops around the country.

Campinguía (www.campinguia.com) Comments (mostly in Spanish) and links.

Campings Online (www.campingsonline.com/espana) Booking service.

Portugal:

➡ Generally, camping grounds run by **Orbitur** (www.orbitur.pt) offer the best services. Some towns have municipal campsites, which vary in quality.

➡ For detailed listings of campsites nationwide, pickup the **Roteiro Campista** (www.roteirocampista.pt; €7),updated annually and sold at *turismos* and bookshops. It contains details of most Portuguese camping grounds, with maps and directions.

Seasons

➡ On the coast, high season is summer, particularly August. Finding a place to stay without booking ahead in July and August in the Algarve or along the Mediterranean Coast can be difficult and many places require a minimum stay of at least two nights during high season.

➡ In ski resorts, high season is Christmas, New Year and the February-March school holidays.

➡ Hotels in inland cities sometimes charge low-season rates in summer.

➡ Rates often drop outside the high season – in some cases by as much as 50%.

➡ In the Pyrenees hotels usually close between seasons, from around May to mid-June and from mid-September to early December.

➡ Weekends are high season for boutique hotels and *casas rurales* (rural homes), but low season for business hotels (which often offer generous specials) in Madrid and Barcelona. Always check out hotel websites for discounts.

ELECTRICITY

220V/230V/50Hz

120V/60Hz

sections of this guide include phone numbers for places that require reservations.

adega (Portugal) literally 'wine cellar', usually decorated with wine castic and rustic ambiance. Expect heavy, inexpensive meals.

asador restaurant specialising in roasted meats

bar de copas gets going around midnight and serves hard drinks

casa de comidas basic restaurant serving well-priced home cooking

cervecería/cervejaria the focus is on *cerveza* (beer) on tap

chiringuito beach bar

churrasqueira (Portugal) restaurant specialising in char-grilled meats

horno de asador restaurant with a wood-burning roasting oven

marisquería/marisqueira bar or restaurant specialising in seafood

tasca tapas bar; in Portugal a *tasca* is an old-fashioned place with daily specials, low prices and a local crowd

terraza open-air bar, for warm-weather tippling and tapas

taberna usually a rustic place serving tapas and *raciones* (large tapas)

vinoteca wine bars where you can order by the glass

Ordering Tapas in Spain

Unless you speak Spanish, the art of ordering can seem one of the dark arts of Spanish etiquette. Fear not – it's not as difficult as it first appears.

In the Basque Country, Zaragoza and many bars in Madrid, Barcelona and elsewhere, it couldn't be easier. With tapas varieties lined up along the bar, you either take a small plate and help yourself or point to the morsel you want. If you do

FOOD

Settling down to a meal with friends is one of life's great pleasures in Spain and Portugal. You'll find a great variety of eateries and drinking spots (food and drink go hand-in-hand in Iberia); categories are listed here. The Eating & Sleeping

Eating Price Ranges

The following price ranges refer to a main course. Unless otherwise stated, the service charge is included in the price.

€ less than €10

€€ €10–20

€€€ more than €20

Tipping Guide

Menu prices include a service charge. Most people leave some small change if they're satisfied: 5% is normally fine and 10% extremely generous. Porters will generally be happy with €1. Taxi drivers don't have to be tipped but a little rounding up won't go amiss.

this, it's customary to keep track of what you eat (by holding on to the toothpicks, for example) and then tell the bar staff how many you've had when it's time to pay. Otherwise, many places have a list of tapas, either on a menu or posted up behind the bar. If you can't choose, ask for '*la especialidad de la casa*' (the house speciality) and it's hard to go wrong.

Another way of eating tapas is to order *raciones* (literally 'rations'; large tapas servings) or *media raciones* (half-rations; smaller tapas servings). Remember, however, that after a couple of *raciones* you'll be full. In some bars you'll also get a small (free) tapa when you buy a drink.

Portuguese Couvert

Throughout Portugal, waiters bring bread, olives and other goodies to your table when you sit down. This unordered appetiser is called '*couvert*' and it is *never* free (*couvert* can cost from €1 to upwards of €8 per person at flashier places). If you don't want it, send it away, no offence taken.

Meal Times

➡ Spaniards rarely eat lunch before 2pm (restaurant kitchens usually open from 1pm until 4pm).

➡ It does vary from region to region, but in Spain most restaurants open for dinner from 8.30pm to midnight, later on weekends.

➡ In Portugal, meal times are typically earlier – from noon to 3pm for lunch, and 7pm to 10pm for dinner. The siesta is not common in Portugal.

GAY & LESBIAN TRAVELLERS

Gay marriage is legal in Spain and Portugal, but lesbians and gay men generally keep a fairly low profile – though people are more out in Madrid, Barcelona, Sitges and Torremolinos. Lisbon, Porto and the Algarve also have a gay scene, but it's fairly low-key. Sitges is a major destination on the international gay party circuit; gays take a leading role in the wild Carnaval there in February/March. As well, there are gay parades, marches and events in several cities on and around the last Saturday in June, when Madrid's gay and lesbian pride march takes place (Porto and Lisbon also have pride fests).

INTERNET ACCESS

Wi-fi is almost universally available at most hotels and hostels, as well as in some cafes, restaurants and airports; generally (but not always) it's free. Connection speed often varies from room to room in hotels (and coverage sometimes is restricted to the hotel lobby), so always ask when you check in or make your reservation. Some tourist offices offer free wi-fi. Others may have a list of wi-fi hotspots in their area.

Internet cafes are rare in this age of smartphones. Big cities usually have a few, with rates around €3 per hour.

MONEY

The most convenient way to bring your money is in the form of a debit or credit card, with some extra cash for use in case of an emergency.

ATMs

Many credit and debit cards can be used for withdrawing money from a *cajeros automáticos* (automatic teller machine – labelled 'Multibanco' in Portugal) that displays the relevant symbols such as Visa, MasterCard, Cirrus etc. Remember that there is usually a charge (around 2%) on ATM cash withdrawals abroad.

Cash

Most banks and building societies will exchange major foreign currencies and offer the best rates. Ask about commissions and take your passport.

Credit & Debit Cards

These can be used to pay for most purchases. You'll often be asked to show your passport or some other form of identification. Among the most widely accepted are Visa, MasterCard, American Express (Amex), Cirrus, Maestro, Plus and JCB. Diners Club is less widely accepted. If your card is lost, stolen or swallowed by an ATM, you can call the following telephone numbers toll free to have an immediate stop put on its use.

In Spain:

Amex (☏900 994426)

Diners Club (☏902 401112)

MasterCard (☏900 971231)

Visa (☏900 991124, 900 991216)
In Portugal:

Amex (☏800 208 532)

Diners Club (☏21 315 98 56)

MasterCard (☏800 811 272)

Visa (☏800 811 824)

Moneychangers

You can exchange both cash and travellers cheques at exchange offices – which are usually indicated by the word *cambio* (exchange). Generally they offer longer opening hours and quicker service than banks, but worse exchange rates and higher commissions.

OPENING HOURS

Following are standard hours for various types of business in Spain and Portugal (note that these can fluctuate by an hour either way in some cases).

banks	8.30am-2pm or 3pm Mon-Fri
bars	7pm-2am
cafes	9am-7pm
nightclubs	11pm-4am Thu-Sat
post offices	9am-5pm Mon-Fri
restaurants	1-4pm & 8.30-11pm Spain, noon-3pm & 7-10pm Portugal
shops	10am-2pm & 5-8pm Spain, 10am-noon & 2-7pm Portugal
supermarkets	9am-8pm

PUBLIC HOLIDAYS

Spain's national holidays:

Año Nuevo (New Year's Day) 1 January

Viernes Santo (Good Friday) March/April

Fiesta del Trabajo (Labour Day) 1 May

La Asunción (Feast of the Assumption) 15 August

Fiesta Nacional de España (National Day) 12 October

La Inmaculada Concepción (Feast of the Immaculate Conception) 8 December

Navidad (Christmas) 25 December
Regional governments set five holidays and local councils two more.
Portugal's national holidays:

New Year's Day 1 January

Carnaval Tuesday February/March – the day before Ash Wednesday

Good Friday March/April

Liberty Day 25 April – celebrating the 1974 revolution

Labour Day 1 May

Corpus Christi May/June – ninth Thursday after Easter

Portugal Day 10 June – also known as Camões and Communities Day

Feast of the Assumption 15 August

Republic Day 5 October – commemorating the 1910 declaration of the Portuguese Republic

All Saints' Day 1 November

Independence Day 1 December – commemorating the 1640 restoration of independence from Spain

Feast of the Immaculate Conception 8 December

Christmas Day 25 December

SAFE TRAVEL

The main thing to be wary of is petty theft (which may of course not seem so petty if your passport, cash, travellers cheques, credit card and camera go missing). Be careful but don't be paranoid.

Scams

There must be 50 ways to lose your wallet. As a rule, talented petty thieves work in groups and capitalise on distraction. Tricks usually involve a team of two or more (sometimes one of them an attractive woman to distract male victims). While one attracts your attention, the other empties your pockets. More imaginative strikes include someone dropping a milk mixture on to the victim from a balcony. Immediately a concerned citizen comes up to help you brush off what you assume to be pigeon poo, and thus suitably occupied you don't notice the contents of your pockets slipping away.

Beware: not all thieves look like thieves. Watch out for an old classic: the ladies offering flowers for good luck. We don't know how they do it, but if you get too involved in a friendly chat with these people, your pockets almost always wind up empty.

On some highways, especially the AP7 from the French border to Barcelona, bands of thieves occasionally operate. Beware of men trying to distract you in rest areas, and don't stop along the highway if people driving alongside indicate you have a problem with the car. While one inspects the rear of the car with you, his pals will empty your vehicle. Another gag has them puncturing tyres of cars stopped in rest areas, then following and 'helping' the victim when they stop to change the wheel. Hire cars and those with foreign plates are especially targeted. When you do call in at highway rest stops, try to park close to the buildings and leave nothing of value in view. If you do stop to change a tyre and find yourself getting unsolicited aid, make sure doors are all locked and don't allow yourself to be distracted.

In some towns fairly dodgy self-appointed parking attendants operate in central areas where you may want to park. They will direct you frantically to a spot. If possible, ignore them and find your own. If unavoidable, you may well want to pay them some token not to scratch or otherwise damage your vehicle after you've walked away. You definitely don't want to leave anything visible in the car under these circumstances.

Theft

Theft is mostly a risk in tourist resorts, big cities and when you first arrive in a new city and may be off your guard. You are at your most vulnerable when dragging around luggage to or from your hotel. Barcelona, Madrid and Seville have the worst reputations for theft and, on very rare occasions, muggings.

Anything left lying on the beach can disappear in a flash when your back is turned. At night avoid dingy, empty city alleys and backstreets, or anywhere that just doesn't feel 100% safe.

Report thefts to the national police. You are unlikely to recover your goods but you need to make this formal *denuncia* for insurance purposes. To avoid endless queues at the *comisaría* (police station), you can make the report on the web at www.policia.es (click on Denuncias). The following day you go to the station of your choice to pick up and sign the report, without queuing.

TELEPHONE

Mobile Phones

➡ Spain and Portugal use GSM 900/1800, which is compatible with the rest of Europe and Australia but not with the North American GSM 1900 or the totally different system in Japan (though some North Americans have tri-band phones that work in Europe).

➡ Check with your service provider about roaming charges – dialling a mobile phone from a fixed-line phone or another mobile can be incredibly expensive.

➡ It's often much cheaper to buy your own Spanish or Portuguese SIM card – and locals you meet are much more likely to ring you if your number doesn't require making an international call.

➡ All the Spanish mobile-phone companies (Telefónica's MoviStar, Orange and Vodafone) offer *prepagado* (prepaid) accounts for mobiles. The SIM card costs from €10, to which you add some prepaid phone time. Phone outlets are scattered across the country. You can then top up in their shops or by buying cards in outlets, such as *estancos* (tobacconists) and newsstands.

➡ In Portugal the process is identical, although the big mobile providers are Vodafone, Optimus and TMN.

Phone Codes

➡ Emergency ☑112 (Spain or Portugal)
➡ International access code ☑00
➡ Spain country code ☑34
➡ Portugal country code ☑351
➡ Portuguese mobile phone numbers begin with 9
➡ Spanish mobile numbers begin with 6

Phonecards

Cut-rate prepaid phonecards can be good value for international calls. They can be bought from tobacconists, small grocery stores and newsstands in the main cities and tourist resorts. If possible, try to compare rates.

TOURIST INFORMATION

➡ All cities and many smaller towns have an *oficina de turismo* (usually signposted '*turismo*' in Portuguese). National and natural parks also often have their own visitor centres offering useful information.

➡ Turespaña (www.spain.info) is Spain's national tourism body, and it operates branches around the world. Check the website for office locations.

➡ Turismo de Portugal (www.visitportugal.com) is Portugal's useful national tourist board.

TRAVELLERS WITH DISABILITIES

Spain and Portugal are not overly accommodating for travellers with disabilities but some things are slowly changing. For example, disabled access to some museums, official buildings and hotels represents a change in local thinking. In major cities more is slowly being done to facilitate disabled access to public transport and taxis; in some cities, wheelchair-adapted taxis are called 'Eurotaxis'. Newly constructed hotels in most areas of Spain are required to have wheelchair-adapted rooms. With older places, you need to be a little wary of hotels that advertise themselves as being disabled-friendly, as this can mean as little as wide doors to rooms and bathrooms, or other token efforts.

Worthy of a special mention is Barcelona's **Inout Hostel** (☎93 280 09 85; www.inouthostel.com; Major del Rectoret 2; dm €18; ❄@🛜🛌; 🚆FGC Baixador de Vallvidrera), which is completely accessible for those with disabilities, and nearly all the staff that work there have disabilities of one kind or another. The facilities and service are first-class.

VISAS

Visas are not required for EU nationals or citizens of Iceland, Norway and Switzerland, and are required only for stays greater than 90 days for citizens of Australia, the USA, Canada, Hong Kong, Israel, Japan, Malaysia, New Zealand, Singapore, South Korea and many Latin American countries.

Language

The pronunciation of most Spanish sounds is very similar to that of their English counterparts. If you read our coloured pronunciation guides as if they were English, you'll be understood. Note that kh is a throaty sound (like the 'ch' in the Scottish *loch*), r is strongly rolled, ly is pronounced as the 'lli' in 'million' and ny as the 'ni' in 'onion'. You may also notice that the 'lisped' th sound is pronounced as s in Andalucia.

Portuguese pronunciation is not difficult because most sounds are also found in English. The exceptions are the nasal vowels (represented in our pronunciation guides by ng after the vowel), which are pronounced as if you're trying to make the sound through your nose; and the strongly rolled r (represented by rr in our pronunciation guides). Also note that the symbol zh sounds like the 's' in 'pleasure'. The stress generally falls on the second-last syllable of a word. In our pronunciation guides stressed syllables are indicated with italics.

SPANISH BASICS

Hello.	Hola.	o·la
Goodbye.	Adiós.	a·dyos
How are you?	¿Qué tal?	ke tal
Fine, thanks.	Bien, gracias.	byen gra·syas
Excuse me.	Perdón.	per·don
Sorry.	Lo siento.	lo syen·to
Yes.	Sí.	see
No.	No.	no
Please.	Por favor.	por fa·vor
Thank you.	Gracias.	gra·syas
You're welcome.	De nada.	de na·da

My name is ...
Me llamo ...   me lya·mo ...

What's your name?
¿Cómo se llama Usted?   ko·mo se lya·ma oo·ste (pol)
¿Cómo te llamas?   ko·mo te lya·mas (inf)

Do you speak English?
¿Habla inglés?   a·bla een·gles (pol)
¿Hablas inglés?   a·blas een·gles (inf)

I don't understand.
No entiendo.   no en·tyen·do

DIRECTIONS

Where's ...?
¿Dónde está ...?   don·de es·ta ...

What's the address?
¿Cuál es la dirección?   kwal es la dee·rek·syon

Can you please write it down?
¿Puede escribirlo,   pwe·de es·kree·beer·lo
por favor?   por fa·vor

Can you show me (on the map)?
¿Me lo puede indicar   me lo pwe·de een·dee·kar
(en el mapa)?   (en el ma·pa)

EMERGENCIES

| Help! | ¡Socorro! | so·ko·ro |

I'm lost.
Estoy perdido/a.   es·toy per·dee·do/a (m/f)

ON THE ROAD

I'd like to hire a ...	Quisiera alquilar ...	kee·sye·ra al·kee·lar ...
4WD	un todo-terreno	oon to·do·te·re·no
bicycle	una bicicleta	oo·na bee·see·kle·ta
car	un coche	oon ko·che
motorcycle	una moto	oo·na mo·to

Want More?

For in-depth language information and handy phrases, check out Lonely Planet's *Spanish* and *Portuguese Phrasebooks*. You'll find them at **shop. lonelyplanet.com**.

child seat	asiento de seguridad para niños	a·syen·to de se·goo·ree·da pa·ra nee·nyos
diesel	gasóleo	ga·so·le·o
helmet	casco	kas·ko
mechanic	mecánico	me·ka·nee·ko
petrol	gasolina	ga·so·lee·na
service station	gasolinera	ga·so·lee·ne·ra

How much is it per day/hour?
| ¿Cuánto cuesta por día/hora? | kwan·to kwes·ta por dee·a/o·ra |

Is this the road to ...?
| ¿Se va a ... por esta carretera? | se va a ... por es·ta ka·re·te·ra |

(How long) Can I park here?
| ¿(Por cuánto tiempo) Puedo aparcar aquí? | (por kwan·to tyem·po) pwe·do a·par·kar a·kee |

The car has broken down (at ...).
| El coche se ha averiado (en ...). | el ko·che se a a·ve·rya·do (en ...) |

I have a flat tyre.
| Tengo un pinchazo. | ten·go oon peen·cha·tho |

I've run out of petrol.
| Me he quedado sin gasolina. | me e ke·da·do seen ga·so·lee·na |

Are there cycling paths?
| ¿Hay carril bicicleta? | ai ka·reel bee·thee·kle·ta |

Is there bicycle parking?
| ¿Hay aparcamiento de bicicletas? | ai a·par·ka·myen·to de bee·thee·kle·tas |

PORTUGUESE BASICS

Hello.	Olá.	o·laa
Goodbye.	Adeus.	a·de·oosh
How are you?	Como está?	ko·moo shtaa
Fine, and you?	Bem, e você?	beng e vo·se
Excuse me.	Faz favor.	faash fa·vor
Sorry.	Desculpe.	desh·kool·pe
Yes.	Sim.	seeng
No.	Não.	nowng
Please.	Por favor.	poor fa·vor
Thank you.	Obrigado.	o·bree·gaa·doo (m)
	Obrigada.	o·bree·gaa·da (f)
You're welcome.	De nada.	de naa·da

What's your name?
| Qual é o seu nome? | kwaal e oo se·oo no·me |

My name is ...
| O meu nome é ... | oo me·oo no·me e ... |

Do you speak English?
| Fala inglês? | faa·la eeng·glesh |

I don't understand.
| Não entendo. | nowng eng·teng·doo |

DIRECTIONS

Where's (the station)?
| Onde é (a estação)? | ong·de e (a shta·sowng) |

Can you show me (on the map)?
| Pode-me mostrar (no mapa)? | po·de·me moosh·traar (noo maa·pa) |

EMERGENCIES

Help!
| Socorro! | soo·ko·rroo |

I'm lost.
| Estou perdido. | shtoh per·dee·doo (m) |
| Estou perdida. | shtoh per·dee·da (f) |

ON THE ROAD

I'd like to hire a ...	Queria alugar ...	ke·ree·a a·loo·gaar ...
bicycle	uma bicicleta	oo·ma bee·see·kle·ta
car	um carro	oong kaa·rroo
motorcycle	uma mota	oo·ma mo·ta
child seat	cadeira de criança	ka·day·ra de kree·ang·sa
helmet	capacete	ka·pa·se·te
mechanic	mecânico	me·kaa·nee·koo
petrol/gas	gasolina	ga·zoo·lee·na
service station	posto de gasolina	posh·too de ga·zoo·lee·na

Is this the road to ...?
| Esta é a estrada para ...? | esh·ta e a shtraa·da pa·ra ... |

(How long) Can I park here?
| (Quanto tempo) Posso estacionar aqui? | (kwang·too teng·poo) po·soo shta·see·oo·naar a·kee |

The car/motorbike has broken down (at ...).
| O carro/A mota avariou-se (em ...). | oo kaa·rroo/a mo·ta a·va·ree·oh·se (eng ...) |

I have a flat tyre.
| Tenho um furo no pneu. | ta·nyoo oong foo·roo noo pe·ne·oo |

I've run out of petrol.
| Estou sem gasolina. | shtoh seng ga·zoo·lee·na |

BEHIND THE SCENES

SEND US YOUR FEEDBACK

We love to hear from travellers – your comments help make our books better. We read every word, and we guarantee that your feedback goes straight to the authors. Visit **lonelyplanet. com/contact** to submit your updates and suggestions.

Note: We may edit, reproduce and incorporate your comments in Lonely Planet products such as guidebooks, websites and digital products, so let us know if you don't want your comments reproduced or your name acknowledged. For a copy of our privacy policy visit lonelyplanet.com/privacy.

AUTHOR THANKS

REGIS ST LOUIS

Many thanks to my co-authors who did such a fine job pouring their passion and expertise into this guide. Thanks to Jo Cooke and Lorna Parkes for inviting me on board. Finally big hugs to my family for all their support.

STUART BUTLER

First and foremost I must, once again, thank my wife, Heather, and children Jake and Grace for their patience with this project. I know it's not easy for any of you. I would also like to thank Itziar Herrán, Oihana Lazpita, Leire Rodríguez Aramendia, Pilar Martínez de Olcoz, Clara Navas, Amaya Urberuaga and everyone else who helped.

KERRY CHRISTIANI

I'm *muito obrigada* to all the welcoming locals, tourism pros and travellers I met on the road. Special thanks go to Jorge Moita in Lisbon and André in Porto. Big thanks, also, to my fellow authors for being a pleasure to work with. Last but not least, thanks go to my husband, Andy, for being a great travel companion.

ANTHONY HAM

Special thanks once again to Itziar Herrán, who brought both wisdom and an eye for detail to her contributions to this book. Thanks also to Marina and Alberto for their unwavering hospitality; to Jo Cooke and Lorna Parkes and Lonely Planet's fine team of editors. And to Marina, Carlota and Valentina –

you are everything that is good about this wonderful country.

ISABELLA NOBLE

Huge thanks to my talented co-authors, especially fellow Andalucía experts Brendan and Josephine. *Muchísimas gracias* to all the *andaluces* (and *guiris*) who shared their wisdom, particularly Antonio, Pepi, Annie, Tessa, Lucy and Ángel. Extra special thanks to Jack and Paps, my faithful white-town roadtripping companions, for laughs and help *por el camino*.

JOHN NOBLE

Muchas gracias a Izzy for sharing the whole experience and keeping my brain busy!

THIS BOOK

This 1st edition of Lonely Planet's *Spain & Portugal's Best Trips* was researched and written by Regis St Louis, Stuart Butler, Kerry Christiani, Anthony Ham, Isabella Noble, John Noble, Josephine Quintero, Brendan Sainsbury and Andy Symington.

This guidebook was produced by the following:

Destination Editors Jo Cooke, Lorna Parkes

Product Editor Alison Ridgway

Senior Cartographer Anthony Phelan

Cartographer Gabe Lindquist

Book Designer Cam Ashley

Assisting Editors Andrea Dobbin, Kate Evans, Victoria Harrison, Ross Taylor

Assisting Book Designer Virginia Moreno

Cover Researcher Campbell McKenzie

Thanks to Sasha Baskett, Grace Dobell, Kate James, Andi Jones, Anne Mason, Jenna Myers, Karyn Noble, Kirsten Rawlings, **Angela Tinson**

JOSEPHINE QUINTERO

Josephine would like to thank all the helpful folk at the various tourist information offices, as well as Sergio Guzman, a valuable contact in Marbella. Thanks too to destination editor Lorna Parkes and to all those involved in the title from the Lonely Planet offices, as well as to all my Spanish malagueño friends who provided endless advice, contacts and tips, and to Robin Chapman for looking after Marilyn (the cat).

BRENDAN SAINSBURY

Thanks to all the untold bus drivers, chefs, hotel receptionists, tour guides, and flamenco singers who helped me in this research.

ANDY SYMINGTON

Numerous people were generous with information, but I owe particular thanks for hospitality and other favours to James and Penny Symington, Rupert and Anne Symington, David and Sara Jane Symington, António Valente, Catrin Egerton, Wil Peters, Ricardo Feijóo, Miguel Amaral, João Valente and Jose Eliseo Vázquez González. A big *obrigado* also to co-author Kerry Christiani and to Jo Cooke and Lorna Parkes for being great editors to work with.

ACKNOWLEDGMENTS

Climate map data adapted from Peel MC, Finlayson BL & McMahon TA (2007) 'Updated World Map of the Köppen-Geiger Climate Classification', *Hydrology and Earth System Sciences*, 11, 163344.

Front cover photographs: (clockwise from top) The Alhambra, Granada, Spain, Alan Copson/AWL; Decorative tiles, Cordoba, Spain, Hemis/AWL; Fiat 600, Lisbon, Portugal, Ian Bottle/Alamy

Back cover photograph: Medieval bridge, Puente la Reina, Spain, Susanne Kremer/4Corners.

INDEX

Josephine Quintero Spain is Josephine's favourite country on earth and she has lived in Málaga province on the Costa del Sol for over 20 years. As well as co-authoring four editions of the Lonely Planet Spain title, she has worked on the Andalucía regional guide, as well as numerous other LP titles. Highlights during this trip including gazing at evocative art at the brand new Pompidou museum in Málaga and discovering still more fine dining venues in the cobbled Marbella backstreets.

Read more about Josephine at: https://auth. lonelyplanet.com/profiles/josephinequintero

Brendan Sainsbury Originally from Hampshire, England, Brendan first went to Spain on an Inter-rail ticket in the 1980s. He went back as a travel guide several years later and met his wife-to-be in a small village in rural Andalucía in 2003. He has been writing books for Lonely Planet for a decade, including four previous editions of the Spain/Andalucía guides. Brendan loves Granada, the writing of Federico Lorca, cycling along via verdes, and attending as many flamenco shows as his research allows.

Read more about Brendan at: https://auth. lonelyplanet.com/profiles/brendansainsbury

Andy Symington Though he hails from Australia, Andy's great-grandfather emigrated to Portugal in the 19th century and that side of his family still calls the country home. This connection means that he has been a frequent visitor to the country since birth, and now nips across the border very frequently from his home in Spain. Andy has authored and co-authored numerous Lonely Planet and other guidebooks.

Read more about Andy at: https://auth. lonelyplanet.com/profiles/andysymington

Kerry Christiani Kerry's love affair with Portugal began as a child clambering along the cliffs of the Algarve. She returned years later and fell for the rest of the country – its captivating landscapes, super-friendly locals, fresh seafood and photogenic light. For this guide, she road-tripped her way through vineyards, over mountains, deep into national parks and along the wave-lashed Atlantic coast. Kerry is the author of more than 20 guidebooks, including Lonely Planet *Pocket Lisbon* and *Porto*. She tweets @kerrychristiani.

Read more about Kerry at: https://auth. lonelyplanet.com/profiles/KerryChristiani

Anthony Ham In 2001, Anthony (www.anthonyham. com) fell in love with Madrid on his first visit to the city. Less than a year later, he arrived on a one-way ticket, with not a word of Spanish and not knowing a single person. After ten years living in the city, he recently returned to Australia with his Spanish-born family, but he still adores his adopted country as much as the first day he arrived. When he's not writing for Lonely Planet, Anthony writes about and photographs Spain, Scandinavia, the Middle East, Australia and Africa for newspapers and magazines around the world.

My Favourite Trip 1 **Castilla y León** for the combination of unforgettable cities and timeworn villages.

Read more about Anthony at: https://auth. lonelyplanet.com/profiles/anthonyham

Isabella Noble Isabella has always thought that learning to drive in central Málaga taught her to cope with roads absolutely anywhere. A London-based, English/Australian travel journalist, she grew up in a white Andalucian mountain village, and spent plenty of summers whizzing across to Cádiz' Costa de la Luz – perfect training for this title. She has contributed to several Lonely Planet guides including *Andalucía*, *Spain* and *India*, and is a Spain expert for Telegraph Travel. She's on Twitter/Instagram @isabellamnoble and blogs at www.isabellanoble.blogspot.com.

My Favourite Trip 23 **The Great Outdoors** for the Costa de la Luz' windswept beaches, Tarifa's Moroccan flavour and Doñana's wild beauty.

Read more about Isabella at: https://auth. lonelyplanet.com/profiles/IsabellaNoble

John Noble Two decades of living in Spain and driving all over it have taught John that it's a great country to drive in! (Outside the city centres, that is – they're best negotiated by other means.) The main highways get better and better and it's now possible to drive from any corner of the country to any other without leaving an autovía. The back roads are even better – low on traffic and usually high on long-distance views over Spain's always dramatic scenery.

My Favourite Trip 13 **Coast of Galicia** You can't beat the ever-changing drama of Spain's most spectacular coastline.

Read more about John at: https://auth. lonelyplanet.com/profiles/ewoodrover

OUR WRITERS

OUR STORY

A beat-up old car, a few dollars in the pocket and a sense of adventure. In 1972 that's all Tony and Maureen Wheeler needed for the trip of a lifetime – across Europe and Asia overland to Australia. It took several months, and at the end – broke but inspired – they sat at their kitchen table writing and stapling together their first travel guide, *Across Asia on the Cheap*. Within a week they'd sold 1500 copies. Lonely Planet was born.

Today, Lonely Planet has offices in Franklin, London, Melbourne, Oakland, Beijing and Delhi, with more than 600 staff and writers. We share Tony's belief that 'a great guidebook should do three things: inform, educate and amuse'.

Regis St Louis Regis first fell in love with Spain and Portugal on a grand journey across Iberia in the late 1990s. Since then he has returned frequently to the peninsula, often splitting his time between his favourite cities of Lisbon and Barcelona. Memorable moments from his most recent trip include earning a few scars at a correfoc in Gràcia and watching fearless castellers build human towers at the Santa Eulàlia fest. Regis is also the author of *Portugal* and *Barcelona*, and he has contributed to dozens of other Lonely Planet titles.

My Favourite Trip 15 **The Costa Brava** I love the combination of wild coastal scenery and great seafood, with jaw-dropping works of Dalí waiting at the end.

Read more about Regis at: https://auth. lonelyplanet.com/profiles/regisstlouis

Stuart Butler Stuart's first childhood encounters with Spain came on a school trip to Parque Nacional de Doñana in the far south of Spain and family holidays along the north coast. Early encounters left lasting impressions and when he was older he spent every summer on the Basque beaches, until one day he found he was unable to tear himself away – he's been in the region ever since. His travels for Lonely Planet, and a wide variety of magazines, have taken him beyond Spain, to the shores of the Arctic, the mountains of Asia and the savannahs of Africa. He's currently writing a book about the Maasai peoples of East Africa. His website is www. stuartbutlerjournalist.com.

Read more about Stuart at: https://auth. lonelyplanet.com/profiles/stuartbutler

← MORE WRITERS

Published by Lonely Planet Publications Pty Ltd
ABN 36 005 607 983
1st edition – Feb 2016
ISBN 978 1 74360 694 0
© Lonely Planet 2016
Photographs © as indicated 2016
10 9 8 7 6 5 4 3 2
Printed in China

MIX
Paper from responsible sources
FSC™ C021741

Paper in this book is certified against the Forest Stewardship Council™ standards. FSC™ promotes environmentally responsible, socially beneficial and economically viable management of the world's forests.